THE
PROFESSOR
AND THE
PUPIL

THE
PROFESSOR
AND THE
PUPIL

The Politics of
W. E. B. Du Bois and Paul Robeson

MURALI BALAJI

Nation Books
New York

THE PROFESSOR AND THE PUPIL:
The Politics of W. E. B. Du Bois and Paul Robeson

Copyright © 2007 Murali Balaji

Published by
Nation Books
A Member of the Perseus Books Group
116 West 16th Street, 8th Floor
New York, NY 10003

Nation Books is a copublishing venture of the Nation Institute
and the Perseus Books Group.
www.perseusbooks.com

Nation Books titles are available at special discounts for bulk purchases in the
United States by corporations, institutions, and other organizations. For more
information, please contact the special Markets Department at the Perseus
Books Group, 2300 Chestnut Street, Suite 200, Philadelphia, PA 19103,
or call (800) 255–1514, or e-mail special.markets@perseusbooks.com.

Library of Congress Cataloging-in-Publication Data is available.

ISBN-13: 978-1-56858-355-6
ISBN-10: 1-56858-355-9

9 8 7 6 5 4 3 2 1

Book design by Maria Fernandez

Printed in the United States of America

*To the legacies of William Edward Burghardt Du Bois
and Paul Robeson and those who continue
in the struggle for our shared humanity.*

CONTENTS

ACKNOWLEDGMENTS

IN THE TWO YEARS it took for me to write this book, I made many new friends, learned more than I could ever possibly hope to know about an era that preceded me, and gained a newfound appreciation of the valuable work of historians.

I have to first thank my parents, who stood by me when I made the very un-Indian decision of quitting my job to write a book. My parents, Kodumudi and Vijaya, along with my siblings, Lakshmi and Arvind, have always been my biggest supporters, even when I didn't think I had the mental stamina to complete this book. Though she came along later in this process, Devi Ramkissoon—the love of my life—has also been a constant source of strength.

My friends come next. Dan Robbins, Donald J. Sanders, Jontue Austin, Steve Bien-Aime, Meera Srinivasan, Erin Uy, and Darrin Rowe made invaluable editorial suggestions while encouraging my development as a journalist turned historian. My cousin Karthik and his wife Sandhya helped me by providing me a place to stay during my frequent visits to Harlem while researching this book. The transition has not been easy, but my friends—including the many I have not named—were instrumental in helping me write this book *and* keep my sanity.

As I began researching Du Bois and Robeson in early 2004, I leaned heavily on the advice of my mentor, Professor Alfred A. Moss of the University of Maryland–College Park. Professor Moss guided me with his insight and with his outstanding writings on black history. My "guardian angel," Joseph M. Selden of Penn State University, encouraged my development as a critical thinker. David Levering Lewis, James Smethurst, Molefi K. Asante, Charles L. Blockson, Kevin Hagopian, and Courtney Young all helped me with their voluminous knowledge about the professor and the pupil and the period of world history I was attempting to re-create. The archivists at Howard University's Moorland-Spingarn Research Center, most notably Joellen El-Bashir, helped me find gems in the Robeson collection. They were extremely dedicated to making sure my research was thorough, accurate, and most of all, personally rewarding. Bev Jarrett at the University of Missouri Press also provided valuable feedback and support along the way.

I'd be remiss if I didn't mention my editor, Ruth Baldwin, and Nation Books for believing in this project.

But the most important people in making this book a reality were the Du Bois–Robeson contemporaries who shared their time and memories with me. I grew very close to James and Esther Jackson, whose commitment to social justice has not diminished after more than 70 years of activism. E. S. Reddy is a pioneer whose contributions to social justice and help in illuminating the lives of Du Bois and Robeson can never be fully expressed in words. Abbott Simon and David Graham Du Bois sadly passed away while I was writing the book, but not before they gave me rich details about the men who played such an important role in their lives. A note of credit is also due to Paul Robeson Jr., who allowed me access to the Robeson Archives. I also wish to thank the Crisis Publishing Co., Inc., the publisher of the magazine of the National Association for the Advancement of Colored People, for use of the Du Bois *Crisis* writings.

May this book add another layer of profundity to the study of Du Bois and Robeson, two men whose lives could never fully be captured in mere words. May it also provide hope to those who continue in the struggle, who stand on principle instead of withering in the face of politics, and who believe that justice, equality, and humanity apply to *all*.

INTRODUCTION

The problem of the twentieth century is the problem of the
color-line—the relation of the darker to the lighter races of
men in Asia and Africa, in America and the islands of the sea.
—W. E. B. Du Bois, *The Souls of Black Folk* (1903)

THE MODEST, TWO-STORY HOUSE on Grace Court in Brooklyn Heights
was the perfect getaway for William Edward Burghardt Du
Bois and his new wife, Shirley Graham, a place where the two
could pen away their frustrations with the Cold War, imperialism, and piecemeal civil rights advocacy at home. For Du
Bois, it was a comfort in the captivity imposed on him by the
suffocating forces of reactionism in the U.S. government. Grace
Court served as a meeting place and sanctum for the Du Boises'
friends on the Left, a circle where access was allowed only by
the fiercely protective Shirley. The house, synonymous with
Foucault's panopticon, was under constant Federal Bureau of
Investigation (FBI) scrutiny and never safe, in Shirley's eyes,
from interlopers who might seek to disrupt its inmates. The Du
Boises' circle of friends shrank during the 1950s, but of the
intimates who regularly made their presence felt at Grace
Court, none loomed larger than Du Bois's longtime student

Paul Robeson. Robeson, himself a Cold War captive, would visit often, and he found solace with his comrades in the struggle. During his frequent house calls, it was not uncommon for Paul to make his way to the grand piano in the living room to sing for W. E. B. and Shirley and other guests who came by.[1]

As their political circle grew smaller during the McCarthy era, both men grew increasingly reliant upon one another, each seeking the moral and collegial encouragement to continue to fight when it seemed futile to do so. For Paul, Du Bois was the elder statesman of the struggle for equality and empowerment, an aging icon who had spent nearly a century fighting discrimination and seeking full dignity for exploited peoples. As Paul Robeson Jr. later recalled, the elder Robeson "simply had infinite respect" for the scholar.

> Dad always called [Du Bois] "the Doctor." It was like a student and a professor, even in private. I had the extraordinary experience of being with Dad coming into a room where Du Bois was sitting. It was 1958, Du Bois was by then in his eighties. He was a very small man and I still see this image of dad, with his huge size, literally settling down on a cushion at Du Bois's feet. It was natural for Du Bois to accept this, and for Dad to do it.[2]

David Graham Du Bois, the Doctor's stepson, added that "Paul, more than anyone, demonstrated that kind of deference and admiration and respect" to the Doctor. But the relationship was more than personal; Du Bois and Robeson forged a strong political alliance out of common views on race, class, international affairs, and the importance of the labor movement in social revolutions. Du Bois and Robeson's politics left a lasting impact on the Left and other schools of thought. They were pioneers of progressivism and pariahs to the establishment, equally revered and vilified for their outspokenness. Though pushed to the fringes of American society, they remain two of the most important figures of the twentieth century, both for their contributions to social and economic equality and the opprobrium that came with their outspokenness during the Cold War.

To UNDERSTAND HOW AND WHY Du Bois and Robeson became outcasts in the mainstream and heroes for the Left, it is important to examine their political and philosophical development during a period of dramatic global change. Both evolved from race liberals (in the traditional definition of liberalism) to leftists whose politics clashed with the American government and the vanguard of black leadership, including the executives of the National Association for the Advancement of Colored People (NAACP). Du Bois and Robeson didn't become staunch Socialists and so-called race radicals overnight, although they occasionally made sudden proclamations that—in the eyes of their peers—seemed to come out of nowhere. Whether it was Du Bois's tacit endorsement of voluntary race segregation (and Garveyism) or Robeson's declaration that blacks wouldn't fight against the Soviet Union, both men strode across the line of "acceptable" discourse without reservations.[3]

For the Doctor and Paul, a militant approach that embraced Socialism and black pride (or nationalism of the oppressed) was an issue of morality after it became clear that capitalism and self-determinism prevented the uplifting of the masses. It was unfathomable to them that rich whites could monopolize global wealth, leaving the rest of the world to suffer economically and racially. The inequality in the United States and in colonized nations could only be remedied, they argued, through a redistributive system that brought up the oppressed. They augmented this Marxist view with the notion that capitalist exploitation created racial subjugation. Exploited workers were essentially enslaved by their lack of economic access, resulting in the degradation of their racial self-worth. Both believed this led to constant conflict among imperial powers over the resources in darker nations; the inhabitants of oppressed nations would in turn fight among themselves for the limited resources remaining after colonial exploitation. "War," Du Bois postulated, "will not disappear until colonialism and quasi-colonialism under the form of investment and industrial control is utterly overthrown."[4]

Both men viewed the struggle against colonialism—and the inherent inequalities in capitalism—as an interracial one, but they asserted that nonwhites suffered disproportionately. "We as colored Americans use little logic if we do not see the basic struggle in the world today," Robeson noted at the start of World War II. "It includes people of every color."[5] He and the Doctor were the most prominent blacks to identify with and publicly support suffrage movements in India, South Africa, the Caribbean, and Latin America. Seeking the answer to global emancipation—physically and psychologically—of the colored masses, Du Bois and Robeson gravitated toward the

Soviet Union as the closest representation of their political idealism. It was hard not to be impressed by a country that banned racial discrimination and "nationalized" minorities through Russification (a process that stripped many tribal peoples of their ethnic identities) when, in comparison, the United States refused to ban lynching or end segregation. Soviet-style government and Stalinism would become a staple of both men's political philosophies, radicalizing them and pushing them further away from the mainstream.

Du Bois and Robeson synchronized their views after World War II when the U.S.-Soviet alliance crumbled and the Cold War began. Convinced that Socialism was the best solution to solve economic disparity and the subjugation of nonwhite people, they espoused political beliefs that bucked traditional "Americanism." This was their response to the United States moving to the opposite extreme in the wake of President Harry Truman's "get tough with Russia" stance and the rise of McCarthyism. However, the more dogmatic Du Bois and Robeson became in defending Russia and criticizing American policies, the more determined the U.S. government and the moderates in black leadership were to get rid of them. During the Cold War, mainstream groups such as the NAACP and Urban League worked closely with the FBI in an effort to discredit prominent leftists and left-wing groups whose political positions threatened to undermine a more accepted civil rights platform—one that Robeson lambasted as "gradualism." Consequently, Du Bois and Robeson lost their right to travel abroad and were blacklisted; they were additionally subjected to other McCarthy-era legal persecution, including Du Bois's indictment under the Smith Act and the forced dissolution of organizations important to both men, namely, the Civil Rights Congress and Council on African Affairs.

In the aftermath of the Cold War, Du Bois and Robeson's legacies were erased and rewritten; they would be "reconstructed" to fit a more acceptable view of African American pioneers. Du Bois continues to be remembered for *Souls of Black Folk* and the idea of the Talented Tenth, despite disavowing the latter following his shift to the extreme Left.[6] What little mainstream recollection there is about Robeson—considered the most famous African American in the world at the apex of his fame in the 1940s—trumpets his achievements as an actor and singer and ignores his contributions to left-wing thought and globalism. In fact, Robeson's destruction by the U.S. government and subsequent censorship by the media is unparalleled. As Du Bois himself noted, "The persecution of Paul Robeson by the government and people of the United States . . . has been one of the most contemptible happenings in modern history."[7]

"IN THE SURROUNDINGS OF MY FAMILY in a little New England town," Du Bois recalled, "I felt myself always as a more or less isolated evangelist, who's going to teach the world what my people meant and what they could do."[8] That evangelism spurred his activism and fueled a lifelong desire to find the answers to the world's social and economic problems. Du Bois's intellectual advancement was so profound that by his late twenties, he had presented himself as the chief adversary of Booker T. Washington. Within a decade Du Bois methodically would debunk Washington's philosophies and advocate a more radical approach that included integration and an emphasis on black higher education. His study of the Philadelphia Negro made him a pioneer of modern sociology, and his notions in the early 1900s of "double consciousness" were later defined and redefined by social scientists and historians as a classic dilemma of African Americans.[9]

By 1918 Du Bois had already achieved what few people could accomplish in several lifetimes. He was a principal member in the Niagara Movement, which led to the creation of the NAACP and the Urban League. Following the founding of the NAACP, Du Bois assumed leadership of the *Crisis*, which became required reading for a new generation of educated African Americans and progressive whites. Du Bois and Alain Locke, his contemporary at Howard University, championed the New Negro and the Talented Tenth, a belief that those blessed with the "natural" proclivity for intelligence and education would lead the uplift of the Negro race. After World War I, Du Bois fathered Pan-Africanism, a concept he would revise several times over the next twenty-five years. But Du Bois's first political awakening came after a visit to the Soviet Union, where he saw firsthand the application of Socialist principles. That was followed by a growing involvement in the Indian freedom struggle, facilitated by his friendships with Lala Lajpat Rai and Sarojini Naidu, an emissary of Mahatma Gandhi. The Doctor became increasingly globalistic and, in doing so, concluded that colonialism was the root of world problems, including the subjugation of African Americans. He wrote, "The determination of our rulers to conquer Asia and hold Africa is but logical prolongation of our despising of Negroes here and eventually the real effective opposition to colonialism, race hate, and war will center in this group of Negroes who know what white domination of dark people really is."[10]

Though initially skeptical about Communism and the Communist Party of the United States, Du Bois became increasingly aligned with noted Communists during the 1940s. One of those Communists, Shirley Graham, would eventually marry the Doctor. Du Bois's increasing radicalism—though aided by leftists such as Robeson, Graham, Louis Burnham, Herbert Aptheker—was also a product of his frustrations with mainstream civil rights advocacy. The NAACP, in his eyes, had outlived its use in finding an immediate remedy for racial discrimination and inequality. He also frequently butted heads with Walter White and Roy Wilkins, especially over his support of left-wing groups, and eventually cut off his ties with the association completely. A frustrated Du Bois wrote radical congressman Vito Marcantonio, "I found that the NAACP organization was almost a complete dictatorship under Mr. White. Without his good-will no one in the organization had any freedom of opinion or of action. . . . We must attack White and his stooges, Wilkins and (Gloster) Current."[11]

Du Bois's departure from the NAACP and his involvement with the Left led to revisions of his earlier philosophies, including his much-ballyhooed notion of the Talented Tenth.

The Talented Tenth did not exist by divine right, that you did not have a group of people of ability coming forward naturally and inevitably so that when you saw the educated and successful man, you saw most of the people who by native ability who should be educated and successful. I began to realize that near all this there was a tremendous amount of pure accident and chance . . . that the

Negroes who were in school and getting an education were not by any means necessarily and
inevitably the Negroes who ought to have had the
chance.[12]

Following his legal and political battles in the 1950s, an
exasperated Du Bois left the country; as a last act of defiance,
he formally registered with the Communist Party. He spent his
final years in Ghana, an honored guest of Kwame Nkrumah—
a Du Bois disciple—and compiled the Encyclopedia Africana.
From Ghana he influenced a new generation of African American scholars; after his death, they carried on and expounded
a legacy of Pan-African thought. Black Nationalists, leftists,
and mainstream civil rights advocates would co-opt different
parts of Du Bois's diverse and prolific political legacy, re-creating
their own versions of Du Bois.

IN CONTRAST TO DU BOIS's lengthy philosophical transformation,
Robeson used one epiphany and years of combined racial experience to make a more sudden (and dramatic) political change.
The roots of Paul's outlook were planted during his upbringing
in New Jersey. "From an early age I had come to accept a certain
protective tactic of Negro life in America," he wrote, "and I did
not fully break with the pattern until many years later. Even
while demonstrating that he really is an equal (and, strangely the
proof must be *superior* performance!) the Negro must never
appear to be challenging white superiority."[13]

Combining steely resolve with magnanimity, Robeson
excelled at Rutgers University, becoming class valedictorian

and earning all-America honors in athletics. Graduation from Columbia University Law School led to a short-lived legal career, but Robeson would find his success onstage. By the mid-1920s, Robeson was hailed as "a man of outstanding gifts and of noble physical strength and beauty."[14] His accomplishments as an actor (*Othello* and the *Emperor Jones*) and singer ("Ol' Man River" and Negro spirituals) afforded him privileges most blacks could only dream of. But the materialistic acceptance of Robeson could not offset the fact that he was still shackled by Jim Crow. That realization led to Robeson's increasing interest in his African heritage and his development as an Afrophile. "I felt as one with my African friends and became filled with a glowing pride in these riches, new found to me," he wrote in his autobiography. "I learned that along with the towering achievements of the cultures of ancient Greece and China there stood the culture of Africa, unseen and denied by the imperialist looters of Africa's natural wealth."[15]

But Robeson's immersion into different cultures still could not prepare him for the shock of visiting the Soviet Union in December 1934. That trip, laden with many revelations on the egalitarianism of the USSR, stirred a political awakening within Robeson. The impact on him was so profound that he would proclaim throughout the rest of his life that "it was only when I made my first trip to the USSR that I felt really that I was a human being."[16] Extolling Russia's model of government as the only answer for a racism- and classism-free society, Robeson began to take more-aggressive political positions that reflected his growth as a Socialist thinker. Robeson attacked colonialism and Fascism, developing close friendships with African, Asian, and Caribbean anticolonials while appearing in Spain to sing on behalf of the republican forces against Franco. Robeson viewed the Soviet Union as the bulwark against Fascism, and his support grew only more pronounced during World War II.

> We must not be talked out of our heritage. We must be proud of our traditions and where possible draw upon them to enrich the contribution we can make to a world which can ill afford to lose whatever value human beings have created. This applies as well to the great folk cultures of the working and peasant masses in Europe, Asia and the Americas. The comradely contribution by different peoples to a common civilization is no longer a dream, for on one-sixth of the earth's surface such a civilization does exist, and these peoples with their rich nationalist cultures firmly bound into one socialist union stand as a bulwark against the forces of reaction and as a leading force in the struggle for peace. Daily it becomes more and more apparent that this struggle for peace, as was said long ago, is indivisible.[17]

Despite Paul's calls for international solidarity against colonialism, capitalism, and Fascism (which he viewed as intertwined evils oppressing colored people), he never forgot his special duty to blacks. Amiri Baraka noted that "Robeson knew, as Du Bois pointed out in *Black Reconstruction in America*, that there had been many other peoples who had suffered similar exploitation and repression—workers and farmers in Asia and Europe—but the difference was that 'none of them was real estate!'"[18] In this regard, Robeson's keen understanding of the uniqueness of the black experience was overlooked and underappreciated by his peers. P. L. Prattis, left-wing editor of the *Pittsburgh Courier*, was among the few who appreciated Robeson's "great intellect." Robeson, Prattis said, "can see so much farther than other men and has the faculty of revealing to them what he sees."[19]

Though Robeson's advocacy antagonized the FBI and hawks in the U.S. government, he remained one of the most internationally beloved figures during the early 1940s. Following a successful run of *Othello*, several publications anointed him America's "number-one Negro."[20] But the tide inevitably turned against Robeson soon after Truman made an atomic statement in Japan, putting Americans on edge for a possible nuclear war with the Soviet Union. Paul became openly antagonistic against what he perceived to be the "reactionary forces" within the U.S. government: namely, Truman advisors Dean Acheson and Edward R. Stettinius. Robeson told a crowd of supporters in 1946 that the coalitions of social justice could "win if the majority of the American people can be brought to see and understand in the fullest sense the fact that the struggle in which we are engaged is not a matter of mere humanitarian sentiment, but of life and death. The only alternative to world freedom is world annihilation—another bloody holocaust—which will dwarf the two world wars through which we have passed."[21] Robeson's involvement with the Council on African Affairs—arguably the most influential American group to advocate an independent Africa—and the Communist-backed Civil Rights Congress also undermined the NAACP's hegemony. The association, which had reached

the height of its influence in the mid-1940s, clandestinely col-
laborated with the government to discredit Robeson.
According to the late actor Ossie Davis, "Paul's capacity to
excite admiration in large groups of people, black and otherwise, here, in Africa, and over the world, made him . . . a real
threat to the powers that be."[22] Following his declaration at
the Paris Peace Conference that he did not wish for a war with
the Soviet Union, Paul's political opponents lined up to attack
him. Facing immense pressure from the grip of McCarthyism,
black leaders distanced themselves from Robeson; some,
including Wilkins and Robeson ally turned FBI informant Max
Yergan, readily condemned him.

The politics of the Cold War demanded ideological conformity. Paul's refusal to go along with mainstream American
ideology would lead to his disenfranchisement during the
1950s. An eight-year battle for his passport would follow,
leaving Robeson confined and censored in the United States.
By the mid-1960s, Robeson was largely forgotten, save for his
followers and a new generation of black nationalists who glorified him as a martyr. In 1976, he died in solitude at his
sister's home in Philadelphia. Robeson's politics—and his
downfall—would inspire various factions within the Left,
ranging from Communists to black nationalists, among them
Malcolm X and the leaders of the Black Panther Party.

THOUGH AN EXPLORATION of Du Bois and Robeson's personal lives
is required to explain their politics, this book isn't a detailed
biography. Instead, it weaves their stories into forty years of
social and political change in the United States and across the

globe, from the Harlem Renaissance and birth of Pan-Africanism to the passage of the Civil Rights Act and post-colonialism in Africa, Asia, and Latin America. The first part of the book discusses how both men became acquainted with each other and became more involved with the Left. The middle explains how they became more entrenched in their leftist views, including their unequivocal support for the Soviet Union, despite a growing tide of conservatism that began infecting American society following World War II. The latter part looks at why Du Bois and Robeson's against-the-grain intellectual activism ultimately led to their downfalls and why the same right-wing ideology that destroyed them has been reincarnated following the September 11, 2001, attacks on America.

Du Bois and Robeson worked well together because of their insistence that the United States be made accountable for its apparent hypocrisy. How could the United States stand for freedom and democracy when it treated more than 15 million of its own people as second- and third-class citizens, supported colonialism and apartheid, exploited the natural resources of "black, brown, and yellow" nations, and installed dictatorships in countries where Communists threatened to take power? That question was the basis of leftist activism, whether it was Popular Front–era Communists who tried to combine Bolshevism with Americanism or black nationalists who espoused Marxism and a mandate for self-determinism. Despite many historians asserting that this symbiosis between an oppressed race and nonmainstream ideology was ephemeral, the Left was more than a passing fancy for blacks; it was a marriage of their frustrations with Jim Crow and the exploitation of capitalism to the idealistic notions of class equality, concepts Du Bois and Robeson emphatically and clearly articulated. Both would in some way influence American Communism, modern-day liberalism, black power, internationalism—more so than even noted black diplomat Ralph Bunche—and the dialogue between moderates and radicals in the black intelligentsia. The common thread among those myriad philosophies was Du Bois and Robeson's vehement stance against oppression and that "a belief in humanity is a belief in colored men."[23]

Racism, classism, and third world exploitation continue to be major themes of global discussion today. Du Bois and Robeson were among the few in their time to take part in the dialogue, and in doing so, sacrificed their reputations. But, as this book seeks to prove, the politics of the professor and his pupil have had a lasting impact on our understanding of social justice and international suffrage.

1

THE HARLEM RENAISSANCE AND THE BIRTH OF A FRIENDSHIP

If we must die, let it not be like hogs
Hunted and penned in an inglorious spot
While 'round us bark the mad and hungry dogs
Making their mock of our accursed lot.
If we must die, O let us nobly die
So that our precious blood may not be shed
In vain; then even the monsters we defy
Shall be constrained to honor us through dead!
O kinsmen! we must meet the common foe!
Though far outnumbered let us show brave,
And for their thousand blows deal one deathblow!
What though before us lies the open grave?
Like men we'll face the murderous, cowardly pack,
Pressed to the wall, dying but fighting back!

—Claude McKay, "If We Must Die" (1922)

IN THE MONTHS FOLLOWING WORLD WAR I, Negroes in the United States were indeed pressed to the wall. After dying overseas for a country that offered them little hope of equal citizenship, black soldiers were welcomed home with the rope. Race violence in the summer of 1919 had reached a new high—so bloody, widespread, and profound that NAACP executive secretary James Weldon Johnson called it the Red Summer. Negroes who beseeched the authorities for justice found their pleas unanswered, as the American legal system, especially in the South, had "degenerated into a machinery for wreaking vengeance upon citizens, and the verdicts of juries are the passions of the mob instead of the voice of justice." A. Philip Randolph's grim assessment of lynching and mob violence concluded "that the civilized world looks upon American democracy as a mockery."[1] Democracy, which the United States had fought so vigorously to defend in Europe, was escaping its own citizens. Economic competition, fears of Bolshevism, and the continued demonizing of black men contributed to racial conflict, with no hope in sight. Violence against blacks had reached levels of barbarism that tested the label of American "civilization."

But more blacks began fighting back, especially in the urban North, where the Great Black Migration strained cities already struggling with tensions among settled whites and European immigrants. The violence—specifically the black backlash—had as much of a psychological impact as a physical one. As Walter White concluded in his investigation of the riots, "One of the greatest surprises to many of those who came down to 'clean out the niggers' is that these same 'niggers' fought back. Colored men saw their own kind being killed, heard of many more, and believed that their lives and liberty were at stake."[2]

With Congress stonewalling the NAACP-led Dyer anti-lynching bill and President Woodrow Wilson's reticence to condemn race violence, black America seemed destined to end one turbulence and begin another.[3] Amid the conflict, a civil rights lion was perched in his Harlem office, contemplating whether or not to maintain hope. Another man, disguising the wounds of racism with a warm smile and captivating presence, was packing his bags at Rutgers University and preparing to make his move to the Big Apple. Although each was unaware of the other, the dreams of Renaissance for William Edward Burghardt Du Bois and Paul Leroy Robeson were about to become reality, cementing one's icon status and making the other an international superstar. When Du Bois returned from the Pan-African Congress—a highly romanticized Paris convention of black scholars and radicals with their own visions of Africa—in the summer of 1919, he had come to the bittersweet conclusion that the United States was still the best hope for blacks and democracy. His own morbid observations on the state of race relations in America were summed eloquently in "Returning Soldiers" prior to the Paris conference. "Make way for Democracy! We saved it in France, and by the great Jehovah, we will save it in the USA, or know the reason why," the Doctor wrote.[4] Despite his misgivings about the staunch integrationist views of James Weldon Johnson and NAACP President Joel Spingarn, Du Bois was convinced that it was the Negro's duty to *become* an American and white America's duty to accept the Negro as such. Robeson, meanwhile, was already an all-American and set his sights on joining the blossoming black professional scene in New York. Having moved past and transcended a racially hostile upbringing in Princeton and Somerville, New Jersey, Robeson embodied the "New Idealism" he so eloquently advocated in his parting oratory to his Rutgers peers. As he looked ahead to a legal career, Paul had no idea that he would become one of the most promising products of the coming decade.

The turbulence of the latter 1910s did pave the way for progress. A new black middle class was growing in the North, and college education among young African Americans had reached an all-time high. For the leaders of the young NAACP, this was progress and testament to their fight, a multipronged effort that espoused equality, an end to lynching, and gradual integration. In the fall of 1919, Du Bois and his cadre of NAACP supporters had seen tremendous progress in the Northeast, opening branches throughout New York and attracting tens of thousands of supporters in their first ten years of existence. Having dispatched Booker T. Washington's notion of accommodation, the Harvard intellectual, schooled in a Eurocentric model of uplift for blacks, was now the prominent voice of black America. Though he had grown increasingly militant during the first twenty years of the century, Du Bois, now fifty-one, still saw the complimentary notions of the Negro and the white coming together in "an ideal of fostering and developing the traits and talents of the Negro, not in opposition to, but in conformity with, the greater ideals of the American Republic, in order that some day, on American soil, two world races may give to each other those characteristics which both so sadly lack."[5] His views, tempered by the cynicism of growing up poor and black in Great Barrington, Massachusetts,

4

seemed to fit the Negro into a Eurocentric frame of advocacy; after all, prominent blacks argued, shunning white America altogether would deny the Negro a model of advancement. It was this philosophy, tied together with the funds of white philanthropy, that governed the mentality of the NAACP and the Urban League. Blacks and whites, working in tandem to attack the ills of race riots, lynching, and systemic discrimination and disenfranchisement of the colored races, would somehow influence the highest levels of government to change the regress of black America following the repeal of Civil War Reconstruction laws. That was the NAACP's modus operandi, but as a result, some blacks called it "a Negro snob affair." Even as hundreds of Negroes hung in public squares, Du Bois and his philosophical allies, such as James Weldon Johnson and Alain Locke, had not lost faith in the American system. They were not "revolutionaries," Du Bois insisted on many occasions, but merely trying to ensure the constitutional protections that had long precluded the darker races of the United States. A mix of militancy and moderation defined the racial philosopher, advocate, and pioneering sociologist, and his own views had a clear impact on the organization and its growing membership rolls.

Many blacks were not as receptive to the idea of wearing the mask of moderation, but urban sophistication had brought them beyond the barrel of a gun. Young Negro intellectuals such as Claude McKay, Jean Toomer, Walter White, and Langston Hughes picked up the pen to capture their frustration with a system that was not working for them. Birthing the Harlem Renaissance with creativity and channeled anger, they voiced their frustration with a broken and unequal system. Taking stock of his own philosophical growth, Du Bois saw the ensuing rise of the intelligentsia as "leaders of thought and missionaries of culture among their people," prophesied in his Talented Tenth manifesto.[6] The New Negro Movement, it seemed, would become the stepping-stone for the advancement of black America, starting from the bustle of Harlem and other big metropolises such as Philadelphia, Boston, and Washington and moving to the South, where the sharecroppers and house servants had never been exposed to the positive elements of blackness. The New Negro—with Du Bois, Johnson, Locke, and young scholars such as Horace Mann Bond and E. Franklin Frazier—was an aggressive counter to the forces of white supremacy and Anglocentrism that dominated the years following World War I. As Du Bois noted at the start of the Harlem Renaissance and the peak of the Great Migration, it seemed that after "years of oppression which at times became almost unbearable, the tide against the Negro in the United States has been turned."[7]

To underscore the Doctor's assertion, Robeson seemed destined to take the mantle of Negro leadership. He had already earned a reputation as a multidisciplinary talent whose effulgence "dimmed the fame of Booker T. Washington."[8] A top debater and an all-American linebacker whom football legend Walter Camp called "the greatest defensive football player of all time," Paul's magnanimity made him one of the most popular people on campus. Expounding his academic talents, Paul was a Phi Beta Kappa and was inducted into the exclusive Cap and Skull society; but his most significant accomplishment may have been mastering the ability to mask his true emotions. As Paul Robeson Jr. would later recall:

Dad became an expert at sitting on his anger. He learned from his father that he couldn't afford the luxury of spontaneously expressing it in a white racist society. It was a Black male rule because we were the ones who got lynched. . . . It was something your parents beat into you psychologically—physically if necessary. It meant your survival. Of course, you still had the rage, but you transformed and transcended it.[9]

In later years white classmates said "Robey" never got angry or expressed his emotions; their ignorance was a testament to Paul's success at keeping a poker face. After all, he did superficially transcend the racism he experienced at Rutgers, including a variety of broken limbs courtesy of opposing players—and even teammates—who went after him. In his valedictorian speech, he boldly predicted a triumph of reconciliation between the black and white races in the United States; moreover, he asserted that those "of the less favored race" must take their destiny into their own hands, a call that echoed Booker T. Washington's notion of self-sufficiency. Robeson went on to say that "neither institutions nor friends can make a race stand unless it has strength; that races like individuals must stand or fall by their own merit; that to fully succeed they must practice the virtues of self reliance, self respect, industry, perseverance, and economy."[10] The graduating class roared with approval for Robeson, capping what seemingly had been a lifetime of accomplishments in a four-year span. The class prophecy printed in the Rutgers *Targum* boldly proclaimed that Paul would become the "leader of the colored race in America."

While Robeson was cool to being a messiah, he embraced the chance to further his debating skills and cultivate a legal mind. With an acceptance letter to Columbia University Law School in hand, Robeson arrived in Harlem during the Red Summer, his attentions focused more on blending into the already world-famous social and political scene. His reputation preceded him, and with the recognition of his athletic exploits and already awe-inspiring voice, Paul had no trouble making friends in the "Negro capital of the world." Robeson was one of "Harlem's darlings," as biographer Martin Duberman later noted, and his daily doings quickly became a fixture in New Negro gossip. Paul's involvement in the nonstop social scene in Harlem, where he was frequently spotted "with a pretty girl on his arm," was not uncommon for an aspiring professional. In fact, it seemed more of a natural calling for any Negro drawn to the enlightened debauchery and glitz of New York, not unlike the lure of Hollywood years later to young blondes with a suitcase full of big-screen dreams. If the political and literary growth of the Renaissance epitomized the artists and activists who envisioned a better day for African Americans, the social aspect of Harlem was Americana, the true embodiment of the Decade of Decadence.

If the Harlem Renaissance helped articulate the Negro plight to urban whites, it also had the latent effect of rein-forcing white stereotypes of blacks as a passionate and primi-tive people. Rich whites delighted in patronizing blacks, if only to assuage their own notions that black art was in fact the African American way of civilizing. The socialite/writer Carl Van Vechten, whose 1926 book *Nigger Heaven*, dropped more than a few jaws among blacks, frequently boasted of his inti-macy with Negro artistic and intellectual circles; like many white aficionados of black culture, he made no secret of his desire to be accepted by the New Negro.[11] But while the vivacious and often ostentatious social climate of the renaissance offered an ideal of integration, the reputation of Harlem as "overcrowded, vulgar, and wicked" only compounded the labels of primacy and incivility attached to its denizens.[12]

Though Robeson quickly wove his way into the Harlem social fabric and drank the soma of the renaissance's extravagance, he fell into two things that would change and define his life: marriage and an acting career. A football injury that sent Robeson to New York Presbyterian Hospital led to an encounter with Eslanda Cardozo Goode, a feisty, olive-complexioned woman whose bloodlines predicted her future success. Essie, as others would later tell Duberman, seemed to jump at the opportunity to meet the incapacitated young law student when introduced by a doctor. Robeson, who had shown no overt indications of affections upon their initial meetings, would eventually fall for Essie, thanks in large part to her almost-methodical efforts to win him over. But it might have been clear to Eslanda from the start that Paul's heart could never solely belong to her; her practicality had trumped even her greatest efforts to idealistically deny the wandering eyes and affections that seemed to be ingrained in his nature. Even after they married in 1921, Eslanda had convinced herself that her husband's stubbornness—a trait that would augment his political convictions in later years—seemed too robust to overcome.

Paul became involved with a theater theater troupe as a law student, seeking to pass the time by earning extra income. He took the stage in featured roles in *Taboo* and *Shuffle Along*, a musical that had grown to become "the most brilliant African American revue New York had ever witnessed." The groundbreaking show was performed at the Sam Harris Theater in Harlem and Robeson's role only expanded both his social rolodex and his geography; Paul signed on to travel and perform in Europe in Mary Hoytie Wiborg's *Voodoo*, the renamed and revised version of *Taboo*. When he returned to the states in late 1922, Paul seized upon his increased fame to find more opportunities on stage; the added roles and singing opportunities, he reasoned, would give him an ample income while he finished up his law studies. The stage exposure gave Paul wider recognition, and it didn't hurt that the Robesons were now a staple of every Harlem party's invite list. It was at these parties where Paul became more acquainted with a young octoroon journalist named Walter White. White, a rising star in Du Bois's NAACP, had been instrumental in helping the organization expose and publicize the damning effects of Jim Crow on Southern blacks and the lack of attention that was paid to lynching. White's friendship was instrumental in introducing Paul to other prominent black activists and would pave the way for a first acquaintance with the venerable Doctor.

Robeson's legal career was cut short by racial reality. Soon after graduating Columbia, he found work at a law firm of Rutgers alum and white liberal Louis William Stotesbury. However, the racial antagonism in the office was too much for even Paul to bear, underscored by a white stenographer telling him: "I never take dictation from a nigger." A meeting with Stotesbury—who was sympathetic but unable to offer anything more than the future possibility of a Harlem office—sealed

Robeson's decision to leave law and pursue acting and singing. When Paul Robeson, Esq., left the legal profession that same year, Paul Robeson the actor finally emerged from the shadows. He joined the Provincetown Playhouse, soon starring in Eugene O'Neill's *All God's Chillun Got Wings*. His breakthrough performance in the play, which received mixed reviews, only furthered his reputation. After playing the lead in the all-black *Roseanne*, critics concentrated more on his individual performance than the plays in which he was cast. *Emperor Jones*, another O'Neill production, gave Robeson a chance to play a flawed protagonist. Brutus Jones, an escaped slave, exuded the "childish and primitive" nature so commonly associated with the black stereotype, but Paul found dignity in the character. Though Robeson worked on developing into an accomplished character actor, it was his physical presence on stage that drew the most response from critics. "His figure on the slave block, in *The Emperor Jones*," one reviewer gushed, "is remembered like a bronze of ancient mold."[13] In later years, historians would assert that Paul's physicality was both sexual and political expression. His instant mainstream success was in no doubt due to the way he promoted his body, drawing instant appeal among women and men. As Jeffrey C. Stewart explained, "The body has been a way for the Black man or woman . . . to negotiate white fantasies of crossing to accept white society to accept as Other. Robeson first crossed over by representing the big Black dangerous man on stage. . . . The next step was to move from inaccessible, sullen Negro . . . to the accessible African American, who incorporated Western values of heroism, universality, and nobility in his body and his personality."[14] Paul believed his physical attributes could be used as a "crossover" tool of his own advancement; by the 1930s, however, he came to view physicality as a vehicle of white capitalist oppression.[15]

THOUGH HE SEEMED PUBLICLY SATISFIED with the black arts movement and the platform of the NAACP, Du Bois was already wading in more militant waters. When *Darkwater: Voices from Within the Veil* was published in 1920, he came out with some of his strongest commentary on the soured state of race relations, challenging the capitalism and racial hierarchy that seemed to doom blacks and other darker races to the lowest levels of global social and economic stratification. *Darkwater* gave voice to Du Bois's building frustrations, especially with the notion that Americans would fight and die overseas for freeing Europe, but would not lift a finger in defense of their own suppressed races. In "The Souls of White Folk," Du Bois placed the blame of the First World War squarely on white greed and exploitation, damning America by its association with European colonizers. "For two or more centuries America has marched proudly in the van of human hatred—making bonfires of human flesh and laughing at them hideously, and making the insulting of millions more than a matter of dislike— rather a great religion, a world war-cry: Up white, down black; to your tents, O white folk, and world war with black and parti-colored mongrel beasts!"[16] The Doctor also bellowed his most damning criticism of the United State as a traitor against its own ideals. "Instead of standing as a great example of the success of democracy and the possibility of human brotherhood," Du Bois lamented, "America has taken her place as an awful example of its pitfalls and failures, so far as black and brown and yellow peoples are concerned."[17]

His frustrations aside, the scholar was still unconvinced that revolution, as seen in the bloody rise of the proletariat under Lenin in Russia, would succeed in the United States. His views often coincided with the domestic and international turbulence he saw, and the last five years would have driven lesser men crazy with philosophical conflict. Despite his growing agitation over the state of affairs and lack of progress in civil rights, Du Bois had grounds for optimism. After all, weren't the advances of the New Negro, coupled with the all-time high for blacks in college, enough to validate the notion that democracy could work if fixed? Wasn't the appointment of Emmett Scott as a special assistant to the secretary of war a small but significant step in the Negro's quest for equality and full emancipation? The Doctor was torn, but the topics covered in *Darkwater* would provide the basis for Du Bois's growing dissatisfaction with the pace of progress in the United States and the "in the framework" methods of the NAACP. His private fascination with left-wing ideologies aside, Du Bois was pragmatic enough to see that his organization—held together by racial idealism and Eurocentric paradigms of uplift—provided the best chance for the race to get its long-overdue equality and eventual integration.[18]

The Doctor's hesitance was reflective of many black activists' wariness of the unknown, especially when it came to the Left. Though black sociopolitical thought had reached new levels of militancy by the end of the First World War, the chosen spokespeople of Negro advancement were not ready to advocate radical social upheaval. The "bit by bit" mentality of black leadership had become a mantra by 1920, a sign of the growing black political elite's unwillingness to go outside of the constructs of acceptable protest; this was to the dismay of some of the offspring of the New Negro movement, poor black intellectuals whose romantic notions of Bolshevism and growing antipathy toward the gradualism of equality were conceiving leftism in Harlem. The Socialist Party was among the early victors in winning over young disenchanted blacks. One of those was A. Philip Randolph, who consistently mocked Du Bois and his peers as the "old-crowd Negroes." Randolph was dissatisfied with what he called "the doctrine of nonresistance" championed by the NAACP. Instead, he called for more militant response to white violence, urging blacks to fight back if attacked. "No one who will not fight to protect his life is fit to live," he wrote. "Self-defense is recognized as a legitimate weapon in all civilized countries."[19] Randolph also showed his ability to unite various fringe groups against a common enemy—the bourgeois Negroes who were out of touch with the common man. He struck a chord with black nationalists, Communists, Socialists, and black conservatives alike by offering his own spin on the New Negro. Calling for the New Negro to lead a social revolution, Randolph wrote that in dealing with "Negro leaders, his object is to destroy them all and build up new ones."[20] Randolph would continue his attacks on Du Bois and the other anointed leaders of black America, stoking a rivalry between the two that would last the next forty years. Randolph and other leftists, including McKay, offered convincing arguments for why the Negro shouldn't settle on a more gradual approach to civil rights and black empowerment. But during the early 1920s, the Left had a difficult time escaping the huge shadow cast by Du Bois and the NAACP. For many educated African Americans who had moved to New York and other big cities, militancy was a zero-sum game that would only create more problems. They were more inclined to accept a path of conciliation, integration, and social equality in white America. Robeson shared this view, feeling that white acceptance was a natural end result of Negro excellence. Professional success, in Robeson's words, equated to bridging what he saw as a reachable gap between the races. "What we have got to do is move forward," he told a reporter in 1924. "I conserve my energies for my work as an actor." His own philosophies still inchoate, Robeson was open to political debate and discussion among friends. William Patterson recalled years later that, from his first encounter with Robeson, "the theme of most of our conversations was political."[21] Publicly, Paul chose to let the organized protest movement of the NAACP and radical organs like Randolph's Socialist-leaning publication, *The Messenger*, do the walking and talking. While he befriended activists from a spectrum of ideologies, Robeson was remarkably uninvolved in the politics of the New Negro. He attended meetings of the NAACP and even made his way to gatherings for the Socialist Party and the Communist Party, but parlayed very little of his empathy into action.

At the time of Robeson's arrival in New York, the new Negro reeked of sophistication and acquired aristocracy—until a portly, dark-skinned Jamaican entered the fray. Charismatic and full of messianic bluster, Marcus Garvey—the pioneer of black racialism and the forebear of afrocentricity and black nationalism—brought with him the idea of a Negro self-improvement organization based on Booker T. Washington's model. Garvey became sensitized to racialism in Jamaica, where blacks were on the lowest rung of a racial caste system run by the British. As he watched blacks compete for scarce resources, Garvey realized that the only way for blacks to gain their full humanity was to destroy white-dominated society or leave it altogether. He chose the latter. Garvey's experiment, the Universal Negro Improvement Association (UNIA), failed in Jamaica, largely because of the influence light-skinned blacks and biracial Jamaicans had in squashing it. "Mulattoes," as Garvey would grudgingly recall, wanted no part of a movement that gave unmixed Negroes an equal weight in West Indian society, especially when the goal of many light-skinned blacks had been to fully assimilate (and intermarry) into the European Jamaica. When Garvey landed in New York in 1916, Washington was dead, the Great Migration was in progress, and urbanization had created new opportunities and new challenges for black America. After a tour of the United States, Garvey got to work in 1917, building his UNIA movement from scratch in Harlem. Garvey had a new strategy for building his movement in the United States: capitalizing on the legacy of slavery and of white blood in the American Negro. Urbanization had changed the dynamics of black life, but Garvey saw that the opportunities that blacks received and how they were treated differed widely based on their complexion. The Eurocentrism of Negro education in America had a profound effect on their psychology. As Frantz Fanon and Robert Smith noted decades later, African Americans had accepted—willingly or unwittingly—an "internal inferiorization" that was predicated on the characteristics associated with race and skin color.[22] White- or light-skinned people with sharp features and "good" straight hair were educated and capable of making moral judgments for the betterment of society. On the other hand, black was corrupt, vile, and uncivilized, and the early study of criminology even suggested that "Negroid" facial features such as wide noses and big lips made those who possessed such traits predisposed to crime and unintelligent behavior. Even as Du Bois and other black scholars blasted the notions of white superiority, they could hardly defend the notion that they were their own prototypes of Negro America. To Garvey, the widespread success of Du Bois was seen in his "mulatto blood," accentuated by Du Bois's light skin and European grooming. As if Garvey's gun of rhetoric was being loaded for him, the treatment of poor, darker-skinned blacks by their richer, more-established, and lighter-skinned counterparts across the country underscored the chasm that existed within black America, even as black leadership preached solidarity following World War I.

Racialism and race pride became the raison d'être, and by 1919, the UNIA had become a force of black mobilization. It wasn't just poor blacks—largely ignored by the NAACP and seemingly etched at the bottom of the American caste system—who rushed to open their wallets to join the UNIA; rich blacks and left-wing groups such as the African Blood Brotherhood and the Hamitic League of the World also jumped at the chance to support a group that glorified blackness. Madame C. J. Walker, the black cosmetics giant, even helped pay for the start-up of Garvey's print mouthpiece, *The Negro World*. The NAACP, which had effectively monopolized the mantle of civil rights leadership, was stunned by Garvey's rise. Rank-and-file members of the NAACP and, not coincidentally, the black bourgeoisie began to petition the government to look at Garvey's activities. Some black leaders tried to stifle UNIA organization by refusing the growing masses of Garveyites from promoting the movement in their churches, through their businesses, and even on street corners. What paralyzed black leadership was their perception that the uneducated hoi polloi, led by a dark-skinned "false prophet" with grandiose schemes of Negrocentricity, would undermine the legitimacy of the NAACP and Urban League. The acceptable forms of militancy and advocacy had to be handled, the bourgeoisie argued, by the established representatives of the race. The interpretations of the Talented Tenth that fueled classism among upper-class and educated Negroes also drove their own racist notions about Garvey and his followers. But the upper-class Negroes' characterizations of Garvey and their attempts to demonize him only galvanized support for the UNIA. By 1922 the UNIA was the largest mass movement ever to organize blacks, and it exposed the deep class division between the NAACP and the poor blacks that were disenfranchised in the struggle for civil rights.

The rise of a popular alternative to the integrationist and almost aristocratic NAACP and Urban League vexed the Doctor, whose *Crisis* editorials on the UNIA were careful at first not to discredit the movement. Initially Du Bois was not antagonistic toward Garvey, calling the UNIA's leader "an honest and sincere man with a tremendous vision, great dynamic force, stubborn determination, and unselfish desire to serve."[23] Though hardly a description that black moderates wanted to hear, Du Bois's assessment reflected his own deep-rooted belief in the beauty of black, a conviction he often felt other NAACP mainstays such as Johnson lacked. But the Doctor offered a less-flattering review of the Jamaican's business and political acumen. He predicted that the "idealist" and his lack of business sense would "overwhelm with bankruptcy and disaster one of the most interesting spiritual movements of the modern Negro world."[24] Du Bois's rebuke of Garvey did little to dissuade many blacks from joining or at least supporting the UNIA. Garveyism offered blacks redemption of their own humanity; rather than fight for an equal standing with the white man, Garvey's alternative allowed Negroes to bask in the richness of their own race. As Du Bois admitted, "Deep in the black man's heart he knows that he needs more than homes and stores and churches. He needs manhood—liberty, brotherhood, equality. . . . Here is Garvey yelling to life, from the black side, a race consciousness which leaps to meet Madison Grant and Lothrop Stoddard and other worshipers of the great white race."[25]

Emboldened by proletarian support, Garvey went on the offensive against Du Bois and the Talented Tenth Negroes, who, in their Eurocentric arrogance, refused to acknowledge the merits of the UNIA. Garvey charged that "Du Bois represents a group that hates the Negro blood in its veins, and has been working subtly to build up a caste aristocracy that would socially divide the race into two groups: one the superior because of color caste, and the other the inferior, hence the pretentious work of the National Association for the Advancement of 'Colored' People." Ironically, Du Bois would later agree with Garvey's assessment of the NAACP, but he was in no mood to discuss racial philosophy with a "demagogue, a blatant boaster, who with monkey-shines was deluding the people and taking their hard-earned dollar."[26] The Du Bois–Garvey personal attacks would escalate as the NAACP and UNIA battled for control to advocate the future of Negroes in America. While Garvey believed that blacks could do without white cooperation, Du Bois proclaimed that America's future was "not in segregation, but in closer, larger unity" and "interracial peace."[27]

Their intense hostility did not prevent the adversaries from agreeing on the importance of Africa, the root of Garvey's movement, and the ideal of Du Boisian uplift of African peoples. Both men romanticized Africa, but their utopian notions of African development clashed as fiercely as their personalities. The dueling Pan-African visions arose from fierce convictions of Christian civility, charity, and self-sufficiency for the Dark Continent. For Garvey, whose bombast overshadowed his sincerity in finding a new construct for black empowerment, Africa was home to Africans and the preordained land of its enslaved expatriates. He likened black Americans' call to Africa to the Zionists' pull to Israel. Africa wasn't just the soil that created the seeds of the black race; to Garvey it was where those seeds would flower and die. The Du Boisian postulate on Africa was based on enriching a continent that had been raped by Europeans, not resettling it. Whether by the hands of the Arabs, Ethiopians, or Zulus who were part of the maze of backgrounds encompassing the land, Du Bois believed in the providence of Africa's eventual success and sovereignty on its own merits. His views on Africa, however, were not wholly different from some white humanitarians such as Albert Schweitzer, whose notions of native African inferiority helped fuel their philanthropy. In fact, early Du Boisian Pan-Africanism smacked of paternalism.

In the Pan-African Congress of 1919, Du Bois and the other assembled delegates—most from the United States and Europe—agreed that African nations should be held in trust until they were ready for self-rule, that "Natives shall have voice in the government to the extent that their development permits," and that "wherever persons of African descent are civilized and able to meet the tests of surrounding culture, they shall be accorded the same rights as their fellow-citizens."[28] Du Bois's bottom-line assessment of Africans was that their civilization did not meet the standards of the modern world, a claim he would later disavow. Garvey, on the other hand, repudiated colonialism and sought to build Africa for Africans, whether by peaceful resettlement or by force. His title of provisional president of Africa added pomp to his claims as he tried to move Negroes to Liberia. Initially welcomed by Liberian president Charles King, Garvey's small but growing UNIA contingent was rebuffed, then banned, after word got out about the Jamaican's grand designs to take over the country.

Garvey's vision for Africa never materialized, and soon he was becoming his own worst enemy. He alienated members of the African Blood Brotherhood—once his primary supporters—and ran afoul of Randolph, who soon eclipsed Du Bois as Garvey's biggest detractor. Moreover, reports surfaced that Garvey had even made an alliance with the Ku Klux Klan. Once the momentum of the UNIA slowed, Garvey was an easy target for the government. He was convicted in 1924 of mail fraud and sentenced to five years in an Atlanta prison before being deported in 1927. Though Garvey's destruction was partly his own doing, Du Bois could not help but pay a backhanded tribute to a man who shook the black elite to its core.

"In a larger field, with fairer opportunity, he might have been great, certainly notorious," Du Bois wrote. "He is today a little puppet, serio-comic, funny, yet swept with a great veil of tragedy; meaning in himself little more than a passing agitation, moving darkly and uncertainly from a little island of the sea to the panting, half-submerged millions of the first world state."[29]

In later years Du Bois would pay homage to Garvey by co-opting some of the central elements of Garveyism into his racial philosophy.

GARVEY'S GROWTH AND HIS DEMISE created opportunities for the Left. Buoyed by the rise of the labor movement, left-wing groups expanded their recruiting to include disaffected Garveyites. Groups such as the American Workers Party, the Socialist Party, and the Communist Party of the United States of America were already building their memberships—though only to a fraction of the extent of Garvey's movement—and honing their message to attract working-class blacks into their ranks. Communist leader Earl Browder was a frequent acquaintance of the New Negro crowd and quickly earned the respect of some of the Harlem artistic circles for his philosophies on race and class. Though the Left still had a ways to go in attracting blacks, there was some appeal for the class conscious. The Communist Party USA, though largely made up of Eastern European nationalistic fraternal agencies, began to feel the squeeze from the Soviet Comintern, which made it clear that recruiting blacks for the revolution was essential to implement the third-period policies of the revolution. By the mid-1920s, American Communist leaders—prodded by their

Soviet shot-callers and dismayed by ethnic and nationalistic factionalism among Communist Party members—began to realize the immediate need to overhaul the party and make interracial unity a top priority. Socialists also had success in bringing blacks into their fold, thanks in large part to Randolph, Eugene Debs, and Heywood Broun. Though the Socialists did not favor revolution, they saw the equal distribution of wealth and a reform of capitalism as the only way to better American democracy. The Socialist Party and Communist Party remained at odds with each other through most of the 1920s and 1930s, jockeying for position among left-leaning whites and disaffected blacks. Some of the prominent New Negroes such as McKay and Zora Neale Hurston felt a pull to the causes advocated by the Socialists and Communists, but for the most part, the upper echelon remained dubious.

During the mid-1920s, those who had given up on Garveyism and the NAACP were beginning to shift their attention to the Left. The foundation for an increase in the ranks of the Socialist and Communist parties existed, in part, because of the presence of UNIA-affiliated groups that had decided before Garvey's demise to pave their own path. West Indian radicals and former Garvey followers Cyril Briggs and Richard Moore, two men driven more by black nationalism than by a deep ideological connection to the labor masses, joined the Communist Party in the early 1920s to augment the presence of existing Harlem groups such as the African Blood Brotherhood. Communists made early inroads with West Indians, a group central to Garvey's rise and largely disconnected from mainstream African American social and political advocacy. Briggs and Moore were charismatic organizers who mixed a "black first" message with Comintern's dictate of racial unity among the proletariat. This marriage of early black nationalism and Communism would be replicated in the 1960s, though the later effort would emphasize black power over class solidarity. The Communist Party's post-Garvey recruitment effort tended to attract members more interested in getting immediate uplift results for the black working poor than reading the works of Karl Marx. There were others, however, who embraced the Communist philosophy and the genius of Bolshevism. One of the most important political converts was William Patterson. Patterson had joined the NAACP in his twenties, but after a trip to London and a meeting with leftists there, he returned to the United States with a more radical philosophy. Moore ultimately convinced Patterson that the democratic structure of the United States would never empower African Americans and other oppressed peoples. At the time of his "conversion," Patterson befriended the Robesons, who were impressed with Patterson's philosophies and soon became acquainted with Moore and other Communist leaders in Harlem. Shortly after their marriage in 1921, Paul and Essie began periodically attending Communist Party meetings and rallies in New York. While Patterson and his Communist Party cadres made a positive mark on Robeson, Paul's interest was purely topical and reflected more his openness to new ideas than a commitment to any political ideology. The repeated efforts of Patterson and other Communists in the 1920s to get Paul to join fell on deaf ears. Their proselytizing might have also failed because of Robeson's innate understanding of what political activism might do to his career. Years later Patterson would play a huge role in Robeson's—and eventually Du Bois's—embrace of the Left.

Though Robeson remained detached from the political transformation of the New Negro, the Garvey–Du Bois debate had a profound impact on him. He would find himself agreeing with some of Garvey's positions on black uplift, especially when it came to taking pride in "Africanness." Robeson later expressed deep admiration for Garvey, whom he credited with urging "the Negro peoples of the world 'go forward to the point of destiny as laid out by themselves.'"[30] Though Robeson had early sympathies for Washington and Garvey's spins on racial self-determinism, he shared Du Bois's belief that a solution to the race problem involved racial cooperation, not separation. Publicly Robeson was careful not to make himself a race advocate, but merely a race artist. "He had no use for color as a weapon, but he felt a great expansion of the soul when he saw the young Negroes, as he did all about him in Harlem, seeking the way not of race abnegation or of race rivalry, but of race consciousness," wrote Elizabeth Sergeant of the *New Republic*. Though he had become friends with anarchist Emma Goldman and radicals such as McKay, Max Eastman, and Gertrude Stein, Robeson avoided incorporating any politics into his artistry. Swayed but not changed by his increased contact with American and European radicals during his stay in Europe in 1925, Robeson's philosophical bent continued to reflect more in his desire to play "dignified" Negro roles. Robeson felt he could represent the best qualities in his blackness through the Negro spirituals and the stage characters he embraced as complex. His portrayal of Brutus Jones showed depth even in a racially caricatured character, and many white critics embraced his "astonishing emotional powers" and his ability to make "the play live."[31] Though he was often asked to play characters whose scripted parts made them no more than simpletons (Brutus Jones and Jim in *Chillun*), Paul had an amazing ability to visualize and personify his role. Robeson would, over the next decade, choose to dignify the Negro rather than politicize him. Sergeant's profile of Robeson fittingly concluded that "if the artist, more than any other, must lose his life to find it, so must the American Negro be born twice into the American universe to live there like a man. In Paul Robeson man and artist now met and voted to take their daily sufferings, their daily nightmare fears, their daily soaring ambitions in common."[32]

DU BOIS AND ROBESON'S EARLY RELATIONSHIP was far from intimate; in fact, they weren't more than casual acquaintances. Having first met in 1923, the two bonded because of their common interest in advancing Negro art and culture. As Robeson recalled, "We often talked about the wealth and beauty of our folk heritage, particularly about Negro music which he loved and found deeply moving. He often stressed the importance of this special contribution to American culture."[33] Both men shared a scholarship of music, which they believed was a testament to the prevailing roots of African culture in America. Robeson noted the "interesting discussions about the likeness of our Negro folk music to many other folk musics throughout the world," conversations that helped mold his feelings on the richness of African culture. Though Paul remained aloof to political involvement, he maintained a professional relationship with Du Bois and the NAACP that was seen as beneficial for both sides. For Robeson, the NAACP's backing of his career—especially White's promotion efforts—only boosted his visibility in black America. In turn the NAACP was no doubt aware that Robeson's crossover appeal—especially among white men—would help promote its activist agenda to a broader audience. Paul banked on the NAACP's support throughout the 1920s, especially after his move to Europe in the later part of the decade. Thanks to White, Robeson's career remained relevant to Negro readers in the United States while he tried to make a name for himself overseas.

Though Du Bois viewed the arts scene as "propaganda," he professed a deep admiration for Robeson as an artist. The Doctor, like many of his fellow New Negro architects, believed in Robeson's success, as well as that of opportunities for the Negro. To Du Bois, Paul was Talented Tenth at work. "As the Negro rises more and more toward economic freedom," Du Bois wrote, "he is going on the one hand to say more clearly what he wants to say and do and realize what the ends and methods of expression may be. We have with this generation just come to the time where there is a very small but very real group of American Negroes with minds enlightened enough and with sufficient fine carelessness concerning their mere bread and butter to be about to be real artists. And their names and works are beginning to appear and to compel recognition."[34] Du Bois was among a group of NAACP leaders who joined White in trying to push Robeson into becoming involved with the association. Their efforts were met with kind rebuffs. Paul remained adamant that his role as an artist not be compromised by politics, though he would later disavow that belief. Undeterred by the New Negro star's objections, Du Bois helped promote Robeson through the *Crisis*; he hoped the latter would at some point reciprocate the assistance. Even in the early stages of their friendship, the Doctor was aware of Paul's interest in other cultures and tried to promote him as more than just the Negro's artist. "These Jewish working folks are very eager to have you sing," he wrote Robeson in a request on behalf of several Jewish organizations. "There is sure to be a large Jewish audience, and as a piece of advertisement for you, I think it would be a fine thing if you could possibly mark it in."[35]

Du Bois likely didn't count on Paul's fascination with the commonality of culture playing a significant role in his political development in later years. And the Doctor himself hadn't come to recognize his own Fabian Socialist thinking would serve as the framework for a more-radical interpretation of Marx and belated acknowledgment of Garveyism. As the Harlem Renaissance peaked, Du Bois and Robeson would come to better understand, if not appreciate, that politics and art were intertwined in the New Negro. Both men slowly built their professional acquaintance, unaware that they were on the verge of parallel epiphanies.

2

DUAL EPIPHANIES

Our hope lies in the growing multiplicity and world-wide push of movements like ours; the new dark will to self assertion.

—W. E. B. Du Bois, *Dark Princess: A Romance* (1928)

WHILE THE NEGRO WAS EXPERIENCING a cultural and political renaissance in the United States, the Soviet Union was completing its own rebirth. With the blood of the revolution not yet dry, Soviet leaders embarked on a daring program of economic reform and integration of Russia's vast cultural and linguistic groups. Though the subsequent "Russification" of the Soviet Union would rob individual cultures and tribes of their primary identity by forced assimilation, the idea of a cohesive society unrestricted by race or class held romantic appeal to leftists in Europe and the United States.

Still privately savoring the downfall of Garvey, Du Bois received an unexpected invitation to visit Russia in 1926. With a European trip already scheduled that summer, Du Bois added Moscow on his itinerary, to see firsthand "the most momentous change in modern human history since the French Revolution."[1] The Soviet visit came at a turbulent time in the formulation of Du Bois's philosophical position. He was vacillating between the NAACP platform he had held to since the beginning of the century and the growing sense of militancy that brewed within. *Darkwater* opened the door for Du Bois's musings on systemic change, and his involvement in the Pan-African Congress and fascination with the Indian freedom struggle only pushed him further to the Left. At the height of the renaissance, political philosophies and movements that threatened to undermine the hegemony of the NAACP and the black church as the vanguards of racial progress were beginning to have a profound impact on the Doctor. Du Bois's writings became increasingly left leaning and offered a glimpse into the ever-changing mind of a genius whose mettle was being tested by racial and political realities.

Robeson, on the other hand, continued to bask in his success, detached from the political changes taking place in the United States and Europe. However, his stay in London would slowly open his eyes and challenge him to be more racially conscious than he had ever been. He began to feel the inextricability of his art and his race and, in doing so, adopted a more racialist approach to his career. With a show-stealing performance in *Show Boat* and a starring role in *Othello*, Paul etched his immortality on the stage. However, his life-changing experience still awaited; he would soon realize the musical and theatrical artistry he had mastered was a mere precursor to his most challenging role yet.

As Du Bois and Robeson came to find out, the Soviet Union would be the catalyst for their political awakening, drawing them closer to the Left.

THOUGH HE HAD PREVIOUSLY BEEN dubious of the grand designs of Bolshevism and dismissed the American Negro's flirtation with Communism, Du Bois expressed admiration for and fascination with the Soviet experiment. He fancied himself a Fabian Socialist, believing that evolutionary social reform was inevitable; revolution, on the other hand, could be avoided.[2] The Doctor had read Marx religiously in his younger years and was no doubt enamored with class parity, but he had reservations about its practicality, especially in the United States. The will of the working class had seemingly triumphed in Russia, but Du Bois was guardedly optimistic about the long-term success of the Socialist state. He questioned whether Soviet leaders would ever make the leap to pure Communism, given that they were the ones now holding the power.

Curious about applied Socialism and its possibilities, Du Bois set sail for Europe and the land of Bolsheviks in August 1926. His arrival in Leningrad came more than two years after a fourth stroke proved fatal for the town's namesake in the midst of upheaval in the Politburo. While Josef Stalin was methodically planning his consolidation of power, Du Bois—oblivious to Kremlin politics—walked the streets of Moscow,

Kiev, and Leningrad with the eyes of a sociologist. The Russian economy and its function as an instrument of wealth distribution immediately struck Du Bois. "We recognize the economic value of small incomes mainly as a means of profit for great incomes," Du Bois observed. "Russia seeks another psychology. Russia is trying to make the workingman the main object of industry. His well-being and his income are deliberately set as the chief ends of organized industry directed by the state."[3] More surprising to Du Bois was the willingness of Soviet bureaucrats to foster such a belief among the common people. Impressed by the hard work of government officials as "servants of the people," Du Bois gushed that "Russia is at work." Though Muscovites ran the streets in hunger and crammed into overworked public transportation to get around, the Doctor was convinced that the Soviet people and their leaders saw that the common suffering would be a sacrifice to move the country forward. "In Russia one feels today, even on a casual visit, the beginning of a workingman's psychology," Du Bois proclaimed. "Workers are the people that fill the streets and live in the best houses, even though these houses are dilapidated; workers crowd (literally crowd) the museums and theaters, hold the high offices, do the public talking, travel in the trains. Nowhere in modern lands can one see less of the spender and the consumer, the rich owners and buyers of luxuries, the institutions which cater to the idle rich."[4] Though he acknowledged that poverty ruled Soviet society, Du Bois reasoned that such conditions allowed necessity to trump luxury. Capitalism created a society of few haves and many have-nots, leaving the have-nots in a constant state of material depression. On the other, Du Bois observed, Russian society was thriving on what the common man *needed*. Such an ideology in the modern industrialized world, he surmised, was unacceptable to the capitalists. "And can we wonder," Du Bois asked, "if modern capital is owned by the rich and handled for their power and benefit, can the rich be expected to hand it over to their avowed and actual enemies? On the contrary, if modern industry is really for the benefit of the people and if there is an effort to make the people the chief beneficiaries of industry, why is it that this same people is powerless today to help this experiment or at least to give it a clear way?"[5] The economic revelation in Russia inspired him to write to James Weldon Johnson that the trip was "a tremendous eye opener." The Doctor's eyes, however, were closed to the sinister designs of Stalin and the politics that would lead to the exile of Leon Trotsky, Lenin's covisionary for the New Economic Program. Incorporating his sense of Russian nationalism into the larger designs of Marxism, Stalin was already planning a coup within the party under the guise of advancing Lenin's original intent. As Stalin biographer Robert C. Tucker would later write, he "was assuming the role of the premier living Marxist philosopher. . . . Stalin was promoting Lenin's primacy in philosophy as a vehicle of his own claim to similar primacy."[6] Clearly unaware of—and likely uninterested in—the "inside politics" of the Soviet Union, Du Bois continued to focus on a society that had undergone both an economic and psychological revolution. He boldly predicted that every country would eventually have to choose either prevalent capitalism or the path the Russians were taking.

> There is world struggle then in and about Russia;
> but it is not simply an ethical problem as to

whether or not the Russian Revolution was morally right; that is a question which only history will settle. The real Russian question is: Can you make the worker and not the millionaire the center of modern power and culture? If you can, the Russian Revolution will sweep the world.[7]

Du Bois wouldn't be the only one to prophesize world revolution. As early as the late 1920s, American foreign policy makers were examining the possibility of a Soviet threat, fearing that Bolshevism would spread to Asia and other parts of the world. Their fears would be etched into Cold War policy twenty years later, with the United States spending millions of dollars to back puppet governments (often brutal dictatorships like Pinochet in Chile or the shah of Iran) in an effort to prevent the spread of Communism. In the meantime Du Bois was slowly warming to the idea of the Soviet Union as the future model of economic advancement for oppressed peoples. "I may be partially deceived and half-informed," he wrote after returning. "But if what I have seen with my eyes and heard with my ears in Russia is Bolshevism, I am a Bolshevik."[8] Though the Doctor had a penchant for hyperbole, his newfound affinity for the Soviet Union was genuine. He soon came to recognize Moscow's importance in reshaping his political, economic, and social philosophies. By the end of the 1920s, Du Bois would become a fervent Russophile, laying the groundwork for his alliance with the Left and splinter from the NAACP.

ROBESON'S ARRIVAL IN LONDON during the mid-1920s thrust him into rarified air among Negroes. After all, how many blacks could fathom the idea of first-class hospitality in some of the finest restaurants and hotels in Europe? How many people, for that matter, could take time off from a seemingly endless onslaught of engagements and revues to vacation in the French Riviera or open expensive wine bottles with Europe's Enlightened Elite? The Robesons also fell in with the European intelligentsia, noting the absence of overt racism in London. "My background at Rutgers and my interest in academic studies were given much more weight than such matters are given in America where bankrolls count more than brains," Paul recalled in his autobiography. "And so I found in London a congenial and stimulating intellectual atmosphere in which I felt at home."⁹ Essie commented that "in London they could, as respectable human beings, dine in any public place." The Robesons joined an already impressive list of black Americans who found the other side of the Atlantic to be far more receptive to their race, including Jean Toomer, James Weldon Johnson, Langston Hughes, Jessie Fauset, and William Patterson. During the extended trip, Paul absorbed conversations on race and class with new friends such as Max Eastman, Emma Goldman, and Gertrude Stein with the ear of a high school student: topically interested, but defiantly unengaged. The exuberant fifty-eight-year-old Goldman, whose book *My Disillusionment with Russia* made her unpopular among fellow radicals, took to Paul immediately, and the two developed a close friendship that would help to open Robeson's political thought process. Goldman would comment later that Paul "fascinated everyone" with his keen understanding of history and of the contemporary forces of change that were fomenting in Europe. During the Robesons' stay in London, British politics was at a crossroads. Facing a growing independence movement in India, the Labor Party battled social conservatives, including Winston Churchill, over the empire's future in domestic and international policy. The Labor Party's inability to appease the workers and indecisiveness over colonial interests emboldened conservative opposition. John Maynard Keynes noted that "it would be for the health of the party if all those who believe, with Mr. Winston Churchill and Sir Alfred Mond, that the coming political struggle is best described as Capitalism versus Socialism, and . . . mean to die in the last ditch for Capitalism, were to leave us."[10] The ensuing political storm would lead to Churchill's rise and the shaping of British politics for the next two decades. Meanwhile, Adolf Hitler—recently freed from a year's imprisonment on treason charges—published *Mein Kampf* (My Struggle), a manifesto of nationalism—guided by the notions of white supremacy and rabid anti-Semitism—for war-depleted and impoverished Germany.

Despite the turbulence in Europe and the United States, Robeson remained coy on the issue of politics and race, even in the company of close friends. Whether or not he truly bought into the fake liberalism of Londoners and Parisians, Paul maintained his feelings about focusing on his art, noting his reluctance to be involved in the "propaganda" of the "race question." One reason for his silence might have been the unwitting influence of Claude McKay. During their 1925 meeting in the French Riviera, Essie did not take kindly to the radical, referring to him as a "monkey chaser," but Paul seemed to genuinely appreciate the conversations of a political activist who was deeply introspective on his discoveries of race and class relations. McKay, like many young black radicals, seemed to jump at the prospect of Communism within the first few years of the Bolshevik Revolution. During his 1922 visit to the Soviet Union, McKay "was welcomed . . . as a symbol, as a member of the great American Negro group—kin to the unhappy black slaves of European Imperialism in Africa—that the workers in Soviet Russia, rejoicing in their freedom, were greeting through me." The renaissance writer was afforded the opportunity to speak at the Kremlin, inspiring him to be "proud of being a propagandist" for the Soviet cause. In "Soviet Russia and the Negro," McKay condemned western Europe's exploitation of blacks in World War I and boasted that "Russia, in broad terms, is a country where all the races of Europe and of Asia meet and mix. . . . Russia is prepared and waiting to receive couriers and heralds of good will and interracial understanding from the Negro race."[11] But McKay soon grew disenchanted with the Soviet Union, feeling, among other things, that the Comintern was using blacks to push its own political agenda. He, Eastman, and Goldman concluded that the Communist Party's promotion of an ideal Russia was a mere cover for a country that exploited its citizens as much as the United States and England. McKay hoped to use his experience as a caveat to other African Americans who had experienced similar naïveté when it came to the Soviet Union. McKay likely told Robeson of his Soviet experiences, but Paul's unwillingness to entertain any ideas beyond the expanse of his artistry played a part in his continued obliviousness to political realities.

Robeson's popularity hit a new high following his appearance in *Show Boat*. Though he was only a supporting character in the Jerome Kern–Oscar Hammerstein musical, Robeson dominated the show with his scene-stealing appearances, most notably in his performance of "Ol' Man River." Robeson (playing the role of Joe, a simpleton boat worker) bellowed the song as a tribute to the endurance of the river. "Ah gits weary / An' sick of tryin' / Ah'm tired of livin' /An' skeered of dyin', / But ol' man river, / He jes' keeps rollin' along." In later years Robeson would change the wording of the song to become: But I keeps laughin' / Instead of cryin' / I must keep fightin' / Until I'm dyin'.

"Ol' Man River" would become a staple of Robeson's repertoire, especially in later years when he became politically active; it evolved into a song of defiance and determination, articulating Paul's belief that you could knock him down, but like the river, he would "just keep rolling along."[12] In 1928, however, Paul was content to keeping most of the original lyrics intact; he had not yet accepted the fact that heightened race consciousness was a duty that no Negro performer could shirk.

What is most amazing about Robeson during the 1920s was his ability to tune out the outside world. Much of his interaction with England's cultured elite created a rosy picture of race relations that belied the true nature of European racial chauvinism. Paul had not yet come to understand that British high society, which treated him like "a gentleman and a scholar," viewed him as an aberration.[13] Perhaps, as some scholars have noted, Robeson was selfish. He was likely aware that racism existed, but was too busy advancing his career to worry about becoming a race advocate, which promised only the scorn of his high-society friends. As Robeson biographers Sheila Tully Boyle and Andrew Bunie wrote, Robeson had merely "given eloquent lip service to the ideal of artistic achievement as a means for improving race relations."[14] Such an attitude has been common for generations among black entertainers, who have taken great pains to present themselves as representatives of their race while not alienating themselves from their white patrons. Many black entertainers—exemplified by Michael Jordan's silence on sweatshop conditions in Nike factories in Southeast Asia and the refusal of most black musicians and entertainers to advocate for heightened race consciousness—are acutely aware that their success is determined by white support; estranging that relationship for racial or political ideals would be tantamount to career suicide.

Besides self-preservation, Robeson was averse to racial advocacy in London because he simply could not relate to it in a larger context. Unlike Du Bois, Robeson was not yet well acquainted with African and Asian anticolonials living in England and France. He was also painfully ignorant of race riots in the Welsh city of Cardiff, fueled in part by jealous white dock workers reacting to African and West Indian immigrants taking both their jobs and their women.[15] The Robesons' ascending social status and the ease in which they seemed to travel through London was in stark contrast to the reality of colored Britons. African migrants squatted in ghettos while Indian and Caribbean students fared no better, subjugated to the same humiliating color tests that prevailed for America's Jim Crow. The irony of Paul's success was that while he wined and dined with the British elite and performed in front of packed concert halls, very few common people of color were afforded the opportunity to see him or appreciate his accomplishments.

Robeson's first revelation on racism in London began with a routine social call. Essie—very much caught up in the adulation of British high society—accepted a late-night invitation for tea with Lady Colefax at the famous Savoy Grill in the trendy Strand of London. The Savoy Hotel, built in 1889 on land donated by King Richard III to Count Savoy, was one of London's signature landmarks for visiting aristocracy and petit bourgeois. The hotel's exclusivity contradicted its centrality; the Thames and the Covent Garden were all just a few steps away, while the insulated walls protected the rich guests from the footsteps of everyday Londoners. The Savoy Grill was even more hallowed, its regular clientele including foreign dignitaries, entertainers, and British parliamentarians. The Grill was defined "by time and observance, the province and playground of men, and the occasional woman . . . who filled their mouths with slices of rare beef from the carving trolley and cigars the size of 16-inch guns on a battleship. They were waited on by old codgers dressed in black tailcoats and they talked about money as freely as they spent it."[16] Paul had dined there several times during his previous London visit; thinking that they would be welcomed again, the Robesons went to the Grill for their rendezvous with Lady Colfax. When they arrived, hotel staff curtly told them that the hotel no longer served Negroes and would not allow them in. In later years, historians have speculated why such a policy came about. The Savoy, while discriminatory, had never implemented a policy of denying service to affluent and prominent nonwhites. Some speculate that American tourists staying at the Savoy objected to the presence of Negroes at the hotel. That might have been the reasoning behind the hotel's refusal to serve Robert Abbott, the African American media mogul whose papers included the influential *Chicago Defender*. Abbott and his wife made front-page news in London when they were denied service at the hotel in the summer of 1929, bringing to light other prominent blacks who were treated similarly there. Despite being cognizant of those preceding events, Robeson was taken aback when he was refused service. After all, this was London, where he and Essie had seemingly been impervious to the racial slights they had received in the United States. This was the city where the richest and most influential whites wanted *them* to be part of their social circles. In later years Paul would tell friends that the Savoy incident was one of his turning points on race relations. For the first time, it seemed, he was a "nigger" outside of the United States.

Robeson's reaction to the refusal seemed to reflect those feelings, though some historians assert that it was Essie who wrote the letter to convey her own disgust at the affront. Paul (or Essie) wrote of having a revelation on the state of race relations in London. "I thought that there was little prejudice against blacks in London or none, but an experience my wife and I had recently has made me change my mind and to wonder, unhappily, whether or not things may become almost as bad for us here as they are in America."[17] After the written statement, Paul was strangely silent on the matter, much to the dismay of some of his British friends and many in the black press in the United States. The Savoy incident had wounded his pride and exposed an ugly side of British hospitality he hadn't seen before. His newfound awareness only heightened during a short return to the United States for a singing tour. Robeson, whose undeniable international fame put him in rare air among blacks, was still a Negro in America, a second-class citizen who was denied accommodations in many cities where he performed. Even for Robeson, the mantra of sitting on anger and keeping a poker face amid racial affronts began to wear thin. In some of the rare moments he had to write down his thoughts, Paul revealed that he felt "oppressed" in the American racial climate. His frustrations with the United States only grew as he began to realize some of the hidden racism of his white American friends and how he felt like only a Band-Aid to their prejudice.[18] The humiliating paradox of being a first-rate actor and singer and a second-class American citizen finally had a noticeable impact on Robeson. "I did not have any fixed ideas in those days," he wrote later, "but one of them happened to be a strong conviction that my own conscience should be my guide and that no one was going to lead me around by a golden chain or any other kind."[19] By the end of 1929, Paul had come to the bitter conclusion that there was little he could do to improve his career and status in America.

Paul's nascent racial consciousness began to develop upon his return to England in 1930. Cast as Othello, Robeson now had the chance to play the complex role he had so long sought in his acting career. As it turned out, *Othello* would be one of the few opportunities for Paul to flex his talents to the fullest potential. The lead of the tragic Moor would define Paul's acting career (and, in many ways, his personal life). The notion of a dignified hero felled by betrayal had more than Shakespearean overtones; it spoke to the idea that a singularly dominant man was vulnerable to the same pitfalls as his peers.

(Shakespeare also brought this point home in *Julius Caesar*.) Robeson seemed to fit Othello perfectly. In addition to his commanding stage presence, his blackness—which he had so often tried to neutralize as a performer in earlier roles—gave an additional depth of humanity and tragedy to the character. Unlike *Emperor Jones*, Robeson did not need to "add" dignity to his role; it was already written in. Perhaps most controversial—and adding to Paul's heightened race awareness—was the kissing scene between Othello and Desdemona, played by young British actress Peggy Ashcroft. Ashcroft later admitted that the experience was an "education in racism." Critics gave mixed reviews of the play, but generally accorded Robeson with high praise. *Othello* did more than add luster to Robeson's acting portfolio; it roused the dormant race advocate from within. Following the successful run of the play, Robeson espoused the idea of championing blackness through artistic imagery. "Some members of my race want to forget that they are Negroes," he told one reporter. "But they should remember that the Negro can no more change his blood than the leopard his spots. A Negro remains a Negro. Then let him be one, with his ideals and energies directed toward the ennoblement of his race. Let him give it a literature of its own."[20] Paul seemed oblivious to the irony of his statements, or simply didn't care. He had for years run away from the very position he was now advocating, but it was apparent that he was no longer just playing lip service. The Savoy incident and *Othello* had profoundly influenced his sense of racial identity, leading to increased involvement with groups he had earlier shunned and planting the seeds of his rebirth as a "political artist."

UPON HIS RETURN from the Soviet Union, Du Bois set to work on his next literary opus, a novel he hoped would combine his newfound political revelations with his established idealism for the colored world. Imbued with the spirit of class suffragist and freedom fighter, an inspired fifty-nine-year-old Du Bois wrote *Dark Princess* in hopes of conveying "the difficulties and realities of race prejudices upon many sorts of people—ambitious black American youth, educated Asiatics, selfish colored politicians, ambitious self-seekers of all races." The book also reflected Du Bois's sentiment that the anticolonial struggle would spring from Asia; he saw India as the model of suffrage. Du Bois opined that India's courage in freeing itself from the bondage of British imperialism would help other countries unite and overthrow their colonial masters. In a 1922 *Crisis* piece, Du Bois gushed that Mohandas Gandhi's method of nonviolence "kills without striking its adversary."[21] The Doctor also gained better understanding of the Indian freedom movement through correspondences with Sarojini Naidu (Gandhi's close counsel) and the legendary Indian writer Rabindranath Tagore. But it was Gandhi's sometime adversary who made the most profound impact on Du Bois. Haughty and passionate, Lala Lajpat Rai was Gandhi's incendiary alter ego in the Indian independence struggle, who incurred the wrath of the British on numerous occasions by actively pursuing social reform and striving for caste unity. The British occupation of India had come largely through dividing the country's religious, caste, and language groups and manipulating them against one another while propping up powerless kings and sultans to enforce colonial laws. Rai consistently defied British laws and expectations,

once reading Urdu instead of English during a welcome cere-
mony for a British lieutenant governor. Unlike Gandhi, who
had mastered diplomacy, Rai came off as rough around the
edges, often appearing confrontational even when he tried to
be charming. He moved to the United States in 1917,
authoring two books (*Arya Samaj* and *England's Debt to
India*) and establishing the Indian Home Rule League. After
becoming acquainted with Booker T. Washington and Robert
Russa Morton, Rai sparked a deep friendship with Du Bois.[22]

Rai's own philosophical transformation, from a practicing
protester to an avowed radical determined to free India of colonial influence, moved the Doctor. It was also likely that in later
years, Du Bois appreciated Rai's struggles with the British government, which denied him a passport to return to India following the infamous Amritsar Massacre. The pair developed a
close correspondence, leading Du Bois to take an active interest
in Hinduism; likewise, Rai paid special attention to American
race relations. Hoping to parallel British subjugation of Indians
with the black experience in America, Rai asked Du Bois for
information "about the treatment of negroes in the United
States" and "the cruelties inflicted on your people by the
whites of America."[23] Du Bois would later write about Indians'
ignorance of blacks, lamenting that "unless they are as wise
and catholic as my friend . . . Lajpat Rai, they are apt to see
little and know less of the 12 million Negroes in America."[24]
Sensitive to Indian culture and the diversity of theological
influence on the Indian freedom struggle, the Doctor soaked in
Rai's critique of the *Dark Princess* manuscript. In December
1927, as Du Bois put the final touches on the book, Rai gave his
final editorial suggestions, asking his friend to be especially

sensitive on issues such as widowhood and caste.[25] He would never be able to fully appreciate Du Bois's final product, however. Rai spent most of 1928 in heated protests against the British, and in late October, was seriously beaten by police. Declaring that "every blow aimed at me is a nail in the coffin of British Imperialism," Rai never fully recovered from his injuries and died several weeks later.[26]

In February 1928, less than a year after Du Bois started work on the manuscript, Harcourt released *Dark Princess: A Romance*. Calling it "a romance with a message," the Doctor clearly envisioned the novel as satisfying both his need to articulate his political beliefs and his desire to invest in the black arts movement. The book left much to be desired as a prima facie fiction piece. Du Bois emphasized the melodrama and was prone to bouts of verbose descriptions of scenes, forcing the reader to stay focused on the deeper meaning of his passages. The book's real strength was its allegory and Du Bois's obvious desire to convey a sense of commonality in the American Negro's struggle for equality and the colonized darker races' quest for sovereignty and emancipation. His 1911 novel, *Quest for the Silver Fleece*, touched upon some of the elements of race and class that inspired his Socialism, but it was hardly a mouthpiece for his personal revelations. *Quest* was also a "an economic study," as Du Bois called it, focusing more on the Mason-Dixon divide and its impact on racism and classism than a universal class struggle. Du Bois would expand on that theme in *Darkwater*, especially in his caustic "The Souls of White Folk," which drew both accolades and alarm on the part of Du Bois's more-moderate peers. In the essay, the Doctor placed the subjugation of the American

Negro in a global context, pinning the hopes of suffrage on the emancipation of "two-thirds of the population of the world. A belief in humanity is a belief in colored men. If the uplift of mankind must be done by men, then the destinies of this world will rest ultimately in the hands of darker nations."[27]

Dark Princess was another incarnation of the new Negro movement, noteworthy for the timeliness of its release rather than its literary merits. But *Dark Princess* gave Du Bois more than just a byline in the ranks of renaissance authors; it was a forum in which he could be his ideal self without having to be the Doctor. Matthew Towns was, for all intents and purposes, an incarnation of Du Bois. From Towns's anxiety toward beautiful women to falling into an unhappy marriage that withered his fidelity, the book's main protagonist personified William's naked humanity. From the time Towns meets Kautilya, it is clear that the author intends to pursue a romantic fantasy that runs parallel to his deeper aim. In their melodramatic scenes of intimacy, Towns and Kautilya are Du Bois's puppets, written to fit how *he* saw the ideal relationship triumphing over global reality and cultural taboo. Like any other fiction piece, Du Bois's protagonists are a manifestation of the author; they live in a world where the dialogue is played out in the author's head long before it goes into print. Du Bois imagined for Towns and the Indian princess an ambience that included "the fire that glowed in the soft warmth of evening. They had their benediction of music—the overture of *Wilhelm Tell*, which seemed to picture their lives. Together they hummed the sweet lilt of the music after the storm."[28] Du Bois—probably recounting his own romantic experiences with Jessie Fauset and others—took great care to create a perfect mood of revolution, allowing his downtrodden protagonists to indulge in an exotic array of cuisines and culture that included "rice with curry that Kautilya had made, and a shortcake of biscuit and early strawberries which Matthew had triumphantly concocted. With it, they drank black tea with thin slices of lemon."

Towns's transformation from an educated Chicago politician to a common laborer, returning to the masses in order to toil for the oppressed people, would parallel Du Bois's own undertaking in later years. Perhaps the Doctor was influenced by one of his own literary creations, taking note of Matthew's Marxist introspective that "they that do the world's work must do its thinking. The thinkers, the dreamers, the poets of the world must be its workers. Work is God." Du Bois as Matthew Towns was not far from the imagination of his readers and his peers. Even confidants such as Mary White Ovington read the book with a smile and winked that the book's hero was an extension of the author, both philosophically and romantically. However, critics, including later reviewers such as leftist historian and Du Bois protégé Herbert Aptheker, did not take into consideration how much of Du Bois was in Kautilya. The Indian princess, while representing everything in the physical beauty that Du Bois imagined in an ideal woman, was a tragic heroine whose life decisions altered the course of world struggle. Both in education and outlook, Kautilya *was* Du Bois. Kautilya, like Du Bois, was an aristocrat reared on modeling her life and her people's destiny after the Europeans. Born in imperial India, Kautilya is spoiled by being the daughter of a maharaja and oblivious to the concerns of the common man. Seizing the opportunity to be educated by the colonizer, she goes to London and experiences firsthand the reality of her color and rank in white society. As she tells Matthew, she quickly learns to accept the indignation of being "colored."

> In the midst of war hysteria, I became the social rage, and I loved it. I forgot suspicion and intrigue. I liked the tall and calm English men, the gracious and well-mannered English women. I loved the stately servants, so efficient, without the Eastern servility to which I had been born. I knew for the first time what comfort and modern luxury meant. . . . Money flowed like water through my careless hands. . . . I was a darling of the white gods, and I adored them.

Kautilya's subsequent realization of her "real" status forces her to question her purpose. "Can I make you realize how I was dazed and blinded by the Great White World?" she asks Matthew. Her lover's response seems clearly to reflect Du Bois's fast-moving philosophical shift in the wake of his Soviet visit. "I quite understand. Singularly enough, we black folk of America are the only ones of the darker world who see white folk and their civilization with level eyes and unquickened pulse."[29] Kautilya's revelation on choosing between the comforts of European paternalism and the struggle for sovereignty in her own land seemed to fit the dilemma of Du Bois's double-consciousness thirty years earlier. Du Bois, then twenty-nine, wrote in *Atlantic Monthly* that the African American was constantly torn between the burden of being Negro and American, "always looking at one's self through the eyes of others, of measuring one's soul by the tape of a world that looks on in amused contempt and pity."[30] The Indian princess is equally reflective on this conflict, telling Matthew:

> I was the only obstacle between native rule and absorption by England in Sindrabad, and the only hope of independence in Bwodpur. . . . Immediately I was the center of fierce struggle: England determined to marry me to an English nobleman; young India determined to rally around me, to strip me of wealth, power, and prerogatives, and to set up here in India the first independent state. . . . Widowed even before I was a wife, bearing all the Indian contempt for widowhood; child with the heavy burden of womanhood and royal power, I was like to be torn in two not only by the rising determination of you India to be free of Europe and all hereditary power, but also by the equal determination of England to keep and guard her Indian empire.[31]

As Kautilya detaches herself from the throne and bears the ostracism for defying expectations, she moves into self-discovery paralleling Matt's own struggle. The Indian princess—a courtesan of English colonialism—becomes a mere factory worker in the United States, taking up common thread with the black and brown masses. Kautilya's political awakening is best summed up when she pronounces that "we will build a world, Matthew . . . where the Hungry shall be fed, and only the Lazy shall be empty." That echoed Marx's proclamation of hunger as intrinsic to the human being. "Hunger is a natural need; it therefore needs a nature outside itself, an object outside itself,

in order to satisfy itself, to be stilled. Hunger is an acknowledged need of my body for an object existing outside it, indispensable to its integration and to the expression of its essential
being."[32] Kautilya and Matthew have other Marxist-tinged
exchanges throughout the book, leading even the most casual
reader to conclude that the author was enamored with the idea
of a new world order.

Dark Princess not only captured Du Bois's growing
embrace of Marxist ideology and romanticism of Afro-Asian
unity in class struggle, but it also acknowledged his own
doubts about the overall goals of his Pan-African vision. Kautilya helps Towns (Du Bois) realize the folly of the Pan-
African Congress's vision for black Africa.

> We had all gathered slowly and unobtrusively as
> tourists, business men, religious leaders, students,
> and beggars, and we met unnoticed in a city where
> color of skin is nothing to comment on and where
> strangers are all too common. We were thousand
> strong, and never were Asia, Africa, and the islands
> represented by stronger, more experienced, and more
> intelligent men. Your people were there, Matthew, but
> they did not come as Negroes. There were black men
> who were Egyptians; there were black men who were
> Turks; there were black men who were Indians, but
> there were no black men who represented purely and
> simply the black race and Africa.[33]

Though Du Bois would later refine his Pan-African philosophy, thanks to the efforts of Robeson and others, he ended the

1920s with a sobering realization: both he and Garvey had ultimately failed in recognizing what kind of sovereignty was best
for Africans. It was a notion that the Doctor would continue to
grapple with through World War II and would ultimately lead
to his embrace of the pre-Afrocentric philosophies of Robeson.
In his second-guessing over the African problem, Du Bois
strengthened his own belief that one way to counter the imperialism of the West was to have an empire of the East. Those sentiments were expressed in the novel's references to Japan, and
Kautilya's description of her friend, the Japanese baron, as "a
man of lofty ideal without the superstition of religion, a man of
decision and action. He is our leader, Matthew, the guide and
counselor, the great Prime Minister of the Darker World."[34] As
the Doctor's impressions of the Left began to change, so did his
own justifications of global imperialism. *Dark Princess* would
give Du Bois's peers and supporters a preview of his defense of
Japanese aggression against China, and his faith in a superpower of the nonwhite races that would ultimately champion
the liberation of the colored world.

The release of *Dark Princess* gave critics a profound insight
into the Doctor's meditations on the changing world and the
impact it would have at home. Well received, though not totally
understood by the Talented Tenth, the book sold three thousand copies before going out of circulation. Going beyond his
base readership, Du Bois caught the eye of many white literary
critics, whose reactions ranged from lauding the book's literary
vision of global unity of colored races to (racially inspired)
rebukes of the content. Perhaps the reception Du Bois most
hoped for was conveyed in Dorothea L. Mann's review for the
Boston *Evening Transcript*. Mann wrote that the book's

strength was "in the revelation it gives to white readers of many grades of Negro life and many problems which are totally unknown to them."[35] She added that the global theme of *Dark Princess* "demands a serious reading." The book hammered home to the Doctor's friends and vexed colleagues at the NAACP that the civil rights icon was not the same. Du Bois's praise of the 1928 decree of the Comintern calling American blacks in the South "an oppressed nation" and those in the North a "national minority," only underscored that point.

His support for the Lenin dream and of the overall mission of the Soviet Union did not alter the Doctor's feelings on communism in the United States. He loathed the notion of ex-Garveyites like Richard Moore and Cyril Briggs spearheading a Moscow-backed social revolution as an alternative to the seemingly entrenched diplomacy of the more-rational civil rights groups. While he kept his penchant for butting heads over the editorial content of the *Crisis* and the causes to which the NAACP aligned itself, William was still, by and large, on board with the overall goals of the organization. His drift to the Left had not prevented him, for example, from downplaying the rise of the Communist Party USA and remaining noticeably silent on the Scottsboro Boys case in 1931. In fact, the Doctor continued to be at odds with the American Communists, suspecting ulterior motives of foreign agents in rallying around black causes and recruiting the black intelligentsia. In a scathing indictment of the CPUSA, Du Bois wrote that the Communists were led "by a number of unprincipled fools" who used the Scottsboro case as a publicity tool to hinder the NAACP's legal defense. He went on to add that:

Communism faces a . . . dilemma: it can rush into revolution following an untested theory and backed by mere handful of blacks and whites, or recognize that the color line is in America a greater problem than the class struggle and one which they must bare first. In other words, before asking Negroes to join white labor the communists must get white labor to join in the invitation. If any considerable proportion of the white laboring class today solicited and desired the cooperation of American Negroes, we as a pre-dominantly laboring class would be compelled to accept and pool our interests with theirs. We have never been invited and we are not likely to be soon.[36]

Du Bois's criticism might have seemed harsh, considering that he praised Russia as "pointing the way which every civilized country will in time follow." But his assessment of American Communists was more of a general response to the party's continued attacks on him and other notable African American leaders. Strangely enough, Du Bois found himself agreeing with black conservative George Schuyler, one of the most outspoken anti-Communists of his time. Schuyler congratulated the Doctor for his "drubbing" of the Communists, noting that "yours was a masterly analysis and criticism to which the Communists will be hard put to reply intelligently." Schuyler added that "if the Communists were intelligent and sincere, they would concentrate their efforts on the white proletariat who need 'emancipating' far more than the Negroes."[37] The fact that Du Bois sided with Schuyler wasn't surprising, given the contentious relationship between

Communist Party and black leadership at the time. As historian James Smethurst observed, "one aspect of 'Third Period' Communist ideology was its ferocious attacks on Social Democratic and liberal 'misleaders' who were even termed 'Social Fascists' at one point."[38] Du Bois and his NAACP peers and Urban League counterparts were subject to such attacks domestically, leading the Doctor to dismiss the CPUSA's criticism as "sectarian" and "personally offensive."[39] His suspicions would only grow as a result of the market crash that led to the Great Depression and paved the way for a new wave of leftists.

PAUL'S SUCCESS IN *OTHELLO* and increased sense of racial pride afforded him the opportunity to become more politically active in the fast-changing world around him. After years of being chided for remaining silent on issues of race by his friends and by the black press, he was more comfortable publicly aligning himself with social activists. There were also few repercussions in Paul's growing need to pronounce his Negro heritage, especially in press interviews. He seemed more comfortable talking about race and expressing the reality of oppression that many of his less fortunate dark-skinned brothers and sisters faced every day. Robeson's increased racial consciousness led him to adopt more of a "race man" mentality. While attaining new professional heights with *Othello* and the film version of *The Emperor Jones*, he embraced his role as a cultural anthropologist and self-appointed spokesman for African peoples. "Culturally speaking, the African negro, as well as his American and West Indian brothers, stands at the parting of ways. The day is past when they were regarded as something less than human and little more than mere savages by the white man," Paul wrote in the *Spectator*. Stepping away from ad hoc advocacy of assimilation that seemed to define his early professional career and personal silence on race issues, he declared that blacks had spent too much time imitating whites.

> But the sufferings he has undergone have left an indelible mark on the negro's soul, and at the present stage he suffers from an inferiority complex which finds its compensation in a desire to imitate the white man and his way; but I am convinced that in this direction there is neither fulfillment nor peace for the negro. He is too radically different from the white man in his mental and emotional structure ever to be more than a spurious and uneasy imitation of him, if he persists in following this direction. His soul contains riches which can come to fruition only if he retains intact the full spate of his emotional awareness, and uses unswervingly the artistic endowments which nature has given him. [40]

Taking baby steps toward activism, Robeson—and Essie as a gatekeeper—began accepting invitations to help with the British Left, singing and speaking when it was to aid his friends. Emma Goldman's influence seemed to make its mark on Paul, as he joined the aging anarchist on several public occasions. At a 1933 luncheon honoring Goldman at the Grosvenor House, Robeson noted that "it takes a great, courageous person who has great faith in the human soul really to feel the human race has so far progressed and really can do the things she wishes to do. I talk to Emma, and in her presence I feel that human love coming out I only get otherwise from the novels of Dostoevsky, the feeling that someone exists whose love really embraces all of humanity."[41] Paul's increased advocacy was probably fueled by his own realization that his adopted country of England would never accept him as a fully entitled Englishmen, much the same way that he felt about his own American identity. So he became a student of Africa, taking Du Bois's notion of Afro-consciousness to another level. Whereas Du Bois continued to view Africa as being deprived and raped and exploited by the savagery of colonialism, Robeson fully immersed himself in the study of African cultures, contending that the American Negro needed to look to Africa as an inspiration and "set his own standards" independent of white expectations.[42] His study, buoyed by his natural curiosity, was aided by his friendships with African and West Indian expatriates in London, the likes of whom included Kwame Nkrumah and Jomo Kenyatta. Robeson studied Swahili and other African languages, believing that cultural linguistics influenced the speech patterns of African-descended people throughout the world. In a way, Robeson was an early proponent of the study of Ebonics that became controversial in the United States sixty years later. Paul wrote that in London, he "discovered Africa." That discovery, he added, "made it clear that I would not live out my life as an adopted Englishman, and I came to consider that I was an African."[43] Conversations with radical African and Indian students in London drew the suspicions of British intelligence agents, who on several occasions questioned him on his ties with the expatriates of colonized nations.[44]

As Paul grew increasingly disenchanted with England and its patronization of minorities, he began to take an avid interest in "the race problem," a subject he had long avoided during his career ascension. With the status of a leading man and an expendable income for travel, Robeson had decided by mid-1932 that he would pay a visit to the Soviet Union, where the romanticism of a nation devoid of racism begged further inspection. Though McKay's realization of Bolshevik brutality and Emma Goldman's frustration with Stalinization of the revolution served as caveats, Paul had come to his own conclusions about the USSR. From Du Bois's praise of the Soviet experiment to the experiences of Essie's brothers, John and Frank Goode, there were more than enough glowing appraisals to warrant a personal validation. The Soviet Union had been active in recruiting American blacks to come and work, offering them equal pay and housing in a land that was already teeming with ethnic, nationalistic, and religious diversity. On paper, the USSR already seemed a utopia to Paul and Essie even before their first visit in December 1934.

The irony of his growing enchantment with Russia was that Robeson was not in Harlem during the rise of the Communist Party there. With the notable exception of Patterson, he had little interaction with the growing ranks of black Communists who flexed their organizational muscle through tenant mobilization and mass protests to free the Scottsboro Boys. Instead, Robeson's education came from the European intelligentsia enamored with Bolshevism and the Russians who entered the Robesons' social circle with glowing testimonials of the revolution. Sergei

Eisenstein proved to be a major influence on Robeson, both in the months before his Russia trip and during his stay in Moscow. The Soviet director corresponded with Robeson about his intent to produce a biopic on Haitian liberator Toussaint L'Overture. Paul's increased immersion into Russian culture also grew from his belief that there were remarkable similarities between the Soviets and Africans, both in language and tribal histories. He was told of the Central Asian tribal group, the Yakuts, who were "successfully" indoctrinated into the Socialist state and became full-fledged Soviets. Robeson's friend William Patterson was impressed with the fact that "Russians seemed to give a man's skin coloration only a descriptive value, looking immediately past this attribute to the significant human differences of character, mind, and heart."[45] Marie Seton—the noted English journalist and close friend of the Robesons—returned from a trip in Moscow in late 1934 and gave the Robesons another positive observation of Russia, paving the way for Paul to book passage on his own journey to Moscow.

On December 20, 1934, Paul and Essie, accompanied by Seton, took the train to Berlin, where they stopped for the first time in four years. In that time, Germany had transformed in accordance to Hitler's vision. The vibrant arts scene that had once greeted visitors was now gone, and the once-flourishing Jewish business district had largely closed down, its proprietors fleeing the country or hiding in the shadows in anticipation of the Nuremberg Laws that would deprive Jews and other minorities of their citizenship. Robeson also saw the overt racism fueled by Hitler youth who walked the streets. Paul recounted many times over the incident at the Berlin train station, where men "with hatred in their eyes" approached

Robeson, who was with Seton and the fair-skinned Essie. "I remembered getting ready for possible attack and determined to take some of the storm troopers with me when I went," he recalled twenty years later.[46] Fortunately the confrontation of glares never escalated, but Seton would later write of how much the incident had traumatized Robeson.

When he set foot on Russian soil, greeted warmly by a welcoming party that included Eisenstein and John Goode, it all came together. The increased sense of racial consciousness that he began to feel after the Savoy incident was now becoming clear in a political sense. Paul could hardly believe his eyes when he saw the multicultural hoi polloi. He played with children who tugged at his coat, in awe of having "never seen such a big man, so dark against the white snow."[47] Paul concluded to Marie Seton that the children "have never been told to fear black men." In his first few hours on Soviet soil, Paul absorbed what he could, having never come close to experiencing such an environment. Not even the racially inclusive parties in Harlem or the leftist social gatherings in London could have prepared Paul for Moscow. He gushed that in Russia, he was "not a Negro but a human being. Before I came I could hardly believe that such a thing could be. In a few days I've straightened myself out. Here for the first time I walk in full human dignity. You cannot imagine what that means to me as a Negro." Average Muscovites seemed genuine in their welcome for the unknown foreign visitor. "I was surrounded in the streets, and friendly feelings were expressed in handshakes," he would later recall. "Muscovites did not know then that I was Robeson, the singer, and treated me simply as a son of the Negro people."[48]

His initial skepticism on whether the Soviet Union was too good to be true dissipated soon after engaging the lively Eisenstein in conversation. Eisenstein, a proud Jew and fierce anticzarist, was deeply conscious of his heritage and had taken a keen interest in developing projects of class and racial liberation. Eisenstein was a visual innovator in Soviet film, using powerful symbols to underscore the themes of his projects. In *Strike*, a movie about the rise of the worker in the face of czarist oppression, the final scene showed a bull being slaughtered against the backdrop of massacred workers, a gripping testament of proletarian sacrifice. His vision for the L'Overture film—consistent with the themes and the ideals of the revolution—seemed to be music to Paul's ears; it was another opportunity to play a dignified Negro lead role and a chance to showcase the life of a man who liberated a nation from colonial oppression.

Robeson spent much of his time in between visits to Soviet cultural attractions with the director, captivated by Eisenstein's musings on labor and his notion of using art to progress a political philosophy. Robeson also visited the Soviet National Minority Theatre, which gave performances in nearly forty languages, including Gypsy, Tartar, and Yiddish. He was also struck by Russia's devotion to writer Alexander Pushkin, who was of Abyssinian (Ethiopian) descent. Within a few days of setting foot in Moscow, Paul was ready to declare his love for the Soviet Union and his commitment to the ideals pushed forth by the revolution. Speaking in his not-yet-fluent Russian and through an interpreter, Robeson told the Soviet press that he intended to return to the USSR for a longer stay and put Paul Jr. in the Soviet School. As Robeson would note four years later, placing his son in a multicultural setting free of racial discrimination was paramount in preparing him for the global struggle against European imperialism. "As he grows up, Pauli cannot fail to realize his good fortune in sharing the common collective life of the Soviet Union, and that he bears a deep responsibility to the oppressed of all peoples in other lands who are struggling to gain an opportunity to live a decent life."[49]

Unlike Du Bois, who viewed the beauty of the Soviet experiment from an economic standpoint, Robeson's initial infatuation had mostly to do with race. Russia, in his view, did not have a race problem. He reasoned that it was a unified society of national minorities driven only by a devotion to furthering Lenin's dream and striving in the name of the proletariat. Paul's whirlwind tour of the cities and the small towns and his meetings with Soviet commissars and peasant villagers during his two-week stay led to his inevitable conclusion that the USSR *was* the global model for modern government and the answer to solving the race question. "These people enjoy complete equality . . . (and on the issue of race) have solved their problems in the Soviet Union. It is logical that the Soviet Union should be playing a major part in the struggle for freedom."[50] As Robeson grew more familiar with Russia, he began to incorporate its economic structure into his racially conscious form of Socialism. He believed the Soviets had perfected a formula for class equity and race equality, declaring that the country represented "the future direction of mankind."[51] Like Du Bois, Robeson was oblivious to Stalin's true motives. Indeed, most Soviets were in the dark about what Stalin was planning, but by the end of the decade, they would see for themselves that megalomania was a main ingredient for genocide.

DU BOIS AND ROBESON'S EPIPHANIES on Soviet Russia and Socialism coincided with domestic and international uncertainty. The start of the Great Depression ushered in a decade-long turf war between the Communist Party USA and the NAACP. While the Communists did not win over the masses, they carved out enough of a following during the 1930s to threaten the NAACP's dominance in civil rights activism. Overseas, Europe braced for an onslaught of fascism spearheaded by Hitler's Germany and Mussolini's Italy, while the rest of Asia was seemingly at the mercy of Japan. More black intellectuals began to connect the international fight for freedom against fascism and colonialism with their own quest for enfranchisement. As a result, many of Du Bois and Robeson's contemporaries came to admire the Soviet Union for its public stance against racism and colonialism, which correlated to greater acceptance of left-wing thought in Depression-era political discourse. The Left's rise to prominence in the struggle for civil rights at home and against fascism abroad expedited Du Bois and Robeson's philosophical shift. As both men would soon find out, there were no U-turns on the road to radicalism.

3

Du Bois, Robeson, and the Popular Front

The question of whether there should be war or peace is a
question of the greatest importance for us, not only for the
Negro people, but for all lovers of peace.
—Paul Robeson, *The Daily Worker* (1937)

THE LEFT'S GROWING IMPORTANCE in the civil rights struggle came at
a time when both Du Bois and Robeson were undergoing major
changes in their outlook on race, class, and the role that economics played in global disenfranchisement. While the Doctor
still harbored deep reservations about the overall effectiveness
of the leftist agenda and the CPUSA's motives, Robeson—who
had become an ardent internationalist thanks to his USSR visit
and the influence of European leftists and anticolonials—

jumped firmly behind the Communist platform. The CPUSA-led Left, which rallied around the Scottsboro Boys case in 1931 and eventually focused its efforts on calling American attention to Fascism abroad, became known as the Popular Front.

Robeson, moved by his own sympathies for Jews and growing allegiance with European leftists, would make antifascism a foundation of his still developing political philosophy. Fascism, in his view, was a philosophy tyrants used "to make serfs of great masses of people, control their labor, and keep them from ever controlling their own destiny."[1] This interpretation would lead to Paul's stronger embrace of Soviet Socialism, inspire his budding anticolonialism and, most importantly, develop his opposition to capitalism. He would come to equate capitalism and colonialism to Fascism; all three, he believed, thrived off exploitation of workers and deprivation of freedom.

Du Bois initially had a more diplomatic take on Fascism, arguing that it was a natural precursor to Socialism. However, he would quickly turn against Germany and Italy following the latter's attempts to annex Ethiopia, the lone African country untouched and unspoiled by colonialism. If Italy succeeded, Du Bois argued, it would be a victory "for those who pin their faith on European civilization, the Christian religion and the superiority of the white race." By becoming an aggressor against a sovereign dark nation, "Italy has forced the world into a position where, whether or not she wins, race hate will increase."[2] As he reshaped his global outlook, Du Bois shocked many of his contemporaries with his newly expounded views on American race relations. An editorial in the *Crisis* endorsing voluntary race segregation would lead to the Doctor's resignation from the NAACP, cutting his ties to the organization he helped create. Searching for a more immediate path for Negro empowerment at home and a more effective solution to stopping colonial exploitation abroad, Du Bois lamented that the NAACP "finds itself in a time of crisis and change, without a program, without effective organization, without executive officers, who have either the ability or disposition to guide . . . in the right direction"[3]

As the fight against fascism abroad became synonymous with the struggle for civil and labor rights in the United States, Du Bois and Robeson found themselves closely aligned with the Popular Front. While Robeson embraced his calling to left-wing causes and wholeheartedly endorsed the CPUSA's efforts, Du Bois resisted his gravitation toward the Left. By the end of the decade, however, the Doctor would soften his resistance, hastening his rebirth as a racial and political revolutionary.

THE GREAT DEPRESSION proved to be a catalyst of the CPUSA's growth in the urban North. Using the sudden economic misfortunes of millions as a rallying cry for national unity against capitalism, the Communists sought to build coalitions among the groups most affected by the Depression: blacks, trade unionists, and immigrants. Buoyed by support from Moscow, the Communist Party was able to piece together left-wing coalitions made up of trade unionists, black nationalists, immigrants, and empathizing liberals in cities throughout the North in the wake of the Depression. As William Patterson correctly noted, the NAACP had no effective counter to the Communist-led mass mobilization campaigns for economic and racial justice.

The (NAACP) had never sought to align the political struggles of the Negro people with those of
another group. They had sought to draw white men
into court campaigns. . . . They organized and led in
behalf of Negroes. But they had mounted no political campaign, participated in no mass demonstrations and had confined themselves to legal action.[4]

Patterson and other Communists—as well as most leftists—
believed that the NAACP lacked the will to fight the government, especially on issues that had as much to do with class as
they had with race. While the NAACP had an almost unim-
peachable record for impacting social change through the
legal system, the Du Bois–Garvey battle and the NAACP's dis-
inclination to challenge the black elite led many in the Left to
conclude that the association was afraid to get its hands dirty.
The Communists mounted a Depression-era offensive against
the NAACP, seizing upon the perception of the NAACP as too
self-absorbed in its reputation to "fight the real fight."[5] The
CPUSA also attacked the credibility of the black church,
accusing many black clergy leaders of essentially kowtowing
to government interests while the masses of blacks suffered.

The party's no-holds-barred attack on the black establishment resonated with younger and poorer blacks who believed
that leaders like Du Bois, James Weldon Johnson, and Walter
White were simply out of touch with the working man. The
Communists also questioned the effectiveness and relevancy
of the NAACP's within-the-system approach to civil rights.
Patterson noted that it was "exhilarating" to see the CP's outreach to the masses as "the order of business." The Depression,

he concluded, had led to black and white workers "sunk in desperate poverty, rise in militant struggle."[6]

Du Bois, however, had a different take. Continuing to believe that party members underestimated the race equation in promoting class solidarity, the Doctor wrote that "while Negro labor in America suffers because of the fundamental inequities of the whole capitalistic system, the lowest and most fatal degree of its suffering comes not from the capitalists but from fellow white laborers. It is white labor that deprives the Negro of his right to vote, denies him education, denies him affiliation with trade unions, expels him from decent houses and neighborhoods, and heaps upon him the public insults of open color discrimination."[7] The disconnect between the white and black proletariat was irreconcilable, Du Bois argued, making a Communist-inspired union of the working classes in America unfeasible and fantastical. If the Negro became actively involved in a proletarian struggle, "the very laboring class with whom he was trying to cooperate and for whom he was fighting would murder him first."[8]

Though publicly affronted by the brazenness of the Communists (he referred to them as "young jackasses"), Du Bois couldn't help but privately admire their idealism. He took notice of the young intellectuals who were turning to the Left for a solution on race and class. One such leftist was a *Crisis* staffer named Abram Harris. Harris was a Marxist who did not buy into the NAACP's advocacy mission, but was nonetheless a fervent admirer of Du Bois and the publication that was more the Doctor's than the association's. Harris quickly began to infuse the publication with his own theories on class exploitation, which caught the ire of both some of the *Crisis* readers and the association's board. But Du Bois had faith in Harris and was increasingly influenced by the young Marxist. The Soviet trip and Du Bois's subsequent political awakening brought the Doctor closer to his protégé, who played a big role in Du Bois's more frequent contact with both the Communists and Socialists. In 1930, sixteen-year-old James Jackson, whose father helped build one of the first black middle-class neighborhoods in Richmond, Virginia, started his own chapter of the Communist Party. What was most surprising about this was the Jackson family's close friendship with Du Bois, after whom they named a street in the community. Jackson recalled with clarity more than seventy years later how someone who grew up reading the *Crisis* could embrace Communism by the time he was a teenager. In Richmond, blacks and whites "waged a militant struggle for equality" that drew people across the color barrier. "There was an advanced consciousness in the struggle for equality . . . and we felt it was still a basic and revolutionary objective that needed to be met."[9]

Underscoring the dichotomy of the NAACP and CPUSA approaches was the 1931 Scottsboro Boys case. The Scottsboro Boys were nine young black men arrested for allegedly raping two white women on a train in Scottsboro, Alabama.[10] Despite what appeared to be an obvious lack of physical evidence and the discrepant testimony from less-than-reliable witnesses (and the "victims"), an all-white jury sealed the men's fate: conviction and death. The NAACP was initially hesitant to jump in, fearing that if the black men *were* guilty, the organization's reputation would be tarnished. Du Bois was surprisingly in sync with the decision.

The Communist Party and their legal wing, International

Labor Defense—the counterpart to the NAACP's Legal Defense Fund—took advantage of the NAACP's hesitance by representing the accused and organizing mass street protests in New York and other cities to win the Scottsboro Boys' freedom. The case would become a rallying call for the Left, and the Communist Party was smart enough to balance their own third-period initiatives, including attacking liberals as "social Fascists," with the need to build coalitions. Riding a wave of national support and international publicity, the Communists would use the Scottsboro case as a stepping-stone for their larger movement against Fascism, the soon-to-be-born Popular Front.

As CONFLICT ESCALATED between the Left and the NAACP, Du Bois was at a philosophical crossroads. Though he remained at arm's length from the Left, the Doctor couldn't help but notice the aggressiveness of the Communist Party in rallying around racial justice issues. Even if the Communist Party was more interested in advancing ideological propaganda than justice for the Scottsboro Boys, its actions continued to out-shine any effort by the NAACP to help them. In short, the association was getting beaten at its own game, and Du Bois privately reveled. His growing tensions with Walter White and other executive officers were slowly bubbling to the surface, and by late 1932 he had convinced himself that nothing short of a dramatic reorganization would save the association from its autocratic arrogance (which he blamed solely on White).

With the release of *Dark Princess*, Du Bois openly stated his affinity for Marxism and the need for a revolution of colored people. His subsequent critiques of American Communists even acknowledged the party's "courageous fight against the color line among the workers. They have solicited and admitted Negro members. They have insisted in their strikes and agitations to let Negroes fight with them and that the object of their fighting is for black workers as well as white workers."[11] It was hard to tell whether Du Bois was dropping hints about his own philosophical sway or merely trying to send a message to White and the NAACP that their efforts were not enough. Whatever the case, Du Bois pined for the kind of militancy that defined the NAACP in earlier years. Times had changed, but he felt the association had not changed with them; instead it clung to antiquated notions of gentlemanly advocacy (for which Du Bois had no use) that did little to coerce systemic change. Du Bois again pointed the finger at White, blaming him for running the organization like an autocrat and not doing anything to rouse the NAACP from its institutional laziness. If the NAACP was sticking to its age-old thesis of pragmatic protest instead of recognizing the current demands of black America, then it was doomed. As Du Bois would note later, the association was "founded in a day when a negative program of protest was imperative and effective, it succeeded so well that the program seemed perfect and unlimited. Suddenly, by World War and chaos, we are called to formulate a positive program of construction and inspiration. We have been thus far unable to comply."[12]

Du Bois hoped he would find an ally in Joel Spingarn, his Niagara Movement comrade and one of the few association executives who agreed a change was necessary. Buoyed by the prospect of Spingarn backing a plan to check White's authority, Du Bois submitted his proposal to a committee of Spingarn, Harry E. Davis, George W. Crawford, Lillian A. Alexander, and Louis T. Wright. "The time has come for a radical and thorough-going re-organization of the NAACP," Du Bois wrote. "If we wish the Association, not simply to survive, but to function during the next quarter century as effectively as it has in the last." Du Bois—whose arrogance in conviction often blinded his pragmatism—outlined his vision for the association, including a more defined economic plan that corresponded with the needs of the economically downtrodden.[13] The Doctor urged more political activism, at least when it came to supporting labor and—when necessary— making alliances with the Left. To his shock, Spingarn shot down the proposal, noting that Du Bois's vision was "neither feasible nor advisable, and that they would inevitably result in the disruption of the Association." Adding injury to insult, Spingarn concluded that while "there must be some kind of re-organization. . . . It must be one that will enlist the support of the colored people of the country."[14]

Du Bois felt his legs had been cut from under him. More important, he believed White would emerge from the association's reorganization alternative even stronger than before. White had already become a one-man show after taking over for James Weldon Johnson. He limited the roles of other NAACP staff, taking a more direct role in handling the association's branches and promotional activities. Those within the NAACP who protested White's actions did not last long. He forced Publicity Director Herbert Seligmann to quit in 1932 and fired Director of Branches Robert Bagnall a year later. William Pickens would follow several years later, lamenting after his departure that in twenty-two years of working together, White did "all in his mortal power to destroy or hurt me in some way."

But White's autocracy and the NAACP's refusal to incorporate radicalism into its mission weren't the only grievances Du Bois had with the association. After years of not bothering with the financial side of the NAACP's operations and how it raised money, Du Bois discovered the source from which the association's agenda sprang: white philanthropy. As brilliant as Du Bois was at interpreting subtleties, his ignorance of the money-buying influence and the steerage of the overall direction of the organization shaped his previous idealism on the association's effectiveness. He began to realize that the NAACP wasn't necessarily advocating a consensus platform for black advancement and equality, but an agenda that the association's executive board—made up of wealthy whites and influential blacks—felt was in the Negro's best interests. To Du Bois, such an approach reeked of paternalism, prompting him to ask more critical questions. Should the NAACP stay on the sidelines when it came to nonglamorous issues such as tenants' rights, medical care for the poor, or urban economic development for Negroes disenfranchised by the Depression? Where was the NAACP when it came to helping the anticolonial rallies in New York and Washington, D.C.? Why was the association—once the unheralded champion of the disenfranchised Negro—now leaving the grassroots organizing to the Left while its resources were being poured into court cases and lobbying? And what of integration? Why was White so insistent on integration when it was clear many blacks might not have the mind-set to become part of white society? Perhaps,

Du Bois concluded, the Garveyites were right in attacking the NAACP and questioning its motives; Garvey might even have been accurate when he predicted that "all the 'gas' about anti-lynching and 'social equality' will not amount to a row of pins."[15] Stunningly, Du Bois would find himself agreeing with his archnemesis that uplifting the race involved collective empowerment, not an oligarchy of the chosen few.

In February 1934, Du Bois—frustrated that his concerns about the association were being ignored—publicly revolted against the NAACP. Penning "The NAACP and Race Segregation" in *Crisis* wasn't just a revealing picture of the Doctor's new mind-set on race; it was a scathing indictment of the association's do-nothingness in responding to the economic needs of the Negro. Du Bois—in an uncharacteristic homage to Booker T. Washington and Garvey—argued that it wasn't segregation that crushed the Negro, but the lack of resources available to black America to build itself up. The Doctor surmised that "the majority of Americans, stand ready to take the most distinct advantage of voluntary segregation and cooperation among Colored people. Just as soon as they get a group of Black folk segregated, they use it as a point of attack and discrimination." Rather than fight for integration, Du Bois wrote, "Our counterattack should be, therefore, against this discrimination; against the refusal of the South to spend the same amount of money on the Black child as on the white child for its education; against the inability of Black groups to use public capital; against the monopoly of credit by white groups."[16]

The NAACP and the black bourgeoisie scrambled when the essay came out, seeking to isolate Du Bois's commentary to the Doctor. White, Schuyler, and Howard University scholar

Kelley Miller were among those quick to lambaste the piece. Bagnall, whose unceremonious firing the year before had left him bitter toward White and the new guard, still found common ground with the association in disavowing the Doctor's commentary that seemed to rebuke the very principles the association was founded upon. Bagnall wrote White to complain of the "defeatist policy" adopted by one of the former champions of blacks having a seat at the white man's table. Adding that the Doctor used "faulty" and "unsound" reasoning to validate segregation, Bagnall claimed that the Du Bois's new stance undermined the Negro's efforts to "break through the wall of compulsory segregation and become an integral part of America's life." Accepting such conditions, Bagnall wrote, would "mean only the hardening of the mold into a caste system."[17]

The backlash forced the NAACP to consider whether they should sever ties with its most venerable member—and the man who had almost single-handedly molded a new generation of thinkers—for the best interests of survival and credibility. As Abram Harris noted, the NAACP's insistence on integration hampered its ability to expand its outreach for the Negro, devoid of "intellectual clarity in accepting a program of action." The Marxist economist would add that the editorial should have given the NAACP a gut check and prompted a review of its policies that would "have resulted in a complete overhauling of NAACP ideology and practice."[18] But as Harris predicted, the association would stick to its course of action, meaning Du Bois would have to go. Knowing his fate was sealed, Du Bois decided to leave with some parting shots for both his nemeses and the Talented Tenth. In "Segregation in the North," the Doctor countered White's criticism with his own offensive.

> In the first place, Walter White is white. He has more white companions and friends than colored. He goes where he will in New York City and meets no Color Line. This is perfectly right and it is what anyone else of his complexion would do, but it is fantastic to assume that this has anything to do with the color problem in the United States. It naturally makes Mr. White an extreme opponent of any segregation based on race.[19]

Du Bois accused Schuyler and Miller of believing "that there is little or no segregation in the North, and that agitation and a firm stand are making it disappear. This, of course, is a fable."[20] The Doctor's apparent realization of just how out of touch the vanguard of Negro leadership was to the plight of common blacks made him more sympathetic to an old adversary. In his last *Crisis* piece, Du Bois paid tribute to militant Monroe Trotter, who had committed suicide that spring. Trotter, according to Du Bois's eulogy, "was not an organization man. He was a free lance; too intense and sturdy to loan himself to that compromise which is the basis of all real organization." But what made Trotter special, Du Bois noted, was his willingness to back up his convictions through action (another shot at White and the NAACP). "He had in his soul all that went to make a fanatic, a knight errant. Ready to sacrifice himself, fearing nobody and nothing, strong in body, sturdy in conviction, full of unbending belief." But in Trotter's death came a caveat: a loner could not champion an entire race. Rather, "the united effort of twelve millions has got to be made to mean more than the individual effort of those who think aright. Yet this very inner organization involves segregation. It involves voluntary racial organization, and this racial grouping invites further effort at enforced segregation by law and custom from without." So that the race would not leap to its death as Trotter did, Du Bois warned that there was no alternative except to "unite to save ourselves."[21]

Before the NAACP could take action, Du Bois offered his resignation. Citing a laundry list of complaints, including the association's unwillingness to organize or modernize in the face of the Depression, Du Bois called the association "a distraction of personalities and accumulated animosities." Taking a jab at Spingarn, Du Bois noted, "I leave behind me in the organization many who have long thought with me, and yet hesitated at action; many persons of large ideals who see no agents at hand to realize them, and who fear that the dearth of ability and will to sacrifice within this organization, indicates a similar lack within the whole race."[22]

Divorced from the NAACP, Du Bois was now free to explore his racial philosophy further. He knew he didn't want to be Garvey; the idea of Negrocentricity and antiwhiteness repulsed him. And he was not yet convinced the Popular Front Leftists had the answer to America's seemingly unbridgeable gulf between poor whites and poor blacks. Street protests in Harlem were one thing; getting the message of revolutionary interracial cooperation to the South—where poor whites were the ones carrying hatchets and guns to keep blacks disenfranchised—was another. Du Bois was inclined to sympathize with Marxist ethos, but he knew those who controlled capital were vested in oppressing blacks legally and poor whites psychologically. He correctly presumed that "the white laborers who lynch Negroes in the South are undoubtedly encouraged in their license by white employers who use race enmity to lower wages and keep them low."[23] Until the Communists in the United States accepted the notion of white privilege as a very real—and almost insurmountable—barrier between poor whites and blacks, Du Bois believed their radical activism would be as futile as the NAACP's. He theorized that whites in power set up and legitimized this division almost immediately after the end of the Civil War.

Such was the premise of *Black Reconstruction*, a telling glimpse of the philosophical and political path Du Bois was taking. In the book he blamed the failure of Reconstruction on the North's unwillingness to recognize Negro equality, as well as the shared interest of white capitalists on both sides of the Mason-Dixon line to keep blacks subjugated and powerless. Du Bois applied a Marxist analysis to race relations, noting that during slavery, blacks were capital. After emancipation, they were no longer part of a white man's wealth; in turn, the white man rendered the value of a Negro useless to American society. Shifting to a general assessment of class, Du Bois asserted that the degradation of labor occurred when the worker was no longer of use to the owner of capital. What was the broader implication in a dark world run by whites? "Immediately in Africa, a black back runs red with the blood of the lash; in India, a brown girl is raped; in China, a coolie starves; in Alabama, seven darkies are more than lynched; while in London, the white limbs of a prostitute are hung with jewels and silk. Flames of jealous murder sweep the earth, while brains of little children smear the hills."[24]

Du Bois turned his attention overseas, intrigued by Nazism, indifferent to Spain, vexed by Japan and China's quarrel, and angered by the plight of Ethiopia. Viewing the global conflict through an anti-imperialistic lens, the Doctor would soon adopt a strategic opposition to fascism fueled by his intense hatred of white colonialism and its devastating impact on colored people.

WHILE THE RADICALIZATION OF URBAN BLACK AMERICA was taking place, Robeson was thousands of miles away, undergoing his own political emergence. Having returned from the Soviet Union, Robeson now embraced the role of "political artist" in London. He became involved with the International African Service Bureau, run by Trinidadian radicals George Padmore and C. L. R. James. Padmore had the typical colonial rearing of a West Indian, groomed to have "the mild inoffensive manner of a Negro professor at a Southern state college." His speech, journalist Roi Ottley wrote, had "a cultivated accent and his manners are graceful. When, in characteristic fashion, he draws a handkerchief from his jacket sleeve, the act is done with all the grace of a courtier."[25] Despite his bourgeois appearance and mannerisms, Padmore was an avowed Trotskyite and had at one time joined in McKay's glowing appraisal of the Soviet Union. But like McKay, Padmore became disillusioned with Stalin's policies, particularly when it came to the Comintern's commitment to helping the Negro. In 1934 he attacked the Soviet Union's decision to align itself with the Western colonial powers against fascism, and a year later, quit the Communist Party altogether. James followed suit, frustrated that Stalin had not done enough to oppose European colonialism in Africa and Asia.

Padmore and James almost certainly tried to convince Robeson that there was more to the Soviet Union than what Paul had seen. They likely pointed out Stalin's collectivization program, which killed thousands, or his diabolical maneuverings to disenfranchise (and ultimately purge) the Trotskyites. And they were sure to have noted that the Soviet Union was using blacks as pawns to win more power and influence, not because of any fraternal bonds with the Negro. But Robeson wasn't having any of it. As James later lamented, "Russia really changed Robeson, and that meant the end for us."[26] He and Padmore came to accept Paul's stubbornness in sticking with the Soviet Union. Instead of trying to talk him about of embracing Russia, they focused their efforts on cultivating his political ideology to include a rejection of imperialism. In later years Padmore would also play a significant role in reshaping Du Bois's vision of Pan-Africanism.

With the help of Padmore and James, Robeson became more active in the African and Asian anticolonial scene in London, intensifying his friendships with Kenyatta, Nkrumah, Nnamdi Azikiwie, and, later, Jawaharlal Nehru. He had a strong interest in their independence struggles, missing the irony of London—the center of the British Empire—being the hub of anticolonial thought and activism. With an increased sense of class awareness, Robeson also made friends with Negro dock workers in Cardiff and Liverpool. As Robeson's involvement with the anticolonial movement increased, so did his belief that the hope for suffrage movements rested with the USSR. He fancied himself a spokesman for Africans, insisting that African culture needed to be preserved and emulated, not exploited and destroyed. "My pride in Africa . . . impelled me to speak out against the scorners," he recalled later in his autobiography. But while Paul had an immense affinity for African culture, he wasn't ready to become an anticolonial advocate. Instead, Robeson set aside his views to back the British government's decision to oppose Fascism (though Neville Chamberlain would soon implement a policy of appeasement toward Germany). "I came to see that the struggle against fascism must take first place over every other interest," he wrote. Paul believed both imperialism and Fascism were evil, but argued that the latter would "destroy the culture which society has created."27 His feelings grew only stronger as German Jews who had escaped Nazi Germany relayed the horrors of living under the Nuremberg Laws. Within a year of his Soviet epiphany, Paul would become convinced that fascism was the greatest threat to mankind.

Though his anti-Fascist involvement prevented him from being more active in anticolonial politics, Paul hoped he could stump for Africa through his acting career. He began seeking out more roles that reflected his desire to portray dignified Negroes. One such role was starring in James's *Toussaint L'Overture*, a play that opened in London in 1935. Though Paul had hoped for a silver screen portrayal of *L'Overture* under the direction of Sergei Eisenstein, James's play provided him an immediate opportunity to re-create the Haitian anticolonial hero. James, who had written the play with a strong contemporary anticolonial undercurrent along with hints of

Marxism, tailored the script to Robeson's acting and singing talents. The performance in London's Westminster Theatre drew mixed reviews, though critics generally raved about Paul's singular performance. One wrote that "the play must have been great pleasure for Paul Robeson to act, for Toussaint's opinion of the necessity of black people being educated has always been a plank in his platform. . . . Robeson made a fine figure of a man as the famous Toussaint."[28]

With *Toussaint* completed, Paul starred in *Song of Freedom*, a movie he hoped would take away the bad taste of *Sanders of the River* in 1934. In *Sanders*, Robeson—for all his claims of dignifying Negro roles and glorifying Africa—played the African warrior Bosambo, whose screen image did nothing to alleviate the image of Africans as savages and lost souls who could only be saved by Christianity. Many historians have wondered why Robeson would take such a role, but in its initial scripting, Bosambo's character was afforded more dignity than what would later appear onscreen. Many black actors charged that Robeson was catering to British imperialism.[29] In *Song of Freedom*, Robeson "rediscovers" his African roots as hero John Zinga, an African-born and Western-trained musician who is captured by a West African tribe. Zinga embraces the tribe's ways and pledges to build and uplift Africa rather than return to London. Ironically the film was shot entirely in England.

Paul continued his African immersion in movie roles with *King Solomon's Mines* in 1936 and in *Jericho* in 1938, but he could never shake the criticism from movie reviewers and anticolonials alike that his films were more or less conceived with a pro-Western bias. Still, Paul sincerely believed that his efforts were creating a better understanding of Africa and infusing the Western image of Africans with both humanity and dignity. As James noted, "Paul was an American and a Westerner, not an African. As an American I don't think he understood what the British had done in the colonies and how wrong it all was, even though it was so like his own situation in America."[30] Only years later would Robeson realize that his efforts to portray Africans in a better light—obstructed by institutional white racism—had failed.

THE SCOTTSBORO BOYS CASE provided the foundation for a larger movement against Fascism and international oppression by the mid-1930s. As Hitler assembled his Nazi military juggernaut and sought to rebuild the German Empire by force, Benito Mussolini rallied Italy around a return to past glory. For Mussolini, that meant going back to East Africa—where the Italians' colonial designs were rebuffed at the beginning of the century—and conquering the land destined to be part of greater Italy.

Italy's plans to attack Ethiopia, which had long been a bastion of African independence amid colonization and exploitation, mobilized an interracial coalition in the United States. By the summer of 1935, a patchwork of Communists, Socialists, black nationalists, Jewish activists, and liberals put the Popular Front into motion. Drawn by myriad causes, the members of the Front flexed their muscle with massive protests in New York and Washington, D.C., and by drawing charismatic speakers such as the Reverend Adam Clayton Powell Jr. Communists spearheaded the effort, including serving in influential anti-Fascist groups such as the American League against War and Fascism. Party luminaries Harry Ward and Earl Browder were the chairman and vice-chairman, respectively, of the group, which supported urgent U.S. intervention to prevent "the most formidable war humanity has ever known."[31] Communists capitalized on their position as the leaders in the fight against Fascism, drawing support from people who traditionally shied away from the party.[32]

Even the NAACP lent some topical support to the cause, but their interest had diminished after White correctly suspected the Popular Front's ties to Moscow. Summing up the association's collective sentiment, Pickens wrote that while he had "the very best wishes for the aim and purposes of the movement against fascism and war. . . . I have learned that in the present effort . . . there is no possibility of a united front."[33] Still NAACP leaders could not help but be worried that the black intelligentsia was being drawn into Communism under the auspices of opposing Fascism. Even many young Jews who grew up supporting the renaissance-era NAACP were beginning to turn to the radical Left, fearful of (and accurately predicting) the consequences if Hitler-inspired Fascism went unchecked. As Abbott Simon, who joined the Communist Party in his teens and immersed himself into Popular Front politics, noted, "I was Jewish to start with, and when Hitler took power in 1933, I made my decision to join [the Communist Party]. I had many friends who saw things the same way I did."[34]

The outbreak of the Spanish Civil War in 1936 only deepened the Left's resolve to stop Fascism. Republican Spain faced an all-out military onslaught led by General Francisco Franco and his strong backing of military elite, rural nationalists, and staunch Catholics who favored a centralized state. Franco received help from Italy and Germany while the Spanish government received tidbits of aid from the Soviet Union and arms from France. Joseph Stalin even helped organize the International Brigades, a regiment that drew thousands of international volunteers, including American blacks. Though Stalin would later withdraw support for the fighters, leftists continued to view the Soviet Union as a supporter of the Spanish struggle. Many black radicals tied Spain's future with their own, fighting for what they believed would lead to "no color line, no Jim-Crow trains, no lynchings." One volunteer in Spain wrote that "if we crush Fascism here we'll save our people in America, and in other parts of the world from the vicious persecution, wholesale imprisonment, and slaughter which the Jewish people suffered and are suffering under Hitler's Fascist heels."[35]

Robeson immediately sprang to Republican Spain's defense. Taking time out of his professional schedule, he sang for Spanish freedom and accepted invitations throughout Europe by anti-Fascist groups. Vexed by the American policy of neutrality and Roosevelt's unwillingness to provide arms to the Spanish army, Paul took it upon himself to help raise money for their cause. He opined that defeating Franco would "give a blow to the world forces of reaction from which they will never recover." Calling on Americans to sign up in defense of Republican Spain, Robeson called it "the greatest importance that the Negro peoples of the world should fully appreciate . . . that 'the Spanish people are defending the whole of society against the ravages of the forces of reaction.'"[36] Paul visited Spain in 1938 and was moved by the commitment of American volunteers (and Soviet philanthropy) in the struggle against Franco.

During the trip, which he would recall as "a turning point in my life," Robeson sang for soldiers and Spaniards who were bracing for the impending attack from the Fascists. His mere presence boosted the morale of the Spanish fighters, some of who had become dispirited and resigned to defeat. As some volunteers recalled, Paul's magnanimity felt like "somebody was reaching out to grasp you and draw you in."[37]

Robeson's accessibility was remarkable considering the danger he faced visiting front-line areas. With his "protecting" troops barely able to fend for themselves in area, Robeson undertook enormous risk in traveling in Spanish land still held by the Republicans. Using his visit as both a call for more international aid and a plug for the Soviet Union, Robeson continued to equate Spanish freedom with that of the Negro. "The artist must take sides . . . to fight for freedom or slavery," he told the *Daily Worker*. "I have made my choice. I had no alternative." As Robeson grew more militantly opposed to fascism, he would connect it to colonialism and capitalism, noting that the latter's history was "characterized by the degradation of my people; despoiled of their lands, their women ravished, their culture destroyed—they are in every country, save one, denied equal protection of the law, and deprived of their rightful place in the respect of their fellows."[38]

While Europe was mired in unrest, the Doctor and Paul also kept a close eye on developments in the Asian Pacific. Japan had become the undisputed power in the Far East, its military prowess drawing the fear of Americans and the awe of Asian nations under colonial rule; its sphere of influence extended into the Hawaiian Islands, where U.S. forces seemed almost certain of a Japanese invasion. In 1937, Japan invaded

China, sparking the bloody eight-year Sino-Japanese War. From December 1937 to January 1938, Japanese soldiers raped more than twenty thousand women and killed approximately three hundred thousand people in Nanking.[39] The widespread looting and arson that accompanied the Japanese takeover of the city prompted calls for international intervention. Soon the Popular Front's activities included an opposition to Japanese aggression. The Left—presumably moved by the presence of Communists in China—quickly lumped the German, Italian, Spanish, and Japanese situations as one common struggle against tyranny. However, Garveyites broke ranks with the Popular Front over Japan; many black nationalists sympathized with the Japanese, rooting for a nonwhite empire that would rival Europe and the United States. The Garveyite-leftist split at the height of the Popular Front would soon lead to other fractures in the movement, culminating in its collapse following the Soviet-Nazi Pact in 1939.

THOUGH ROBESON IDENTIFIED closely with Socialism, his major political outlook was based on opposition to Fascism. Following his visit to Spain, Paul resolved to fight Fascists on a global level, whether they were Mussolinis and Hitlers in Europe or the Dixiecrats in the United States. Robeson would become convinced that capitalism and colonialism were the offshoots of Fascist ideology; all three, he believed, sought to deprive common people of their freedom. As he firmed his anti-Fascist resolve, Paul—like many leftists—grew increasingly infatuated with the Soviet Union, especially after Josef Stalin began sending arms to Spanish freedom fighters and the German resistance. For Stalin, the move was both promotional and strategic: the Soviet Union could enhance its international reputation, particularly among Communist-wary liberals, while keeping his enemies at bay. However, in Robeson's eyes, such an action only cemented the USSR as "a bulwark against the forces of reaction and as a leading force in the struggle for peace."[40] Paul had been drawn to the Soviet Union based on its formula of racial equality; he was now a loyalist because of Russia's commitment to stop Fascism. The same could not be said, however, of Paul's feelings toward the United States and Great Britain. He was vexed by the U.S. government's unwillingness to get involved in the European conflict, despite the reports of atrocities committed against Jews in Germany and Spaniards in Guernica.[41] Even more appalling was Great Britain's about-face in dealing with Hitler. Neville Chamberlain's policy of appeasement allowed the Nazis to take Czechoslovakia without opposition. Paul and other anti-Fascists correctly predicted that conceding anything to Hitler would only embolden him to take more.

Paul viewed the events in Germany, Spain, Italy, and Japan as evidence that power-hungry dictators sought to exploit the weak and disenfranchised. In his political development, such a motive was similar to the actions of capitalists in the United States and the European colonialists in Africa and Asia. Robeson saw exploitation as a common theme of Fascism, capitalism, and colonialism; he soon incorporated them into one giant evil that needed to be stopped, again relying on the Soviet model as his paradigm. Paul began to use the term *fascist* to describe anyone he deemed reactionary. In later years, he would call McCarthyism a product of American Fascism.

Du Bois was not as quick to become an anti-Fascist. Morbidly impressed with the initial stages of Fascism, he postulated that its application was really an incarnation of Socialism, given that the state held the primary responsibility for employing, educating, and nationalizing its citizens. During Du Bois's visit to Germany in 1935, just months before the enactment of the Nuremberg Laws, the Doctor found that Hitler's dramatic improvements to the battered German infrastructure were rebuilding the people's national confidence. He noted the efficiency of the German bureaucracy, once just a withering hulk of ineptitude and inaction, as one of the fuhrer's triumphs. Du Bois was quick to point out how the Germans used the Russian model for state-controlled economic distribution and expanded it into a more-efficient means of nationalized production, with the support of the private sector. "Unless England and the United States follow the foot-steps of Germany," the Doctor concluded, "they can never expect to rival her in technical production and distribution." If Socialism was the desired result, why not allow Fascism and its nationalization of industry to continue in Germany? At least from the economic side, Du Bois saw Fascism as a possible solution to disenfranchisement.[42]

Du Bois changed his mind about applied Fascism when Italy attacked Ethiopia, a nation that served as "an example and a promise of what a native people untouched by modern exploitation and race prejudice might do." Italian aggression and the unwillingness of the League of Nations to intervene on Ethiopia's behalf struck Du Bois as the insidiousness of white colonial mentality. He argued that while France and Great Britain condemned Fascism, they allowed Italy to expand its colonial influence unchecked and subjugate an independent Negro nation. Du Bois also recognized the ramifications of this mentality: that Europe would allow Italy and Germany to annex colonial land in exchange for peace with the colonial powers. "But if Italy takes her pound of flesh by force," Du Bois wrote, "does anyone suppose that Germany will not make a similar attempt?"[43] No longer believing that fascism held any benefit for the colored world, Du Bois asserted that allowing Italy to invade Ethiopia would only spread racial chauvinism in the white world.

> Moreover, while some of them see salvation by uniting with the white laboring class in a forceful demand for economic emancipation, others point out that white laborers have always been just as prejudiced as white employers and today show no sign of yielding to reason or even to their own economic advantage. This attitude the action of Italy tends to confirm. Economic exploitation based on the excuse of race prejudice is the program of the white world. Italy states it openly and plainly.[44]

Du Bois threw his support behind the Popular Front, though he remained skeptical of American Communists and their objectives. Like Robeson, he would come to view Fascism as another white political ideology that propagated colonialism and exploitation in the darker world.

Du Bois opposed European Fascism for the same reason he supported Japan's invasion of China. Du Bois defended Japan so fervently that rumors circulated that he was a Japanese propagandist, an allegation he vehemently denied. "I have never received a cent from Japan or from any Japanese and yet I believe in Japan," he angrily wrote. "It is not that I sympathize with China less but that I hate white European and American propaganda, theft and insult more. I believe in Asia for the Asiatics and despise the hell of war and the Fascism of capital, I see in Japan the best agent for this end."[45] This justification of Japanese aggression put Du Bois in the same corner as Garveyites, who romanticized the notion of a colored nation entering the imperial fray to challenge white domination of the world.

Robeson, however, viewed Japan's invasion in the same light as the conflict in Europe. He bristled at the notion that blacks should support Japan because of Japanese were not white. In unpublished notes, Robeson upbraided black nationalists—and possibly Du Bois—for their "rally around the colored nation" mentality.

> As persecuted minority we are on side of other persecuted minorities of the persecuted and colonial peoples—whether source of persecution Hitler . . . or Japanese militants, we are on side of Jewish people, the Chinese, the Koreans . . . the people of Dutch East Indies. As far as any sympathy (for the Japanese) because they make some dent in white civilization—this is fantastic. The suffering of Koreans, of Chinese people, of people of Philippines, of Hawaii, of Malay States, shows that they have no regard for color. After all, they took their early civilization from China.[46]

If the Japanese had "no regard" for the Chinese, how could they have any regard for African Americans? Robeson would argue this point as he became more absolute in his opposition to colonialism and Fascism. By the time the United States entered World War II, Robeson led the charge to demonize Fascists, who existed "not only in Germany, Italy (and) Japan, but in Canada, the United States, the West Indies, (and) Africa."[47] Paul advocated the use of any means necessary to destroy Fascists at home and abroad; ironically McCarthyists would later follow the same rationale to hunt their enemy—leftists.

Why did Du Bois and Robeson differ when viewing Japan's aggression? For one, the Doctor was a more of a racialist than a "pure" anti-imperialist. His sentiments on Japan arose from a fundamental belief that the darker races deserved every bit of the material success of Europeans, even if it came by exploiting one another. As Abram Harris observed, Du Bois's growing sense of race nationalism was "nothing more than the objective manifestation of the intellectual racialism of . . . Woodson."[48] In Du Bois's view, that meant any victory against the overwhelming sway of Anglo imperialism on the world. The man who penned the collective frustration of the colored races toward the inhumanity of whites, who dared read into their souls, and who questioned whether the Negro's role was to fight for a place at the dinner table or resolve to make his own food, was enthusiastically behind any plan to offset white dominance. In obliterating the case of Italian aggression against Ethiopia, Du Bois absolved Japan of any wrongdoing.

Japan is regarded by all colored peoples as their logical leader, as the one nonwhite nation which has escaped forever the dominance and exploitation of the white world. No matter what Japan does or how she does it, excuse leaps to the lips of colored thinkers. Has she seized Korea, Formosa and Manchuria? Is she penetrating Mongolia and widening her power in China itself? She has simply done what England has done in Hong Kong and France in Annam, and what Russia, Germany and perhaps even the United States intended to do in China. She has used the same methods that white Europe has used, military power and commercial exploitation. And yet in all her action there has been this vast difference: her program cannot be one based on race hate for the conquered, since racially these latter are one with the Japanese and are recognized as blood relatives. Their eventual assimilation, the accord of social equality to them, will present no real problem. White dominance under such circumstances would carry an intensification of racial differences. Conquest and exploitation are brute facts of the present era, yet if they must come, is it better that they come from members of your own or other races?[49]

Du Bois's ignorance on the Japanese-Chinese situation was understandable, given his generalization of East Asian culture (a common mistake among many Westerners who believe Japan and China have strong cultural and linguistic ties). Du Bois stressed the similarities between Japan and China (the influence of Buddhism in both countries), noting that both societies shared a "magnificent heritage of courtesy, pride, hard work, and efficiency."[50] Du Bois predicted Japan would usher in a new world order and that "when China got over the birth-pains of evolving a new order, she was going to be a self-ruling nation freed of white dominance."[51] Furthermore, Du Bois added, those "who watch the development of Japan from afar, with sympathetic eyes, and the curious tie of color with all its memory of insult, slavery, and exploitation can but hope that her possible leadership of the world will make for industrial democracy and human understanding across the color line on a far larger scale than the world has yet seen accomplished."[52]

Though Du Bois would change his mind about Japan during World War II, his meditations on Japanese imperialism were the framework for racialist internationalism during the late 1930s and early 1940s. Du Boisian logic would be reincarnated in later years by prominent blacks opposed to U.S. intervention in Vietnam, Iraq, Panama, and Afghanistan.

Du Bois and Robeson solidified their opposition to Fascism by the end of the decade, convinced that slaying a three-headed monster of Fascism, colonialism, and capitalism would lead to greater freedom among oppressed people. By becoming more active in the anti-Fascist struggle, both men grew closer to the Soviet Union and the Left. But as they came to learn, Germany, Italy, Spain, and Japan weren't the only nations engaging in brutal oppression.

4

STALIN'S PURGE, THE PACT, AND FALSE JUSTIFICATION

*The comradely contribution by different peoples to a
common civilization is no longer a dream, for on one-sixth
of the earth's surface such a civilization does exist, and
these peoples with their rich nationalist cultures firmly
bound into one socialist union stand as a bulwark against
the forces of reaction and as a leading force in the struggle
for peace.*

—Paul Robeson, 1938 speech in London

DURING HIS 1937 VISIT, Robeson publicly declared his love for the
USSR, noting how the Soviets—through the adoption of the
new Socialist constitution—had successfully eliminated racism
and class division. "I must say that all of my earlier impressions have been confirmed, my understanding of the Soviet

ideal has been broadened and many features of Soviet society not so well understood by me, made more clear," he told the *Soviet Worker*. Having enrolled Paul Jr. in school there, he gushed that his son would not "fail to realize his good fortune in sharing the common collective life of the Soviet Union." Learning among diverse students who all considered themselves Soviets (or were conditioned to believe they were), Robeson said his son's schooling would foster "a deep responsibility to the oppressed of all peoples in other lands who are struggling to gain an opportunity to live a decent life."[1]

While Robeson raved about the "freedoms" of the Socialist state and the Negro's ability to live there without fear of discrimination, Josef Stalin's methodical purge of the Soviet Union was at its peak. More than eight hundred thousand people had already been killed, and hundreds of thousands more would follow; average Soviets lived in daily fear of being implicated as enemies of the state. Soviet sympathizers justified the Great Purge as an ideological cleansing necessary to the survival of Russian society and successful continuation of the revolution. Robeson, who was likely personally devastated by news of the purge, was among those who condoned it as a necessity for the Soviet state's survival.

Du Bois's racial militancy and more fundamentalist interpretations of Socialism following his split from the NAACP segued to his public defense of the USSR during World War II. While Du Bois continued to favor Japan as the battering ram against European imperialism, his admiration for the Soviet Union grew with Stalin's support of Spanish freedom fighters and Russian opposition to colonization in Africa. The Doctor was quietly impressed with the Soviet model for minorities, and despite his reservations about such a paradigm being successful in the United States, acknowledged that "there was something rather splendid in the way in which this great new land slashed at Negro prejudice throughout the world."[2] He also concurred with Robeson's assessment that Soviet Russia stood "four-square for the cause and the rights of all the oppressed peoples of the world."[3]

Du Bois and Robeson's defense and justification of the purge was understandable, given their belief that Fascism and colonialism, which had degraded and subjugated millions of people worldwide, were far greater evils than Stalin's political executions. Like many on the Left, they lionized the Soviet Union for being the only country to oppose Fascism and provide moral (and in Spain's case, financial) support to anti-Fascist resistance. Though the first wave of Purge Trials made news in the United States, and Paul—through information from his young son and other friends—came to know that others were being killed, the general silence among Leftists was an indication that any scrutiny of the purge would be seen as a victory for conservatives, colonials, Fascists, and capitalists. Many also supported the Soviets out of ignorance, unaware of the true extent to which genocide was taking place.

The Left's unquestioned support for the Soviet Union rapidly evaporated after the signing of the Soviet-Nazi Non-Aggression Pact, which opened the door for Germany's invasion of Poland and the start of World War II. Those who had spent the entire decade fighting Fascism could not justify the Kremlin's decision to sign an agreement with Hitler; as a result, the Popular Front collapsed. However, Du Bois and Robeson remained in Russia's corner, convinced that Soviet-style

Socialism and international diplomacy offered the best hope of equality and freedom for oppressed peoples. As Robeson tried to explain, the "pact was an attempt on the part of the Soviet Union to prevent the war already threatening and which has broken into the bloody battle between imperialist powers which we witness today."[4] By defending the pact and its ramifications, Du Bois and Robeson made clear their desire to support the USSR unconditionally, even if it meant contradicting themselves in the process.

As Du Bois continued to debate the future success of the Russian experiment, Robeson grew more infatuated with the Soviet Union, thanks in large part to his flattering assessment of its leader. While Joseph Stalin might have engineered a diabolical consolidation of power, killed or forced into exile hundreds of key Communist leaders, and began what would be a forceful reshaping of the Soviet political and cultural landscape over the next decade, he was still cast as the leading voice against colonialism, Fascism, and capitalistic oppression. Robeson sincerely believed that Stalin "patiently . . . labored for peace and ever increasing abundance—with . . . deep kindliness and wisdom."[5] Robeson, like American Communist leaders and other black radicals, vehemently defended Stalin in the United States, even if the kindly and paternal Father Joseph's actions clearly showed his proclivity toward oppression and willful destruction of dissenters.

The real Stalin was the antithesis of the ideal Stalin created by Soviet propagandists, romantic leftists, and other anti-colonials at the height of the Popular Front. He was not, as some called him, a political revolutionary seeking to build upon the Communist ideals of Marx and Engels, but a despot whose sole objective was political survival and the accumulation of more power. Stalin was a nationalist first and foremost, paying mere lip service to the idea of international Communist revolutions envisioned by Vladimir Lenin and Leon Trotsky. Stalin carried out his nationalism by ingraining it into the governance of the Comintern. Stalin biographer Robert Tucker noted that Stalin fancied himself more Peter the Great than Lenin; in Stalin's eyes, the revolution needed to be molded by one dominant figure. Eager to escape Lenin's shadow, he tried to reach that iconic status "by leading the [Communist] party and country in a revolution of Socialism's construction and thereby saving Mother Russia from the fate of once again being beaten by foreigners."[6]

Stalin knew his vision was in direct conflict with Leninism, which called for the continuance of the revolution through a plurality of ideas. Trotsky advocated an even more radical stance than Lenin, believing that class warfare was inevitable and that political genocide was an effective tool against the obstinate ruling class. Trotsky called for Russia to lead a worldwide class revolution, an idea popular among such anti-colonial thinkers as Padmore, James, Mexican painter Diego Rivera, and Vietnamese Communist Ta Tu Thau. Stalin, on the other hand, sought to perfect Socialism by centralizing the state. Because Trotskyism threatened the Comintern, Stalin engineered Trotsky's expulsion from the party and the Soviet Union in 1929. Following the ejection of nearly half a million party members during the early 1930s, Stalin became even more determined to consolidate his power. Like Hitler using the Gestapo, he directed the NKVD (the forerunner to the KGB) to weed out potential opposition, sanctioning the use of torture to get confessions. Stalin set out to wage ideological war against the rest of the world while conforming Soviet society to *his* desires. But in order to justify such bold moves, he would need a martyr.

Three weeks before Robeson's revelatory first visit to the Soviet Union, party leader Sergei Kirov was assassinated in his office. Soviet officials quickly revealed a Trotskyite conspiracy led internally by Grigory Zinoniev, one of Stalin's chief opponents within the Comintern. Zinoniev and fifteen others, including former Bolshevik luminary Lev Kamenev, were arrested and charged with conspiring with Western powers to destabilize the Soviet state. Many of those charged, including Zinoniev, were complicit in their own arrests; they had been led to believe that the trials would be a message to the foreign imperialists that the Soviets used a heavy hand to deal with subversion.[7]

The first of the Moscow Purge Trials began with heavy media publicity in August 1936. The accused had confessed, some believing their lives would be spared and that they would be exiled to start new lives in other parts of the Republic. The defendants seemed at ease, according to courtroom witnesses, leading Western observers to believe that a fair trial was actually taking place.[8]

Though Zinoniev and a few of his codefendants may have believed that the court's foregone decision would be followed by a "mock" execution, they would soon find out that the NKVD used real bullets. Russian playwright and Stalin biographer Edward Radzinsky noted that Zinoniev went to his grave still convinced that he could somehow spare himself and get back into Stalin's good graces. But for Stalin, forgiveness could only come in the form of sacrifice.[9]

Others would follow. In January 1937 and March 1938, the Soviets conducted two show trials against alleged conspirators, many of who had been high-ranking party officials and close associates of Lenin. Among those executed was Karl Radek, a former Bolshevik Revolution leader who had become one of Stalin's staunchest allies. However, Radek became more valuable as a political oblation to Stalinism; the Soviet government would use Radek's arrest to point out that when dealing with enemies of the state, *no one* was above suspicion.

Ironically, leftists and Communists worldwide used the Moscow Trials to show the successes of Stalinization as an effective counter to capitalism and colonialism. Stalin became the world's leading anti-Fascist, anticolonial, and antiracist, the *generalissimo* of oppressed peoples. Black writers, including Langston Hughes and Richard Wright, canonized him in their works, while New Deal liberals—still cautious of the Communist influence in the United States—began taking notice of the Soviet Union as a potential ally. Stalin's exportation of arms and military advisor to the Spanish republicans was even more ample evidence that the Russians were serious about fighting fascism, further legitimizing the Popular Front.

The growth of the antifascist movement seemed unhindered by Congressman Martin Dies's (the predecessor to Joseph McCarthy in instigating anti-Red paranoia) examination of "Communist penetration" in New Deal agencies.[10] Even the most ardent Popular Front supporters—including Robeson—were unaware that Stalin's real motives for intervening in

Spain were to destroy Trotskyites and swindle money from the Spanish treasury.[11] Similarly, the Soviets' portrayal of the political killings as a necessity to keep the Socialist state free of Fascist infiltration made the purge seem like a noble action to Stalin loyalists.

The Great Purge would include an expansive effort to destroy kulaks (wealthy landowning peasants) and "fifth column" national minorities, deemed too backward for assimilation into the Soviet machine. But while Stalin secretly destroyed minorities, the public signing of the Socialist constitution became another feather in the cap of the Soviet Union and another effort, many black leftists believed, to shame the United States into ending Jim Crow. The Soviet constitutional provision banning racial discrimination read, in part:

> The equality of the right of citizens of the USSR, irrespective of their nationality or race, in all fields of economic, state, cultural, social and political life, is an irrevocable law. Any direct restriction of these rights, or conversely the establishment of direct or indirect privileges for citizens on account of the race or nationality to which they belong, as well as the propagation of racial or national exceptionalism, or hatred or contempt, is punishable by law.

Robeson boasted that "this expression, broader in scope or loftier in principle than ever before expressed, is particularly appealing to Negroes for it comes at a moment when in almost all other countries, to a greater or lesser degree, theories concerning the superiority and inferiority of this or that people, and especially the inferiority of my people, are propagated even in the highest schools of learning."[12] Many black intellectuals living in the United States agreed, temporarily throwing aside their skepticism about the Communists to join the Popular Front. The CPUSA was able to win support from unlikely candidates, including Alain Locke, Lester Granger of the Urban League, and Robert Vann, the influential but conservative publisher of the *Pittsburgh Courier*. By cobbling together alliances among black moderates and church leaders, the Communists were able to exercise considerable influence on the Left and recruit more supporters to their pet causes.

However, disenchanted Russophiles escalated their guerrilla war against the Popular Front and Stalin. McKay, Padmore, and James—respected black leftists who once had an all-access pass to the Kremlin and had been groomed to become the next leaders of the revolution—lambasted the Moscow Trials and the Soviet Union's commitment to the Negro. CPUSA leaders summarily dismissed them as black nationalists.[13] Though it was the Communists who had popularized the notion of the "Black Belt thesis" in order to attract former Garveyites, they now found themselves trying to separate the notions of black pride and black self-determinism, the principal factors of black nationalism. To do this, they relied on well-respected intellectuals such as Hughes, Richard Wright, and Adam Clayton Powell, as well as Robeson, whose popularity in the United States had not dimmed despite his self-imposed exile in Europe. What made the impact of these men so much more profound was their ability to reach young people, including white bohemians, black college students, and those moved to activism by their religious duty. Even though some black leftists opined that the link between nationalism and the black experience was inextricable, they were willing to incorporate their natural militant tendencies into a greater push for enfranchisement.

Powell wrote that the Popular Front and its offshoots, namely the National Negro Congress and the Southern Negro Youth Congress, fostered "a nationalism that aims toward solidifying our race into a militant oneness and to cooperate with other groups in the fight for social justice."[14] It was this kind of outreach that aimed to integrate race pride and economic justice for all, a platform that appealed to a wide range of black intellectuals. By keeping the focus on social justice at home and opposition to fascism abroad, the Communist Party–led Left minimized the negative impact of the Moscow Trials and the purge.

THOUGH ROBESON PROBABLY HAD more inside information about the real extent of the Great Purge than any other American, he remained committed to the Soviet cause. His denial of the atrocities in Russia might have stemmed from his unwavering belief that the Soviet Union was still a better option than the open discrimination of Jim Crow in the United States. However, Paul privately asked his son, who was enrolled in the Soviet School, to tell him everything he knew about the purge. Paul Jr. recollected in a book years later that he gave his father "fragmentary insights into the unfolding Soviet tragedy." Paul Jr. got his information from classmates, some of whose parents went missing at the peak of the purge. He would later rationalize his father's continued support of the Soviet Union as choosing between the lesser of two evils. Paul Jr. claimed that the 1,116 people killed in 1936 during the first purge was "not an abnormal number in those days for a population," adding that during his father's lifetime, "the number of African-Americans killed by white mobs exceeded this number—for example, during the 'Red Summer' of 1919."[15] Without much fanfare, Paul and Essie pulled their son from the school, not knowing whether they would be next to get caught in the political storm brewing within Mother Russia.

Paul was also not untouched by the trials. His friend Ignaty Kazakov, a physician who spent time with the Robesons during their visits to the Soviet Union, was arrested for murdering Communist Party leader Vyachslev Menzhinsky. Robeson met with Kazakov in August 1937, though he quickly realized that his friend—who came with two Soviet agents—was in some sort of trouble. The two met for lunch at a Moscow hotel and had a normal conversation, given the circumstances, but it became clear to Robeson that Kazakov was doomed. The physician thanked Paul and left with his "bodyguards; Robeson would not see him alive again."[16]

Although Kazakov and other Soviets whom Paul knew became victims of the middle-of-the-night arrests, hastily conducted trials, and even faster executions over the next few years, his obstinacy when it came to his feelings on the Soviet Union seemed to fall in line with the rebelliousness in his character. As Robeson grew more attached to the Soviet Union, he became more vehement in its defense and could never bring himself to publicly admit any of its shortcomings, despite the devastating impact of Stalinization. His defense of the Moscow Trials reflected that public stubbornness Paul showed at critical times in his life and career. He might have felt betrayed, but questioning the USSR would only validate his critics and the reactionaries in the United States. So he stayed loyal, proclaiming that the Soviet Union's lead in the global freedom struggle and their fair treatment of minorities made it the one nation that valued human dignity. Robeson, in one of the rare public comments he made on the trials, told Ben Davis the Soviets "ought to destroy anybody who seeks to harm that great country."[17]

Paul also seems to have been caught up in the "personality cult" that drew so many Western intellectuals to Stalin, who, in their eyes, was an omnipresent father to the Soviet masses. As Robeson recalled of Stalin: "Here was a clearly a man who seems to embrace all . . . so kindly (I can never forget that wonderful sense of kindliness) and too a feeling of sureness. . . . Here was one who was wise and good . . . the world and especially the Socialist world was fortunate indeed to have daily guidance."[18] Not even James or Padmore could convince Robeson that Stalin's increasing boldness in arresting Communist Party members as conspirators against the state needed further examination. The West Indian radicals were now—at least on ideological terms—the enemy, banished to the fringes with other Trotsky loyalists. Though the 1937 Dewey Commission exonerated Trotsky of any crimes against the USSR, Robeson was adamant that Stalin was right in his handling of the "Trotskyite" element.[19] Not until Nikita Khrushchev's revelation twenty years later would Robeson recognize that Trotsky was just an excuse for a madman to destroy a society and rebuild it in his image.

Du Bois continued to view the Soviet Union with distant

admiration, still uncertain of its success in a world dominated by Western imperialism. During the mid-1930s, he was not as excited as Robeson and Hughes about the prospect of Russia leading the way for black America and other oppressed nations. "Perhaps sometime when this great experiment finds its feet," the Doctor wrote skeptically, "it will again essay to stretch rescuing hands to the dark submerged millions of the world."[20] Du Bois began to come around to the Soviet Union after Stalin's offer of support for the Spanish Civil War. Maybe the USSR was ready—both socially and militarily—to become a catalyst for world change against capitalism, colonialism, and Fascism. Maybe, Du Bois thought, the Japanese had a potential ally in breaking the monopoly of Western Europe. But Japan, the Doctor lamented, "has declared her enmity toward Russian communism although that forces her to give too much power to her military party and to turn her back upon perhaps the greatest effort to raise the economic level of the common people which the world has ever seen." He held out hope that if Japan could be made to see that the Soviet Union was their ally against imperialists, then it would escape "the lap of fascist Germany and Italy who represent today war, tyranny, reaction and race hate on the most dangerous scale."[21]

During the Moscow Trials, Du Bois became even more convinced of the Soviet Union's legitimacy and sincerity as an anticolonial power. The Doctor's one-week visit to the Soviet Empire in 1937 as the first part of his justification tour (the latter being his trip to China to inspect Japanese "leadership" there) yielded very little information about the purge, but he came away convinced that Stalinization was working. In noting how things had changed for the better (the quality of life had improved dramatically, thanks to Stalin's economic policies), Du Bois did not take note of how much worse things had become from a morale standpoint. Moscow, which boomed with a widespread optimism in 1926 under Lenin's New Economic Program, was now replete with quiet paranoia. Even as Du Bois jotted his sanguine assessment of Russia more than twenty years after the end of oppressive czarist rule, many Muscovites kept their heads on swivels in fear of being fingered as conspirators. It is hard to believe Du Bois was completely oblivious to the culture of fear that Stalin had created, but his acceptance of this path as the alternate to American history of exploitation and racism seemed to outweigh any potential concerns he might have had. As David Levering Lewis noted, Du Bois had his misgivings about Stalin, but he had faith that it was the system, not the man, who would ultimately be responsible for the success of the Soviet machine. He believed the "Russian people . . . needed more (Karl) Radeks and fewer Stalins, and they would stumble and retreat many times on the road to Socialism."[22]

Du Bois did not yet share the same hope for American Communists. Though white racists labeled him as a "Red radical preaching dictatorship of the proletariat," the Doctor was still far from a party supporter.[23] He admired their initiative, particularly in organizing the Popular Front. He had even befriended several Communist Party members, including Doxey Wilkerson and James Ford, expressing gratitude for their support after his resignation from the NAACP. But the Doctor still held to the belief that "in the case of the American Negro, the communist program for him as laid down by the American Communist Party and by the Russian dictatorship is in my opinion fundamentally wrong. . . . I do not believe any such program will emancipate the American Negro."[24] Du Bois was convinced that younger writers like Hughes and Wright were drawn to the Communist Party out of naïveté over a desire for practical civil rights advancement. He would, however, side with his younger counterparts in defending the purge, accepting Stalin's genocide as more digestible than the atrocities of colonization and fascism. As the Doctor sharpened his opposition to the seemingly immovable citadel of white chauvinism, he would come to find that the USSR, in spite of its imperfections, was a much-needed ally in his fight.

A HANDSHAKE AND TOAST at the Kremlin signaled the end of the Popular Front. The CPUSA-led struggle against racism and Fascism crashed with the signing of the Nazi-Soviet Non-Aggression Pact in August 1939. For Communists in other parts of the world, the pact, which seemed out of the question only six months earlier, meant either supporting the Comintern's logic or leaving the party. Many chose the latter. CPUSA leaders, including Earl Browder, Ben Davis, and William Patterson, tried to explain the Soviet rationale, but were hard pressed to offer any plausible justification for a Communist-Fascist coexistence. Robeson, who returned to the United States in 1939 after more than a decade away, offered his own take, saying, "The Soviet Union relies upon its growing economic, political and cultural standards and upon the mutual friendship of the nations. . . . In the opinion of the Soviet Union these new, good relations between the USSR and

Germany were tested in practice in connection with events in Poland and their strength was then proved."[25]

Their spin doctoring did little to slow the exodus from the party, especially among Jews who had joined because of the Communist Party's stand against Fascism. Black leftists, including Powell, Bunche, E. Franklin Frazier, and Abram Harris, also broke ranks with the Popular Front. Bunche, whose career track destined him for a diplomatic post, would soon distance himself from the Left altogether. Within three years, Hughes and Wright joined him as critics of the Communist Party. The pact essentially drained the CPUSA of prominent black intellectuals who had, by official membership or loose affiliation, advanced the party's message to black America. Though Robeson continued to vocally defend the Soviet Union and the party, the Stalin-Hitler truce had done irreparable damage to the Kremlin's reputation among many left-leaning blacks and Jews. Faced with an increasing vacuum in allies, the Communist Party would shift its focus away from internationalism and become more involved in the wartime labor movement in the United States. America's entrance into World War II would create another opportunity for the Communist-led Left to capitalize, while Du Bois and Robeson would become more publicly adamant that the fate of oppressed Negroes was inextricably tied to others around the world. Ignoring the brutality of Stalin, they would embrace the Soviet Union as the torchbearer of peace and freedom.

5

WORLD WAR II AND THE DOMESTIC BATTLEFRONT

There are words like Freedom
Sweet and wonderful to say.
On my heartstrings freedom sings
All day everyday.

There are words like Liberty
That almost make me cry.
If you had known what I know
You would know why.

—Langston Hughes, "Words Like Freedom"

IN THE SPRING OF 1939, Rushton Coulborn—Du Bois's colleague at Atlanta University—predicted that Fascism would become ingrained in American society the way it had in Germany and Spain, subjecting blacks to the same treatment as Jews under Hitler and Spanish leftists under Franco. "When the American South goes fascist," Coulborn wrote, "look for something native to the soil, a movement which quite possibly will not even use the word *fascist*, since the word is unpopular." He reasoned that Fascism, especially in the South, did not need "foreign inspiration" to take root, noting that "the beginnings of such a system . . . are present in the 'Jim Crow' laws."[1] Du Bois agreed with Coulborn's grim postulate. "As the Negro develops from an easily exploitable, profit-furnishing laborer to an intelligent independent self-supporting citizen," he wrote, "the possibility of his being pushed out of his American fatherland may easily be increased rather than diminished. We may be expelled from the United States as the Jew is being expelled from Germany."[2] Though most of the Doctor's progressive contemporaries did not share such a fatalistic assessment of the Negro's future, they believed the United States couldn't fight a war against Fascism overseas unless it fought Fascism at home, too. "The fight now is not to save democracy, for that which does not exist cannot be saved," Ralph Bunche wrote. "But the fight is to maintain these conditions under which people may continue to strive for realization of the democratic ideals. This is the inexorable logic of the nation's position as dictated by the world anti-democratic revolution and Hitler's projected new world order."[3]

Fighting a two-front war for freedom galvanized African Americans. Spurred by their sense of loyalty to the United

States and dissatisfaction with continued second-class citizenship, blacks became more actively involved in advocacy than ever before. Blacks joined unions in record numbers, while the NAACP and Urban League reestablished themselves as the prominent voices of civil rights progress. The NAACP would increase its standing in Franklin D. Roosevelt's administration, thanks to the support of Eleanor Roosevelt and high-profile cabinet members. Though the Popular Front era had passed, the Left would bounce back by becoming a force in the labor movement. The Communist Party USA, which would take control of the National Negro Congress in 1940, led efforts for greater opportunities for African Americans in the American Federation of Labor (AFL) and the Congress of Industrial Organizations (CIO). As Du Bois happily noted, "American Negroes . . . are much more radical and broad-minded than they were a generation ago and wish to go far in cooperating with the labor movement."[4]

At the start of the war, Du Bois and Robeson were the most prominent African Americans in the world, revered equally for their professional accomplishments and their activism. The Doctor had now influenced several generations of black thought spanning parts of two centuries, and he showed no signs of letting up. With the release of *Dusk of Dawn*, he gave black America a guidebook for militancy while accelerating his own immersion into the Left. Robeson, who returned to the United States in 1939 following more than a decade in Europe, would soon overtake Joe Louis as the most popular black man in the United States. Though his political activities raised Red flags among FBI officials and conservatives, Robeson continued to be celebrated for his artistry. By 1944, he starred in a record-breaking run of *Othello* and sung the "Ballad for Americans," accomplishments that would earn him the label America's number-one Negro.[5]

Though initially noninterventionists, Du Bois and Robeson joined the war bandwagon after Germany broke the pact and invaded the Soviet Union. The ensuing alliance between Moscow and the West—highlighted by the 1943 Tehran Conference—engendered hope for a lasting U.S.-Soviet alliance. "At long last," Robeson said, "we have a real united drive against Hitler. . . . Therefore the Negro people will give all support to the present drive to smash Hitler and free the world from the threat of his domination."[6] Robeson, like many of his peers on the Left, knew warm relations between both countries could only lead to better conditions for blacks in the United States. Wonderstruck by the possibility of such an alliance, Robeson and Du Bois devoted their energies to wartime activism, inspiring a new generation of leftists and creating political enemies in the process.

THOUGH THE NAZIS appeared to be on the verge of vanquishing Europe, Du Bois and Robeson opposed U.S. participation in World War II, arguing that intervention equaled tacit support for colonialism. After all, Great Britain had despoiled the better part of three dark continents and continued to resist colonized natives' demands for self-determination. France held Southeast Asia and much of North Africa in its clutches and, despite being overrun by the Nazi machine, refused to grant its colonies independence. Robeson publicly opposed the American intervention on these grounds, arguing that many blacks had been misled to believe that they were supporting a cause for freedom. If the United States aided Great Britain, it would mean America's own complicity in global imperialism. Robeson summed up these sentiments at the Win the Peace Conference in 1940:

> We can choose between the end of colonial tyranny in India, China, Indonesia, Africa, and Iran—or its continuance under a new or highly developed kind of benevolent Anglo-American imperialism. So this conference has a tremendous task in working out ways to get the facts to the American people. When they know they will force our government to cease its policy of propping up fascism—and on the other hand, to help, not hinder the development of governments with new democratic forms, answering the needs of ever expanding liberal, cooperative, socialist and communist democratic societies. [7]

Paul also feared inevitable wartime concessions would have devastating effects on the Negro. "The decision that must be made, and remade, by the American people as issue after issue comes before them is this: In what direction are we going? And the maxim that must be remembered is that concessions to the forces of reaction are a double blow," he wrote. "They both weaken the giver and strengthen the opposition. In the name of national defense, great concessions—the sacrifice of civil and human rights—are being demanded from the people of America." Sensing that black America was at a crossroads as war loomed, Robeson cautioned that "democracy cannot be defended through self-imposed death. It must be defended by its own strengths and all steps backward can add only to the forces of enslavement."[8]

The Moscow factor also weighed heavily in Paul's decision to oppose intervention. Though he despised Fascism, Robeson was painfully aware that the Nazis were the Soviet Union's allies for the time being. He held out hope that the USSR could stop the Nazi advance through peaceful negotiations, thereby avoiding the need for the United States to enter the war on behalf of a colonial power. The pact remained in effect, and Paul's loyalty to Moscow and the Communist Party overcame his antipathy toward Nazi Germany. Falling in line with other Communist Party leaders like Browder and Ford (who formed the party's presidential ticket in 1940), Paul called for a peaceful solution to the struggle overseas. Fascism needed to be defeated, he believed, but not by saving imperialism. Robeson would reverse course the following year, when the Germans broke the agreement and attacked the Soviet Union by way of Finland.[9] The CPUSA, which had been constrained by the pact, now became one of the most vocal groups in advocating American intervention. "The Communists will do their full share to bring about victory," Ford declared. "Unless the Negro people play their part in helping to win the war, the war effort will be less effective. . . . They now know that this war for the military destruction of fascism is *their* war."[10]

Du Bois's explanation for withholding support reflected his staunch adherence to racialist internationalism. Like Robeson, the Doctor reviled European colonialism and felt it partly to blame for the rise of Fascism in Germany and Italy. After all, England and France had plundered the Dark World, emasculating the Germans and Italians with their colonial conquests. Du Bois saw the tedious peaceful coexistence between the Soviets and Germans, as well as the alliance between the Germans and Japanese, as a sign that the world order was shifting against the old guard of colonial powers. He had also come closer to Robeson's view that Russia had more to offer the world than any of the imperial powers, including the United States. "No matter how much the Fascism of Mussolini and the National Socialism of Hitler, the New Deal of Roosevelt and the appeasement of Chamberlain and the new World War, may assert and believe that they have found ways of abolishing poverty, increasing the efficiency of work, allowing the worker to earn a living and curtailing the power of wealth by means short of revolution, confiscation and force," Du Bois wrote, "every honest observer must admit that human civilization today has by these very efforts moved toward Socialism and accepted many of the tenets of Russian communism."[11]

This was not the same Du Bois who had asked his fellow blacks to "close ranks" during World War I, or the venerable NAACP leader who dismissed black nationalists as "buffoons" at the height of the UNIA's popularity in the 1920s. Experimenting with black nationalism, Socialism, and textbook Marxism, Du Bois now found himself agreeing with iconoclast George Schuyler, who in later years would become the forerunner to Clarence Thomas, Stanley Crouch, Larry Elder, Alan Keyes, and other black conservatives. Schuyler was as cynical as Du Bois when viewing the war's impact on blacks, noting:

> Maybe peace will see an end to the discrimination
> and insults Negroes suffer under the Stars and

Stripes, Union Jack, Tri-color, the banner of Savoy, etc. I hope so. But when I see a great nation like the United States engaged in a struggle for its life and still determined to continue and even expand the racial distinctions forced upon the whole nation by the fanatically Negrophobic South, I am doubtful, to put it mildly. And unless some changes are made pretty soon in the direction of real improvement, the disinterest of the Black masses in the outcome of the current fight for democracy is going to become tremendous.[12]

Du Bois would also base his opposition on international relativism. What Hitler was proposing to do with Eastern Europe, what Italy was doing in Ethiopia, and what Japan was doing in China was no different than what the United States had done to the American Indian and the Negro, and what Western Europe had continued to do with the nations of Africa and Asia. And when the Soviets invaded Finland, Du Bois was incredulous at the West's response. "England has been seizing land all over the earth for centuries with and without a rightful claim," he wrote. "The United States seized Mexico from a weak and helpless nation in order to bolster slavery. . . . This is the sort of world that has grown suddenly righteous in defense of Finland."[13] Du Bois was equally unambiguous when it came to Japanese subjugation of China. While he felt Japan overstepped its bounds, "he would never permit himself to be misled by the capitalists and missionaries who wanted to keep Asia as the backyard of European commerce and civilization."[14] But his opinions about America's role in the war rubbed hard against the grain, especially as his peers—including Randolph, Bunche, Mary McLeod Bethune, and now, Robeson—stumped for intervention. He continued to withhold support for the war until the Japanese attack on Pearl Harbor, which would effectively squash his hopes for peace between the United States and Japan.

Once the United States jumped into the conflict, Du Bois fell in line with other black Americans, albeit more grudgingly. Even though he felt a deep-down conviction that the war was wrong, and that Negroes were being used as pawns yet again to advance the causes of imperialism and racial superiority, Du Bois concluded there was nothing black America could do. He felt blacks were called to duty and forced to support the war "under the sad weight of duty and in part . . . the inheritance of a slave psychology which makes it easier for us to submit than to rebel. Whatever all our mixed emotions are, we are going to play the game."[15] And so, unwilling to accept U.S. entry into World War II yet resigned to its inevitably, the Doctor decided to let the chips fall.

PREWAR MOBILIZATION COINCIDED with full implementation of New Deal programs seen as beneficial to blacks. The passage of the Fair Labor Standards Act had begun to give African Americans in blue- and white-collar industries better economic opportunities. However, the bill did not cover agricultural and domestic workers, who made up most of the black workforce in the South. Still, New Deal programs such as the National Industry Recovery Act and the Work Projects Administration provided increased—albeit limited—economic opportunities for African Americans, paving the way for black America's exodus to the Democratic Party. The gains of black wage earners during the New Deal also strengthened the labor movement.

Though the American Federation of Labor continued to resist integration, many unions in the Congress of Industrial Organizations welcomed blacks into their ranks. Some, including the National Maritime Union (NMU), had significant black membership, making them among the leaders of a progressive effort to get African Americans fair representation in industry. The growing labor movement provided the Left another chance to play a key role in domestic advocacy. Having stumbled significantly as a result of the pact, the Communist Party quickly sought to make amends through the labor organization. Communists began to take key roles in union leadership, influencing a diverse collection of labor groups ranging from the NMU and the International Long-shoremen's and Warehousemen's Union (ILWU) to the Fur and Leather Workers Union. These unions would be important in promoting Robeson's labor advocacy, and in later years, some of their members would be among his and Du Bois's biggest supporters during the McCarthy era. The Left became a force in the drive to integrate unions, despite encountering fierce resistance from white workers. White workers often went on strike to protest integration of unions and the hiring of blacks. As Du Bois observed, "White labors in the South would rather submit to disenfranchisement and starvation than be put on an equality with black labor."[16] But the Communist-led Left continued to press for unionization. Even Harry Bridges, the longtime leader of the ILWU, backed the Left's call for integration. By 1941, black representation in unions had made small but significant gains.

As the Left led the battle for integration of unions, the National Negro Congress (NNC) was in a fight for its soul. The congress, which had been cofounded by a number of progressive civil rights organizations during the Popular Front, now faced the prospect of being coopted by Communists. Many of the congress's initial supporters, including Howard University President Mordecai Johnson and Adam Clayton Powell, had left, fearing that the party's growing influence would damage their own careers. Bunche, who had been a proponent of the congress during its inception, attended the third convention of the NNC in spring 1940. He had already concluded that the congress was turning into a "Communist cell," and kept his distance, only attending as part of a study commissioned by Swedish sociologist Gunnar Myrdal.[17] But he wasn't the only one who feared that the Communists were using the organization as a front to advance their own interests. A. Philip Randolph, whose Brotherhood of Sleeping Car Porters had been an important member of the congress, decried the use of the NNC as a tool for Soviet interests. After his speech at the NNC convention, Randolph walked out, terminating his membership with the congress and paving the way for an official Communist takeover. Bunche also disavowed his connection with the NNC, offering a scathing portrait of the organization in his study of Negro organizations. NNC members now knew they had made their choice to align themselves with the party. As Thelma Dale Perkins recalled, "The moment Randolph walked out with the Pullman porters, we knew things had changed significantly."[18] Perkins found out immediately how right she was. Max Yergan and Revels Cayton took front-and-center control of the organization, mirroring the NNC's platform with the Communist Party's. By the mid-1940s, the congress would become a puppet for the Communist Party, losing much of the support and goodwill it had originally gained among moderates, fraternal organizations, and churches.

Randolph did not have time to begrudge the NNC. As war loomed in the spring of 1941, he was preparing a Washington, D.C., march of "100,000 Negroes" as a way of demanding equal rights and integration for black workers. This was new territory for black activism, which for years had held firm to the NAACP paradigm of lobbying, with limited participation of the masses, or the mass protests sprung from narrow causes and contained to one city at a time. Randolph's call for national unity, as well as the government's willingness to negotiate with him, culminated in Franklin Delano Roosevelt's signing of Executive Order 8802. Whites would continue to resist, however, and some companies who refused to hire blacks were taken over by the military to ensure compliance with Roosevelt's order. While African Americans made inroads in labor, they continued to suffer hostile treatment in the armed forces. Roosevelt's desegregation order did not apply to black servicemen and servicewomen, despite the best efforts by the NAACP. Blacks in the service often faced humiliating conditions, though the U.S. military continued to deny any discrimination had taken place. "I can assure you that there has been and will be no discrimination against the colored race in the training of the national forces," General Douglas A. MacArthur insisted to NAACP Legal Counsel Charles Houston.[19] Despite the military's denials, African Americans who fought for the

United States presented a completely different picture. "They treated us no better than animals," recalled Littleton Mitchell, one of the Tuskegee Airmen. "I think the general attitude among whites in the armed forces was that we weren't competent to do anything, and they wanted us to know that."[20] In the latter stages of the war, and after, Du Bois and Robeson would make segregation in the armed forces the crux of their argument against U.S. foreign policy, questioning how a country that segregated its own soldiers was fit to defend democracy abroad. As Robeson would lament, black progress was "pitifully small . . . when measured against the loss of manpower, the lowered morale, the inter-racial friction and national disunity which characterize America at war."[21]

ROBESON RETURNED TO THE UNITED STATES in 1939, infused with a passion for the labor movement. In arguably his most successful role (in terms of political artistry), Robeson starred in *Proud Valley*. He later recalled that living among Welsh miners while filming the movie instilled him with class-consciousness and fueled his commitment to the working man. Artistically, Robeson might have failed to land dignified race roles on the big screen, but he managed to become a labor icon in film and onstage. *Proud Valley* and *Stevedore* exemplified his desire to be a man of the people, at least among British crowds. However, Robeson had been away from the United States at the height of the Popular Front, and his links to the labor movement were primarily Communist Party members who had kept in contact with him during his European exile. He immediately sought to get involved with the Left-led effort to integrate blacks and other minorities into unions. Robeson felt the future of working-class solidarity rested with multicultural labor organizations. He visited Camp Wo-Chi-Ca (Workers' Children Camp), an interracial camp conducted by the International Workers Order (a leftist workers' insurer), where he met with poverty-stricken youths of different backgrounds. His first visit to the camp in 1940 had a profound impact on him; he would visit the camp every year until 1954, when it was forced to shut down under pressure from McCarthyites.[22] Though he remained opposed to interventionism until mid-1941, Paul saw prewar industrialization as a boon to blacks. Robeson strengthened his ties to labor by making friendships with black unionists, including John P. Davis of the Negro Industrial League and NNC and Ferdinand Smith of the NMU. Davis and Smith were Communists, and their ties to Robeson had a twofold mission of making him both a vocal labor advocate and an unofficial party spokesman.[23] But Robeson didn't need Communists to tell him how important unionization was to the Negro. While in Europe, he had already concluded that the labor movement was paramount for economic emancipation and greater political suffrage for oppressed peoples. Robeson believed strong *integrated* unions were the best hope for working-class uplift; consequently, he endorsed the CIO. As he told Ford workers in 1940, "I am against separate unions for Negro workers. All should belong to the same organization." Paul did not believe "the Negro problem cannot be solved by a few of us getting to be doctors and lawyers. The best way my race can win justice is by sticking together in progressive labor unions." Robeson declared that it "would be unpardonable for Negro workers to fail to join the CIO."[24]

Robeson continued to blend his political beliefs with his artistry. In *John Henry*, Paul personified the labor struggle in his onstage depiction of the black folk hero. Critics raved that Robeson "scored a brilliant personal success" with his portrayal of Henry, "the giant roustabout who died when he tried to lick a steam engine totin' cotton bales."[25] Though the play itself has been lost in the sea of Robeson's career accomplishments, the role epitomized Paul's desire to incorporate larger-than-life figures into his political ideology. If Othello was Robeson the dignified royal and Toussaint L'Overture was Robeson the anticolonial, then John Henry clearly showed Robeson as the labor icon. In many ways, the mere physical presence of Robeson emphasized the enormousness of Henry—a giant in his own mythical right—and the growing labor movement. That fact was not lost on Robeson, who had transformed his physicality into a political weapon onstage and onscreen.

Paul's alignment with the labor movement drew him closer to the Communist Party, which took an active lead in union organizing among blacks and other minority groups. Robeson began to rely on NNC leaders like Max Yergan and Revels Cayton, who would soon become his key political advisors during the 1940s. He also remained close with Ben Davis Jr. and William Patterson, who continued to play active roles in the party's ILD. Robeson joined Communist Party leaders in calling for the release of Browder, who had been jailed in 1940 on passport irregularities. Following Germany's invasion of the Soviet Union, Robeson told a Free Browder rally that "there can be no more honest evidence of a sincere decision to defeat Fascism along with the sending of tanks and every possible aid to the Soviet Union, than the freeing of Earl Browder, so that he may take his rightful place in the vanguard of the cohorts against fascism."[26] By 1942, many of his closest political allies, including Browder, Davis, Patterson, Yergan, and Abner Berry, were active Communists. That fact was not lost on the FBI, which opened an active file on Robeson. His profile had become a growing cause of concern for the bureau, and by the end of the war, agents would have enough information about Robeson's "subversion" to make him one of the most scrutinized public figures on their Red watch lists. Paul made defending the Soviet Union an integral part of his speeches and public performances, and he was never remiss in mentioning the link of the Bolshevik credo to the uplift of colored peoples throughout the world. Though the United States and USSR had become allies in the war against fascism, J. Edgar Hoover was a bottom-line anti-Communist. Hoover's growing paranoia over the Left's influence on American politics would prompt the bureau to open dossiers on almost every prominent African American, including Bunche and Judge William T. Hastie.[27]

Robeson, meanwhile, expanded his ties to a new generation of leftists. In the midst of mobilizing sharecroppers in the Deep South, the Southern Negro Youth Congress (SNYC) needed a headliner for the 1942 convention. Hoping to secure the most prominent Negro entertainer of the decade, SNYC executive members Esther Jackson, James Jackson, and Louis Burnham called on Paul Robeson to give a performance in Tuskegee, Alabama. Paul initially refused. The reason? Despite being home to the college that had trained generations of black men under the founding principles of Booker T. Washington and stewardship of Robert Russa Morton, the town strictly enforced Jim Crow. The SNYC members finally convinced Robeson, promising him that the concert venue would be fully integrated. As promised, Robeson's concert that spring was a mix of black and white, of businessmen, college students, and sharecroppers who filled the venue. "It was a huge turnout," Esther Jackson recalled more than sixty years later. "So many people wanted to see Paul." Esther idolized Paul, and like many young women in her generation, had developed a fanlike devotion to the larger-than-life political artist. "Some of my friends asked me if I had a crush on Paul. I said that it was hard not to," she quipped. Following the concert, the diminutive young woman stood side by side with the 6-foot-4-inch Robeson. The concert was a landmark event on two levels. First, the Southern Negro Youth Congress's success in integrating a Jim Crow venue proved that despite the rigidity of the Deep South, segregation *could* be overcome. The second was the start of a friendship between Robeson and the congress, namely its dynamic young leaders. Three years later, Esther Jackson met Du Bois in London for the World Youth Conference, wowing the venerable civil rights warrior with her zeal, political acumen, and organizing abilities.[28] By expanding his contact with Southern advocacy groups, Robeson also overcame his own perceptions of Southern blacks, changing his initial impressions of them as "beaten, subservient, cowed." Instead, he now saw it as a moral obligation to support them, vowing to return often "to be with my people and to refresh my soul with their strength." Robeson also likely understood that black leadership was largely out of touch with the needs of Southern blacks, who had, for the most part, remained in abject poverty in rural areas and were the most oppressed by Jim Crow. "We must come south to understand in their starkest presentation the common problems that beset us everywhere," he told a desegregated crowd in New Orleans. "We must taste the bitterness, see the ugliness. . . . We must expose ourselves unremittingly to the source of strength that makes the black South strong!"[29]

Paul reached the height of his fame in 1943, starring in a record-breaking run of *Othello* on Broadway.[30] He had finally mastered his defining role, portraying Othello in such a manner that has not been equaled since. With a strong supporting cast of Uta Hagen and Jose Ferrer, Robeson was able to infuse heightened political consciousness into an already dignified character. As a result, *Othello* was another opportunity for Robeson to demonstrate his political artistry. The play, he noted, was "a play which is of great interest to us moderns today as we face the whole problem of relations of peoples between different races and cultures." Robeson also used the play to promote his stance against segregation, refusing to perform in cities that enforced Jim Crow. Langston Hughes wrote that "the Negro race ought to give a big hand and a couple of 'Bravos' and a million fan letters to Paul Robeson for standing up for his own professional decency, and for his implied protest against American theatre Jim Crow."[31]

With the success of *Othello*, Robeson no longer shied away from using his international superstardom to advance his far-left-of-mainstream political message. Viewing the Tehran Conference as a breakthrough in U.S.-Soviet relations (he wasn't the only one to believe this), Robeson began to push for militant, multiethnic coalitions in the fight for civil and labor rights. "I deeply believe the whole future of America stands or falls with the complete unity of the American people, including the minorities of black, Mexican and Chinese," Robeson told the Conference on Racial and National Minorities. "It will not be able to stand in the world after the war unless we do achieve this unity."[32] Like his friends in the Communist Party, Paul was convinced that minorities and working-class people were one Popular Front away from full integration and emancipation. Cognizant of the power that came with his popularity, he coolly dismissed conservatives' attacks on him as "Red-baiting." Appearing overconfident at times, Robeson began to escalate his criticisms of American domestic and foreign policy. "I feel it is my duty as an American citizen to press the need for collaboration and friendship now and in the post-war world with the great peoples of Soviet Russia," he said at a war forum sponsored by the *New York Herald Tribune*. "For Negroes hate Fascism to the death, and of all its destroyers the Soviet peoples have been the most potent and self-sacrificing."[33] In his address at the *Tribune* forum, Robeson also fired a warning shot to the U.S. government, implying that Negroes might not be as patient with the New Deal as they had been in the past.

There are three things in the American scene which today arouse the bitterest resentment among black Americans and at the same time represent the greatest handicap upon his full participation in the national war effort. First is their economic insecurity which they know to be the result of continuing discrimination in employment even now, coupled with other forms of economic exploitation and social discrimination in urban communities such as Harlem. Second is the segregation and inferior status assigned to Negroes in the armed forces, and their complete exclusion from most of the women's auxiliary services. Added to this are the insults and acts of physical violence nurtured by the segregation policy, which have been inflicted upon them in many of the camps and camp communities, even in areas which, before the coming of the army camps, had been free from racial prejudice. This is a shameful condition. Several appeals have been made to the President, from whites as well as Negroes, urging him to issue an executive order against racial discrimination and segregation in the armed services. Such an order is as essential to the morale and fighting spirit of our war machine as to the morals and productive capacity of our industrial machine. Third, is the poll tax system in the South, which operates to maintain undemocratic elements in places of authority not only below the Mason-Dixon line but in our national life as a whole.[34]

Though Robeson found supporters in Roosevelt's administration, namely Vice President Henry A. Wallace, his increasingly confrontational remarks during the war paved a path diverging from mainstream civil rights advocacy. Within two years, Paul would deepen that chasm and become firmly entrenched in the Left.

DESPITE CIVIL RIGHTS PROGRESS in the early 1940s, Du Bois was torn between reformation and revolution. Though he had long distanced himself from the NAACP, convinced that its program would never work, the Doctor wanted to believe that New Deal reforms could somehow lead to greater significant social changes down the road. But he had not yet bought into the mantra of Communists, keeping a safe distance from what they proposed through a united front black and white labor—a union the Doctor had deemed impossible. Du Bois chuckled at the idea "that the class solidarity of laborers in the United States will hold across the color line and that the union of black labor with white labor will consequently bring a solution to the race problem."[35] Living in the heart of Jim Crow Atlanta, Du Bois figured the Communists were either out of touch or simply out of their minds. While Communist Party leaders like Ford insisted that "Communists are Americans, steeped in the traditions of America's struggle for liberty, and fighters for the interests of the American people," Du Bois guessed that the party had a hidden agenda.[36] Despite his lionization of Marx, the Doctor insisted that the Communists and the Left were wrong in believing interracial labor organization could ever lead to black emancipation. Like many of his predictions, Du Bois was tragically correct: labor groups have long struggled with racial chauvinism, and in recent years, many whites have left unionized jobs altogether, leaving a marginalized base of mostly minority workers with little political clout.

Clouded by pessimism, Du Bois viewed the black struggle for integrating into the armed forces, as well as the persistent calls by Southern Negroes to end Jim Crow, with a sense of detached empathy. How could he fully immerse himself into these fights, which he felt would not achieve a greater victory for the Negro? He had immense respect for the work of Bunche, Mary McLeod Bethune, Channing Tobias, and other black New Dealers, but he generally saw African Americans mired in tunnel vision when it came to their emancipation. Du Bois began to recognize his own folly in championing the Talented Tenth, an idea that did little to uplift the masses. By 1948, Du Bois would abandon the concept completely, frustrated by the fact that the Talented Tenth consisted of more bourgeois Negroes than true race leaders. His feelings on black nationalism and segregation, which shocked the Talented Tenth, alienated many of his white liberal supporters, and expedited his departure from the NAACP a decade earlier, had only coagulated since the start of the war. In *Dusk of Dawn*, Du Bois reiterated his position that African Americans could never gain full emancipation unless they empowered themselves first. He blamed the Negro intelligentsia for lacking the foresight, indicting the NAACP for pushing a platform of integration without realizing that black America lacked infrastructure. "From the eighteenth century down the Negro intelligentsia has regarded segregation as the visible badge of their servitude and as the object of their unceasing attack," Du Bois wrote.[37] Castigating the NAACP and other black intellectuals for denying their fundamental right to blackness, the Doctor asserted that another path needed to be taken. In laying out a path of Negro self-improvement, Du Bois would parallel the ideas of Washington, Garvey, and Randolph, who, in their own ways, advocated the construction of a black foundation.

I began to emphasize and restate certain implicit

aspects of my former ideas. I tried to say to the American Negro: during the time of this frontal attack which you are making upon American and European prejudice, and with your unwavering statement and restatement of what is right and just, not only for us, but in the long run, for all men; during this time, there are certain things you must do for your own survival and self-preservation. You must work together and in unison; you must evolve and support your own social institutions; you must transform your attack from the foray of self-assertive individuals to the massed might of an organized body. You must put behind your demands, not simply American Negroes, but West Indians and Africans, and all the colored races of the world. These things I began to say with no lessening, or thought of lessening of my emphasis upon the essential rightness of what we had been asking for a generation in political and civic and social equality.[38]

By early 1942, Du Bois was an admitted nationalist, at the brink of shunning any idea of black advancement coming via white philanthropy. If he were young again, Du Bois opined, he would "devote more time and advice to consumers' cooperation and consumers' protection; stressing the absolute necessity for Negroes to plan for a new economy of consumer control of production and production for use and not for private profit."[39] Du Bois felt the silliness of fighting integration battles and ignoring the education and economic needs of blacks had arguably kept the entire race hamstrung while its leaders were calling for the desegregation of the wartime public sector. In readjusting his views, he might have even tipped his hat to Garvey, who died two years earlier without realizing how close Du Bois had come to acknowledging his genius.

Though skeptical about the long-term success of the New Deal, Du Bois couldn't help but admire FDR, who "gave a social and political recognition to the American Negro greater in effect than that granted by any president of the United States since the Civil War."[40] Du Bois watched how Roosevelt methodically silenced the reactionary Democrats, and by doing so, changed the ideology of the party altogether. But the Doctor was more interested in the politics of Eleanor Roosevelt. Mrs. Roosevelt—the most activist first lady of the twentieth century—supported progressive causes, often acting as an intermediary between the White House and civil rights groups. She befriended many radicals over her husband's time in office, entertaining NAACP dignitaries such as White and providing a receptive audience to radical organizations such as the Southern Negro Youth Congress. The Doctor was moved by Mrs. Roosevelt's handling of the Marian Anderson–Daughters of the American Revolution fiasco, and her subsequent willingness to stand by her convictions. He gushed that Eleanor Roosevelt, more than her husband, "insists on thinking in public. She consorts with Negroes and Communists and says so." But Du Bois didn't fool himself into believing that a progressive president and first lady could alone be responsible for the uplift of blacks. He still viewed the battle with conservatives and segregationists as an uphill battle, no matter how much social progress had been achieved during the New Deal. Du Bois felt Roosevelt "was losing ground," and that "the tremendous inner struggle with his own Southern allies as well as the Republican Party of wealth and privilege shortened his days by at least a decade."[41] His words would prove prophetic. In 1948, Southern Democrats opposed to the party's civil rights platform broke ranks and became the Dixiecrat Party, running Strom Thurmond as the new party's candidate. The temporary revolt set the stage for conservative Democrats to move to the Republican Party.

While concerned about Roosevelt's fight against the "forces of reaction" within his own party and dubious of the effectiveness of New Deal liberalism, Du Bois took a more sanguine outlook on Russia. Like Robeson, he felt the Tehran Conference provided an outstanding opportunity for closer ties between the United States and the Soviet Union. Stalin, whom he had labeled a dictator only three years earlier, was now "helping to rescue the world from the greatest disaster that has ever threatened civilization."[42]

The Doctor now penned glowing reviews of Russian sacrifice for the preservation of democracy and the struggle against fascism. The Soviet Union offered Du Bois, who had lost in Japan, another chance at salvation; he would become more enamored with the Russian model of anticapitalism and anticolonialism, a paradigm that he believed could lead to Africa and Asia's freedom from white European domination. While he remained less optimistic about such a path for American Negroes, Du Bois believed that Roosevelt and his New Deal cabinet could be pragmatic in advancing federal programs to end poverty and racial inequality if the Soviet Union offered its support and allegiance. However, the Doctor was aware that the U.S.-Soviet ties were not popular among Western leaders, most notably Winston Churchill. The political storm was brewing, and Du Bois envisaged "every effort, conscious or unconscious, is being made to estrange the United States and Russia, and to make a pattern of future war between the two greatest countries in present power on earth."[43] Within a year of his gloomy forecast, U.S.-Soviet ties would chill considerably, and by 1946, Churchill's "Iron Curtain" speech would start the Cold War.

As THE WAR SHIFTED decidely to the Allies' favor in early 1944, Du Bois and Robeson began to look ahead to a postwar America. The progress of the New Deal, though slowed, seemed irreversible. Du Bois began preparations for another Pan-African Congress, radically changed by the last two decades of social and political change in the United States and abroad. The Doctor now borrowed Garvey and Washington's notion on racial self-determinism, but at the same, leaned more toward the Russian model of Socialism as a formula for economic emancipation. He had come to believe that there were very few "genuine" black groups that could overcome the silent oppression of white benefactors to advance a truly "black for black" agenda. Despite those misgivings, Du Bois would return to the NAACP in July 1944 after being forced out of Atlanta University. His "retirement" from academic life would propel him into the radical activism that would shape his late-life philosophy.

Despite Du Bois's racialism and long-held admiration for Japan, he was noticeably silent on the U.S. internment of

Japanese-Americans. In fact, most prominent blacks, including Communists, did not emphatically speak out against Roosevelt's decision to hold 110,000 Americans of Japanese in camps throughout the Southwest.[44] Perhaps, as Du Bois noted nearly thirty years earlier, blacks knew best when to protest and when to close ranks, even if it meant turning a blind eye to injustice. Robeson, however, was more vocal about the mistreatment of Japanese-Americans, offering to testify to their loyalty in 1942. While scholar Greg Robinson has written that Robeson was a staunch advocate for Japanese-Americans throughout World War II, it appears that Robeson's most vocal support for them came after the war ended.[45]

While advocating on behalf of Japanese-Americans might have been risky for other African-American luminaries, Robeson was unfazed by the political consequences of supporting unpopular causes. Having created an aura of invincibility, Robeson strode across the line of tolerable protest. By 1945, he knew that the end of the war abroad meant focusing his energies on fighting domestic Fascists who opposed racial progress and close ties between the United States and Soviet Union. He and Du Bois readied themselves for the conflict that lay ahead, not knowing that they would soon be flung into a protracted ideological war.

6

AFRICA, ASIA, AND THE GLOBAL VISION

I am not at all sure how much American Negroes know about India or realize the great fight that Indians, as well as African and Asiatics, are making for recognition in the modern world.

—W. E. B. Du Bois, "India" (1946)

A LETTER FROM THE UNITED STATES arrived in the Calcutta office of Manmohan Gandhi of the Indian Chamber of Congress in 1931. The sender claimed to have "almost personal acquaintance" with Gandhi through a mutual friend, adding that Gandhi had been kind enough two years earlier to write a note to the *Crisis* magazine representing the sentiments of Indians toward the struggle of "twelve million Negroes." The sender asked Gandhi for another statement of support, which would "do much I am sure to encourage the American Negro." Gandhi, perplexed at who the sender was and why he would write such a letter, replied with a note that said, in essence, he was the *wrong* Gandhi. Manmohan Gandhi asked the American to write to Mohandas Gandhi for a statement.[1]

The mistaken letter writer was Du Bois, who, despite his confusion over Gandhis, was in tune with the Indian freedom struggle. From his relationship with Lala Lajpat Rai in the 1920s, Du Bois had become enamored with Indian efforts to break away from British rule. His veneration would only grow through his acquaintance with Indian freedom struggle leaders such as Rabindranath Tagore, Jawaharlal Nehru, and Vijaya Lakshmi Pandit during the 1930s and 1940s, leading him to proclaim that Indians "must always stand as representatives of colored races, of the yellow and black peoples as well as of the brown—of the majority of mankind."[2] Robeson came to a similar conclusion during his stay in London during the 1930s, expressing deep admiration for India's ability to maintain its culture despite British domination. He developed a strong connection with the Indian independence movement (sparked by his friendships with Nehru and Krishna Menon), along with freedom struggles in Africa, Eastern Europe, and the Caribbean. Buoyed by his visit to the Soviet Union, Paul also become one of the foremost speakers in defense of preserving the cultures of Africa and Asia, seeing their past as essential to building their future after colonialism.

Anticolonial advocacy became a centerpiece of Du Bois and Robeson's political philosophies, helping them become giants of twentieth-century internationalism. Both made significant

contributions to the African, Asian, and Latin American suffrage movements by advocating similar global outlooks: rejection of colonialism and capitalism and embrace of Soviet-style
Socialism. Du Bois, who entered the 1930s with racialist-
internationalist perspective, incorporated anti-Fascism into his
worldview following the Italian invasion of Ethiopia. Though
initially skeptical of the Soviet Union's role in the anticolonial
struggle, he became convinced during World War II that
Moscow was an important ally for international suffrage. Du
Bois joined Robeson and the Communists in calling for the
United States to support the Soviet Union's efforts to promote
independence among colonized people, an effort that fell short
after the postwar shift in U.S. foreign policy. However, the
Cold War only cemented the Doctor's belief that Marxism and
scientific Socialism were the salvation for darker nations.
Robeson had reached that conclusion much earlier, incorporating his ardent pro-Soviet stance with budding anticolonialism during the 1930s. During the war, Paul only became
more outspoken in his belief that the future of colonized
nations needed to be aligned with the interests of the Soviet
Union. He based this argument on the rapid economic development of the USSR under Stalinism, which he believed
would work in underdeveloped countries in Asia and Africa.
Robeson also argued that Socialism built a collective sense of
cultural and nationalistic identity among darker peoples,
whether in their own lands or as minorities in other nations.
In advocating this hoi polloi internationalism, Paul became
one of the most outspoken proponents of uniting the forces of
labor and racially oppressed peoples into a greater suffrage
movement.

Du Bois and Robeson were not the only black internation-alists, but they were most vocal in tying the fate of African Americans with that of oppressed people throughout the world. Their commitment to the emancipation of darker nations helped cultivate an international following among anticolonials. As E. Franklin Frazier noted, Du Bois and Robeson represented "the new understanding on the part of the American Negro that his battle for freedom and equality is a part of the battle of colored colonial peoples in Asia and Africa and the battle of the serfs in Eastern Europe against feudalism."[3] By developing lasting friendships with future nation leaders such as Nehru, Kwame Nkrumah of Ghana, Jomo Kenyatta of Kenya, and Eric Williams of Trinidad, the Doctor and Paul served as black America's spokesmen to other oppressed peoples even before Ralph Bunche rose to prominence as a U.S. diplomat.

Through their involvement with numerous anticolonial advocacy groups, including the Council on African Affairs, Du Bois and Robeson would become close political allies and comrades-in-arms in a larger international struggle. Their shared worldview would lead to convergence of social and political circles that for years had been peripheral to both; however, it would also hasten their radicalism, estrange them from many of their former friends and allies, and plant the seeds of their downfall in the United States.

DU BOIS ENTERED THE 1930s with dueling notions of postcolonial advancement. The first dealt with the growth of Japan as an imperial force and its ramifications on a free colored world, while the other focused on Indian independence as a model and precursor to freedom for the rest of Asia and Africa. On one hand, the Doctor wanted Japan to become the driver of a global movement by colored nations to reclaim what was theirs from Europeans and Americans, a sentiment that grew from his friendships with Japanese expatriates such as Hikida Yasuichi, who was reputed to be a plant.[4] But Du Bois couldn't help but privately condemn the course of action Japan was taking in becoming the next global superpower. Japanese aggression in the mid-1930s and Chinese resistance to it only exacerbated his fears that the European conspiracy of dividing and conquering was coming to fruition. In 1933, an exasperated Du Bois wrote:

Colossi of Asia and leaders of all colored mankind: for God's sake stop fighting and get together. Compose your quarrels on any reasonable basis. Unite in self-defense and assume that leadership of distracted mankind to which four hundred millions of people entitle you. Listen to a word from twelve little black millions who live in the midst of western culture and know it: the intervention of the League of Nations bodes ill for you and all colored folk. The real rulers of the world today . . . are bloodsucking imperial tyrants who see only one thing in the quarrel of China and Japan and that is a chance to crush and exploit both Shanghai and Manchuria or lead them to rub hands with more solemn unction or practiced hypocrisy. Unmask them, Asia; tear apart their double faces and double tongues

and unite in peace. Remember, Japan, that white
America despises and fears you. Remember, China,
that England covets your land and labor. Unite!
Beckon to the three hundred million Indians; drive
Europe out of Asia and let her get her own raped
and distracted house in order. Get together and
wire word to Asia. Get together China and Japan,
cease quarrelling and fighting! Arise and lead! The
world needs Asia.[5]

Du Bois would change his attitude about Japanese imperialism over the next few years, excusing it as a natural gateway
of empowerment for darker races. Japan, as the Doctor had
noted years earlier, was the prime minister of a new world
order that would eventually see India and China take their
places alongside Europe and the United States, and would one
day lead to the independence of Asia. The Doctor became even
more convinced of this belief as he saw fascism spread in
Europe. Japan, he reasoned, was a buffer against the
inevitable rape of the darker peoples of the Far East by colonial interests. "Unless [Japan] warded off the communism of
Russia to the north and the imperialism of England at the
South, China would never survive and Asia would never
become independent," he told a crowd at Morehouse College.
"Slowly she is turning toward understanding with China
although that involves the danger of European interference
since China still has naïve confidence in the philanthropy of
the West." Still, Du Bois held out hope for a "union of Japan
and China and eventually India," which he believed could
"easily dominate the world with a leadership of mankind such

as Western Europe could never accomplish."[6] Du Bois admired the Japanese juggernaut that grew in the face of Western domination, but would find it more difficult to justify and defend after the start of World War II.

Though he oscillated on the significance of Japanese imperialism in the Pacific Rim, the Doctor consistently held the Indian struggle as a paradigm of colored emancipation, including that of black America. Despite his awe of Japan's development, Du Bois knew that at the very basic level, African Americans could not relate to the Japanese. Blacks, he believed, needed inspiration from another subjugated group by seeing how they handled white chauvinism and attempted to free themselves from the bondage of second-class citizenship. Du Bois saw such a fraternity with Indians. He had read of the history of colonization in India, of how the country was duped by British traders and how the money and military might of the British replaced Indian rulers with puppet princes who acquiesced to the wishes of their white masters. India had been divided and conquered by manipulation, its people forced into servitude and acceptance of an inferior status. But the Doctor believed that the Indians' struggle for self-government would resonate with black America, if only to prove that a united front against oppression was the key to suffrage. He felt the only factor dividing Indians from African Americans was mutual ignorance. "The Negroes taught in American schools and reading books and articles by American writers, have almost no conception of the history of India," Du Bois wrote. "On the other hand, the knowledge which educated Indians have of the American Negro is chiefly confined to the conventional story spread by most white American and English writers: ignorant black savages were enslaved and made to do physical labor which was the only thing they could do." Du Bois argued that white interests were using "deliberate and purposeful propaganda" to keep Indians and African Americans apart. If only they could meet and collaborate, "not necessarily for action, but for understanding, and especially for emphasizing these people have common aims."[7]

There was more to Du Bois's interest in India than admiration of the country's quest for independence. The Doctor was genuinely confused as to why many Indians, whose skin color was often as dark, if not darker, than blacks, considered themselves removed from the plight of the colored nations. He was troubled by the notion of the caste system, which he equated to the long-held desire by blacks to be drawn to lighter skin and shun darker skin (though he himself was afforded European features). Du Bois's concerns were validated by Rai and other Indian expatriate leaders, who argued that the caste system in its modern form was a tool of the British to reinforce control over Indian society by using the lighter-skinned Brahmins to subjugate the dark-skinned majority of non-Brahmin Indians. India, the Doctor observed, "has long wished to regard herself as 'Aryan' rather than 'colored' and to think of herself as much nearer physically and spiritually to Germany and England than to Africa, China, or the South Seas." Du Bois dismissed such a belief as ludicrous, noting that "European exploitation wishes the black sharecropper, the Chinese coolie, and the Indian laborer for the same ends and the same purposes, and call them all 'niggers.'"[8] In this vein, Du Bois regarded his friendships with "enlightened" Indians such as Rai and Bengali literary giant

Tagore as paramount in breaking down the communication and perception barriers between Indians and blacks, and in doing so, erasing the desire by both groups to emulate whites. Du Bois's admiration for India and his belief of its importance in becoming a leader of colored nations would dramatically increase in the next decade, thanks to his introduction to a new generation of Indian leaders.

India was exceptional to Du Bois's thesis on dark colonies, which he generally considered "the slums of the world. They are today the places of greatest concentration of poverty, disease, and ignorance of what the human mind has come to know. They are centers of helplessness, of discouragement of initiative, of forced labor, and of legal suppression of all activities or thoughts which the master country fears or dislikes."[9] This brutal assessment was especially applicable to Africa, where centuries of European exploitation had robbed the natives of any opportunity to control their own destiny. Du Bois was repulsed by the brutal repression of South African blacks and Indians by the racialist policies of James Hertzog and Jan Christian Smuts and felt betrayed by constant broken promises of Great Britain and France to grant more autonomy to their African colonies. He knew European powers would never give autonomy to the natives unless forcefully compelled. He noted, "The colony is conducted for the defense and aggrandizement of home countries and for the profit of owners and investors, and to mulct the victims of this process for the cost of their oppression is indefensible in morals and short-sighted in politics."[10]

Du Bois became even more convinced of European ruthlessness in Africa following the League of Nations's complicity in the Italian invasion of Ethiopia. Had all of Europe ignored the pleas of Haile Selassie to prevent a fascist invasion? Was the Western powers' opposition to fascism only based on its spread in Europe, oblivious to the ravaging of darker sovereign lands? The Doctor assessed the plundering of Africa as both an economic and racial issue. He surmised that Western views on civilization already deemed Africans incapable of self-rule based on long-held notions of black inferiority. He also correctly assumed that labor conditions in Africa were such that European imperialists could maximize their profits off the land without sacrificing much in wages; natives were already near slaves in their own nations. Though Du Bois hoped Japanese imperialism would somehow influence the African freedom struggle and wished increased interaction among Indian and African anticolonials would lead to a diplomatic solution for autonomy, he knew both possibilities were not practical. However, he was not yet willing to recognize the Soviet Union as a possible savior; "Russian Soviets, the Doctor opined, "have appeared in Africa chiefly as deliberate troublemakers without waiting to study local conditions."[11] But soon after the start of World War II, Du Bois would change his stance about Soviet intervention, ultimately leading to a revision of his Pan-Africanism.

ROBESON'S FRIENDSHIP WITH GEORGE PADMORE and C. L. R. James, combined with his newfound faith in the Soviet experiment, provided the catalyst for his learning of African and Asian cultures while he was in London. Already an Afrophile, Paul took stronger interest in the politics of colonial Africa. He became active in the discussion circles of African, Caribbean, and Indian expatriates living in London, absorbing everything he could on their emancipation struggles. Although Robeson biographers Boyle and Bunie claim that Paul turned his back on the independence movements in Africa during the 1930s, Robeson believed that the anticolonial fight was inextricably linked with the battle against Fascism. However, Robeson rejected Padmore and James's nationalistic anticolonialism, choosing instead a more uplift-through-labor and common cause approach to suffrage. For example, in a 1938 London speech advocating Jamaican freedom, Paul said:

> All the Progressive forces in this country are one in condemning the terrible conditions in the Islands, and in demanding drastic action. You must help them, not only for general humanitarian reasons, but because their struggle is connected with your struggle. They are part of the great Peasant and Working Mass. If they are denied the right to collective bargaining, the right to decent wage, to better conditions, there will be serious repercussions here. As I have said on previous occasions, we are engaged in a struggle for a richer and more decent life, for democratic liberty—a struggle which is one and indivisible.[12]

Robeson worked extensively with British leftists and Western missionaries in London during the 1930s, drawing heavily from their views about African economic development and its eventual emancipation. Some scholars have interpreted

Robeson's views on Africa during that time as paternalistic, based on interviews and speeches he gave about the "primacy" of African culture. "Africa, like the culture of the East, has a culture—a distinctive culture—which is ancient, not barbarous," he told a Christian missionary in 1936. Robeson, however, did not want to endorse the more-militant anticolonial platform of James and Padmore, perhaps cognizant of the impact it would have on his career. Instead, he made veiled suggestions for African independence through a cultural lens. "In the past, African communities developed along their own lines, in their own way, to reach a point of order and stability which may well be the envy of the world today."[13] Robeson maintained an active but subtle approach to anticolonialism until his departure from Europe, when he felt that his career would not be affected by his shift to more-radical advocacy.

Paul was a student of Asia's culture before he became aware of its politics. Prior to his trip to the Soviet Union, he stressed that the Negro had a common cultural bond with the Chinese, who had successfully managed to incorporate some of the influence of the West into their long-standing culture. Part of Robeson's understanding of Chinese culture came through his education at the Institute of Oriental Languages in London. There, he took a scholarly interest in how the connection of languages and culture led to common themes of expression among different cultures. Paul came to believe that African Americans had much to learn from the Chinese, who were proud of their ancestry and unwilling to let go of ancient beliefs despite being colonized by Europeans, and in the early twentieth century, the Japanese. As he tried to look at the "natural" traits of blacks rooted in African tradition, Paul pointed out that by understanding China, "we know enough of history to be aware that great cultures do not completely die, but are soil for future growths."[14] Though he considered himself a scholar of Chinese culture and language and an aficionado of Eastern philosophy, Robeson did not identify closely with the Chinese political struggle until after the Japanese invasion of Nanking. During the 1940s, however, his public support for China would grow, particularly for the integral role Communists were playing in the country's emancipation.

During the 1930s, Robeson—as Du Bois had in the previous decade—"discovered" India and its independence struggle, which to him seemed so similar to the fight of the American Negro. He became close with Nehru, a Kashmir-born and Britain-educated lawyer who had been imprisoned numerous times in India by the colonial government. Nehru had for much of his politically active life been a follower of Gandhi, but he also clashed frequently with his mentor when it came to the best tactics needed for a free India. Nehru embraced the notion of Indian nationalism as the key in governing a free India. In advocating self-rule, Nehru noted that "India could not be a mere hanger-on of any country or group of nations; her freedom and growth would make a vital difference to Asia and therefore the world. That led inevitably to the conception of full independence and a severance of the bonds that tied her to England and her empire."[15] Nehru returned to London in 1938 as part of a rallying effort among British anticolonials and the significant Indian expatriate community there, but he met one of his biggest supporters in Robeson. Paul quickly grew fond of Nehru, agreeing wholeheartedly with the latter's stance that a free India should look to the Soviet Union for guidance in

managing its diverse and divided population. Nehru became a
role model to Robeson, a leader who had seen the beauty of
religion as being essential to the lives of everyday man but the
ideal of Socialism as being necessary to run the state. In a
London rally for Indian independence, Robeson lionized Nehru
as the navigator to global freedom:

> We in Black America and other parts of the world
> have closely watched the Indian struggle and have
> been conscious of its importance for us. . . . The
> struggle of the Indian people, their courage, the
> emergence of leaders like Nehru, give the lie to tales
> of a hopelessly backward people of a decayed cul-
> ture . . . and there is one thing it seems to me we
> peoples of long oppression must remember: We
> must not be talked out of our heritage. We must be
> proud of our traditions and where possible draw
> upon them to enrich the contribution we can make
> to a world which can ill afford to lose whatever
> value human beings have created. This applies as
> well to the great folk cultures of the working and
> peasant masses in Europe, Asia and the Americas.
> The comradely contribution by different peoples to
> a common civilization is no longer a dream, for on
> one-sixth of the earth's surface such a civilization
> does exist, and these peoples with their rich nation-
> alist cultures firmly bound into one socialist union
> stand as a bulwark against the forces of reaction
> and as a leading force in the struggle for peace.
> Daily it becomes more and more apparent that this

> struggle for peace, as was said long ago, is indivis-
> ible. . . . And I am certain that under the leadership
> of men such as Nehru the people of India will
> undoubtedly remain in the front rank of the pro-
> gressive human forces of our time.[16]

Robeson's friendship with the future prime minister of India would last until the latter's death, though they would experience a brief rift in the late 1940s over Nehru's alleged suppression of Communists following independence. Paul also befriended Krishna Menon, a young neo-Marxist whose involvement with the India League and the Labour Party made him a key liaison between the Indian people and the British during his twenty-one-year stay in London. Menon, who was influenced by the teachings of Socialist Harold Laski, was more radical than Nehru and embraced a more rigid view of Socialism and how it should be applied to a free India. Menon was also pro-Chinese, a stance that also endeared him to a like-minded Robeson. Over the next three decades, Robeson and Menon would grow very close, even as Paul's relationship with Nehru cooled following Indian independence. Like Du Bois, Robeson also had strong admiration for Gandhi, marveling at how a man of such diminished stature could rally an entire nation of people for their independence. Though the two had never met, Robeson believed Gandhi had a profound understanding of the dilemma of the American Negro, an insight Paul attributed to Gandhi's stay in colonial South Africa and the beginnings of the Satyagraha (nonviolence) movement there. Gandhi himself noted that his treatment as a colored man in South Africa, as well as the treatment of Africans there, inspired his call to duty. "The hardship to which I was subjected was superficial—only a symptom of the deep disease of color prejudice," he wrote. "I should try, if possible, to root out the disease and suffer hardships in the process. Redress for wrongs I should seek only to the extent that would be necessary for the removal of color prejudice."[17]

Robeson became increasingly militant in his anticolonialism after returning to the United States in 1939. Without fear of backlash from British theatergoers, Robeson delivered scathing critiques of Western imperialism, which he partially blamed for the start of war. He no longer agreed with many British leftists on the theory of gradual emancipation and repudiated the missionary mentality of the West when it came to self-determinism. Like Du Bois, Robeson concluded that colonialism was not only an economic oppressor, but also a racial one as well. The subjugation of native cultures, Robeson argued, was inexcusable in the wake of Great Britain and France's stand against Fascism. "We can choose between the end of colonial tyranny in India, China, Indonesia, Africa, and Iran—or its continuance under a new or highly developed kind of benevolent Anglo-American imperialism," he told the Win the Peace Conference in 1940. Within two years, Paul's involvement with the Council on African Affairs would propel him into the role of spokesman for colonized peoples everywhere, a paradox considering that—with the exception of Egypt—he had never set foot on African or Asian soil. His growing philosophical affiliation with the Soviet Union would profoundly shape his anticolonialism during the war, so much so that Soviet Socialism and the emancipation of darker nations would become intertwined in his advocacy.

The hostility between Japan and the Soviet Union, which Du Bois could not fathom, was better comprehended in Robeson's worldview at the start of World War II. Paul felt the USSR stood against *all* types of colonialism, even if it meant challenging another colored nation's ascendance to power. His political naiveté when it came to competing hegemonies caused him to overlook Stalin's influence on Chinese nationals in an attempt to win them over to communism, and in turn, convert a "liberated" China into a Socialist state aligned with Soviet interests.

Their differences over Japan and China aside, Du Bois and Robeson were philosophically in-sync when it came to India. The desire of Indian revolutionaries to repudiate imperialism, have warm relations with Moscow, and take the role of leadership of the colored world appealed to Robeson. He hoped that warm relations between India and the Soviet Union would also carry over to the United States, which sought to reach out to Indian freedom movement. Robeson looked at the hesitance of many Indians to fight for the British as a sign of hope for other colonial nations, which were sending thousands of natives to fight in overseas battles where there was nothing to be gained. To Paul, the dilemma of Indians in fighting in World War II was similar to the long-standing plight of American Negroes: *If we are to fight, what are we to fight for, and why?* Despite his public support of American intervention against fascism during the war, it made no sense to him that colonized peoples were sacrificing their lives for the freedom of Europeans, only to return to their countries and be treated as second-class citizens. The tacit support that Moscow offered India in its efforts for home rule heartened Robeson, who declared that "in the Soviet Union, so-called backward peoples are fighting alongside their brothers for freedom. . . . We are fighting a war for the freedom of all peoples and certainly the Indian people have a right to their freedom as well."[18]

AS THE WAR PROGRESSED, African American intellectuals began to stress the connection of the domestic fight against Jim Crow with independence movements abroad. Intellectuals such as Bunche, Langston Hughes, Richard Wright, and Rayford Logan of Howard University (one of Du Bois's allies in Pan-Africanism) advocated a closer relationship among black activists and anticolonial nationalists of other countries. Roosevelt took a more subtle approach to anticolonialism, although some of his high-profile administrators, including Vice President Henry A. Wallace and Secretary Sumner Welles, endorsed the drafting of the Atlantic Charter as a precursor to freedom for all colonized peoples. Though Roosevelt was hardly a racial progressive, he seemed to favor the anticolonial stance of his American liberals and leftists over the more racialist assumptions of Winston Churchill, who was determined to hold onto colonial lands at all costs.[19] Wallace noted that after a 1943 meeting with Churchill, he came to realize that democracy was a subjective term to the British prime minister—reserved for only whites. Wallace recounted the meeting in his diary:

> I said bluntly that I thought the notion of Anglo-Saxon superiority, inherent in Churchill's approach, would be offensive to many of the nations of the world as well as to a number of people in the United

States. Churchill had had quite a bit of whiskey, which, however, did not affect the clarity of his thinking process but did perhaps increase his frankness. He said why be apologetic about Anglo-Saxon superiority, that we were superior, that we had the common heritage which had been worked out over the centuries in England and had been perfected by our constitution. He himself was half American, he felt that he was called on as a result to serve the function of uniting the two great Anglo-Saxon civilizations in order to confer the benefit of freedom on the rest of the world.[20]

With Churchill not backing down on the colonial question, Roosevelt found himself in a dilemma. He wanted to be supportive of independence movements abroad, but realized that British sensitivity to the matter would complicate his anticolonialism. In 1942 Roosevelt planned to send a delegation of African Americans to help Indian freedom leaders work out a solution with Sir Stafford Cripps, the British liaison to India who had proposed slight modifications to colonial rule after the war. That effort failed, Walter White told Du Bois, because "of Mr. Gandhi's assertion that the chief interest of the United States in India is that of preserving and perpetuating 'British imperialism.' The President feels that any action by the United States right now would be interpreted by Mr. Gandhi and would be utilized by the Japanese as proof of this."[21] The Indian National Congress subsequently rejected the Cripps proposal and adopted the Quit India resolution; however, the British government arrested Gandhi, Nehru, and other freedom leaders for going against imperial will. Ironically the Communist Party in India backed the Cripps plan, leading the CPUSA to do the same. The CPUSA based its support for Great Britain on the country's role as an ally of the Soviet Union and the United States, hoping that publicly and unconditionally backing the Allies during the war would continue to win the party influence. However, Robeson—in one of his rare breaks with party platform—castigated the British position. He, Du Bois, and Richard Wright (who was already on the outs with the Communist Party) vehemently attacked the Cripps proposal as another effort by European paternalists to determine the future of a colonized nation. Though many black intellectuals felt the same, their influence among the masses was ephemeral at best. As historian Gerald Horne noted, "Jim Crow was an insular, all-consuming reality; it was so oppressive and suffocating that by its very nature those who were ensnared by it often had neither the time nor the inclination to peer across the oceans."[22]

The black press tried to bring the international struggle home. The *Pittsburgh Courier* published dispatches from anticolonials such as Kumar Goshal of India, Liu Liang Mo of China, and Prince A. A. Nwafor Orizu of Nigeria in an effort to show commonality in struggle among colonized groups and African Americans. Goshal was especially instrumental in rallying support among Negro intellectuals, including Du Bois and Robeson, for the freedom movement in India and the political suffrage struggle in South Africa. Goshal became involved with the Council on African Affairs during the war, helping to connect black intellectuals to visiting Indian delegates such as Vijaya Lakshmi Pandit, Nehru's sister and one of the architects of an Afro-Asian union during the formation of the United Nations. Though affiliated with the Communist Party, Goshal was a fervent Indian nationalist who did not back down from attacking the British government. Many contemporary scholars have overlooked Goshal's influence in swaying some prominent Communists, including Alphaeus Hunton and Max Yergan, away from the party's kid-glove stance on Western imperialism. Goshal likely played some role in Robeson's decision to publicly disagree with the Communist Party over the future of India.[23] Despite his and other leftists' best efforts, however, the United States could not advance an anticolonial agenda without the support of Great Britain and France. Instead, they would back a more modest proposal of United Nations trusteeships of colonized nations. The trusteeship plan was considered a partial victory for some black advocates, including White and Bunche, who called for a more pragmatic internationalism. Bunche, who joined the State Department in 1943, agreed with anticolonials that the United States needed to do more to promote independence, but he viewed trusteeship as the lesser of two evils. "Even during the war the native African in a British colony, as badly off and oppressed as he may be, has more liberty, more rights, more hope for a free future, than does an Aryan in Germany," he noted.[24] Leftists condemned his stance as defeatist, increasing pressure on the United States to force a solution that would be on the terms of colonized people, not the colonizers.

While a conflicted Du Bois stood on the sidelines of the Sino-Japanese conflict, Robeson became a vocal proponent of the Chinese nationalist struggle. Influenced by the nationalist teachings of Sun Yat-sen and by the visible role that Communists were playing in the war against Japan, Paul called on the United States to offer financial and moral support for Communist-trained guerrillas. His advocacy for China was twofold: while he championed Chinese independence, he also tried to get international pressure on Chiang Kai-shek to cease military operations against the Communists. "China's plight is critical," Robeson told Chinese nationalist supporters in New York. "We cannot permit either selfish isolationism or a misguided sense of democratic propriety to prevent Americans and America from speaking out on this issue. . . . The entire might and strength of China's 400 millions must be united."[25] In speaking on behalf of Chinese Communists, Robeson became close to Soong Ching-ling, also known as Madame Sun Yat-sen, who would later become an influential member of Mao's Communist government. He also noted the Soviet Union's backing of the Chinese freedom fighters, more evidence in his eyes of Moscow's commitment to the anticolonial struggle.

Paul was equally optimistic about the Soviet model for Africa, believing that the Dark Continent could rise quickly after colonialism if it used the same Socialist methods in industrialization and mass agriculture. In 1944, Robeson, speaking in his capacity as chairman of the Council on African Affairs, argued that Africans did not need trusteeship because Soviet guidance ensured modernization. He noted that the USSR showed "how, with systematic planning, a vast territory can be transformed in the space of a couple of decades from the most primitive, feudal agricultural economy into a modern agricultural and industrial economy; and of how many millions of peoples of different languages and cultures can be raised from illiteracy, poverty, and degradation to a high level of development with flourishing social, cultural, and political institutions of their own."[26] He even lauded British handlers in Africa for recognizing the Soviet success.

"Notable signs of this new understanding, born of the war, are the proposals of Colonel Oliver Stanley, British Secretary for Colonies, and the delegates at the French Colonial Conference at Brazzaville to study methods of social improvement in the Soviet Union, particularly in the field of mass education, with a view toward applying these methods to African society."[27] Du Bois, however, was not as optimistic about the possibility of postcolonial Africa. If the British and the French—besieged by fighting a war against fascism in Europe—still did not relinquish their claims to Africa and Asia, then why would they agree to giving up said land in peace time? The Doctor acknowledged the closeness of Indian independence, but he was extremely skeptical about Africa's chances of freeing itself from foreign rule without some sort of revolution. In *Color and Democracy*, Du Bois was unambiguous about the course of action that anticolonials in Africa needed to take.

> In this way the modern world after this war may easily be lulled to sleep and forget that the exclusion of something between one-fourth and one-half of the whole population of the world from participation in democratic government and socialized wealth is a direct threat to the spread of democracy and a certain promise of future war—and of war not simply as justifiable revolt on the part of colonial peoples who are increasing in intelligence and

efficiency, but also of recurring wars of envy and greed because of the present inequitable distribution of colonial gain among civilized nations. Moreover, the continuation of the belief of vested interests in the theory of racial inferiority and their dislike of minorities of any sort will be encouraged by failure to face the problem of the future of colonies—the problem of those hundreds of millions of people on whom the world long has walked with careless and insolent feet.[28]

Du Bois made this philosophy the centerpiece of his revised Pan-Africanism, a notion that he had revised numerous times over a twenty-five-year period. The Doctor had abandoned his 1920s paternal approach to the future of Africa, choosing instead to back a more radical notion of immediate independence devoid of white intervention and guardianship. He now found himself agreeing with Robeson and Yergan, who argued that the "question of the status of millions of Africans and their right to a better life is at the heart of the present world struggle."[29] Du Bois would find a fraternity among African anticolonials in the Pan-African Congress shortly after the war.

With the outcome with of the war decided by early 1945, the Allied Powers turned their focus to shaping the postwar world. Roosevelt and Stalin continued to press Churchill for some kind of concessions on the colonies, but Churchill resisted at the Yalta Conference. Bunche was among those who tried to steer the U.S. government toward a tougher stance toward Great Britain and France (which refused to give up its colonies at Brazzaville conference in 1944), but found his efforts filibustered by U.S. military officials, who believed that the United States should also enter the colonial game to strengthen its strategic interests.[30] He and other black internationalists were privately dismayed by the Dumbarton Oaks Conference the previous summer, in which the United States had to shelve its plans for a postcolonial solution based on conflict between FDR's stance and the U.S. military's strategic interests agenda. Du Bois upbraided American diplomats, accusing the United States of "siding with the fascist elements in South America" and "with Great Britain, that must have colonies or die, with France that thinks she must." While expressing some hope that the planned United Nations conference would bring a solution to the table, Du Bois labeled Dumbarton Oaks a colossal failure in postcolonial dialogue:

> Vague promises were made concerning human rights and the development of peoples toward self-government and social uplift, but promises only without implementation. The actual decisions permit increase of colonial empire, perpetuation of poverty and organization of military power against Asia. This result is because those at present in power in the British Empire are determined to preserve its organization substantially as it exists despite any cost to the world or its people; because other colonial powers are following Britain's lead, they and Americans forget the laborers and real thinkers in Britain, France, Holland, Belgium and oppose the colonial system. Finally, colonialism was untouched because of the indifferences of the

mass of people in the United States as to the fate of
the darker peoples within or without the United
States and their utter inability to conceive that anything that can happen to Africans or Asiatics can be
of any immediate and pressing concern to the white
people of North America.[31]

Du Bois and Robeson joined other anticolonials in promoting a stronger U.S. stance on the future of colonized
nations during the United Nations Conference in San Francisco. Though FDR passed away nearly two weeks before the
conference, Germany's surrender provided hope that the international body could focus its efforts on reshaping the globe
post-Fascism *and* postcolonialism. Du Bois attended as an
NAACP representative, joining White and Mary McLeod
Bethune, whom Du Bois considered more of an annoyance than
an asset. Bunche and Eleanor Roosevelt also made their presence known by taking a nonoffensive stand on the future of colonized nations. The conference included representatives from
colonized Asian countries, including India, which was determined to make its anticolonial presence felt. Du Bois learned
that some of the "Indian" delegates who were seeking out the
Americans were really British puppets. As a result, he avoided
contact with the delegates until meeting with the true representative of Indian aspirations, Vijaya Lakshmi Pandit. A
former provincial legislator and brilliant diplomat, she was
keenly aware of the importance of the conference and the right
of Indians to speak without British interference. Her conversations with Du Bois captivated the latter with her words and her
physical presence. "She is a charming woman in every way,

physically beautiful, simple, and cordial, and she represents as few people could, nearly 400 million people, and represents them by right of their desire and her personality, and not by the will of Great Britain," Du Bois wrote, perhaps ruminating about the comparison between the real-life Vijaya and his fictional Kautilya.[32] The question of India was constantly looming over the conference, but in the end, there was little resolution over its fate and that of other colonized countries. One of the key items Du Bois had hoped to pass in the conference was a resolution calling colonialism "undemocratic, socially dangerous, and a main cause of wars." Of course, such a document never saw the light of day among the powers negotiating the charter of the world assembly.

Discouraged by the inaction of the imperial powers in determining the free futures of the darker nations, Du Bois came away with two smaller victories: the alliance building among the delegates of colonized countries and the condemnation of colonialism by the Soviet delegation. During the conference, Pandit (who would serve as India's ambassador to the Soviet Union after independence) coordinated networking circles among the Asian and African delegates. In Du Bois's eyes, the seeds were being planted for an alliance among the darker nations after the inevitable end to colonialism. Watching Vijaya's skillful bridge building among oppressed nations was almost prophetic for the Doctor, who had predicted such a course of events in *Dark Princess* nearly twenty years earlier. The other token triumph was Soviet foreign minister Vyacheslav Molotov telling the conference that "from the viewpoint of international security we must first of all see to it that dependent countries are enabled as soon as possible to

take the path of national independence." The Doctor raved
that Molotov's admonition of the imperial countries was "the
most straightforward designation made at the San Francisco
Conference. It will not be followed because the British are sitting tight on Churchill's determination."[33]

Like Du Bois, Robeson was equally encouraged by the
Soviet stand, which reinforced his ideals about Moscow's support for darker nations, but he was deeply disturbed by the
unwillingness of the United States to press the colonial issue
further. He appealed to Secretary of State Edward R. Stettinius, who headed the U.S. delegation. Stettinius, who would
resign after the conference to become the country's first representative to the United Nations, assured Robeson that "we
have at all times insisted that the Conference should agree to
the inclusion in the Charter of provisions for the political, economic, and social advancement of peoples who are not yet
self-governing." However, Stettinius did not make any promises about a stronger anticolonial stance, backing away from
his predecessor's prediction about the end of imperialism. "We
shall continue to support the traditional American principles
which have been so well exemplified in our relations with the
Philippines," he wrote Robeson. "I would add that we have
pressed the Conference to accept as one of the basic objectives
of the trusteeship system the promotion of the political, economic, social, and educational advancement of the trust territories and their inhabitants and their progressive development
toward self-government or independence as may be appropriate to the particular circumstances of each territory and its
people and as may be provided in each trusteeship arrangement."[34] Stettinius's claims did little to assuage Robeson, who

joined in the nation's collective shock two months later with the U.S. nuclear bombing of Hiroshima and Nagasaki, which effectively ended the war. Truman's atomic statement would be an emphatic start to the Cold War and a dramatic reversal of Roosevelt's anticolonialism.

BUOYED BY AN INCREASINGLY ORGANIZED and vocal anticolonial movement in the mid-1940s, Du Bois and Robeson used the momentum of the United Nations charter conference to push for a concrete vision for independent Africa, Asia, and Latin America. The first major issue at hand was the future of Africa, which was largely divided among the British, Dutch, French, and Belgians. Though British troops helped restore Haile Selassie to power in Ethiopia, Great Britain was not as benevolent in addressing the futures of its territories in West Africa. European resistance to African autonomy, coupled with white minority rule in South Africa, set the stage for another Pan African Congress. Du Bois had initially relied on White and Bunche to help organize the congress, but Bunche backed out after it became clear to him that the conference was too narrowly focused on African problems and had the potential to be seen as pro-Communist. After losing faith in White, Du Bois turned to George Padmore, who resurfaced as a muse to postwar Du Boisian Pan-Africanism. Padmore, who had been instrumental in cultivating Robeson's anticolonial and Pan-African thought in the previous decade, corresponded with Du Bois from London to help plan the congress and became a galvanizing force for the diverse collection of interests that were involved in organizing the congress. Though he had long lost his love for the Communist Party, he became a gateway of sorts for anticolonial Communists and trade unionists in planning the agenda. Padmore also was a powerful liaison to the vehemently anticommunist groups in London, including the League of Coloured Peoples led by Jamaican-born missionary Harold Moody. The League of Coloured Peoples was initially viewed as the British counterpart to the NAACP, but its influence had waned by 1945 because many anticolonials viewed Moody as a sellout to British imperialism and Christian interests in colonized countries. Still, Padmore and Du Bois viewed Moody's cooperation as indispensable to a wide-encompassing agenda. In the months before the congress, Du Bois warned Padmore that, "we should be very catholic and cooperative and avoid to push people too far or get any particular set of ideas adopted too quickly. It would be very easy in a case like this for us to get split up before we begin."[35]

The planning for the congress became near disastrous, as organizers could not pick a host location or agree on a date. After deeming Africa out of feasibility and deciding against Paris, the congress settled on the country that was the axis of imperialism and subjugation of colored people. As it turned out, the Pan-African Congress became a platform for left-wing interests despite Padmore's best efforts to moderate the agenda. Most of the ninety attendees were fierce anticolonials who had embraced Socialism as the best fit for the future of their countries. Joining Padmore, Du Bois, Nkrumah, and Kenyatta were Hastings Kamuzu Banda (who would later go on to become the dictator of Malawi) and Marcus Garvey's first wife Amy Ashwood. Du Bois presided over the four-day gathering and was introduced by a reverent

Padmore as "the father of Pan-Africanism." The Doctor saw in the young radicals what he had long hoped for in the development of Africa—a core of able leaders whose commitment to African uplift rejected the notions of European "civility" that had ravaged the continent for nearly four centuries. Nkrumah, Kenyatta, and Banda were the radicals who emerged from the Du Boisian Pan-Africanism, and their presence at the congress exhilarated the Doctor. The union of Socialists and black nationalists had been coming for years, but the congress wedded the sides in an unofficial marriage of convenience against colonialism. The congress delegates, riding a wave of anti-imperialist sentiment, issued a Marxist-inspired main resolution that condemned "the monopoly of capital and the rule of private wealth and industry for private profit alone." Another resolution, modeled after the Soviet Constitution, called for racial discrimination to be punishable by law. In the spirit of shared struggle, delegates also passed resolutions supporting the freedom struggles in Vietnam (led by Communist revolutionary Ho Chi Minh) and the West Indies. The congress was emphatic in its demands, and not even the Doctor could have been prepared for the overwhelmingly radical and militant attitudes of the delegates as a whole. The Manchester gathering was deemed a success and set the tone for a new Africa that was to be free of colonialism. As one Pan-Africanist noted years later, the congress "was the springboard from where some of the most significant national liberation struggles in Africa were launched in post–Second World War era."[36] It also marked the start of an intimate friendship between Du Bois and Padmore, whose innovative

Pan-Africanism greatly influenced the Doctor over the next two decades.

REENERGIZED BY THE LABOUR PARTY'S VICTORY in postwar elections and the Pan African Congress's new direction, Du Bois turned his attention to the World Youth Conference in London. By attending the gathering of young radicals, Du Bois felt partially validated in his long-held belief that the union of students from around the world would be the key in the struggle for global freedom. It was there he met Esther Jackson, who, at the age of twenty-four, was already a civil rights veteran and an influential member of the CPUSA. Jackson said an "energetic" Du Bois had "a real enthusiasm, particularly meeting with the young people. He wanted to know our suggestions." Jackson organized a dinner during the conference with the Doctor and members of the India delegation, who had already concluded that independence for their country was soon at hand.[37]

That optimism became a reality nearly two years later, when the subcontinent finally broke away from British rule. Indian independence was the natural precursor, anticolonials assumed, of a larger emancipation of colonized lands. Both the Doctor and Paul hoped India's perseverance in attaining freedom would be the blueprint for all colonized and oppressed peoples, including African Americans under Jim Crow. "India knows well the ambition of the real leaders of the United States is to succeed Great Britain as the ruler of the Colored World in Asia and Africa and the control of their raw material and cheap labor," an emboldened Du Bois wrote shortly after India's emancipation. "For that reason we urge India to know and maintain contact with Negroes in this Nation which will call for initiative on India's part since ordinarily is not apt to be aware of our existence. This group has watched with interest and sympathy the efforts of India in the United Nations for World Peace."[38] Robeson sent congratulatory notes to his friends Nehru and Menon, expressing his hope that they would inspire others to freedom.

But the euphoria and elation over independence ended several months later when a Hindu nationalist shot and killed Gandhi. A crestfallen Du Bois looked at the assassination as part of a bigger picture, directing the blame at British imperialism. "The hypocrisy and violence of the British spawned the violence that killed Gandhi, and in the long run . . . national peace is going to come through the broad principles which Mohandas Gandhi laid down," the Doctor opined, adding that it would be prudent for the West "to acknowledge that it took a heathen to show Christians the way of life and to refuse to be carried further in this insane discrimination to commit suicide through a Third World War."[39] Gandhi's assassination validated Robeson and Du Bois's feelings about the evil of colonialism and pushed them further Left in their global outlook.

IN EARLY 1937, PAUL AND ESSIE entertained two notable guests for an evening at their flat in London. One was Earl Browder, whose farm-boy charm and stated passion to fight for the equality of African Americans and the global rise of Fascism endeared him instantly to the Robesons. The other guest had become an instant friend to Essie during her life-changing experience to

South Africa the year before. Dr. Max Yergan, a charismatic former missionary with the YMCA, was already an entrenched leftist with Communist Party affiliations. Yergan had spent more than a decade in South Africa, and within his first few years of studying the economic and social conditions there, became convinced that nothing short of revolution would lead to the betterment of native Africans. Yergan had already been acquainted with Du Bois and agreed on many of the basic principles of Du Boisian Pan-Africanism, but his more radical notions of economic change for Africans using the Bolshevik model was congruent to Paul's budding global philosophy. Yergan was in London to ask Paul's assistance to help put their idealism into practice: Would Paul be willing to help start an organization devoted to helping African and Caribbean nations win self-government by acting as a trustee in their best interests? The idea appealed greatly to the Robesons, especially Essie, whose firsthand trip to South Africa while Paul was filming *Song of Freedom* accelerated her development into a Pan-Africanist on equal footing with her husband. With the enthusiastic support of the Robesons, Yergan set out to establish his goal, and within a year, the Council on African Affairs (CAA) was born.

The Council, funded in part by the Communist Party, was as anticolonial as it was pro-Marxist in its basic philosophy, but Yergan was skillful in his dissemblance of the latter. This would prove necessary as the council enlisted support of many moderate black leaders, whose distrust of anything deemed "pro-Red" was based on their fears of becoming regulars on the FBI watch list. The council's early focus was on conditions in South Africa, where racialist politics had created conditions for blacks and Indians that were as oppressive as Jim Crow segregation. Unlike the United States, however, the oppressing whites in South Africa were the minority. Yergan believed that South Africa would be the best place to advocate an "Africa for Africans" agenda, given the high education levels among black and Indian freedom fighters and Marxist leanings. The African National Congress (ANC) and Gandhi's Natal Indian Congress were highly organized groups well versed in protest tactics. The ANC, which for years had been considered nothing more than a suppliant to philanthropic whites, underwent an organizational upheaval in 1940, leading to the recruitment of young and more aggressive nationalists such as Oliver Tambo and Nelson Mandela. These younger generation activists expressed a stronger inclination toward militancy, which Yergan believed could be cultivated into an effective weapon for insurgency. The council became black and brown South Africa's representative in the United States, advocating fierce opposition to white minority rule and political representation for darker people.

Ironically, the CAA's wartime advocacy against colonialism went in direct opposition to the Communist Party, which had refrained from attacking British imperialism out of fear that it would be seen as unpatriotic. Yergan and Hunton, however, shaped the council's mission to oppose all forms of colonialism. Robeson enthusiastically supported this effort, believing that the CAA could give voice to the concern of disenfranchised Africans. He wasn't the only one who backed the council's stand during World War II. Bunche, Adam Clayton Powell, E. Franklin Frazier, and Channing Tobias were among the black luminaries who were actively involved with the CAA; Bunche, however, withdrew his support when he realized that the council was becoming increasingly pro-Soviet and irresponsible in its advocacy.[40] The CAA expanded its influence during the war, attracting a wide array of intellectuals to the myriad causes it supported. The council kept regular contact with Yusuf M. Dadoo, the charismatic leader of the Communist Party of South Africa, relaying the concerns of South Africans to sympathetic American liberals.

In this regard, Robeson was correct in assuming the council's ability to facilitate change. The CAA, thanks to Robeson's chairmanship and Yergan's charismatic (and as later proven, quixotic) leadership, emerged as the foremost advocate for African peoples. For Paul, the involvement with the council also meant striking out on his own as a political activist; he had for the better of a decade followed the Communist Party line, but decided that his anticolonialism bested any strategic refrain preached by Party leaders. The CAA became a liaison to Africa and served as a voice for the independence struggles in Asia and Latin America. E. S. Reddy, who became involved with the council in 1946, noted that the council became a mandatory stop for foreign visitors from colonized nations. With the help of Goshal, the CAA even organized a party for Pandit during her stay in New York. Reddy credited the CAA for invoking a sense of common struggle among oppressed peoples. "African Americans felt very happy that Gandhi, a colored man, had stood up to Britain," he said. "There was a feeling of kinship in the struggle."[41] Paul felt the same way, hoping to highlight Africa as a place of untapped strength in the fight against colonialism. "Many Negroes think of Africa with pain, and many white people with condescension, because both believe that Africans are inferior—they're supposed to be savages," he wrote in *New Africa*, the council's newsletter. "Actually, they are in the same cultural level as many millions of Chinese and Hindus and Indians. The Soviet Union has show that these peoples can catch up with modern technology and culture within a generation."[42]

Shortly after the war, Robeson and the CAA stepped up their anticolonial rhetoric, employing a full-scale media blitz to highlight disparate conditions in colonized Africa and the "fascist-like" policies of South Africa. Paul also saw the strong parallels between African subjugation and the continued oppression of African Americans, especially in the segregated South. In a letter to the *New York Herald Tribune* in 1946, he wrote:

> We have learned bitterly, that where there is slavery, Fascist or Fascist-like, there is potential and eventual war. To mould the peace and keep it, there must be a free world, a world freed from any semblance of slavery—Jim Crow, colonial, or any other kind. That free world, that freedom can be won through the United Nations, through Big Three unity, through keeping the pledge which the major European powers and our United States have given to all peoples everywhere: Self-determination and freedom for all peoples in one free world.[43]

In 1946, Du Bois joined the CAA, convinced that it could advance the principles of the Pan-African Congress. The Doctor, in his increasing affinity for the Soviet Union, found like-minded members in Robeson, Hunton, Yergan, Herbert Aptheker, and Doxey Wilkerson (the latter four being Communist Party members). Du Bois's views on postcolonial Africa began to mirror Robeson's. Both felt increasingly certain that the Soviet model was destined to work in African nations, where they believed the framework for Socialism was inherent to the tribal structure in most African countries. In revising his thesis on Africa to more closely resemble Robeson's beliefs, Du Bois had reversed his belief on the haplessness of the Dark Continent; he now agreed with Robeson and other anticolonial leftists that an implemented Marxist formula would emancipate Africa politically and economically. Du Bois's activities vexed his colleagues at the NAACP, which had distanced itself from any organization deemed Communist. The Doctor was oblivious to their concerns, however, finding the council to be a perfect fit for his newfound optimism on Africa. Du Bois was also impressed by the council's willingness to highlight cruel conditions in colonized nations and its intrepidness in pointing out American capitalist investment in South Africa. However, he wasn't as certain about Yergan, whose behavior became increasingly self-promoting. Gathering information from Padmore, the Doctor seems to have guessed that Yergan was being duplicitous in his day-to-day management of the organization; he and other CAA members would find out just how far Yergan would go to save himself from a sinking ship.[44]

In 1947, the council was active in pushing for a United Nations petition on anticolonialism that reiterated the stance of Du Bois's 1945 effort in San Francisco; like the previous incarnation, this one was doomed to die. But even in failure, the CAA kept its profile, attracting the support of the black press while maintaining strong contact with anticolonials in Europe and Africa. But the more activist the council and Robeson became in Cold War politics, the further it created division with the moderate wing of black leadership. With leaders such as White, Bunche, and Randolph distancing themselves from the council, the lines were being drawn for acceptable dissent; the CAA, as it turned out, was too radical for its time. The FBI had already accumulated a healthy dossier on the council's activities, as well as its frequent contacts with Communist leaders in African, Asian, and Latin American countries. The bureau also kept track of Robeson and Du Bois's public speeches praising the Soviet Union as a paragon of anticolonialism. Keeping close watch of the council, the feds might have known that the group was about to implode even before its members did.

By late 1947 the CAA was beginning to show cracks. Hunton, who had by now become Robeson's spokesman in CAA-related correspondence, grew to believe that Yergan was using the council as nothing more than a vehicle of self-promotion. This was a charge that the left-wing faction of the council began to repeat more vigorously in the coming months, hastening Robeson's decision to begin an inquiry of Yergan's performance as executive director. There were rumors of financial mismanagement, an allegation Yergan vehemently denied.[45] When an audit validated key CAA members' suspicions, Robeson was devastated. He felt that Yergan, whom he had come to rely upon as a right-hand man for the better part of a decade, had led him astray, seducing him with a shared political vision and ultimately conning him. Had years of tireless campaigning for the right of colonial peoples, as well as political organizing in South Africa, been nothing more than a glorified front for Yergan's bourgeois lifestyle? Robeson was determined not to let the organization sink with Yergan, but by early 1948, the CAA was in disarray. Yergan and his supporters now faced off against Robeson and the left-wing faction of the group. Robeson, Wilkerson, and Hunton asked Du Bois to lead the special committee investigating the executive director's activities. The Doctor accepted, on condition "that . . . Yergan must be replaced. If he continues as director or with any position of power in the council, it will be impossible for me to take part."[46] Yergan tried to sidestep the investigation by calling a meeting while Robeson and Du Bois were out of town, asserting that he was acting within his powers as the council's executive director to do so.[47] However, that only increased Robeson's ire, prompting him to call for Yergan's resignation.

A defiant Yergan had one card up his sleeve. In March, Yergan—sensing his star was soon to crash and a possible indictment on blackmail charges near—went to the FBI as an informant. Considering that he had been a longtime Communist Party member and the one who introduced the Robesons to Communist Party leaders such as Browder, Yergan's decision to "flip" was, in the eyes of the Left, unmitigated treachery. Now in the good graces of Hoover, an emboldened Yergan held a press conference, declaring that he intended to wrest control away from the Communists and "restore the Council to its true function of enlisting American support for the improvement of conditions among the indigenous population of East, West, and South Africa."[48] He also charged that the council was a partisan tool of the Progressive Party and the presidential campaign of Henry A. Wallace. His public posturing infuriated both Paul and Essie, who noted that they helped Yergan conceive the idea of the council. Essie countered that if the function of the council had ever strayed from its original mission, Yergan was to blame. "Max Yergan . . . has kept the political, financial, and social direction of the Council's affairs exclusively in his own hands, and we have not been able to say as much as we would like about them."[49] Paul was less eloquent, confronting Yergan outside of the council's offices in late April. Their "showdown" purportedly came to near blows, but Yergan escaped unharmed. Though the council subsequently censured Yergan, condemning his claims about the council as "complete distortions," the damage to the council's reputation had been done. By summer, more than half of its advisory board members, including Powell, Judge Hubert T. Delany, and Channing Tobias of the NAACP, resigned or distanced themselves from the organization.[50]

After the upheaval, Du Bois accepted the token position of vice-chairmanship, in part to try to restore the credibility the CAA lost with Yergan's betrayal and the resignation of most of the council's moderate members. The council was now unabashedly procommunist, hampering its efforts to build coalitions during the Cold War. However, the CAA limped along, guided by Du Bois and Robeson's spirited protests against colonialism. The Doctor wrote that though "the wave of European control and conquest has deprived black African populations of all independence except in Ethiopia and Liberia . . . the apparent demand for autonomy and even separation is growing."[51] The CAA rallied in support of the budding independence movements in Libya and Morocco, which would gain sovereignty in 1951 from Italy and 1956 from France, respectively. It also called for the end of Belgian control of the Congo and the right to self-determination in Kenya and Nigeria, two of Britain's most valued colonial possessions in Africa. However, Du Bois and Robeson directed most of their advocacy toward South Africa, where Afrikaaner prime minister D. F. Malan's racialist politics subjected blacks and Indians to brutal repression and de facto slavery while essentially formalizing apartheid, the country's mandate for the next forty years. Du Bois wrote, "It seems almost unbelievable that in the middle of the 20th century the Union of South Africa is widely recognized as a civilized nation." A disgusted Robeson likened Malan's rule in South Africa to the Nazi government, describing the treatment of nonwhites as borderline genocide. Simply put, Robeson said, "South Africa is now the stamping ground of all the evil forces which many decent, progressive people believe the war was fought to destroy. The disciples of Streicher and Goebbels are unashamedly and insolently boasting about their foul creed. They are brazenly persecuting three quarters of the population. They degrade mankind by their policies and practices and consequently they are deserving of the severest censure of decent men and women everywhere."[52]

Paul's best efforts couldn't dissuade the United States from making South Africa a key Cold War ally. Under Truman's containment policy, the United States began sending aid to South Africa in the late 1940s, an economic relationship that would last until the government finally caved into international pressure and enacted sanctions in the late 1980s.

Robeson continued public protests against the U.S. alliance with South Africa while pleading with the Truman administration to reverse course on the Soviet Union. He pointed to America's support of imperialism and apartheid as evidence that the U.S. government was not interested in civil rights and the principles of the Atlantic Charter.

> Go and ask the Negro workers in the cotton plantations of Alabama, the sugar plantations in Louisiana, the tobacco fields in south Arkansas, ask the workers in the banana plantations or the sugar workers in the West Indies, ask the African farmers who have been dispossessed of their land in the South Africa of Malan, ask the Africans wherever you find them on their continent: Will they fight for peace so that new ways can be opened up for life of freedom for hundreds of millions and not just for the few; will they fight for peace and collaboration with the Soviet Union and the new democracies; will they join the forces of peace or be drawn into a war in the interest of the senators who have just filibustered them out of their civil rights; will they join Malan in South Africa who, just like Hitler, is threatening to destroy eight million Africans and hundreds of thousands of Indians through hunger and terror; will they join their oppressors or will they fight for peace? There can only be one answer: We want peace. We have the chance to know who are our true friends.[53]

Despite Du Bois and Robeson's best efforts to promote a united front against colonialism, Cold War politics muted the Council on African Affairs. Labeled a Communist front organization by conservatives, the CAA could do little to enter the mainstream political dialogue of the 1950s. Groups that had backed the notion of black internationalism, including the NAACP, refused to have anything to do with the council. Bunche disavowed his connection a decade earlier, disgusted by Yergan and likely cognizant of the fact that the council's radical stance was putting it on a crash course with the U.S. government. Meanwhile, Yergan would become a Schuyleresque conservative, going so far as to defend apartheid from a Cold War strategic point of view.

Though the council was forced to disband in 1955 under the McCarran Act, it would have a lasting impact on anticolonial activism. The CAA provided international recognition to the ANC, Natal Indian Congress, and Communist Party of South Africa. By the 1980s, Nelson Mandela was a household name to many African Americans, embodying the South African struggle for human dignity. Reddy, one of the CAA's members and a close friend of Hunton, would go on to lead the UN Centre Against Apartheid, which applied international pressure against South Africa for more than twenty years. "I was destined to spend most of my working life on South Africa," he noted.[54] Reddy would spearhead efforts in the 1970s to honor Du Bois and Robeson for their commitment to the struggle against colonialism.

BY THE TIME YERGAN had left the CAA, Du Bois and Robeson's international views had fully converged. Both believed the

Soviet Union held the promise of a free world and promoted their anticolonialism hand-in-hand with endorsements of Soviet foreign policy. Following the war, Robeson once again became the unofficial spokesman of Communist Party internationalism, condemning the Truman administration's invocation of the Monroe Doctrine and the implementation of the Truman Doctrine in Turkey and Greece.[55] But supporting the Communist Party's efforts in postcolonial countries also put Robeson at odds with Nehru, who sought to consolidate the Indian Congress Party's power following independence. Paul believed that Communists needed to be an important player in shaping postcolonial India, a sentiment that few Indian leaders shared. Nehru, who distrusted the Communist Party's motives, jailed many suspected Communists at the height of a Maoist rebellion in India's Andhra Pradesh state, which led to a reported feud with Robeson.

According to Robeson biographer Martin Duberman, Paul was extremely upset by Nehru's handling of the rebellion, so much so that he refused to meet with Nehru during his visit to the United States in 1948. However, Paul Jr. and E. S. Reddy dispute this claim, arguing that Robeson was looking out for Nehru's interests. By that time, Paul was acutely aware of FBI and State Department surveillance of his activities and was concerned for friend. To underscore their assertions, Nehru would later play an important role in helping Robeson win back his passport. But while Paul walked the line between his loyalty to the Communist Party and his old anticolonial friend, Eslanda pulled no punches. Following a return from China in 1950, Essie accused Nehru of establishing a "police state" in

India; furthermore, she added, "he has established Hitlerite concentration camps where hundreds of our militant peasant fighters have been driven to a slow death and even murdered. The Anglo-American imperialists have put Nehru in Chiang Kai Shek's shoes, but the battle cry of the countryside is 'We shall go the Mao Tse-tung way!'"[56] Essie later recanted her criticism of Nehru after acknowledging the latter's efforts to recognize Robeson in India during the Cold War.

Du Bois was equally disappointed in India following independence. The country he had held as an example to the American Negro had seemingly turned its back on the rest of the dark world. Though he had hoped Nehru would succeed in implementing Socialism, the Doctor guessed that Americans would help Indian capitalists exercise increasing influence in postcolonial India. He also lamented the apparent about-face of his friend Pandit when it came to identifying with African American struggle.

> Mrs. Pandit realized that while it was popular here to defend Indians in South Africa, it was never popular to defend Negroes anywhere. It was not long ago that the head of one of our colored sororities invited Madame Pandit to a celebration which was beautifully carried out. There were lovely colored women becomingly gowned and the Basileus, who had fought a good fight for freedom, over many years congratulated Madame Pandit on her defense of Negroes and their cause. Madame Pandit demurred: she said that she had been misunderstood that; she did not go along wholly with what Negroes in American were

saying and trying to do; that she advocated patience
and waiting, etc. She took the path only too familiar
to us. The ladies of the sorority felt humiliated and
cruelly disillusioned. But all this is perhaps natural
and to be expected.[57]

Du Bois, however, would applaud India's role in the 1955
Conference of Asian and African nations in Bandung, where
Nehru called for unification of interests against white imperi-
alism in the dark world.

In assessing China under Mao, the Doctor had a far more
sanguine outlook. Sometime during World War II, he had privately abandoned his racialist internationalism, choosing
instead to side with the Chinese in their struggle against
Japan. That support only grew following the civil war that
eventually established China as a Socialist republic. Du Bois
had immense respect for Mao, whom he considered a populist
capable of inspiring mass uplift of China's peasant classes. Du
Bois began to view China as a success story in implementing
Soviet-style Socialism, unaware that Mao's Great Leap Forward would eventually kill millions in Stalinesque collectivization. The Doctor would even excuse China's occupation
of Tibet, dismissing the Dalai Lama's right to rule.[58] Du Bois
visited China in 1959, meeting Mao and becoming convinced
that the country would become an international crusader for
Socialism and mass peasant uplift. In his autobiography, he
wrote a glowing account of his visit.

You won't believe this, because you never saw anything like it; and if the State Department has its

way, you never will. Let *Life* lie about communes;
and the State Department shed crocodile tears over
ancestral tombs. Let Hong Kong wire its lies
abroad. Let "Divine Slavery" persist in Tibet until
China kills it. The truth is there and I saw it. . . .
Fifteen times I have crossed the Atlantic and once
the Pacific. I have seen the world. But never so vast
and glorious a miracle as China. This monster is a
nation with a darktinted billion born at the beginning of time, and facing its end; this struggle from
starved degradation and murder and suffering to
the triumph of that Long March to world leadership. Oh beautiful, patient, self-sacrificing China,
despised and unforgettable, victorious and for-
giving, crucified and risen from the dead.[59]

Robeson was equally enamored with China, calling it the
greatest success in Soviet foreign policy. "China has shown the
way, no argument about that, but some people don't pay
enough attention to one of the most important facts about
China's successful struggle for liberation," he wrote in
Freedom. "I mean the great truth, proclaimed by the Chinese
leaders and masses alike, that their victory could not have
been won without the strong friendship and support of the
Soviet Union."[60] Though China's relations with the USSR
cooled considerably by the end of the decade, Du Bois and
Robeson seemed to be validated in their international outlooks
by the mid-1950s. Communists were playing an important
role in African, Asian, and Latin American independence
movements. In 1954, the Vietnamese, led by Communist

leader Ho Chi Minh, defeated the French. Robeson hailed Ho Chi Minh as a modern "Toussaint L'Overture" and warned the United States not to interfere in the Vietnamese independence struggle. Robeson could not fathom how blacks in the United States—given their treatment under Jim Crow and segregation during the Korean War—would back America's support of French colonialism in Southeast Asia. "Shall Negro share-croppers from Mississippi be sent to shoot down brown-skinned peasants in Vietnam—to serve the interests of those who oppose Negro liberation at home and colonial freedom abroad?"[61] Du Bois implored African Americans to understand the importance of Socialism as a world-changing force.

> We American Negroes can no longer lead the colored peoples of the world because they far better than we understand what is happening in the world today. But we can try to catch up with them. We can learn about China and India and the vast realm of Indonesia rescued from Holland. We can know of the new ferment in East, West, and South Africa. We can realize by reading . . . how Socialism is expanding over the modern world and penetrating the colored world. So far as Africa is concerned we can realize that Socialism is part of their past history and will without a shade of doubt play a large part of their future.[62]

Though the promise of a world governed by democratic Socialism never came to fruition, Du Bois and Robeson's internationalism became a force in leftist thought in the latter half of the twentieth century. Both preached the need for Americans—especially blacks—to identify with the struggles of other oppressed peoples. In doing so, they built valuable bridges with the international anticolonial movement, helping to establish long-term ties between the American Left and the leaders of postcolonial nations in Africa, Asia, and Latin America. The Doctor and Paul's global outlooks, though changed over a twenty-five-year span of shared activism, still conformed to their basic convictions that all people should walk in full dignity. Whether they were overidealistic is a subject for argument, but what is beyond debate is their lasting impact on anticolonial thought and international relations, especially among formerly colonized nations. Du Bois and Robeson would leave behind a powerful internationalist legacy matched only by Bunche's achievements as a diplomat. As Esther Jackson eloquently noted, "Dr. Du Bois and Paul had this unshaken faith in the power of humanity. They truly believed the world could become free through common understanding."[63]

7

CONVERGENCE AND DIVERGENCE

It is possible to win if the majority of the American people
can be brought to see and understand in the fullest sense
the fact that the struggle in which we are engaged is not a
matter of mere humanitarian sentiment, but of life and
death. The only alternative to world freedom is world
annihilation—another bloody holocaust—which will
dwarf the two world wars through which we have passed.
                                    —Paul Robeson, CAA speech (1946)

THOUGH WINSTON CHURCHILL'S "Iron Curtain" speech might have
officially kicked off the Cold War, Robeson's Spingarn Medal
acceptance speech in October 1945 might have been the first
major warning shot. The NAACP, after much debate, decided

to award Robeson its highest honor; in doing so, board members picked Paul over boxer Joe Louis and longtime YMCA stalwart (and NAACP board member) Channing Tobias. Though Walter White and Roy Wilkins expressed some concern about Robeson's political affiliations, they could not deny his accomplishments as an entertainer. The medal committee announced that it had given the award to Robeson for his "distinguished achievements in the theater and on the concert stage, as well as his active concern for the rights of the common man of every race, color, religion, and nationality."[1] Marshall Field III, the business magnate and powerful editor of the *Chicago Sun*, introduced Paul at the award banquet at the Biltmore Hotel in New York. A long list of prominent blacks and liberal whites showed up for the event, which the NAACP also marked as a celebration of the thirtieth anniversary of the Spingarn Medal. Even some Communist Party members, including Davis, Max Yergan, Esther Jackson (who would leave for the World Youth Conference a few weeks later), and Thelma Dale, attended. Jackson said she had heard that there had been "a big battle within the NAACP over whether to give Paul the award."[2] Paul's supporters won the debate. Walter White presided over the event, hoping that Robeson would praise civil rights progress during the war and promote the NAACP's role in fighting for oppressed people. Paul did neither. In a speech that shocked most of the several hundred attendees at the banquet, Robeson ripped into American policy following the war. He said he could not believe that the United States was cooling off ties to the Soviet Union after both had successfully defeated Fascism. And in a rebuke of the U.S. government's handling of mass uplift, Robeson noted,

"Full employment in Russia is a fact, and not a myth, and discrimination is non-existent."[3] His speech caused White to "turn red," according to some of the attendees.

Robeson's remarks not only drew visible gasps, but they drew the lines for an imminent battle between ideologies.[4] Paul was making himself very clear that the world was changing, and that unless the United States sided with the USSR, Americans would be "again on the edge of destruction." His apocalyptic speech also opened the rift between him and the NAACP; as it turned out, the Spingarn Medal speech would be the last time Paul would work with the NAACP in any official event.

Du Bois, who was across the Atlantic presiding over the Pan-African Congress, enthusiastically agreed with Robeson's stance. He might have even chuckled at the notion of White and Wilkins turning red-faced during the acceptance speech. Like Robeson, Du Bois concluded that the real was fight at home, against conservative policy makers who would endorse imperialism over communism and restore racial progress to the pre–New Deal era status quo. He believed the first target of criticism needed to be Truman, who was far from an outspoken advocate for civil and labor rights. Despite continuing many of Roosevelt's social programs, Truman allowed the powerful Southern wing of the Democratic Party to dilute—and in some cases, destroy—policies designed to integrate blacks into the economy. He refused to be heavy-handed in making permanent the Fair Employment Practices Committee (FEPC), despite support from liberals in his own party, including Mrs. Roosevelt, to do so. Not even pressure from a wide-encompassing interracial coalition led by A. Philip Randolph could convince the president that FEPC needed an immediate resolution. Truman also dallied on antilynching legislation and the poll tax, both of which became pet causes for influential black politicians Powell, Perry Howard of Mississippi, and William Dawson of Chicago. The appointment of James F. Byrnes—who would go onto become one of the architects of U.S. foreign policy—as secretary of state rankled some of Truman's most diehard supporters. Wilkins called Byrnes (who was a Supreme Court justice under Roosevelt) a "shameless white supremacist."[5]

Despite Truman's questionable commitment to civil rights, the NAACP stood by him, confident that he would advance a social platform that was amenable to black progress. As Wilkins noted, "Truman's own views on race were border state, not Deep Dixie: he didn't believe in social equality, but he did believe in fair play. No one had ever convinced him that the Bill of Rights was a document for white folks only."[6] From Du Bois and Robeson's vantage point, however, the post-Roosevelt era heralded a return to "gradualism" that offered blacks some, but promised nothing in the way of meaningful progress. After returning from the Pan-African Congress, Du Bois took an increasingly hostile stance toward the Truman administration. Like Randolph and Powell, he accused the president of caving into pressure from Republicans and conservative Democrats and ignoring millions of blacks who had sworn allegiance to the New Deal. "President Truman," Du Bois complained, "can implement no program of reform as long as the South, with political power based on disenfranchisement and caste, can out-count the majority in the presidential election and in Congress."[7] In the spring of 1946, the Doctor guessed Churchill's bluff when it came to the Communist threat, calling the "Iron

Curtain" speech nothing more than an imperialist's bogey. Despite public pledges to honor the Atlantic Charter, Du Bois noted that "the idea persisted that no matter what the cost in cruelty, lying and blood, the triumph of Europe was to the glory of God and untrammeled power of the only people on earth who deserved to rule; that the right and justice of their rule was proved by their own success and particularly by their great cities, their enormous technical mastery over the power of nature, their gigantic manufacture of goods and systems of transportation over the world."[8] His involvement with the Council on African Affairs would only intensify his antagonism toward the doctrine of "Anglo-American" supremacy.

Though Truman was reticent on civil rights, events in Columbia, Tennessee, in February and Monroe, Georgia, in July brought antilynching legislation to the national forefront. In February a race riot in which two blacks were killed by local authorities led to the arrests of more than two dozen black men in Columbia. Though the men—who were defended by Thurgood Marshall—were later exonerated, the riots brought to light the continued racial hostility in the South. But what happened in Monroe shocked the entire nation. On July 25, two black couples, including a World War II veteran, were tied up and shot hundreds of times by twenty-five men carrying pistols and rifles. The Georgia Bureau of Investigation and the FBI went to the town to interview residents, but came away with nothing.[9] However, press reports of the gory killing prompted black leaders to call on immediate action from Truman. Robeson demanded that Truman "take immediate effective steps to apprehend and punish the perpetrators of this shocking crime and to halt the rise tide of lynch law." The

National Negro Congress, which would soon fold into the Civil Rights Congress, criticized the president for his "continued silence over the renewed wave of terror directed against the Negro people of the South."[10] The NAACP made plans to mobilize a national coalition against lynching, but stopped short of criticizing Truman or the U.S. government. Truman would not act on the Monroe case until the fall, when Attorney General Tom Clark launched an investigation into the killings. However, no arrests were made in the case.

Fed up with the lack of action on the lynching issue, Robeson helped lawyer Bartley Crum—a staunch Marxist who helped lobby for the creation of the state of Israel—mobilize a new grassroots effort against lynching. Their efforts were in response to what they considered a repeat of the "Red Summer" more than twenty-five years earlier. In addition to the Columbia and Monroe cases, at least fifty blacks, including several war veterans, were killed by white mob violence in the South. Robeson and Crum wanted federal intervention, which they believed wouldn't happen with the masseuse-type pressure the NAACP was applying on the Truman administration. Thus, the American Crusade against Lynching (ACEL)was born. Hoping to make waves immediately, ACEL leaders planned a mass gathering in Washington, D.C., to show full-scale support for legislation that would criminalize lynching. Robeson envisioned the crusade to reflect "the determination of the American people that the lynchers be apprehended and prosecuted and that the Congress of the United States enact a federal anti-lynch law."[11] Du Bois joined the crusade at Robeson's behest, feeling that a mass mobilization against lynching (backed by the Left) would yield equal, if not greater, results than what the NAACP had been able to achieve up to that point. The rally also drew the support of Albert Einstein, whose passion for antiracist causes was only overshadowed by his scientific brilliance. Comparing discrimination toward blacks with his own experience as a Jew, Einstein believed the United States had "a heavy debt to discharge for all the troubles and disabilities it has laid on the Negro's shoulder." In becoming an active member of the antilynching crusade, the Nobel physicist became close to both men and would remain one of their staunchest allies until his death in 1955. Health troubles prevented Einstein from attending the protest, but he wrote a letter to Truman assailing the government for not passing legislation to ban lynching.[12]

Though the actual gathering drew only three thousand people (perhaps out of fears that the FBI was taking names of invitees and attendees), the seven-person delegation headed by Robeson secured a meeting with Truman after the rally. Other notables in the group included Aubrey Williams, former head of the National Youth Administration under Roosevelt; Harper Sibley, president of the United Council of Church Women; and Rabbi Irving Miller of the American Jewish Congress. Their "conference" was tension-filled, with Robeson repeatedly asking Truman to make a formal declaration on lynching. Williams warned that "a reign of terror" existed in the South. Truman, infuriated by the delegation's assertion that not enough was being done to end white violence against blacks, countered that the issue needed to be dealt with "in political terms and strategy." However, he abruptly ended the meeting after Robeson intimated that blacks might have to defend themselves if no federal lynching ban was enacted.[13] The delegation left the White House with no promises of assistance, and the FBI would act quickly against the leader of the purported "Communist front." Two weeks after the rally, the Joint Fact-Finding Committee on Un-American Activities in California, formed to investigate "subversive" groups and individuals, called Robeson to testify. Members of the committee, headed by Senator Jack B. Tenney, "interviewed" Robeson about his involvement with the Left. The hearing was almost lighthearted, with committee members at times joking with Robeson. Tenney laughed when he asked Robeson if he was a member of the Communist Party. "I ask it of everybody so don't feel embarrassed," Tenney added. Paul noted that though he wasn't a Communist himself, he could "just as conceivably join the Communist Party, more so today than I could join the Republican or Democratic Party." Members of the committee thanked Robeson for his time and dismissed him, ending—at least for the next couple of years—any further congressional scrutiny of his involvement with the antilynching efforts.[14]

But the fallout from the crusade didn't end there. Robeson and Du Bois's involvement with the movement drew strong rebuke from Walter White and the NAACP, which had long claimed sole ownership of the lynching issue. White, whose relationship with Robeson had been strained long before the Spingarn Medal speech, told Robeson that the crusade paralleled the association's own antilynching efforts and was unnecessary. After all, White noted, the NAACP had spearheaded its own coalition, the National Emergency Committee to End Mob Violence, which included Max Yergan. In fact, the committee met with Truman the same month as the Robeson delegation and received a more positive response from the president. As Wilkins recalled:

> During the meeting, Walter briefed the President on the mayhem in Columbia, Tennessee, and gave Truman a rundown on other eruptions around the country. The one I recall best was the case of Isaac Woodward, a young black soldier who mustered out of uniform down South only to have his eyes gouged out three hours later by a white sheriff. Walter returned and told us that Truman had listened, fists clenched on the arms of his chair, as the delegation told its horror stories. Finally, the President stood up and said, "My God, I had no idea that things were as terrible as that. We've got to do something."
>
> So we had the President's ear, a good beginning.[15]

The NAACP-led meeting would set the tone for the association's close relations with the Truman White House over the next six years, but in the meantime, the ACEL was simply unwanted competition. White told Robeson that championing the same cause would be tantamount to redundancy and would "create confusion in the public mind and would also give comfort to our enemies who would believe that there are rival groups fighting for anti-lynching legislation." But White's letter to Robeson was nothing more than a polite warning when compared with his response to Du Bois's involvement with the crusade. Referring to the "unfortunate conflict between two groups," White told the Doctor that lending his name to the crusade only caused confusion among NAACP members, who believed "that the Association is participating in this Washington meeting because of your name on it." Adding that Du Bois should have consulted the national office about the lynching campaign, White wrote that "it would just save all of us time and headaches if the facts are obtained before decision is made." Du Bois bristled at White's suggestion, firing back that his cooperation from the NAACP was "evidently not needed." The Doctor excoriated White for suggesting that he needed to consult with the association before committing to Robeson's effort. "I have been fighting lynching for forty years, and I have a right to let the world know that I am still fighting. I therefore gladly endorsed the Robeson movement which asked my cooperation. This did not and could not interfere with the NAACP program. The fight against mob law is the monopoly of no one person and no one organization." White was taken aback by Du Bois's response. "I had sought to make my memorandum to you explaining the complication which had arisen as friendly as possible so that you would understand the facts," an agitated White wrote. "You can imagine, therefore, my surprise at the manner in which you received my memorandum." [16]

The lynching issue was only part of a larger tug-of-war between White and the Doctor, who was incensed by what he perceived to be the NAACP's limitations on his outside involvement. As he would tell Arthur Spingarn two years later, had he realized that "re-joining the NAACP meant an end to my writing and speaking I would have never come back."[17] But Du Bois was not going anywhere, at least while he could use the association's name to advance his own Left-leaning causes. It was no accident that his involvement with the American Crusade to End Lynching, the Council on African Affairs, and other organizations far outside the scope of the NAACP was tied to his "official" work. In fact, the Doctor's title—no matter how superficial—was just as important in lending name recognition and credibility to myriad leftist groups as it was in restoring postwar black America's faith in the NAACP.

IF THE CAA HAD BECOME Du Bois and Robeson's platform for foreign policy, the Civil Rights Congress (CRC) would become their vehicle for domestic issues. The CRC was formed in 1946 as a result of the CPUSA's merger of the International Labor Defense and the National Federation for Civil Liberties. By 1948, the sinking National Negro Congress, headed by Robeson friend and Communist Party stalwart Revels Cayton, would also assimilate into the group. Formed in order to combat discrimination against blacks, labor, Jews, and social progressives in the wake of the Cold War, the CRC quickly emerged as a militant counterpart to the NAACP, employing aggressive legal representation on civil liberties issues. Though Robeson joined William Patterson as one of the founding members of the congress, he was far from the most recognizable name involved in the group's initiation; a wide array of prominent American figures, including Powell, Mary McLeod Bethune, and nationally renowned leftist philanthropist George Marshall were among those who helped launch the CRC. As the organization took shape, other high-profile members would join the group's branches, including fiction writer

Dashiell Hammett (author of *The Maltese Falcon* and *Red Harvest*), playwright Rockwell Kent, scrappy New York Congressman Vito Marcantonio, radical writer Jessica Mitford (whom *Harry Potter* author J. K. Rowling calls her role model), and actor Gregory Peck. Though increased scrutiny of suspected Communist activity would lead many of the organization's early members to take a backseat or leave altogether, the CRC managed to piece together a large coalition of moderates, liberals, and left-wingers who shared a common concern about the direction of Cold War America. Du Bois joined the CRC unofficially in 1946, and became more involved after his dismissal from the NAACP in 1948. The congress was ambitious from the start, taking aim at the NAACP's inability to get antilynching legislation passed and at legislators who supported segregation.

Their first major target—and victory—was a drive to unseat Mississippi Senator Theodore Bilbo. Bilbo was somewhat of an anomaly as a political figure. He was a staunch supporter of the New Deal, yet he was religiously devoted to the notion of white supremacy. Bilbo had ties with the Ku Klux Klan and published a lengthy racial discourse, *Take Your Choice, Separation or Mongrelization*, which called for blacks to be deported to Liberia. Bilbo might have found common cause with Garvey, but he was equally in favor of keeping blacks disenfranchised at any cost; he began calling for extralegal actions to prevent Negroes in the South from voting or seeking employment. Civil rights activists rightfully demonized Bilbo, shocked that a man who had helped promote the New Deal in the South would openly advocate violence against African Americans. The CRC—led by Robeson and Patterson—formed a National

Committee to Oust Bilbo, which included Powell, Einstein, Alain Locke, and Oscar Hammerstein II. The "Oust Bilbo" campaign garnered widespread support, even leading to cooperation between branches of the CRC and the NAACP. At a rally against war on September 12 (the same one where Henry Wallace would deliver his fateful "The Way to Peace"), Robeson called on all Americans to focus their efforts on attacking Bilbo and other segregationists.

> This crusade and the general campaign against discrimination must not be regarded as the special or exclusive concern of Negroes. I call particularly upon organized labor, because of its organizing drive in the South, as well as for other reasons, to throw into full strength into this fight to end lynching and discrimination. Death to the lynchers! Oust Bilbo from the Senate! Free the country of the poll tax menace! There must be the cry of us all. There is my possible comparison to be made with the Soviet Union in its treatment of minorities. For they have no minorities in our sense of the word. There, all people, of whatever color or culture, enjoy complete equality. It is painfully obvious that this is not true in our United States—neither for the Negro, the Spanish American, the Jewish American people, the Americans of Asiatic descent, nor for millions of underprivileged of all colors.[18]

A month later, Robeson almost called for Bilbo's assassination: "Every section of the American people—black and white,

Jew and Gentile, Catholic and Protestant—has felt the venom of this enemy of democracy and should see to it that he is driven from the Earth."[19] While some of Paul's comments might have contradicted his peaceful nature, they reflected his deep hatred for Bilbo and others who threatened civil rights progress. The CRC—choosing a more socially accepted approach than violence—enlisted the support of politically savvy lawyers, including Emmanuel Bloch (who would later represent Julius and Ethel Rosenberg), to lobby political leaders to remove Bilbo. The Oust Bilbo campaign collected more than half a million signatures and played a major role in the Senate's decision not to automatically seat Bilbo following his reelection; as a result, he was forced to stand aside and died several months later. The campaign proved to be a high point in the CRC's existence, mobilizing a diverse coalition of figures and providing hope for progressives that they could force change through their activism. But while the congress reveled in its victory, the FBI already began to keep close watch of its activities. As Gerald Horne noted in his historiography of the organization, the bureau began to infiltrate the CRC, which played a major part in the congress's downfall in the 1950s.[20] Buoyed by the support of labor and liberal groups, the congress continued its advocacy on national and local levels. Hammett, who led the New York chapter, called for an investigation of police misconduct in New York City. That spurred a national campaign against police brutality among CRC branches. Though Robeson—overwhelmed by his involvement with the CAA and the labor movement—took some time off from political activity in 1947, and Du Bois was still bound to the NAACP, both lent their public endorsements of the congress's activities.

Over the next few years, the Civil Rights Congress passionately fought for the freedom of the Trenton Six, the Martinsville Seven, and Willie McGee. In January 1948, an elderly white shopkeeper was bludgeoned to death during a holdup. His wife, who survived the attack, identified the assailants as white or light-skinned blacks. Police subsequently canvassed Trenton's black neighborhoods and arrested five men. Another was arrested when he went to the local police station to find out what had happened to his brother-in-law. The arrested men—Collis English, McKinley Forest, Ralph Cooper, Horace Wilson, John McKenzie, and James Thorpe Jr.—eventually signed confessions to the murder, despite not having any physical match to the suspects. In fact, Thorpe—the lone light-skinned man of the group—had only one arm; witnesses had told police that all of the assailants had two arms. However, New Jersey authorities pressed forward with the case, and on August 6, the six were found guilty and sentenced to death. The CRC quickly mobilized on behalf of the convicted men, dubbing the case a "Northern Scottsboro." Patterson led a team of lawyers to appeal the conviction while the CRC organized demonstrations and petitions with the motto: "They Shall Not Die." The congress took the Trenton Six case to the international stage; newspaper accounts in Europe and Asia described the case as political persecution of blacks. Despite the bad publicity that the U.S. race relations received abroad, Truman and Attorney General Clark refused to intervene in the case. However, Du Bois and Robeson did, as well as writer Howard Fast and folksinger Pete Seeger. Under substantial pressure from the CRC and other groups, including the NAACP and ACLU, the New Jersey Supreme Court reversed the conviction in 1949 and ordered a new trial. Subsequent trials led to five of the men serving about three years each; English died before the third trial.

The following year the CRC tried to save the Martinsville Seven. In that case, seven black men in Martinsville, Virginia, were arrested for allegedly raping a mentally retarded white woman. The congress once again mobilized, arguing that an all-white jury would never give a fair trial to the accused. However, the CRC's efforts fell short, and the men were executed in February 1951. At the same time, the congress rallied in the defense of a black trucker named Willie McGee, who was tortured into confessing that he had raped a white woman in Laurel, Mississippi. Despite a spirited defense by the CRC and international appeals from the likes of Robeson, Du Bois and Einstein to save his life, the state of Mississippi executed McGee in May 1951.

By that time, the congress had been smeared with the "Red" label, which as critics argued, severely hampered defense efforts for McGee and the Martinsville Seven. As *Time* wrote shortly after the execution, the McGee case "had become surefire propaganda, good for whipping up racial tension at home and giving U.S. justice a black eye abroad. Stirred up by the Communist leadership, Communist hardliners and manifesto-signers in England, France, China, and Russia demanded Willie be freed."[21] In the end, the combination of black and Red doomed McGee. Patterson, dejected over the back-to-back court losses involving McGee and the Martinsville Seven, sought some injunction from the continued imprisonment and state-sanctioned killings of blacks. "State prisons in the South were really reservations, concentration camps for Black political prisoners,' he wrote in his autobiography. "Millions of Black Americans are aware that when they leave home in the morning they may not return at night if by chance their general demeanor or manner of response to a question rubbed a white person the wrong way. This offense could and often did mean death or imprisonment for a period of years."[22] Within seven months of McGee's execution, Patterson, Robeson, and the CRC would deliver a petition to the United Nations charging the United States with genocide against blacks.

The CRC's increasing involvement with the defense of Communists and other Leftists would invoke backlash by 1948. Mary McLeod Bethune and Benjamin Mays, two of the congress's early supporters, left that year because of fears that they would be connected to the Communist Party.[23] The congress didn't help its image by filing an amicus brief on behalf of the CPUSA leaders arrested under the Smith Act. The congress would also suffer significant damage to its reputation after several Communists it had defended skipped bail. Though Paul and the Doctor took on more active roles with the CRC in 1949, it began to suffer a loss in membership. According to Horne, many of the congress's members across the country fled to the NAACP, which was seen as less radical and not as scrutinized by the FBI. Arrests of CRC leaders, including Hammett and Patterson, also hampered the organization's efforts.

Undaunted by increasing federal pressure, the congress scored several major victories in the early stages of McCarthyism, including the successful effort to convince Michigan Governor G. Mennen Williams not to extradite Haywood Patterson, one of the jailed Scottsboro Boys, who had escaped an Alabama chain gang. Du Bois and Robeson helped draw international attention to the Civil Rights Congress, paralleling its defense of minorities and workers to the anti-colonial movement. Du Bois had become especially convinced that the tactics of the CRC were far better suited to achieve results than those of the NAACP; while the association remained on good terms with Truman, Du Bois developed a deep admiration for an organization that rolled up its sleeves in vigorous defense of the voiceless. Despite its dynamic style, the Civil Rights Congress would soon become a fixture on the government's list of subversive organizations, paving the way for its vilification.

THE POLITICAL SHIFT IN AMERICAN SOCIETY was not lost on Du Bois and Robeson. In June 1947, Congress passed the Taft-Hartley Act, overriding Truman's veto. Truman called the bill "slave-labor," and the provisions of the law stunned labor activists and Leftists alike. The act greatly diminished the power of unions, which had been such a force during the New Deal, by prohibiting "closed shops" and secondary and sympathy strikes. Du Bois and Robeson instantly jumped against the Taft-Hartley Act, alarmed at its implications on free speech and right to assembly. Robeson joined progressive unions in protesting the act, calling its passage one of the first signs that fascism was creeping into American politics. He told a meeting of ILWU workers that "Taft-Hartley means death to the trade union movement" and that the act would "not only break the back of the labor movement but would set back the whole struggle of the American people for generations."[24] The Doctor viewed the act as a victory for the same capitalists who had ravaged Africa and Asia and were determined to destroy the labor movement in the United States. If Americans were about to "let DuPont, the Steel Trust, General Motors or General Electric plan our industry while we are declaiming that we are free in our industrial initiative and in our enterprise, then . . . we are not acting like intelligent members of a democracy."[25] But their attempts to rally widespread support to fight against Taft-Hartley fell short, mainly because of the resurgence of conservatism and the labeling of act's opponents as "Communists." The conservatives' use of the media, including *Time* magazine, to vilify union sympathizers set the precedent for contemporary efforts by neoconservatives to attack the mainstream media and antiwar activists.

The Taft-Hartley was just the first of many setbacks for the Left. Du Bois and Robeson's hopes for international diplomacy governed by cultural relativism vanished with the U.S. government's endorsement of Henry R. Luce's "American Century" concept. Luce, the influential editor of *Time* (which many liberals accused of being an arm of the State Department), advocated a missionary mentality when it came to spreading democracy. He argued that Americans needed to "accept wholeheartedly our duty and our opportunity as the most powerful and vital nation in the world and in consequence to exert upon the world the full impact of our influence, for such purposes as we see fit and by such means as we see fit."[26] Luce's approach would become a blueprint for American unilateralism, followed in later years by John F. Kennedy, Ronald Reagan, and George W. Bush. Robeson believed such a mind-set would destroy America's international reputation, wasting the goodwill it had accumulated during World War II and the Yalta Conference. At a Council on African Affairs rally in April 1947, Paul simplified the domestic battle over American foreign policy as good versus evil. "But now, as I say, today we have a restatement of the Luce spiel—the American century all over again. And we will go very wrong, unless we in America examine very carefully all our ideas, unless we examine very carefully the nature of this fascism that we have just defeated . . . that has, again, begun to march."[27] Du Bois might have agreed with the Luce approach thirty years earlier, when he vehemently argued the case for defending democracy abroad. But as he became increasingly in accord with Robeson's stance and immersed in leftist thought, Du Bois concluded that Socialism and the Soviet Union were the buffers against the imperialistic evangelism of the West. He had forsaken Christianity as a solution to world economic and racial disparity and the disenfranchisement of the American Negro, arguing that "the Christian Church during its two thousand years of existence has been foremost in war and organized murder." Du Bois rejected the anti-Communist rhetoric against Stalin and showed even more repulsion for the government's endorsement of Luceism, which he believed was "in direct contradiction to the ethics of the Christian religion. It is as far as one can conceive from the Christ doctrine of turning the other cheek, or self sacrifice, of peace and goodwill."[28] The Doctor, who had based much of his earlier philosophy on Christian notions of advancement, had in fact become an atheist by the late 1940s.[29]

While conservative backlash made it more difficult for Communists to operate, the party was also partly to blame for its alienation from the mainstream. It had tried to "Americanize" under Earl Browder during the Popular Front and World War II, and in doing so, subordinated most of the Comintern's mandates. Browder rejected many of the tenets of Stalinism, choosing instead to shape the party as a prolabor movement that attached itself to the work of trade unions. During the 1940s, the party became a champion of Roosevelt's domestic policies and advocated a lasting alliance among the Big Three (despite Britain's obstinacy on colonialism). Browderism, as it was later known, also advocated a coexistence between communism and capitalism, a notion that had won support during the New Deal. The CPUSA, reconstituted as the Communist Political Association in 1944, advocated reform, not revolution. But the mainstreaming of the party ultimately failed, leading to Browder's removal as its head in 1945 (and his expulsion a year later). In a letter allegedly ghostwritten by Stalin or his advisors and signed by Jacque Duclos, the head of the French Communist Party, Browderism was indicted for selling out to pro-imperialist and capitalistic interests. The CPUSA (which switched back to its original name after Browder's ouster) reverted to its pre-1930s platform, bringing back sixty-three-year-old William Z. Foster, who led the party until his heart attack in 1932 paved way for Browder's rise to general secretary. Foster was a hard-line Stalinist who was a strong critic of the party's efforts at compromise with the American political establishment. Foster essentially propagated pro-Soviet and anti-American rhetoric, establishing a clear signal that the party had ceased its attempts at peaceful coexistence with the political establishment. The Communists were no longer willing to pledge "its loyalty . . . labor and . . . last drop of blood" for the United States.[30]

Foster wielded considerable influence among older Communists, particularly those who hadn't abandoned the idea that the party's goals should be working toward revolution and endorsing the Soviet doctrine throughout the world. If Truman's actions following the end of the war drove a wedge between U.S.-Soviet relations, than Foster and his return to pre-Browder Party ideology was ready to make a clean cut. Paul endorsed the party's decision to appoint Foster, especially in the wake of American foreign policy shift. As the United States became more conservative, Robeson would become more staunchly aligned with the party, reflecting his desire to counter the political grain. But he was more philosophically aligned with Browder when it came to presenting the party as a legitimate political option for American voters. He also supported Browder's willingness to let black Communists tout their Afro-consciousness while promoting the ideals of the party. Members such as Patterson and Revels Cayton had been allowed to advance a notion of blackness under the Browder rules for the party that would set the stage a new generation of black Communists.

The "new" Communist Party members were a far cry from the party veterans who had made their names by being politically confrontational and openly antagonistic to gradualism. Instead, they worked behind the scenes as labor and civil rights organizers, often subjecting themselves to the threat of serious physical harm and death. James and Esther Jackson, Louis and Dorothy Burnham, Edward Strong, and Jack O'Dell cut their activist teeth as leaders of the Southern Negro Youth Congress (SNYC). James Jackson referred to SNYC members as "eagles in buzzard country." Abbott Simon was a young

New York lawyer who had committed himself to social uplift, and in the words of David Levering Lewis, "knew that good people had to dream lest bad people force most of humankind to live long nightmares."[31] All would become integral members of Du Bois and Robeson's inner circle in later years and would give rise to the New Left. However, the young Communists were not as tied to party dictum when it came to advocacy. SNYC was unaffected by the Soviet-Nazi pact because its mission was helping to organize rural workers in the South, not extol the virtues of Stalin's global vision. To Du Bois and Robeson, they represented the future vanguard of the Left and the civil rights struggle as a whole.

While Robeson remained loyal to the old guard of the party, Du Bois was drawn to the younger members. James Jackson engaged the aging civil rights icon on the merits of the Talented Tenth thesis, as well as finding similarities between Du Boisian racialism and neo-Marxism. Esther Jackson had already made a dramatic impression on the Doctor several years earlier with her ability to organize a diverse number of delegates during the World Youth Congress.[32] The Jacksons, Doxey Wilkerson, Louis and Dorothy Burnham, and Abbott Simon were among the young radicals who proselytized the party to the Doctor, adding to the efforts of Robeson and Shirley Graham, who were convinced that Du Bois would find salvation in a new political philosophy. Graham told Browder that Du Bois "needs the assurance which comes from hope and the realization of united strength. He can be a powerful force. Once thoroughly convinced—he will be a powerful force."[33] Thus, Shirley tied her emotional pursuit of the one man she loved unconditionally to a political objective. Though Graham felt the party could provide "guidance" to Du Bois, she was cognizant that he wouldn't be inclined to listen to the likes of Davis or Yergan, whose personal advice would be seen by the Doctor as a transparent attempt in political indoctrination. The party's efforts to lure Du Bois rested with the younger members, who blended political idealism with a sense of pragmatism during the Cold War. And unlike the older members of the party, who frequently clashed with the NAACP during the renaissance and the Depression, the younger generation believed the association was an inspiring force of change, particularly in the Jim Crow South. Esther Jackson said that as an undergraduate in Oberlin College, she viewed the NAACP "as a militant and progressive organization. They were the ones leading the fight."[34] Such admiration moved Du Bois, who had become convinced that the association would move beyond gradualism with White and Wilkins at the helm. Over the next few years, Jackson and her husband would play a pivotal role in the Doctor's "conversion" to the Communism.

IN 1947 THE FBI DEVOTED more manpower to tracking Robeson, aware that his temporary retirement from the stage would only intensify his left-wing activities.[35] By spring, Paul—who just three years prior had been named "America's number-one Negro"—was beginning to feel the heat from reactionaries. His planned speech in Peoria, Illinois, was canceled after the city council there voted to bar any "avowed propagandist for Un-American ideology" from making a public appearance. The council's decision (apparently influenced by a House

Un-American Activities Committee [HUAC] citation) appalled Robeson, who saw the signs that a witch hunt was looming. At a CAA rally several days later, he called the incident "no clearer example of fascism that I have ever seen— and I have seen a lot of it in many parts of the world—than I saw in Peoria the other night. Nor did I see, have I seen, a clearer example of what Americans must weigh very carefully—the use of certain fascist techniques to confuse the people." Robeson likened the HUAC's influence to "terroristic control" that had rendered Peoria's liberals powerless.[36] As Robeson forecast, the Peoria incident was just the beginning. Encouraged by the FBI and the powerful HUAC, which was expanding its influence on Capitol Hill, conservative groups began taking aim at liberals, accusing them of being Communist sympathizers. The Red threat—no matter how greatly exaggerated—was now America's number one security concern, and conservatives such as Robert A. Taft, J. Edgar Hoover, Patrick McCarran, and a recently elected senator from Wisconsin named Joseph McCarthy began pressuring the Truman administration to weed out domestic Communists and take a hard-line stance on Russia. Truman, aware that public opinion was shifting to the right, acquiesced, replacing Byrnes (whom Truman considered soft on the Soviets) with George C. Marshall, a former soldier. Truman allowed Marshall to essentially reshape American foreign policy, leading to the implementation of the Marshall Plan and the policy of containment authored by George F. Kennan.

The increasingly antagonistic foreign policy of the United States toward Russia did not set well with New Deal liberals, including Wallace, who was secretary of commerce under

Truman. Like Du Bois and Robeson, Wallace guessed the "Iron Curtain" speech was a mere red herring so that conservatives could increase their influence in Washington. The idea that Churchill—whom Wallace believed was playing up the Communist threat in order to uphold imperialism—would dictate American attitudes toward Moscow was especially galling. After all, Wallace argued, hadn't the Soviets help American forces wear down the Nazi juggernaut, and in doing so, help win the war? He and other progressives believed Great Britain's intentional meddling in U.S. affairs was responsible for the rift between Washington and Moscow. Wallace cautioned that "the British imperialistic policy in the Near East alone, combined with Russian retaliation, would lead the United States straight to wax unless we have clearly-defined and realistic policy of our own."[37]

Wallace believed the only way to lasting peace was warm relations with Russia, which was music to the ears of Du Bois, Robeson, and many on the Left. "We have no use for namby-pamby pacifism. But we must realize that modern inventions have now made peace the most exciting thing in the world and we should be willing to pay a just price for peace," he said at a progressive rally in New York. "We must not let our Russian policy be guided or influenced by those inside or outside the United States who want war with Russia."[38] His sentiments were not shared by others in the Truman administration who pressured the president to oust him. Wallace's subsequent resignation in September 1946 became a rallying call for liberals and Left-wingers, and by early 1947, supporters were mentioning him as a candidate for president.

Wallace hardly seemed like the typical politician. He was a

folksy and idealistic liberal from Iowa whose personality and activist zeal invoked comparisons to a real-life Mr. Smith.[39] A former student of George Washington Carver, Wallace (who grew up on a farm) was passionately prolabor, proagriculture, prointegration, and just about pro-anything else that protruded from the jacket of liberalism. His views on race relations were two decades ahead of the 1960s white progressivism that helped changed the landscape of American society. Wallace publicly backed Robeson's antilynching crusade, calling civil rights for African Americans a foundation to world peace. "Hatred breeds hatred," Wallace warned. "The doctrine of racial superiority produces a desire to get even on the part of its victims. If we are to work for peace in the rest of the world, we here in the United States must eliminate racism. . . . Merit alone must be the measure of man."[40] And unlike Truman and Eleanor Roosevelt, who did not believe in social equality, Wallace was committed to the notion of uplifting the social status of blacks.

Du Bois and Robeson joined in an increasingly loud chorus of Leftists and disaffected liberals calling for Wallace to run as a third-party candidate in the 1948 election. Both the Doctor and Paul believed that if Wallace ran, he would undoubtedly win the majority of the black vote, since African Americans would remember him as a coarchitect of the New Deal. By fall of 1947, Wallace, who had taken the editorship of the *New Republic*, attracted an eclectic following of social moderates, progressive internationalists, leftists, and trade unionists, as well as the scrutiny of the FBI and the hardliners in the Truman cabinet. In December, Wallace—backed by a coalition of labor groups, left-wing civil rights organizations, and several black churches—announced his intent to challenge Truman. The newly formed Progressive Party's primary tenets were peace with Russia and an ambitious civil rights agenda that included a federal lynching ban and an end to Jim Crow. Deciding not to field a candidate, the CPUSA officially endorsed Wallace—a move that likely doomed the Progressive Party even before the campaign got into gear. The American Labor Party of New York also backed the Wallace ticket.

The formation of the Progressive Party represented the splintering of the Democratic Party. Liberal Democrats such as Powell initially backed Wallace, while Southern Democrats— led by Senator Strom Thurmond of South Carolina—broke away from the party to form the Dixiecrat ticket. Thurmond was nominated as the Dixiecrats' presidential candidate, running on a policy of states rights and segregation. With the Democratic Party in crisis, many early political prognostications predicted the Republicans would win with a ticket with New York Governor Thomas Dewey. Progressives, however, were equally optimistic that the Wallace campaign would galvanize New Deal liberals and the Left against the "forces of reaction." Paul enthusiastically jumped behind Wallace, traveling throughout the country stumping for his friend. The FBI, not surprisingly, followed Robeson everywhere, including his trip to Honolulu to speak on behalf of union workers there. Paul painted Truman as a closet conservative and Red-baiter, accusing him of cowing to pressure to get rid of Wallace. But in fairness to Truman, it should be noted that Robeson never wanted him to replace Wallace as FDR's vice president in 1944. Claiming that Wallace had become a victim of his own progressivism, Robeson called him a bulwark against the rising tide of reaction in the United States.

> Wallace is the man who might be [in the White House] had he not in 1944 said "Jim Crow must go," had he not fought so hard for the rights of labor. He is the one public leader who has come out at once to say that the hiring hall must remain and that these men must be fought to the teeth: the people who are trying to break our backs. And so I trust that you will realize the depth of that struggle, that you will not separate them, that they cannot be separated, that they go hand in hand, that the one way that this can be beaten is to give your energy, to give your time, to give your money, to see that we can put representatives in Congress and a President in the White House and a Vice-President who will represent our interests.[41]

Du Bois concurred, lending his support to Wallace. In fact, the Progressive Party campaign marked a zenith in Du Bois's political activism. Long content to observe and record the changing world around him without jumping into the fray, the Doctor became more of a hands-on advocate and political activist in the months leading up to the election. He made regular public appearances on behalf of Wallace, extolling the candidate's civil rights commitment and desire for peace with the Soviet Union. Like many leftists, Du Bois believed Wallace was the true heir to the FDR legacy and needed black America's full support to get into the White House. He agreed with Robeson's assessment that Truman was nothing more than a Dixiecrat feigning liberalism on civil rights.

The Wallace candidacy—and Du Bois's backing of it—did not set well with the NAACP, which knew the Progressive Party would hinder its efforts to promote the president's civil rights agenda. The NAACP, thanks to the support of Eleanor Roosevelt, had become a fixture in the White House; moreover, the association was turning into a partisan organization, pledging to back Truman in exchange for substantive efforts at advancing black rights. But Truman reciprocated the NAACP's loyalty, aware that promoting a measured civil rights agenda would keep blacks from defecting en masse to the Progressive Party. Perhaps his most significant action to promote his relations with Africans Americans was appearing at the NAACP Convention in 1947; by doing so, he became the first president to address the association, starting a tradition among presidents and presidential hopefuls every four years since. Wilkins described the momentous Truman speech in his autobiography.

Truman was no FDR. He wasn't an aristocrat; he wasn't slick; he couldn't wrap Congress around his finger or get people to love him. But he was direct where Roosevelt had been slippery, open where Roosevelt had always kept his flanks protected. He spoke with a Midwestern twang, a plain-spoken, no-frills delivery. He said that it was his deep conviction that the country had reached a turning point in its long history of efforts to guarantee freedom and equality to all citizens. "Recent events in the United States and abroad have made us realize that it is more important today than ever before to ensure that all Americans enjoy these rights," he observed. Then he paused, and said, "When I say all Americans, I mean *all* Americans." . . . There it was—an unequivocal pledge. For the first time, the president was putting himself and the government where they should have been all along: at the head of the parade, not on the sidelines.[42]

Truman also rewarded black patronage by giving key supporters roles in his administration. In 1946 Truman established a civil rights committee, headed by White, Bunche, and Mary Church Terrell, to look into solutions for advancing black rights. A year later, the committee issued its radical civil rights manifesto, aptly titled, *To Secure These Rights*. The report took on the administration for leading the call to democracy overseas but ignoring the pleas of African Americans for safeguards against lynching, segregation, job discrimination, and unequal access to housing. Though the committee was hardly militant, its overall mission was radical given the reactionary political climate. Using *Rights* as a background, Truman issued an historic civil rights address on February 2, 1948, pushing for a broad legislation that included federal protections against lynching, strengthening the FEPC, naturalization for immigrants, and some restitution for Japanese-Americans who had been interned during the war. Perhaps his most radical suggestion was the creation of a civil rights division in the Justice Department, which had long been accused of one-sided investigations in race-related crimes (some blacks joked that FBI investigations of lynchings and race riots would undoubtedly end up indicting the victims). In his most vehement speech for civil rights since taking office, Truman said the government had "a clear duty to see that constitutional guarantees of individual liberties and of equal protection under the laws are not denied or abridged any-where in our Union.[43] Later that year, Truman—using the Cold War as justification to push for civil rights—signed an Executive Order guaranteeing minorities equal rights in the civil service and establishing the Federal Employment Board.

Though Truman hardly placated the Left (Robeson and Du Bois dismissed the civil rights legislation as mere token ges-tures with no real power), his actions transformed him into a progressive chief executive in the eyes of many African Amer-icans. The civil rights measures were a monumental victory for the NAACP, which had seen Robeson's ACEL, SNYC, the Civil Rights Congress, and the NNC as threats to its hege-mony. The lynching measure was especially a coup de grâce for White, who had been engaged in a power struggle with Du Bois over the direction of the NAACP. Despite three decades of service to the association and masterfully positioning it as a militant force in the black community and a trusted friend of the White House, Walter's biggest challenge was escaping the giant shadow cast by the Doctor's return. In securing passage of Truman's executive orders and his endorsement of *Rights*, White emerged, in the eyes of many blacks, as a leader on equal footing with the venerable Du Bois. The election results several months later would only serve as validation for White and the NAACP's agenda.

Despite Du Bois and Robeson's vigorous campaigning on behalf of Wallace, the Progressive candidate couldn't offset Truman's civil rights measures. It became clear to many African Americans that the president had made enough of a commitment to civil rights—despite enormous pressure from conservatives—to warrant reelection. The Wallace campaign also suffered a mortal blow in July 1948, when CPUSA leaders were arrested under the Smith Act. The Communist Party had backed the Progressive Party, making Wallace guilty by association. During the stretch run of the campaign, Wallace tried to promote his platform while fending off constant attacks by anti-Communists.

Though Robeson and Du Bois led the calls among Wallace supporters to paint the Smith Act arrests as politically motivated, their efforts were hampered by the fact that very few non-Communists publicly denounced the arrests. The NAACP, hoping to shake rumors that it had been infiltrated by Communists, added insult to injury by praising steps to remove the Communists through legal measures. White even boasted of the NAACP's own hard-line stance against communism, noting that the "national Board of Directors and staff have been empowered and directed to revoke the charter of any of the organization's thirteen hundred branches should any such local unit come under the control or influence of the Communists."[44] The Communist Party's involvement in the campaign also damaged the reputation of the unions that supported the Progressive Party. By 1950, most unions would ban Communists from membership, aware that any semblance of Communist Party influence would harm the labor movement. As the election neared, the Progressive Party had radicalized itself from contention. The specter of Communist involvement, coupled with the lack of support from moderates, doomed Wallace in November. By contrast, Truman's civil rights pledge had earned him the endorsements of most prominent African American leaders, including Powell, who had earlier backed Wallace.[45]

The black vote helped Truman defeat Dewey, despite predictions of the latter's landslide victory. In a rare win for centrists during the Cold War, Truman captured twenty-eight states, compared to sixteen by Dewey and four by Thurmond. Wallace barely made a dent in the election, capturing only 1.1 million votes and no states. The diehards who stayed with Wallace were progressive labor supporters and Leftists, hardly a ringing endorsement of the Progressive Party's ability to attract a diverse following. The party would remain in the fringes of U.S. politics, unsuccessfully running Vincent Hallinan and black journalist Charlotta Bass in 1952. But Wallace himself would bow out of the Left, recanting his support for the Soviet Union in the 1952 book *Why I Was Wrong*. In effect, the Progressive Party became another casualty of the Cold War, its platform out of tune with the reality of a society that had become fearful and intolerant of radicalism.

THE OVERWHELMING DEFEAT of the Progressive Party in 1948 proved to Du Bois and Robeson that "the forces of reaction" had bullied and scared most Americans into ideological conformity. This revelation only emboldened them to do more. Both men believed that they could galvanize liberals and the Left for the important 1950 congressional elections, and so doing, reverse the trend of conservatism on Capitol Hill. Though Wallace's defeat was crushing to Paul, he didn't lose hope that voters would eventually see through the deliberate "Red-baiting." Paul believed the election was a wake-up call to liberals and would serve as a rallying cry against reactionaries. "The workers' job is now depending upon the question of peace or war, so the political campaign can now be conducted on the terms of Wallace," he said. "And let me say here that it is easy to show that the speeches of Wallace have already saved the peace by disorganizing the plans of reaction. Millions who were certainly with us, but who were fooled by Truman, will come back. They put Wallace on the ballot and they see now that he was right."[46] Despite his overly optimistic assessment, Robeson didn't fool himself into believing that Wallace's paltry showing at the polls represented any moral victories. He knew that in a high-stakes political climate, the majority of blacks had wagered that siding with Truman offered more than abandoning the Democratic Party for a third-party candidate. Most black leaders seemed willing to go along with Truman, knowing that any signs of going against the grain would shut them out of political influence and potentially mark them as targets of government scrutiny.

The NAACP, Urban League, and the prominent black scholars who held sway in numerous colleges around the country had chosen the less damning path. Du Bois believed their failure to back Wallace and the Progressive Party was an affront to old-fashioned liberalism. Why were black leaders afraid to associate with Communists and other Leftists? It was a question that weighed heavily on Du Bois. "Every Liberal is bound to be a fellow-traveler with the Communists in a large number of things for which Communism and Socialism stand," the Doctor wrote. "And too, there is no question about the fact that however large a section of our present capitalistic organization we retain, if we are going to succeed in reforming this system in industry, in accordance with the best thought of mankind, we have got to subordinate the profit motive to the motive of the social welfare of the mass of men." He called it the duty of the "sane liberal" to promote values of peace and global enfranchisement, issues he felt the majority of black leaders such as Bunche, White, Wilkins, Powell, and Lester Granger (head of the Urban League) conveniently ignored during the election.[47]

Du Bois and Robeson might have missed the point altogether on why the NAACP and most African Americans had gone with the Democrats. While the Progressive Party and the Communist Party boasted of utopian ideals for blacks, laborers, and other disenfranchised people, they offered little in the way of actual progress. Many blacks agreed with Richard Wright's sentiment that being black was already a handicap, and that getting labeled as a leftist or Communist or Progressive was even more debilitating to a race that was still being fought everyday to prove citizenship.

By making their choice to go along with the Democrats and support the government's anticommunist stance, the vanguard of black leadership had essentially cut ties to the Left, including Du Bois and Robeson. The Doctor's acrimonious second run with the NAACP ended on the last day of 1948, divorcing him from the mainstream civil rights struggle he had helped create a half-century earlier. Robeson, already distanced from most African American leaders, remained unapologetic and stubborn on his stance that full enfranchisement required going beyond conventional liberalism. "You need only look at the actual conditions of the ten million Negroes in the south," he said. "They are still living near the starvation limit and without civic rights. There is a tremendous resistance and deep feelings among these people."

Robeson believed the failure of black leadership in acting on the frustrations of Negroes was indicative of the disconnect between the community and the organizations and officials that claimed to represent them. In a jab at his friend turned nemesis, Paul claimed "the Negro population is much more progressive than some of their leaders like (Walter) White."[48] But in reality, most African Americans were willing to accept any progress; White's successful guidance of the Truman civil rights agenda earned him the right to help dictate the politics of black America. He, Powell, William Dawson, Terrell, Granger, Bunche, and William T. Hastie were insiders whose clout within the halls of government went far beyond the scope of influence any outside agitators—namely those in the black Left—had. Du Bois and Robeson were now part of that outside, pushed to the fringes of civil rights advocacy and increasingly shut out of the dialogue in progressing the rights of African Americans. Within a year of the 1948 election, they would find that speaking out against the government and mainstream black leadership carried a heavy price.

8

THE "WITCH HUNT" AND THE NAACP'S BETRAYAL

We have built in the NAACP a magnificent organization of
several hundred persons, but it is not yet a democratic
organization, and in our hearts many of us do not believe
it can be.

—W. E. B. Du Bois memo to NAACP (1946)

THE ANNOUNCEMENT AT THE 1944 NAACP CONVENTION in Chicago
was as shocking as it was exhilarating for the several hundred
delegates gathered from around the country. The most venerable name in the civil rights struggle was returning to the
association he had helped sculpt into the dominant advocate
for black America. In an ode to the improbable, Du Bois had
signed on for another go-around with the NAACP, ten years

after what appeared to be a permanent split from the association. The Doctor's unceremonious departure from academia necessitated his return, and the NAACP leadership was happy to accommodate him in order to use his name and larger-than-life status once again. Shirley Graham told her seventy-six-year-old lover that the "fact you were returning to the Association . . . gives me a better opinion of average human beings! I am really so very happy you are coming to New York. I believe you will find much of genuine enjoyment."[1] But Graham's optimism and the Du Bois–NAACP honeymoon would not last. Over the next four years, Du Bois's growing immersion into the Left and his desire to exert more influence over the association would lock him in a bitter power struggle with Walter White and Roy Wilkins.

Robeson's rift with the NAACP began the same evening he received its highest honor, and would only widen during the nascence of the Cold War. Paul was frustrated by the association's unwillingness to extend itself into a global agenda anchored by militant anticolonialism and advocacy for better U.S.-Soviet relations. He saw more opportunities in promoting his views through the Civil Rights Congress, the Council on African Affairs, and other left-wing organizations that defied ideological conformity. Robeson and Du Bois made their decision to stay with the Left, despite a political climate that was incubating reactionaries and hawkish anti-Communists.

The same forces that kept Paul and the Doctor ensconced in radicalism were pushing the NAACP to the right. Faced with increased scrutiny of its activities and accusations that it harbored Communists, the association adopted a hard-line stance against the Left. White and Wilkins believed that

Communists threatened to overtake the NAACP and destroy the progress achieved under the association's stewardship of the civil rights struggle. White asserted that "had the Communists captured the NAACP—the largest, most militant, and most successful of America's civil-rights organizations—the perilous quarter of a century following the stock market crash of 1929 would have been far more strife-ridden. Democracy would be far less secure than it is."[2] As the association became more aligned with the Truman administration, it acquiesced to the government's gradualism on civil rights and tacit endorsement of colonialism. Its anti-Communism would lead to a relationship of convenience with the FBI, which had honed in on Du Bois and Robeson as the most prominent voices of the Left. The NAACP's collusion would enable the government to act against both men.[3]

DU BOIS'S REMARRIAGE to the NAACP wasn't prompted by the willingness of either side to make up. In fact, it would have never come to pass had the Doctor and White not found themselves in the precarious position of needing each other. Du Boisian thought—now more closely aligned with that of Robeson and Ben Davis Jr.—and the association's philosophy were heading in seemingly opposite directions. Du Bois had become an uncompromising race militant, convinced that he was nearing an equilibrium of black nationalism and Marxism. While the Doctor had grown more radical, the NAACP doggedly held to its doctrine of pragmatic protest. During the war, the association redoubled its efforts at better access and opportunities for African Americans in the public sector. Having Eleanor Roosevelt as an ally didn't hurt. White guided the NAACP on a carefully mapped agenda of legislative lobbying and mass mobilization in major cities. The New York headquarters tightly controlled the association's branches, made up mostly of well-to-do business and church leaders. If Du Bois had resigned ten years earlier because of the NAACP's ideological rigidity, bureaucracy, and autocratic governance (which he blamed on White), he found little improvement in the current state of affairs of the organization. White had only strengthened his hold on power, squeezing out the last open resistance with the forced departure of William Pickens in 1942. Joel Spingarn died in 1939, and Mary White Ovington had reduced her role with the association in order to focus on her writing. Wilkins and Gloster Current were White's right-hand men on the executive staff; ironically, White was the most liberal of all three. Wilkins and Current both had strong disdain for Communists, and in later years, would lead the effort to ban any contact with the Left on a national or local level.[4]

So why did Du Bois return? Simply put, he had little choice. The Doctor's increasing clashes with Atlanta University (AU) President Rufus Clement made him a marked man. When Clement took over AU in 1938, the university's board had already committed to re-upping Du Bois for another five years, with the intent of extending the Doctor's term for as long as he was willing and able. AU's wink-and-nod approach with the Doctor's tenure seemed an affirmation to Du Bois that he was welcome to stay there as long as he wanted. Leaving would be on *his* terms. But Du Bois ran afoul of Clement, who grew annoyed by the Doctor using his faculty position as a bully pulpit for his own radical research. By 1943, Clement was determined to rid himself of Du Bois, whose antagonism toward the administration was common knowledge on campus. Conversely, Du Bois viewed Clement as an incompetent who did not grasp the changing dynamics of the United States and the world. Atlanta, Du Bois believed, was primed to become a Mecca of racial study and progress. He lobbied hard for an AU-sponsored consortium of land-grant colleges to assess the economic impact of the war on the Negro. Though the Doctor's ambitious plan had received a round of yeas from leaders of other southern black institutions, Clement had other ideas. In late 1943, he convinced the board to let Du Bois's contract expire, effectively ending the Doctor's tenure.

The humiliation of "retirement" found Du Bois in the unlikely position of looking for work. He was a household name in black and white households, and even as a septuagenarian, held as much sway with teenagers as he did with the children of slaves. Yet the icon of black America, the man who had helped mold several generations of black intellectuals, artists, and activists, was unemployed. His militant philosophies on race and class, along with his age, made him unattractive to many colleges. Though several offers to teach trickled in, the Doctor seemed to want more than the security blanket of academia. At seventy-five, he saw himself as more of an activist than an academic, a sentiment motivated by his restlessness and the private realization that he was in the twilight of his career.[5]

Du Bois's employment predicament came at the same time that the NAACP found itself on the outside of the anticolonial struggle. The Council of African Affairs, led by Robeson and the shrewd Yergan, had positioned itself as *the* voice for colonized peoples of the world. Its effectiveness drew young idealists eager to facilitate change that would benefit more than just African Americans. Eager to become a player in the anticolonial movement, the association voted to send White to the Peace Conference in 1944. Arthur Spingarn and Louis T. Wright lobbied the NAACP board to hire Du Bois as a special consultant, seeing that his expertise would undoubtedly aid White while providing employment to an old friend in need of face-saving. White was less than thrilled, but in deciding what was best for the association, went along with the arrangement. In May, he offered Du Bois the task to preparing "material to be presented on behalf of the American Negro and of the colored peoples of the world to the Peace Conference or to Peace Conferences, at compensation and under conditions which are mutually agreeable."[6] Spingarn followed up with his own note, asking his old civil rights comrade to "give this proposal your most serious consideration; not only the future of the colored people of the world, but the peace of the world, is at stake and there is no one in America who is as qualified as you to do it. I earnestly hope that you will make a favorable decision."[7]

Du Bois wasn't ready to accept the offer. The position held no guarantees, and for a man whose pride was unwavering, a role with no formal title bordered on condescending. In a letter to Spingarn and White, Du Bois demanded directorship of a bureau or department, noting that he needed "an office for myself and for a secretary; salaries for both, and an expense account for postage, books and periodicals; and for some travel." Du Bois assured the men that his request for an official role wouldn't undermine the executive staff. "I should not want in any way to have part in the policymaking activities of the NAACP, the editing of the Crisis or any of the regular literature," he wrote. But the Doctor was disingenuous in this regard. He knew the NAACP's malleable international agenda was the perfect opportunity to exert his influence on policy. Du Bois, whose move to the Left had been ongoing since his 1934 exit from the association, was also keenly aware that his presence might offset some of White's control. After the NAACP board relented and offered him a formal title, the new director of special research set to work on organizing another Pan-African Congress and implementing *his* vision for the association.

In rejoining the NAACP, Du Bois soon fell victim to his vanity and idealism, the same factors that were partly responsible for ending the first relationship. He believed Spingarn and Wright's support was all he needed to accelerate the militancy of the association, and in doing so, supplant the outdated White vision with a more aggressive platform. However, he greatly underestimated the importance of White as a liaison between the NAACP and the Roosevelt administration. After all, White was a New Deal liberal whose pragmatism stopped him from going any closer to the Left. Du Bois also failed to give White proper due for the NAACP's resurgence. The association's membership had grown to nearly half a million by 1944, and would reach close to six hundred thousand by the late 1940s.[8] Though the NAACP was still run by the same "black-tie" Negroes who had driven Du Bois out, its local branches had great success in recruiting blue-collar workers and forming valuable alliances with trade unions. The NAACP had come to realize that its survival depended on mass membership, not just the select few who had deep pockets. The association's wartime registration drive success-fully added new members while reaching out to working-class blacks who might otherwise have joined more leftist groups. Instead of developing a better understanding of why the NAACP had succeeded in attracting more proletarians (the association's strong connection with the black church, the anti-Communist sentiment among poor blacks in the South), the Doctor figured the increased membership was a mandate for the association to adopt a more radical approach to civil rights. He also thought his reappointment would allow him opportunities to travel abroad on official business. However, the budget-minded White quickly admonished Du Bois for his outside travel, setting the stage for a renewed confronta-tion over the direction of the association.[9]

The Du Bois–White acrimony manifested itself in the poli-tics of the association. White viewed the Doctor's refusal to be a company man as a direct threat to his authority, as well as an act of biting the NAACP's generous hand. After all, the association had rescued Du Bois from purgatory; in White's eyes, the department director was showing his thanks by rou-tinely overstepping his bounds. He threatened to dismiss Du Bois for failing to go along with association guidelines, expressing dismay that the Doctor—in his official role as the director of special research—involved himself in other left-wing organizations. The Doctor's gushing report about the Southern Negro Youth Congress, and his subsequent involve-ment with the group, alarmed White and Wilkins, given the rapidly changing world dynamics. Equally unnerving was Du Bois's decision to join the Council on African Affairs, which had been tied to the Communist Party. Du Bois's best efforts to bridge the gap between the NAACP and the Left were falling short. The NAACP leadership, perhaps privy to what was coming, maintained a safe distance—and in some cases, broke away—from Leftist groups and figures. If the Robeson Spingarn Medal speech had left a sour taste in the mouths of White and Wilkins, the Doctor's continued affiliation with and support of known left-wing organizations was cause for legitimate concern. How could the association, which had managed to hold court with the Truman administration, publicly separate itself from its most beloved member?

White's dilemma was only compounded by Du Bois's insubordination. In the fall of 1946, Du Bois sought to gain an edge in the battle of wills by going on a public offensive against White. Having lambasted the executive secretary for questioning his involvement with Robeson's antilynching crusade, Du Bois prepared a long memorandum to the NAACP executive board on implementing a long-term strategy. The Doctor's "report" was, in actuality, a manifesto and a transparent attack on White's autocratic leadership style. In true Du Boisian form, the special report on the state of the association was equal parts academic and bully pulpit. The Doctor indicted the NAACP for its failure to keep with dramatically changing times, accusing the forty-six-year-old organization of sticking with an archaic formula for racial progress. Du Bois complained that the association had been "curiously reticent on the matter of education." Claiming the association's insistence on integration was hurting young blacks, Du Bois wrote, "The NAACP should start a crusade for Negro education, and while not for a moment relaxing their fight on race segregation in schools, insist that segregation or no segregation, American Negro youth must be educated." He went on to state the need for economic literacy in the black community, recommending "study of economic organization by lectures and forums and lead the masses of Negroes and their children to clear comprehension of the problems of industry; we must not be diverted by witch-hunting for Communists, or by fear of the wealthy, or by the temptation ourselves to exploit labor, white and black, through business, gambling, or by industrial fascism."[10] Du Bois saved most of his venom for the issues of executive leadership and the NAACP's long-standing adherence to nonpartisanship. In a not-so-masked critique of White's leadership, Du Bois assailed the "concentration of power and authority in the hands of a small group which issues directives to the mass of members who are expected to be glad to obey. . . . Always the leader wants to direct and command; but the difficulty is that he does not know enough; he cannot be experienced enough; he cannot possibly find time enough to master the details of a large group widely distributed." He said the NAACP's fight for democracy was hypocritical given its own totalitarianism. In what was the most damning assessment of the NAACP's current state, Du Bois wrote:

> [The NAACP] has regarded the demand of regions and branches for increased autonomy as revolt against the New York headquarters while in truth it has been a more or less crude attempt to teach New York the things New York must know in order to cooperate with Texas or California or New Jersey in

the Advancement of Colored People. The NAACP should set out to democratize the organization; to hand down and distribute authority to regions and branches and not concentrate authority in one office or one officer; and then to assure progress by searching out intelligent, unselfish, resourceful local leaders of high character and honest, instead of being content with the prominent and rich who are too often willing to let well-enough alone.

He finished his memo with a call to political action, challenging the association to stop hiding behind the shield of neutrality. Noting that "party government in this nation has definitely and disastrously broken down," the Doctor urged the association to "ignore all party labels and vote for candidates solely on their records and categorical promises." Such issue-based support of candidates would not make party labels an incentive or hindrance, Du Bois noted. "The NAACP should lead in such political reform, all the more because no other American group has yet had the foresight or courage to advocate it."[11]

Response to the Du Bois memo went as expected. Board members, though sympathetic to what the Doctor had to say, summarily dismissed the report's merits as legitimate fodder for policy. But the wily research director had another trick up his sleeve. Shortly after sending the memo to the NAACP board, the Doctor "leaked" a copy to George Streator, who was now working for the *New York Times*, and George Schuyler. White blew his top. In a letter admonishing Du Bois and dropping not-so-subtle hints about the Doctor's employment with the association, the executive secretary claimed public dissemination of the memo would have proved disastrous. "Fortunately," White added, "Mr. Wilkins was able to convince Mr. Streator that this was strictly an inter-office memorandum and that the conference was one of staff members solely to discuss ways and means of improving our machinery and that it was not a matter which should have gone outside of the office."[12]

Du Bois was unapologetic. He refused to acquiesce to the board's wishes that he take a lesser role and simply coast until retirement. Despite Spingarn and Wright's attempts at mollifying the angry giant, Du Bois only grew more aloof of the association. He refused to hold back his criticism of the NAACP, especially to what he considered a milquetoast approach to fighting colonialism and capitalist exploitation. In a letter to White, the Doctor questioned whether the association was committed to taking the lead in the struggle against colonialism.

> The NAACP has taken no stand nor laid down any program with regard to Africa. I have repeatedly urged this since my return from the Pan-African Congress. Individually I have done what I could but I have neither the help, funds, nor authority to accomplish much. If we are to enter into conference with regard to Trusteeships or other problems we should be prepared with a policy or clear statement or our position. As an organization we have nothing of the sort. I asked two years ago to have authority to collect and publish the various demands of Africans for freedom and autonomy. Permission

was never given me. Such a series of documents now would be of invaluable use before the Assembly of the United Nations.[13]

Du Bois correctly assumed that the NAACP was backing away from its original intent of becoming an international mouthpiece for suffrage. Du Boisian internationalism was too radical of a philosophy for the association to adopt, and White had concluded that the "Iron Curtain" speech would make it difficult for the NAACP to go along with anything that seemed even close to a tacit endorsement of Soviet foreign policy. The association, in effect, abandoned its international advocacy role, ceding such a task (and the scrutiny that came with it) to the CAA. White also trusted that having Bunche in a diplomatic position gave a more sympathetic ear to the freedom struggles of colored people outside the United States. Bunche's internationalism was more in tune with the NAACP's global outlook, making him a reliable ally when it came to ascertaining the role of black America in the struggle of colonized people.

Undaunted by the increasing resistance to his policy suggestions, Du Bois began his most radical indictment of colonialism and racism. *An Appeal to the World: A Statement on the Denial of Human Rights to Minorities in the Case of Citizens of Negro Descent in the United States of America and an Appeal to United Nations for Redress* was intended to call international attention to white mistreatment of blacks and other colored citizens in the United States. The report's aim was to incorporate themes that the NAACP had built its reputation on: antilynching and forced segregation. At around the same time, Du Bois, guided by the influence of Robeson, stepped up his immersion into the Left. He had frequent correspondence with pro-Soviet groups, offering articles for *Soviet Russia Today* and signing up in support of the National Council of American-Soviet Friendship, one of the most scrutinized left-wing organizations during the Cold War. A grateful Howard Melish (the chairman of the organization) wrote Du Bois that his support was invaluable to the "activities which are being planned to reaffirm American-Soviet friendship—the keystone to maintaining the peace of the world."[14] Du Bois and Robeson's endorsement of the Left and of Soviet policy did not diminish their popularity in black America, to the dismay of the NAACP. Du Bois's affiliation with the NAACP made it that much more difficult for White to keep the association out of harm's way. The FBI was already making a list of potentially "subversive" groups, and the NAACP leadership had no desire to join the CPUSA, the Civil Rights Congress, Council on African Affairs, National Negro Congress, and the numerous other left-wing groups whose actions were being closely watched. Du Bois hoped *Appeal* would give the NAACP some backbone in addressing the longstanding grievances of black America. White backed *Appeal*, despite its subtle proclamations of support for the Soviet Union. The report stated that "it is not Russia that threatens the United States but Mississippi, not Stalin and Molotov but Bilbo and Rankin."[15] The NAACP even printed pamphlets of the petition to circulate to the U.S. media, but did not formally endorse it to the United Nations.

By late 1947 Du Bois was aware that *Appeal* would never be sponsored by the NAACP, a casualty of Cold War politics and the association's decision to formally distance itself from its most radical member. Though several other countries offered to support the document before the United Nations, the U.S. delegation—led by Du Bois's old friend Eleanor Roosevelt—successfully scuttled those attempts. The following year, Du Bois's efforts to press for the petition to be heard were met with private reproach from Mrs. Roosevelt. The world body would never hear the *Appeal*.[16]

After tolerating Du Bois's involvement with the Wallace campaign (despite the association's support for Truman) and his public speeches openly going against association policy, the leadership of the NAACP had privately concluded that Du Bois needed to go by the end of 1948. Even his former supporters, including Channing Tobias and Wright, were beginning to grow weary of the Doctor's impassioned speeches and incisive editorials praising the Soviet Union and denouncing the United States. Du Bois refused to change his position when it came to segregation, maintaining the same racialist view that led to his departure in 1934. Du Bois asserted that when "Negroes are suffering disabilities because of segregation, I think that a deliberately segregated economy would eventually be the best way toward attacking economic injustice." Though he felt segregation was "an evil," he was convinced it was a lesser evil than "poverty, ignorance, and disease. While segregation increases these evils in most cases, nevertheless, it would not be sensible to wait for doing away with segregation before attacking these fundamental evils themselves, even if in that attack you were working within segregated limits."[17] The Du Boisian justification of voluntary segregation was as offensive to White and Wilkins as it had been fourteen years earlier. As Wilkins would note years later, "Racial separation is the basic requirement for control. . . . Racial segregation, preached and urged by a . . . minority of Negro Americans, can be the means of plunging their race back behind the barbed wire of restriction, inferiority, persecution, and death to both the spirit and the body."[18]

By mid-1948, most of the association's board members felt the Du Bois redux was a failed experiment. The final straw came in September, when the association board voted to send White—alone—to the UN General Assembly in Paris. The Doctor protested, charging that White's participation as a U.S. consultant "ties us in with the reactionary, war-mongering colonial imperialism of the current administration."[19] To underscore his dissatisfaction, Du Bois provided a copy of his scathing memo to Streator, who published it in the *New York Times*. The Doctor's divulgence would be his last action as an officer of the NAACP. In a letter to branch officers, Wilkins relayed the board's motion to terminate Du Bois's employment on September 13. The board, having run out of patience with Du Bois's belligerence, agreed that "it will not be in the best interest of the association to continue the employment of Dr. Du Bois." Arthur Spingarn summed up the sentiments of the board by noting, "The Board could not retain Dr. Du Bois and still remain the administrative authority of the Association."[20] Spingarn's comments reflected the collective exasperation of board members, who felt they could no longer coddle Du Bois, no matter how important he had been to them in the past.

Reaction to the association's decision was swift, and, as expected, overwhelmingly negative. Leftists seized the opportunity to chide the NAACP for what they viewed as succumbing to pressure from conservatives and Cold War witch-hunters. "When a man like Du Bois is dismissed because of his policies and principles," James Malley of the American Labor Party wrote, "this, in these times, is cause for worldwide apprehension." Malley complained to Wright that the Du Bois dismissal "represents a ruthless attempt to silence the protesting voice of large sections of the outstanding Negro organization in America, against the wanton exploitation of the colored peoples of the world by imperialist, reactionary Truman administration and its advisers, leaders and allies in the Republican Party."[21] Hunton, on behalf of the CAA, beseeched Spingarn and the board to reconsider the decision to let go of Du Bois. "Is the NAACP to be wedded, even though by indirect means, to the imperialist bi-partisan foreign policy of our government?" Hunton wrote, adding that the association "cannot continue to serve the interests of the Negro people if it tails along with the . . . Truman administration."[22] An unbending White accused leftists of using Du Bois and his dismissal for their benefit. His overall assessment of the situation, however, seemed to reflect a genuine concern that African Americans were damned if they did, damned if they didn't when it came to taking a stand on the Cold War. "The U.S. and Russia are both playing power politics, and we Negroes are caught in the middle," he said.[23]

Du Bois knew he had strayed far to the left of the association's politics, but remained adamant that *his* views were right. "It was quite impossible to get on with Walter White and other reactionary elements of the NAACP," he told Padmore. "The NAACP is supported by working people and yet is gradually developing into a bourgeois set-up, afraid to do anything that is not respectable. I advocated the election of Henry Wallace which they resented; and in addition to that I protested against White's going to the meeting of the United Nations in Paris without any preparations or real authority from the Board."[24] He had made his choice to support the Soviet Union, defend the maligned Communists in the United States, and attach himself to radical causes that promised immediate liberation for colonized and exploited people. In four years replete with conflict, Du Bois only confirmed his long-held suspicions that the NAACP's activism would only go so far.

His dismissal had at least one silver lining. He was no longer bound to the "limitations of expression" that the NAACP had imposed, intensifying his decade-long courtship with the Left. In leaving an association that could not support his worldview, Du Bois found comfort in the company of Robeson, Doxey Wilkerson, Esther and James Jackson, Louis Burnham, Alphaeus Hunton, Herbert Aptheker, and Abbott Simon. Robeson welcomed the Doctor to a new office in the CAA headquarters in January 1949, initiating Du Bois's "official" relationship with the Left. The eighty-year-old CAA vice president was as fiery as ever, determined to join Robeson in the struggle for global freedom. Both men were among the few who stood in the tunnel as the speeding train of anticommunism and conservative politics sped toward them. White, Wilkins, and the NAACP were not willing to stand on that same track, aware that any future involvement with the Doctor and Paul was tantamount to political suicide. In effect, Du Bois and the NAACP had, once and for all, chosen sides for the looming battle that would turn friends and allies into enemies.

In his scathing critique of the NAACP and its markedly conservative attitude toward the Left, Du Bois seemed to forget his own anti-Communist sentiments during the 1930s. Like White and Wilkins, the Doctor had assumed that the Communists were simply trying to "discredit the present thought of leadership of the black folk" with "idiotic falsehoods."[25] However, the Doctor became more of an admirer of the Communist Party during the war, especially after Browderism created a new generation of Afro-conscious and patriotic black Communists. Through his increased involvement with Robeson, Davis, Wilkerson, and Graham, Du Bois concluded the Communists and leftists' efforts in the emancipation of the oppressed was sincere, that even if the CPUSA was under a Kremlin mandate, its advocacy was going a long way in articulating black America's grievances with white oppression. Du Bois did not need further convincing that leftists represented black America's best hope for immediate civil rights advancement; and on the world stage, he believed Communists were "leading the world in the fight against poverty, ignorance, and disease and against the worst of diseases, race prejudice."[26] While the Doctor had adopted a more estimable view of the Left, his NAACP brethren remained highly distrustful.

The NAACP's embrace of anti-Communism was undoubtedly reflected by the changing political climate, but the association had long held a conservative view when it came to "outside agitators" in the civil rights struggle. Over the years, the association had viewed the UNIA, Urban League, the National Negro Congress, the Socialist Party, the Southern Negro Youth Congress, and the Civil Rights Congress as legitimate threats to its autocracy over the destiny of black

America's freedom. The NAACP's survivalist instinct was fueled by the paranoia that it would one day lose appeal among the majority of blacks and the wealthy whites who had helped bankroll it. White and Wilkins felt the association had earned its place as the leader in advocating civil rights. They scoffed at Communist leaders' efforts to work with the NAACP during the 1940s, perhaps aware that segregationists would seize the opportunity to paint the association as a Communist front. Though the NAACP wasn't immune from attacks by conservatives, it had earned enough political capitol to command respect from Democrats and Republicans alike. Even Joseph McCarthy, whose Ahab-like quest for Communists would start witch hunts in almost every sector of American society, did not openly attack the NAACP, perhaps aware of White and Wilkins's acquaintance with Hoover.[27]

During the early part of the Cold War, the NAACP was especially defensive of the idea that it harbored Communists. In his paranoia-inducing article, "The U.S. Communist Party," historian Arthur M. Schlesinger Jr. surmised that the NAACP was vulnerable to Communist infiltration. However, Schlesinger soft-pedaled on his prediction when White confronted him.[28] The association's national office did not view Communist infiltration as a major issue; White correctly guessed that no more than a handful of the association's branches harbored Communists during the late 1940s. However, the national office—cognizant of what might happen if local branches operated autonomously—began to centralize branch operations. No branches were allowed to take a stance on foreign policy or national issues without clearing it with headquarters. Such a rigid philosophy bred resentment among local leaders and infuriated Du Bois, but White and Wilkins reasoned that it was a far more practical approach than allowing the association to be a collection of independent branches.

As early as 1948, the NAACP also began cracking down on branch collaboration with the Civil Rights Congress (CRC). The CRC's successful collaboration with NAACP branches in San Francisco, Los Angeles, and Philadelphia was not only a cause for concern among the association's national leaders, but also a red flag for FBI officials. The association tried to rectify this by replacing branch officers who had strong leftist sympathies.[29] White arrogantly believed that the Communists were beholden to foreign interests more than those of Americans. He downplayed the work of the SNYC and the CRC, noting that Communists had presented an infeasible plan for black emancipation. White had long ridiculed the "Black Belt" thesis advocated by the CPUSA during the 1920s and 1930s, and believed the party still clung to that notion of separatism; had he investigated further, he would have known that the "Black Belt" disappeared under Browderism. Still, White used the apparent disconnection between the party and black America as evidence that the Communists could never understand the Negro's true desires. "Had the Communist theoreticians been less doctrinaire," he wrote, "they would have seen that the Negro's goal in the United States has always been integration and not separation from the main stream of American life and culture."[30] Wilkins expounded this theory after taking over for White in 1949. He believed that the spirituality of black America, coupled with the optimism most blacks shared about their eventual integration into society, would successfully prevent any mass exodus to the Communist Party. He was partly right. The black church held much influence among blacks, and though some religious leaders such as Adam Clayton Powell Jr. and Bishop R. R. Wright Jr. were sympathetic to the Left, the overwhelming majority of church leaders saw communism as a threat to Christianity. As Wilkins noted in his autobiography, "the comrades made a fundamental mistake":

> Negroes were oppressed, but they were first and foremost Americans. No amount of Marxist flattery could turn them away from the United States toward the Soviet Union. . . . I have often wondered how the Communists ever thought they would crack the black churches. There were 15 million Negroes in the United States in 1950, and of these, nearly 6 million were Baptists. Any comrade who thought he was going to turn those folks away from Jesus and on to Joseph Stalin had to be smoking his own opium. Negroes wanted good jobs and good homes, the opportunity to raise children and educate them, room to love and grow old. These things could all be had if the Constitution was honestly applied. *Das Kapital* didn't have a chance of competing with the Declaration of Independence or the Bill of Rights.[31]

Wilkins might have been right in assessing black America's loyalty to the church over Marx, but he exaggerated the optimism many blacks felt about the pace of progress in the United States. Indeed, many African Americans were frustrated by the continued oppression of Jim Crow and U.S. unwillingness to guarantee the rights of all of its citizens; however, most believed that joining the Left at a time when the threat of political backlash was real was not the most sensible option. As disenchanted leftists such as Richard Wright and Ralph Ellison would note, the Communist-led Left could not offer much more than promises of racial egalitarianism. Ellison had rightly concluded in *Invisible Man* that the Negro needed to find his own way.[32]

Though Wright and Ellison's disparagement of communism seemed hardly a ringing endorsement of the NAACP, the association would use their sentiments as ammunition to undermine the Left. White boasted that "the basic condescension of white Americans in general toward Negroes played a part in creating the notion of a segregated area for Negroes in the 'Soviet America' toward which the Communists were working, and in the stubborn adherence to the idea even against the advice of Communist Negroes." He added that the underlying premise of Communist was a notion of paternalism. "Along with many other mistakes made by the Communists, this thinly disguised condescension alienated intelligent Negroes."[33] The NAACP's public belief that blacks would reject Communism on merit contrasted its private actions. As early as 1946, association leaders began working with the FBI to "clear the air" about suspected Communist infiltration in branches and cooperation with leftist groups such as the CRC. At the same time, the NAACP amplified its patriotism, claiming to be the leading *American* voice in the civil rights struggle and disparaging the Communist-led effort as a propaganda instrument of the Kremlin.[34] White and Wilkins correctly assumed that no matter how bad things got in the United States, most blacks would never abandon their loyalties to the country. In reshaping the

NAACP from a militant advocate for civil rights into a patsy for the Truman administration following World War II, the association's leadership deftly positioned it for survival over the next few years of extreme political turbulence and regressive attitudes on civil rights. In essence, the Cold War NAACP sought higher ground as the wave of anti-Communist backlash engulfed other left-of-center groups. The association also proved its loyalty to the government by denouncing or publicly disagreeing with any African American critic of the United States. When Robeson would make his infamous Paris Peace Conference speech in April 1949, the association would respond accordingly.

LONG BEFORE DU BOIS'S second split from the NAACP, Robeson had concluded that the association was paying mere lip service to militant advocacy of global suffrage and anticolonialism. After the war, Paul believed the struggle for African American civil rights and opposition to colonialism and capitalistic exploitation were inextricably intertwined causes. To win back freedom, Robeson believed, meant a steadfast rejection of American Cold War policy. As evidenced by reaction to Robeson's Spingarn Medal speech, such a radical platform was something the NAACP was unwilling to endorse. Paul gave up on the association by early 1946, becoming a key member in the Communist-backed rival organizations that were willing to take risks and adopt an in-your-face approach to advocacy. The Civil Rights Congress and the National Negro Congress were two of the radical domestic groups to which Robeson lent his name and support. Calling for a Soviet-style ban on racial discrimination, both congresses positioned themselves as more militant alternatives to the NAACP, which had done little to dispel criticism from younger blacks and leftists that it was out of touch with the poor and disenfranchised. Robeson was equally active on the international front, working with Yergan (until the 1948 fiasco) on making the Council of African Affairs a force in advocating the freedom of colonized peoples.

Though the FBI's scrutiny was relentless, Paul remained an idol to many Americans, especially the social progressives and constitutionalists who applauded his use of the First Amendment. By 1947, he was as admired for intellectualism as he was for his activism and entertaining abilities. "You could see that to Paul Robeson . . . the revolutionary forces at work in the world today were as real as integers and that he observes as much," noted black journalist P. L. Prattis wrote. "But, in a larger sense, he is not free until all those like him, white, black, yellow or brown, are free."[35] With a fervent desire to have all oppressed races "walk in full dignity," Paul was a strong proponent of colonized nations following the Soviet model of government, even as the architects of American foreign policy were formalizing what would be the lasting doctrine of U.S. anti-Communism.

By 1948, Robeson's political views were antithetical to U.S. policy. Paul watched with horror as the Truman Doctrine, the Marshall Plan, and the reemergence of the Monroe Doctrine provided tacit support to dictatorships that swore allegiance to the United States and its fight against the spread of communism. The embrace of such a conservative absolutist stance put others on edge as well. "Our domestic and foreign policies are so closely tied together and the various moves of late are so politically oriented, I feel some very clear sighted thinking is needed," a worried Eleanor Roosevelt wrote to Truman. "I do not believe that the Democratic Party can win by going the Republican party one better in conservatism on the home front. Nor do I believe that taking over Mr. Churchill's policies in the Near East, in the name of democracy, is the way to really create a barrier to communism or promote democracy."[36] Truman defended the doctrine, noting that the safeguarding of American interests was integral in preserving peace abroad. "I am determined that the instructions to our mission will be worthy of the 'support of all democratic nations,'" he wrote, "and will give no basis for the fear that it may be solely a 'futile attempt to stop communism without offering anything better than the strengthening of autocracy and dictatorship.'" He went on to assure the former first lady that "I shall continue to take every action within my own power to see that the United States has a progressive domestic policy that will deserve the confidence of the world and will serve as a sound foundation for our international policy."[37] But Truman's justification did little to assuage the fears of most liberals. The Truman Doctrine was, in the words of foreign policy advisor George F. Kennan, a policy of containment, not a framework for international democracy. Over the next decade, the U.S. government would endorse Malan's apartheid government in South Africa, back Shah Mohammad Reza Pahlavi's brutal reign in Iran, and provide aid for French control of Vietnam—the precursor to U.S. involvement in the Vietnam War. The Robeson worldview that democratic government and Socialist economic structure could coexist was crumbling amid the rise of authoritarian regimes that used Socialism and capitalism as tools to stay in power.

As murmurs of another war were growing louder, Paul became increasingly zealous in his defense of the Soviet Union. Was it not the embodiment of hypocrisy for the United States to oppose Communism abroad while continuing to subjugate blacks and other colored citizens at home? Robeson warned that following the hardliners who crafted American foreign policy was tantamount to sheep being led to slaughter.

> It is possible to win if the majority of the American people can be brought to see and understand in the fullest sense the fact that the struggle in which we are engaged is not a matter of mere humanitarian sentiment, but of life and death. The only alternative to world freedom is world annihilation—another bloody holocaust—which will dwarf the two world wars through which we have passed. We have been hearing a lot of talk about a coming war. It has been defined by some of the bolder reactionaries in brutally clear terms as a war of the United States and Great Britain against the Soviet Union. This war mongering is the logical consequence of the get-tough-with Russia policy preached and practiced by those who direct American and British foreign policy.[38]

Paul's insisted that an embrace of Russia and its governing ideology put him at odds with not only foreign policy hawks in the U.S. government, but also with other black leaders. White, for one, believed Robeson was being misled and used by the Communists. Randolph and Powell would later echo

White's sentiments. Even Richard Wright distanced himself from Robeson, concluding that his onetime friend had become a mere tool for Communist propaganda.[39]

But Robeson stuck to his belief that the hunt for Communists in the United States was an attack on democracy. The arrest and indictment of the "Communist Twelve" under the Smith Act was only more evidence to Robeson that the U.S. government was intent on suppressing free speech and civil liberties. In early 1949, he and Vito Marcantonio (or Marc, as he was affectionately called by fellow leftists) began an aggressive campaign to free the jailed Communists, or at the very least, ensure a free trial. Marcantonio complained to Du Bois that the jury system had been set up to preclude "fair trial by systematically excluding workers, Negroes, Jews, other minority groups."[40] Robeson met with the jailed CPUSA leaders, declaring that he was on trial as well for his supporting their right to their political beliefs. He also offered support for the "Hollywood Ten," the blacklisted Hollywood filmmakers whose left-wing ties had made them prominent targets of the anti-Red backlash in California. Robeson was among the few entertainers willing to publicly support his peers in the motion picture industry.[41] More than forty prominent Hollywood figures, including once Democrat Ronald Reagan, would testify against the Hollywood Ten and name others in the industry as being agents of the Left.

In March, Robeson embarked on a European concert tour. There, he continued to criticize the Truman administration for its soft stance on lynching and for allowing the Fair Employment Practices Committee, signed in 1941 by Roosevelt, to expire. He also accused the United States of abandoning

democracy for the sake of supporting anticommunist governments that held "millions of people of non-European race in
permanent subjection. At the head of the aggressive forces in
this cold war . . . stands the United States. But occupying a
prominent place by its side is the Union of South Africa. They
are at once agreed in their policies of racial discrimination,
but they differ in their practical approach."[42] One month into
the tour, Robeson attended the Congress of the World Partisans of Peace in Paris. He joined Du Bois, Pablo Picasso, and
Frederic Joliet-Curie (the French scientist) as the headliners of
the conference. By this time, Robeson and Du Bois were
clearly in sync in both their domestic and international outlooks. They had bucked the trend of growing conservatism in
the United States and had refused to moderate their philosophies on race, class, and exploitation. The Doctor, fresh off his
divorce from the NAACP, spewed a venomous diatribe against
U.S. imperialism and Jim Crow. The crowd had already been
worked into a frenzy when Paul took the stage. He opened by
expressing hope that his words would "show the world that
the people can direct their own destinies and come together
for the well being of humanity."

> I have come here on behalf of my black brothers and
> Progressive America, and I bring to you the message
> of the Coordinating Committee of the Black People
> of the Colonial Countries. These people want to
> have a decent life. They want to see elaborated, new
> programs of human emancipation, programs to
> fight the enemies of Peace. They know these black
> people and other people of colonial countries who

aspire to human life; they know about the so-called new and bold program of Mr. Truman and this invasion of Africa extolled by Mr. Stettinius and the trusts, which spending billions of dollars, can lead only to a new slavery against which we are fortifying ourselves. The black people, the people of Colonial countries, want fighting programs which will give them the right to be men. Now it was only when I made my first trip to the USSR that I felt really that I was a human being. We in America do not forget that it is on the backs of the poor whites of Europe, on the backs of those who came from Europe to build America, and on the backs of millions of black people that the wealth of America has been acquired—and we are resolved that it shall be distributed in an equitable manner among all of our children and we don't pay any of that hysterical stupidity about our participating in a war against anybody no matter whom. We are determined to fight for Peace. We do not wish to fight against the Soviet Union. We are opposed to those who wish to restore imperialist Germany and establish fascism in Greece. Peace we want against fascism with Republican Spain. We shall maintain peace and friendship with all peoples, with Soviet Russia and the popular Republics.[43]

The speech would be Robeson's Waterloo. While attendees of the conference roared with approval over the speech, news of the Robeson declaration was being transmitted across the Atlantic. The Associated Press reported that Robeson compared the U.S. government to "that of Hitler and Goebbels." The dispatch also quoted Robeson as saying, "It is unthinkable that American Negroes would go to war on behalf of those who have oppressed for generations against a country which in one generation has raised our people to the full dignity of mankind."[44]

Black leaders—some at the behest of the U.S. government—lined up to denounce Robeson. Powell dismissed the notion that Robeson spoke "for all Negro people." Tobias, who had stepped down from the Council on African Affairs a year earlier, called Robeson an ingrate. Though many prominent blacks spoke out against Paul out of fear that they would become government targets if they didn't, one person seemed to revel in condemning him. Max Yergan, adopting an "I told you so" platform since his humiliating departure from the Council on African Affairs and National Negro Congress, was the first and most vocal to lead the anti-Robeson crusade in the days after the Paris speech. Conveniently denying his previous connection with (and leadership in) the Communist Party, Yergan slammed Robeson for purporting "to speak not just for that Communist minority, but for one-tenth of the American population, some fourteen million Americans of Negro extraction." No patriotic Negro American, he claimed, would heed Robeson's statements, which "had as their purpose the vicious and cynical effort which Communists in America have for a long time been putting forth to drive a wedge between American Negroes and their fellow American citizens." Adding to his own reputation for twisting reality, Yergan contended, "The counterpart of Mr. Paul Robeson's Russian idol, the American Communist Party, certainly has not 'raised our people to the full dignity of mankind.' I know some Negro Communists. Few of them are individuals who have experienced 'the full dignity of mankind.' Most of them are, by every test, the slaves of slaves." Yergan put a blowtorch to his past alliances, alleging that the party's "so-called leaders . . . resorted to the most abject groveling, the most undignified concealment of their deeper personal convictions and the grossest denial of the ordinary principles of decency when their party bosses cracked the whip." In a final insult, he lambasted Robeson "for his slavish following of Communist instructions with regard to (the Council on African Affairs). I count it as one of the most important actions of my entire lifetime when, along with the majority of the individuals within that organization, I left it. Our leaving it," the CAA founder and longtime executive director boasted, "established the fact that today it is what it is, an instrument of the Communist party, Communist intrigue and Communist use of it, not in the interest of the people of Africa, but in the interest of the Kremlin masters of Communists everywhere."[45] Despite its dramatic appraisal of Robeson and the Communist Party, the editorial was transparently disingenuousness. Yergan's denunciation was generally dismissed as vitriol from a very bitter man; he had lost credibility with moderate blacks long before he had fallen out of favor with the Left, rendering his commentary trivial to anyone outside of FBI offices.

Though White had been ruthless in his attempts to get rid of Du Bois, he initially refrained from attacking Paul. However, as pressure to denounce Robeson grew, he jumped into the fray against his old friend. "[Robeson] is naïve in refusing to recognize the only freedom in the U.S.S.R. today is the freedom to obey uncritically and absolutely what the men in the Kremlin tell the people of Russia and Communists the world over to do, think and say," White wrote. "It is because I have known him so long and well that, sharing as I do his criticism of white hypocrisy and the glaring weaknesses of democracy as they are manifested in bigotry and colonialism, I believe him in grievous error in his thinking that the Communism of today's Soviet Russia offers the way out for Negroes and other exploited minorities."[46]

His criticism was not enough to quell the anti-Robeson sentiments of conservatives, who put enormous pressure on the NAACP to take more substantive action against Robeson. Wilkins spearheaded an effort to discredit Robeson by helping mobilize black leaders, including A. Philip Randolph and Lester Granger, head of the Urban League, to collectively denounce the Paris speech. Their goal was to reiterate that Robeson spoke for himself and not the entire race. Wilkins, in his own attempt to defray the controversy, said blacks would "fight loyally for this country no matter how many of us they lynch."[47] He also met privately with J. Edgar Hoover to assure him that the association (or the majority of black America, for that matter) did not endorse Robeson's message. Under Wilkins and White, the NAACP would soon become a key player in the collaborative effort to ostracize Robeson.

THE ROBESON SPEECH resonated with black America on many levels. Paul had bluntly articulated the long-held sentiment among many blacks that they would never fight and die for a "white man's army." Randolph made similar statements to that effect before, but his calls for a black boycott of the U.S. armed forces were deemed more of a militant stand against segregation. Paul had specifically mentioned the Soviet Union, which *happened* to be U.S. Enemy Number One. Many blacks lauded Robeson's courage in opposing the idea of sending Negroes to die overseas when they were barely afforded the right to live in the United States. The black press especially took note of the poignancy in his stand, even if his politics did not reflect the beliefs of most African Americans. "If I must condemn Robeson," *Pittsburgh Courier* columnist J. A. Rogers wrote, "what must I reserve for those who create and keep alive those conditions that have aroused Robeson's anger? Let those whites who condemn Robeson . . . ask themselves what they would do if they were in the Negro's place."[48]

Robeson's comments struck at the very core of a debate that continues today: Should blacks go along with the program or resist in an effort to promote their own survival within America? Du Bois—and many Black Nationalists after him—theorized that the "sheep-like mentality" of African-Americans was rooted in slavery; that a Negro's willingness to accept a white man's orders satisfied an unconscious desire to serve.[49]

Robeson broke from a cardinal rule of interracial dynamics by daring to speculate the willingness of blacks to fight against an enemy, putting their patriotism—and their citizenship—into question. Ironically, black war veterans were among Robeson's biggest supporters. One veteran claimed he put his "life on the line in World War II for nothing but three long years ducking bullets," and he said Negroes owed Paul for his comments. "Unless there is a lot of changes made in the near future, I am 99 and 44/100 percent with him," the vet wrote.

"Negroes have one of the greatest weapon of all time: threatening to turn (Red). They should thank Mr. Robeson for giving it to them, and use it. Now we have that great Paul Robeson and don't know how to appreciate him."[50]

Amidst the debate over Robeson's remarks, the NAACP dropped a bomb in its May issue of the *Crisis*, publishing a scathing editorial that Ben Davis called "a gutter attack." Likely written just days after the Paris speech, the unsigned diatribe belittled Paul's civil rights record while emphasizing that "Mr. Robeson, if he represents any group at all, speaks for the fellow travelers of Communism and it is well-known that these are overwhelmingly white." Overlooking Robeson's involvement with the CRC, SNYC, and the National Negro Congress, the editorial's writer also blasted the political artist for "lavishing his attention on an outfit called the Council on African Affairs, long ago labeled a Communist front by the Department of Justice. While his people in Mineral Wells, Tex., and Bossemer, Ala., and Waycross, Ga., were battling as best they knew how and yelling for help, Mr. Robeson was writing and talking about Africa, singing Russian folk songs, and dispensing the comfort-to-be when and if the Soviet cabal replace the Talmadge-Rankin deal." The editorial concluded that "Mr. Robeson must have fancied himself a general (or at the very least a colonel) in the Communist-led army of the proletariat, but if he takes occasion to glance behind him he will find but a thin sprinkling of American Negroes following the banners and parroting the monotonous slogans."[51]

Robeson supporters were incensed. They expected attacks from the white press, and even some of the more conservative elements of the black press, but the *Crisis* piece was tantamount to fratricide. Progressive Party leader (and former NAACP leader) Charles P. Howard offered an immediate rebuke to Wilkins (whom he believed to be the author of the piece), claiming that the NAACP had become "a tool of the Democratic Party" and was "being used to destroy progressive forces among the Negro people." Howard also noted the irony of awarding "the Spingarn Medal to one with none except sentimental roots among American Negroes. Nobody may have ever heard it around NAACP Headquarters, but Paul Robeson is recognized by the great masses of the Negro people as more nearly their ideal leader than all of the Walter Whites and Roy Wilkins in the country and he doesn't get a dime for doing it, only the kicks of Negroes who ought to be appreciating him."[52] Hunton said the *Crisis* editorial read "like something written by George Schuyler or someone his type." Wilkins later admitted he authored the piece on Paul's speech, explaining that "it was a wrongheaded thing for Paul to say, and I had called him on it."[53]

Though Wilkins asserted that the "Robeson matter died" right after the NAACP's denunciation, the battle of public opinion raged for the next few months.[54]

A *Des Moines Tribunal* editorial claimed, "It doesn't help Negro rights in America to have one of the race's most distinguished sons show how naïve politically and sociologically a Negro with a law degree can be." The *Columbia* (S.C.) *Record* gloated: "Of the 10,000,000 Negroes most of them have not been interested in Communist blandishments. . . . Robeson has made his choice, and although it is a sad thing to witness the disintegration of any person under the Communism malignancy, he may hereafter be dismissed and forgotten."[55]

Du Bois, Shirley Graham, Essie, Howard, Howard Fast, and William Patterson led the counterattack against the white media and the "so-called representatives of the Negro race." The Doctor condemned "certain Negro leaders" who "beat the gun in denouncing Robeson before they even knew with certainty what he said or what he meant. This was the old plantation technique which hastened to outdo 'Ole Massa' himself in denouncing any slave who dared lift his head for a minute out of the dirt of slavery.'"[56] Howard fired off editorials admonishing white journalists who had judged Robeson. "Paul Robeson has seen the truth," he wrote, "and with God's help, he will help the rest of his people to see the truth."

Robeson returned to the United States in June, only to discover how much of a furor he had caused in Paris. As Paul continued to defend his statements (both his actual speech and the words that had been wrongly attributed to him), more blacks came out of nowhere to denounce him. James Bellanfant, head of the Mutual Association of Colored People in the South, claimed he "had covered 13,000 miles" across several southern states and collected 750,000 signatures condemning Robeson.[57] Bellanfant was one of those arrested in the Columbia, Tennessee, race riots in 1946, and his efforts to denounce Robeson might have been quid pro quo for the NAACP's successful efforts to exonerate him. [58]

The rush by many Negroes to denounce Robeson and pledge loyalty to the country could not stop the government's own investigation. Gearing up what would be a decade-long witch hunt against Communists and other leftists, the House Un-American Activities Committee announced it would convene during the summer to get information about possible

Communist infiltration of Negro organizations. Some black journalists ridiculed the premise of the hearings. "There might be some 'Red' Negroes around but they aren't Red the way the House Committee on Un-American Activities would have it," wrote *New York Age* Managing Editor Dan Burley. "The kind of 'Red' Negro I'm talking about is raw inside from being made to drink the segregated waters of Georgia and Mississippi and eat the hot dogs of race hate in Alabama and Tennessee where they also whip the outside of his hide with blackjacks and pistol butts and . . . clubs and sometimes barbed wire to be doubly sure he'll be 'Red' all over."[59] The committee's chairman, Representative John S. Wood of Georgia, tried to allay the fears of the NAACP and other black organizations that the hearings were a test of Negro loyalty. Quite the contrary, Wood claimed. He told NAACP leaders that the investigation was to allow prominent Negroes to counter the statements of Robeson. The committee invited several notable African Americans, including Lester Granger, Tom Young of *The Journal and Guide*, George Hunton of the Catholic Interracial Council, and Charles Johnson, head of Fisk University, to speak. Also slated to testify was the HUAC's own Negro investigator, Alvin Stokes. Surprisingly, the committee did not invite Yergan, who would have undoubtedly relished the opportunity to publicly condemn Paul and paint a story of Communist conspiracy.

The HUAC hearings began in mid-July, and committee members hoped for someone of Robeson's stature to discredit him. Wood turned to Brooklyn Dodgers star Jackie Robinson, asking him "to give the lie to statements by Paul Robeson." Dodgers executive Branch Rickey also sought to persuade his star player to testify.[60] However, Robinson was initially reluctant at first to speak out against Robeson, whom he credited with helping him break the color barrier in Major League Baseball. He was also keenly aware that his testimony would be used to pit one prominent Negro against another. "I didn't want to fall prey to the white man's game," Robinson wrote years later. "I knew that Robeson was striking out against racial inequality in the way that seemed best to him."[61]

While Robinson and his wife Rachel deliberated on what to do, the parade of African Americans lined up to speak on black America's sentiments about communism. Manning Johnson, a Judas of the Communist Party who would become one of the most prominent government informants of the Cold War, was among the most damning witnesses against Robeson and the party. Johnson, once a key party organizer and a confidant of James W. Ford, testified that the fundamental goal of the party "was the complete destruction of the American government and the establishment of a soviet system of government in America. The system, of course, in America that we had planned and envisioned is a dictatorship of the proletariat in the transition from Socialism to world communism." Johnson's testimony when it came to party affairs only seemed to underscore the fears of many Americans that there was an insidious Communist plot—backed by Russia—to take over the United States. He told committee members that "once the Communists come to power the Constitution will be burned on the public square and the liberties and freedoms now enjoyed will be completely suppressed. . . . Everybody will be governed according to the dictates of the Communist Party, which will be the party in power." When asked about Paul Robeson, Johnson claimed that Robeson was under confidential orders from the party "to work among the intellectuals, the professionals, and artists that the party was seeking to penetrate and influence along Communist lines." Summing up his attestation, Johnson likened Robeson to a "Black Stalin" who "sought to play the role of an exploiter of the injustices and ills of American democracy in the interest of a foreign power."[62]

Johnson's comments were by far the most extreme, but in the eyes of HUAC members, were effective in depicting Robeson as an outside agitator. Others offered more general criticisms of Robeson and the party. Granger said that while he believed the Communist Party should be driven underground, the HUAC needed use the hearings to investigate the Ku Klux Klan in order to assure black America "that while it is fighting against one enemy of this country, Communism, our Government is helping to fight off the other, Racism."[63] Robinson, meanwhile, had come to a decision. Wilkins and Granger—who helped draft Robinson's statement to the committee—purportedly convinced him to testify, and the baseball star finally accepted the HUAC's invitation to speak as the committee's last witness.[64] "In those days," Robinson recalled, "I had much more faith in the ultimate justice of the American white man than I have today. I would reject such an invitation if offered now."[65] On July 18, the Negro "who never had it made" sat before a committee of white lawmakers eager to hear his rebuttal of Robeson. But Robinson did not go to the lengths of Johnson and some of the other "witnesses" to denounce Paul. Instead, he told the committee that the issue of "Communist activity in the United States wasn't a matter of partisan politics," and that "every Negro worth his salt hated racial discrimination, and if it happened to that it was a Communist who denounced discrimination, that didn't change the truth of his charges." He did, however, question Robeson's right to act as the global mouthpiece for black America.

> I can't speak for any fifteen million people any more than any other person can, but I know that I've got too much invested for my wife and child and myself in the future of this country, and I and other Americans of many races and faiths have too much invested in our country's welfare, for any of us to throw it away because of a siren sung in bass. I am a religious man. Therefore I cherish America, where I am free to worship as I please, a privilege which some countries do not give. And I suspect that nine hundred and ninety-nine out of almost any thousand colored Americans you meet will tell you the same thing. But that doesn't mean we're going to stop race discrimination in this country until we've got it licked. It means that we're going to fight it all the harder because our stake in the future is so big. We can win our fight without the Communists and we don't want their help.[66]

While Robinson refrained from attacking Robeson, his testimony served a greater purpose for conservative policy makers and Communist witch hunters by highlighting the importance of religion to most Negroes. Using the comments of an all-star Negro baseball player who also was a "good Christian," anti-Communists were able to simplify the cold war as a battle between the faithful and those who sought to impose an atheist society. The United States was defending Christian ethos and safeguarding the right to religious freedom; by siding with the Soviets, Paul Robeson was calling for an end to the right of free worship. Robinson's statements, along with the vitriolic testimony of Rabbi Ben Schultz (head of the American League Against Communism), seemingly justified the "get tough with Russia" policy. As conservatives would argue for the duration of the Cold War, religious freedom and the importance of faith—the founding principles of the United States and bedrocks in the black community—were under attack by the Soviet threat.

Though white newspapers bought into the reframing of the Cold War and the urgency of denouncing Robeson, some in the black press vilified Robinson for playing right into the hands of conservatives. "We wish he would just shut his big mouth and get back on 2nd base," one black columnist wrote, adding that "when Jackie speaks of what he has gained he is thinking of himself. When Paul Robeson speaks of what is happening to colored people in the name of democracy, he is thinking of a race."[67] Paul himself did not go after Robinson publicly, perhaps aware that his friend was under enormous pressure to testify. "I am not going to permit the issue to boil down to a personal feud between myself and Jackie," he told reporters. "To do that would be to do exactly what the other group wants us to do. Let's not fall for anything like that."[68] Robinson would later regret testifying against Robeson after having "grown wiser and closer to painful truths about America's destructiveness." He added that he had an "increased respect for Paul Robeson who . . . sacrificed himself, his career, and the wealth and comfort he once enjoyed because, I believe, he was trying to help his people."[69]

Robinson's testimony, coupled with the premise of the HUAC hearings and the increasingly humid political climate, proved devastating to Paul's reputation. By the end of July, an increasing number of organizations and concert halls either canceled or indefinitely postponed Robeson appearances. Unfazed by a growing public sentiment against him, Robeson continued his political involvement. He actively solicited support for the reelection campaign of Ben Davis for New York City Council and remained the public face of the Civil Rights Congress and the Council on African Affairs (which both he and Du Bois had been trying to salvage since Yergan's departure). Robeson also didn't shy away from press interviews, aware that any attempt to escape the spotlight would only leave his reactionary critics unchecked. He used every opportunity to expound his feelings about the Soviet Union, lambasting American politicians and the mainstream press as "warmongers." "Moscow and Stalingrad of 1949 convinced me of the fact that your people, as distinct from the Wall Street reactionaries, think of one thing only: of peace and happiness for the millions of common people in the world," Paul wrote. "Every Soviet person, every Muscovite whom I had the occasion to meet in those thrilling and happy days, thirsts for peace and creative labor in the name of progress."[70]

Despite the backlash generated by his Peace Conference comments, an undaunted Robeson agreed to perform at a prolabor concert sponsored by a leftist arts organization, People's Artists, Inc. The concert was to be held just outside of Peekskill, New York, a small town about forty-five miles from New

York City. Peekskill's demographic makeup was a volatile mix of working-class "townies" and summer residents—most of who were liberals from the city. The townsfolk had an under-belly of anti-Semitism, but the limited interactions among year-round residents and summer visitors created a tenuous peace. The concert was slated for August 27 at the Lakeland Acres picnic grounds, and organizers announced proceeds would benefit the Harlem chapter of the Civil Rights Congress. When news of Robeson's visit reached the town, it proved to be the catalyst for combustibility. An editorial in the Peekskill *Evening Star* stated that Robeson wouldn't receive a hero's welcome. "Time was when the honor (of receiving Robeson) would have been ours—all ours. As things stand today, like most folks who put America first, we're a little doubtful of that 'honor,' finding the luster in the once illus-trious name of Paul Robeson now almost hidden by political tarnish." Townspeople quickly mobilized against the concert, calling for "group action" to thwart the Robeson visit. The concert was uniformly condemned by the town's Chamber of Commerce and numerous veterans groups. Sensing that vio-lence was imminent, Robeson supporters appealed to Westch-ester County district attorney George Fanelli to prevent the violence. Concert organizers planned to bring their own "pro-tection" as well, with a cadre of unionists to be on hand in case of heightened tensions.

Dreams of a peaceful Saturday concert were shattered hours before Robeson was slated to take the stage. In the late afternoon, a crowd of men had converged on the scene, deter-mined to prevent the concert from happening. Trouble began at about six P.M., one hour before the start of the concert.

Howard Fast, who went to the concert by car, reported that he was allowed access by "the organized fascist mob." Fast said "40 or 50 carloads of fascists" were already at the picnic grounds, with hundreds of others arriving on foot. Within minutes, physical altercations started between the anti-Robeson crowd and the handful of his supporters who arrived early. Fast reported that in the melee, "two of our boys were hurt, quite badly."[71] Peekskill sheriff deputies arrived on the scene, but did little to dissuade the increasingly rowdy crowd. By 7:30, the skirmishes had erupted into an all-our riot, with attackers using clubs, knives, rocks, and other blunt objects against Robeson supporters. According to Fast, a group of men burned a twelve-foot cross on the picnic grounds. Unionists formed a circle against the converging mob, singing, "Freedom is our struggle, we shall not be moved." Just as the pro-Robeson crowd seemed confident that they had contained the mob, a new wave of attackers appeared. Some youth reportedly cried, "We're Hitler's Boys—out to finish his job," as they moved in on the unionists. More than twenty Robeson supporters sustained injuries in the melee and in a subsequent barrage of rocks thrown by rioters. State police only arrived after ten P.M. to break up the riot, leaving the picnic grounds in ruins. Robeson, who was made aware of the violence, never came near Lakeland Acres.

Within minutes of the restoration of calm and order, fingers began pointing at each other. Robeson supporters condemned the violence, blaming right-wing extremists, town officials, and the state for endorsing the mob attacks. The New York chapter of the NAACP sidestepped the issue of Robeson, but chapter president Lindsay H. White wired Governor Thomas Dewey expressing concern about the cross burning on picnic grounds. White wrote "the barbaric practice of burning and destroying works of art must not be tolerated as it was in Nazi Germany. Your failure to punish the offenders will be an open invitation to hoodlums for a petition of this disgrace." Others, including Henry A. Wallace and Patterson, also called for a full investigation of the matter. On September 1, a group of Robeson supporters met with Lawrence Walsh, Dewey's assistant counsel, in Albany and demanded a specially appointed district attorney to file charges against those who incited the violence at Peekskill. Supporters, including Robeson friends Sam and Helen Rosen, claimed that leaving Fanelli in charge of the matter was akin to "having a man investigate his own guilt." But Dewey was inclined to leave it in Fanelli's hands. Fanelli, under pressure from veterans groups, announced he would look into pressing charges against the event organizers after a published photo showed a black man holding a knife during the melee. Fanelli's announcement only emboldened locals to boast of their attack. Many summer residents fled the area after hearing townies talk of "the job they had done on the 'Commies,' 'Niggers,' and 'Jews.' " Reports of violence against Jews grew in the days after the melee, with numerous homes and businesses vandalized. One Jewish resident who had survived the Holocaust claimed the violence recalled Poland shortly before the Nazi invasion in 1939. "There was the same rock throwing with intent to kill at Peekskill as there was at Andernach," the man wrote. "But even more striking for me was the psychopathic hatred, the hysteria of the hoodlum mob. Both acted and looked exactly the same."[72] Locals began placing signs that read: "Wake Up America—Peekskill Did!" Townsfolk appeared confident that they had scored a victory in keeping Robeson away, and local and state officials were relieved that any "threat" of a Robeson appearance had disappeared. But on the same day as Robeson supporters met with Walsh in Albany, organizers of the Peekskill concert announced that it would be rescheduled to September 4.

One of the defining qualities of Robeson, as noted earlier, was his stubbornness in the face of pressure. He had openly defied what he was told *not* to do, whether it meant siding with unpopular political figures or having extramarital relations with white women. Paul was determined not to let the "Fascists" get the best of him. Backed by the leadership of the Communist Party and the CRC, he decided to revisit Peekskill, if only to prove that he wouldn't be intimidated. "This thing burns in me and it is not my nature or inclination to be scared off."[73] He felt invulnerable when it came to espousing his views, fully believing that he could walk into a hornets' nest without getting stung. Perhaps Paul had overestimated his support base, but he remained optimistic that America would "wake up" and rally against Fascism, racism, anti-Semitism, and reactionary foreign policy. Another Peekskill, he believed, would show his supporters that they could have the courage to speak out about their convictions. "I am well equipped now . . . to make the supreme fight for my people and all the other underprivileged masses, wherever they may be," Robeson said in an interview with Dan Burley. "I speak of those bereft of uncompromising, courageous leadership that cannot be intimidated, and cannot be swerved from its purpose of bringing true freedom to those who follow it." True to his word, Robeson returned to Peekskill, this time with a heavily armed contingent of unionists, Communists, and several members of Harlem's underworld. Fearing more violence, Dewey called upon state police to secure the perimeter of the concert to prevent a repeat of the August 27 fiasco. He also announced he would hold Fanelli "strictly accountable" for any violence. Veterans groups assured town officials that they would stage a peaceful demonstration against the concert.[74]

The concert took place at two P.M., with more than nine hundred police officers "protecting" a crowd of about twenty-five thousand concertgoers. An entourage of unionists surrounded the stage, forming a human wall to add extra security for Robeson. David Graham Du Bois was among the guards who provided a buffer between Robeson and the audience. "We weren't going to let anything happen to him," Graham Du Bois recalled. "There was this feeling that if something was going to happen, it should happen to us before it even came close to Paul Robeson." Graham Du Bois and other unionists kept the phalanx while Robeson and other performers, including singer Pete Seeger, entertained the crowd. Veterans groups were on the embankment of the concert grounds holding their own "concert" of sorts, blaring instruments in an attempt to drown out Robeson.[75] It didn't work. Paul sang his trademark spirituals, his voice booming over Lakeland Acres as if broadcasting to the surrounding areas that he and his supporters had won. The concert ended without violence, and Robeson was hurried off the stage and whisked away by caravan of unionists and black mobsters. However, as concertgoers attempted to leave, they were confronted by an angry mob made up of townies and out-of-towners eager to send a message to Robeson. Assailants began hurling rocks at the departing crowd, attacking cars and the buses used to bring out-of-town Robeson supporters to the concert. State police, who were charged with protecting the concertgoers and safeguarding against violence, joined with the anti-Robeson crowd in attacking the Peekskill II attendees. Police arrested many of Robeson's guards while allowing anti-Robeson rioters to go unchecked in their assaults on concertgoers. Police and townies joined forces in singling out blacks and Jews, beating them with clubs and hurling rocks. Attempts at getting Dewey to intervene proved unsuccessful, and by the early morning hours of September 5, the riot left more than fifty people injured and thousands of dollars in property damage.[76]

Peekskill II, as it turned out, damaged Robeson's reputation more than that of the anti-Communist forces who appeared to have started the violence. Fanelli promised a full investigation of the matter, but within a month, a special grand jury concluded that Communists had incited the riots. Several legal watchdog groups, including the American Civil Liberties Union (ACLU), pressed for an impartial investigation, but Dewey rebuffed their attempts. Press reports painted the rioters as patriots who were merely responding to an actual Communist threat, a sentiment that echoed to a lesser degree by Dewey and Fanelli. The backlash against Robeson and his supporters resulted in the departure of most of Peekskill's liberal residents. Some, like Sam and Helen Rosen, closed up their summer home after receiving death threats. Robeson's attempt to galvanize liberals against the "forces of reaction" had backfired, only strengthening the claims of conservatives that Robeson and his cadre of "alien Communists" were incendiaries bent on disrupting the stability of American democracy. Paul countered by accusing conservative veterans organizations such as the American Legion for fomenting trouble against peace lovers. "I told the American Legion that I have been to Memphis, Tennessee, the stamping ground of such Negro-haters as Ed Crump and others of the cracker breed, and I have been to the lynch belt of Florida. I told the Legion I would return to Peekskill. I did. I will go North, South, East or West, Europe, Africa, South America, Asia, or Australia and fight for the freedom of the people."[77] A week after the concert, Paul told a rally of fur and leather workers in New York that "we can and will lick these forces of fascism in America . . . by making Peekskill a symbol of both of our unity and of our determined and unyielding struggle."[78] Though he spun Peekskill II (the concert itself) as a victory for perseverance, he ignored the consequences of his defiance. The lives of some of his supporters in the small New York town had been ruined, and those who dared to speak in his defense were being implicated as Communist coconspirators. The events in Peekskill, and the local and state government's tacit justification of the violence, would only reaffirm anti-communists' beliefs that they were above the law when it came to handling the "Communist threat." Peekskill only fueled Robeson's belligerence and stoked government officials' beliefs that he needed to be dealt with immediately.

AS THE TURBULENT DECADE came to a close, Du Bois and Robeson stood on the edge of American society, having been cut off from the mainstream. Both men were now so far against the grain that for many prominent blacks, supporting them had become too impractical and dangerous. The NAACP divorced Du Bois and disavowed Robeson, choosing to steer clear of any government backlash from affiliating with known "Communist conspirators." As David Levering Lewis noted, the association was "in a fight for its survival." In an attempt to advance its own agenda, the NAACP "thought it necessary to sacrifice Du Bois and Robeson by throwing them over the side."[79]

There was no hope of reconciliation; both men had gone too far to the Left to be accepted as spokesmen of black America. By the end of 1949, Du Bois and Robeson had alienated the likes of Bunche, Powell, Wilkins, William Hastie, Randolph, and Granger—leaders who could have helped salvage their reputations in the eyes of many Americans. In a six-month span, Robeson had gone from a hero to a pariah, while Du Bois barely clung to the reputation he had earned as one of the century's most passionate civil rights fighters *before* 1940.

9

CRASH

Three centuries of oppression in the United States placed
the Negro people in a position where they refuse to have
anything to do with the sickening "theories" of gradualism.
We want our freedom and we want it now.

—Paul Robeson remarks during Negro History Month
(1952)

THE INTENSIFICATION OF ANTI-COMMUNIST sentiment during the summer of 1949 proved to be a crushing blow to American progressives. As Robeson acquaintance James H. Gilliam Sr. recalled, "Anything you did that wasn't by the book—that made you a Communist."[1] The events at Peekskill marked a boiling point in the tensions between conservatives and the

Left. Violence was no longer just a threat, but a real and viable option for anti-Communists emboldened by the conclusions of a Westchester County grand jury in October 1949. Concerts in several U.S. cities, including Cincinnati, were canceled immediately after the Peekskill episode because local officials feared the likelihood of violence.[2] Paul pointed to the willingness of anti-Communists to use force as an attempt "to silence any criticism of our land for the injustices that daily happen to us—lynching, persecution, denial of the right to work, police brutality."[3] But he found very little sympathy among most Americans. Society's dramatic swing to the Right following the 1948 election created such a hostile atmosphere that Robeson's message was limited to left-wing loyalists and small groups who clandestinely supported him.

The government's patience with Robeson had also worn thin. Since his confrontation with Truman in the White House, Paul became a prime target for federal investigators. The FBI had a mountain of evidence linking Robeson to the Communist Party, including information from confidential informants within various leftist groups. Despite mounting pressure from conservatives and representatives of veterans' organizations to take action against Robeson following the Paris speech and Peekskill, J. Edgar Hoover was content to wait a little longer. A California resident complained that the bureau wasn't responding quickly enough to prosecute "the lover of the Russian people" and that Robeson needed to "be deported to Russia and black-listed from the U.S. forever!"[4] An anonymous veteran also wrote Hoover to "send [Robeson] over there—also his *son* and *white wife*."[5] Hoover had other plans. The FBI built enough of a case against Robeson to move the matter to the U.S. State Department, which had begun its own investigation of "subversive" individuals and groups. A bureau fact sheet sent to the State Department identified Paul as a member of no less than twelve suspected Communist Party front organizations.[6] The bureau also kept an active file on Du Bois, carefully noting his active involvement with Robeson and suspected Communist organizations. Special agents collected newspaper clippings from around the world that quoted Du Bois and Robeson praising Russia while denouncing American domestic and foreign policy. By 1950, the files of both men were overflowing with articles connecting them to known Communists.

Du Bois and Robeson, by virtue of their international prominence, were viewed as legitimate security threats. Their adherence to a pro-Soviet agenda, which angered many leftists who began to view Stalinism in the same regard as Hitlerism, only made conservatives more determined to destroy them. As the government closed in on Du Bois and Robeson, the hammer dropped on the Left. The McCarran Act of 1950 placed a Scarlet Letter on prominent leftists and left-wing organizations, forcing them to register as "subversives."[7] The leadership of the CPUSA also remained in flux during the trial of the Communist twelve. Making matters worse was the conviction of Alger Hiss (Ralph Bunche's mentor at the State Department) on perjury after he had been accused of being a Communist spy for the Soviet Union. The crackdown spurred an exodus of Communist Party members, many of whom abandoned their left-wing sympathies altogether. Others went into hiding. The Doctor and Paul, however, still loomed large as the spokesmen of the oppressed, traveling the world to endorse a Soviet-style government and rally the working classes against capitalism. "The Soviet socialist program of ethnic and national democracy" was, in Robeson's eyes, "precisely the opposite of the Nazi, Fascist, South African and Dixiecrat programs of racial superiority."[8] Such declarations would prompt legal action against Robeson and Du Bois, part of a concerted effort by federal authorities to neutralize them.

SHORTLY AFTER HIS RETURN from Europe (and the World Partisans of Peace Conference), Robeson—seemingly undeterred by the consequences of his speech—expounded his pro-Soviet beliefs and defense of Stalinism. Though Communist Party members increasingly spoke out against Stalin's harsh repression of Trotskyites and other opposition figures, Robeson was adamant that the Kremlin was safeguarding Russian "democracy." Paul's subsequent defense of the Soviet Union would become part of a public relations chess match with U.S. foreign policy makers. He was confident that he could checkmate anti-Communists on the subject of racial discrimination. Despite Truman's civil rights mandate, the United States was still a segregated country, with the majority of blacks living in oppressively unequal conditions. Could American politicians justify protecting foreign countries from Soviet influence when they were unable to protect fifteen million of their own citizens from being lynched? Of course not, Robeson argued. In speeches during the summer of 1949, he continually implied the superiority of the Soviet Union over the United States when it came to foreign policy and race. Stalin, he argued, was defending democracy against the Dean Achesons, Henry

Luces, and Winston Churchills. No longer bothering to even clarify his Paris speech, Robeson *did* suggest that Negroes would find it difficult to fight for a country the refused them full dignity. "In the United States," he wrote, "tolerance is displayed to but a small group of eminent Negroes." On the other hand, "Moscow and Stalingrad of 1949 convinced me of the fact that [Soviet] people, as distinct from the Wall Street reactionaries, think of one thing only: of peace and happiness for the millions of common people in the world. Every Soviet person, every Muscovite whom I had the occasion to meet in those thrilling and happy days, thirsts for peace and creative labor in the name of progress."[9]

Paul considered his uniform defense of the Soviet Union a pillar of his anti-Fascist philosophy. The importance of anti-Fascism in Paul's worldview was as important of a coping mechanism as it was a political argument, especially as revelations about Stalin's regime came to light. Robeson remained overly idealistic on the state of affairs in the USSR, ignoring the fact that the Soviet Union was now a totalitarian state. He dismissed Eastern Europe's efforts to fight against "Russification" as the work of Fascists to undermine peace in the region. The "real" Romanians, Bulgarians, Hungarians, Albanians, Czechs, and Polish, Paul claimed, had—by Soviet guidance—become "masters of their own lands—a sum-total which means that the world balance of power has shifted in favor of the forces of peace and democracy."[10] Those forces only hardened U.S. foreign policy. The Truman administration stepped up its export of arms and supplies to colonial governments in Southeast Asia and Africa in an effort to quell rising nationalist freedom movements. Some American policy makers conceded that the support of repressive regimes against nationalist and Marxist freedom fighters was not helping U.S. interests. Ho Chi Minh's Soviet-backed militia had made tremendous gains in Vietnam, threatening the French colonial government's hold on Indo-China. Though the U.S. government continued its aid to the French, some foreign policy makers had already concluded that nothing short of American military intervention could stop Ho Chi Minh from defeating the French. State Department officials had reached an even grimmer conclusion about their longtime support for Chiang Kai-Shek. In August, Acheson issued a memorandum essentially calling the U.S. backing of Chiang futile. The White Paper, as it was later known, was a major embarrassment to Right-wingers while giving the Left one of its few victories during the Cold War. Robeson saw Acheson's memo as an admission of U.S. hypocrisy in supporting Chiang. In October, Mao announced the formation of the People's Republic of China, and several months later, signed the Sino-Soviet alliance. Truman, following Acheson's advice, chose not to defend Formosa, the last stronghold of Chiang's nationalist government.

While Paul hailed the Communist victory in China as a strike against fascism, he found it much more difficult defending Russia's development of the atomic bomb. In late September, the Soviets announced they had successfully tested an atomic device two months earlier, sparking widespread fears across the Atlantic that a nuclear war was imminent. Robeson was among only a handful of leftists who publicly supported Russia's newly acquired weapon. In a statement that alarmed even some of the most ardent left-wingers, Robeson claimed the Soviet atomic bomb would become "a

powerful force for intensifying the peace struggle in America."
He went on to add, "Now that the American people know the
Soviet Union has the bomb, I believe they will demand our
national leaders start talking in terms of peace, not war. For
they realize the atom bomb means destruction and nobody
wants to be killed."[11] FBI agents took special note of Robeson's
statements. He had effectively firebombed the bridges that led
back to moderate America, and more important, had indicted
himself as a Soviet apologist. His increasingly irrational justifications of Russia only validated the claims of black leaders
such as Wilkins that Robeson was out of touch with the sentiments of the majority of Negroes.

Paul did little to help himself on the domestic front. He
remained loyal to his friends in the Communist Party,
appearing on behalf of the jailed CPUSA leaders less than two
weeks after Peekskill. Judge Harold Medina sustained most of
prosecutor John McGohey's objections about the relevance of
defense attorney George Crockett's questions, limiting
Robeson's testimony to a few sentences admitting that he
knew the defendants. Paul's appearance at the Foley Square
Trial—and his willingness to testify for party leaders—further
tarnished a reputation that had taken a beating in the last
nine months; it also added legs to Manning Johnson's damning
HUAC accusation about Robeson's Communist Party membership. The Robeson cameo in Medina's courtroom was more
than fodder for the press. In Washington, lawmakers wondered aloud if there was any way to sanction Robeson for his
behavior. Several U.S. congressmen brought up the issue of
Robeson's involvement in Peekskill. Georgia Representative
Gene Cox called Robeson a "Communist agent provocateur,"

suggesting that Paul had wantonly incited the riots in Peek-skill.[12] While others questioned his allegiance to the country in the wake of Peekskill and Foley Square, Paul moved on, actively stumping for his good friend Ben Davis's bid to return to the New York City Council. He viewed the Davis campaign as a microcosm of the Cold War—an election victory for the Communist Party stalwart would, in Robeson's eyes, strike another blow against Fascism. Paul (ironically agreeing with those on the opposite end of the political spectrum) said the events at Peekskill were a landmark in the Cold War.

They go to the root of the whole struggle for freedom of speech and freedom of assembly, but they especially concern the struggle of we Negro people. Twice they attempted to silence any criticism of our land for the injustices that daily happen to us—lynching, persecution, denial of the right to work, police brutality. And these KKK acts of terror go far beyond the local scene. They have their roots in hysteria, aroused by the House Un-American Committee in an attempt to outlaw one of the great political parties of our nation, the Communist Party, to imprison its twelve courageous leaders. . . . Today America stands at the crossroads. Yesterday's Peekskill and now Foley Square, a threat equal to a thousand Peekskills, challenge every decent-thinking citizen. Shall we defend our true heritage or shall we allow ourselves to be destroyed by American fascism parading as defenders of the democratic faith? One powerful answer must be

Ben Davis' election to the City Council—that he
may continue his fine contribution. Together with
that answer must be provision of immediate bail,
and demand for arrest of judgment and a new trial,
based on the true traditions of democratic justice.[13]

Despite Paul's best efforts, however, the Foley Square
defendants were doomed by the politics of their era. Medina
allowed hearsay evidence and irrelevant information into the
trial (including the testimony of alleged Communist Hebert
Philbrick, who testified about an imminent "armed insurrec-
tion"), thus stacking the deck against the Communist twelve.
On October 14, Davis and the other indicted Communist
leaders would be found guilty of plotting to overthrow the
U.S. government. With the exception of Robert Thompson,
who received three years, the defendants were sentenced to
five-year sentences and fines of $10,000 each. British leftist
writer Cedric Belfrage called the trial an "inquisition," noting
that the "trial set two important precedents. One was the
'Aesopian language' thesis which, proving that Communists
never meant what they said or wrote, made it idle for them to
cite their actual words. The other was that lawyers defending
heretics were guilty of contempt if, in what they thought to be
the line of duty, they sought to confine a trial to the indictment
and to have normal rules of evidence enforced."[14] Anti-
Communists hailed the convictions of the Communist twelve
as an important legal victory in the war against subversives.
Medina was the judicial star of the day, and McGohey was
soon promoted to a federal judgeship.

In his unswerving defense of the Foley Square defendants

and the Soviet Union, Paul became one of the most polarizing figures in the United States. A groundswell of anti-Robeson sentiment, particularly in the South, forced the cancellation of scheduled concert appearances. No Robeson visit went without at least the threat of violence. In October, Paul performed in front of fifteen thousand people in Los Angeles, despite calls by the City Council to boycott the concert. Despite numerous death threats and promises by anti-Robeson forces to repeat Peekskill, the concert was an immense success. It was also a huge personal boost to Robeson, who saw that his popularity was undiminished among many progressives, particularly younger blacks. "I have sung many times in Los Angeles," he told the *Daily People's World*, but no appearance has meant so much to me. I have never felt so much like singing and saying the things I did."[15] A few days later, he performed in Washington, D.C., where his arrival prompted extra security. In a rare showing of public support during anti-Red hysteria, prominent blacks in Washington issued a statement backing Robeson's visit. The statement, signed by Charles Houston, Mary Church Terrell, E. Franklin Frazier, W. C. Hueston, and Rayford Logan, noted that "many of us find ourselves in sharp disagreement with the position this great concert artist has taken on certain issues." But their bottom line was "vigorously and without qualification, we defend the right of Paul Robeson, whose voice has been heard in every land on earth, to sing and speak in the Nation's Capital."[16] In a speech before the concert, Frazier took the added step of defending Robeson, offering a rare justification of the maligned political artist's worldview.

For those who would invoke sociology and anthropology to bring understanding to the Negro problem let me remind you that in the American culture the Negro male has never been permitted to play a masculine role. There has always been a restriction upon his role as husband and father. He has been supposed to dance and sing or preach the Christian virtues of humility and forgiveness. This is partly why white America has become incensed at Paul Robeson. Mr. Robeson represents the Negro man in the masculine role as a fearless and independent thinker. He represents the new understanding on the part of the American Negro that his battle for freedom and equality is a part of the battle of colored colonial peoples in Asia and Africa and the battle of the serfs in Eastern Europe against feudalism.[17]

But Frazier was a plant in the forest when it came to advocating on Robeson's behalf. With the exception of the usual supporters (Communists and other marginalized individuals such as Du Bois), most of Paul's former allies refused to speak out. In January 1950, NBC canceled a scheduled Robeson appearance on Eleanor Roosevelt's Sunday program, *Today with Mrs. Roosevelt*. The last of the prominent New Dealers, Eleanor Roosevelt remained a hero to many in the Left. At a time when many liberals clammed up about the Communist witch hunt, she publicly preached discretion and denounced the HUAC as infringing upon the civil liberties of Americans. The cancellation of the Robeson appearance was seen as a blow to Paul and a victory to conservatives, who pressured the network into rescinding its invitation. The silence in the ranks of black leadership was equally telling; the NAACP did not issue a statement until several days after the announcement, while other prominent groups, including the Urban League and the National Council on Negro Women, didn't register a protest. The Left, as expected, rallied in support of Robeson, but the outcry was muted compared with the widespread praise of NBC for denying him the airtime.

As the calls to censure him increased, so did Paul's vehemence in defending his position. He blasted NBC for caving in to Right-wing pressure, pointing to the incident as more evidence that "warmongers" were openly persecuting progressives. But the TV show cancellation was a prelude to a more widespread effort by the white press in the 1950s to exclude Paul. By 1958, Robeson's name would be an afterthought in most white publications. Robeson turned to the black press to spread his message about U.S.-Soviet friendship, claiming that American politicians intentionally ignited conflict with the USSR to prevent Russia's "freedom" from reaching Negroes in the United States. "They (politicians) can shut me up. I'll gladly shut up tomorrow if the poor colored worker is freed of discrimination and can stand up with dignity and be a man," he told the Baltimore *Afro-American*. "I don't expect to recant what I have said about Russia, because I feel too deeply that Russia's program of raising the little people of all races to basic equality in their nation and in the world is the opposite of what our country and England and the fascists stand for."[18] Robeson also saw black publications as more sympathetic to him as a Negro, not an alleged Communist. He would become a fixture in several major black newspapers—including the *Afro-American*, the California *Eagle*, the *New York Age* and the *Pittsburgh Courier*—in the 1950s, taking advantage of their loyalty to promote his undiluted political philosophy.

Robeson used the sympathies of many African-Americans to paint his persecution as part of a larger-scale effort to victimize Negroes and other oppressed people. He claimed the Cold War was about more than just Paul Robeson, W. E. B. Du Bois, Ben Davis Jr., and a handful of other black leftists—it was about the future of a race. In February, he addressed the Progressive Party Convention, calling the foreign policy initiatives a curse to black America.

> We progressives must understand that the Negro people are in the forefront of every struggle in this land today—of the attacks on all minorities, foreign born, of the Jewish people and other religious groups. The Negro people today is the first to be lynched, the first to be terrorized in the mass, the first to be unemployed, the first to have relief cut, the first to lose his freedom and his basic civil rights—the first to be deprived of all his rights and citizenship.[19]

Paul's unambiguous stand on race issues in the United States came just as the Cold War heated up. With the ink on the Sino-Soviet alliance still drying, China was helping to train the forces of Kim Il Sung in North Korea for what would be their inevitable excursion into American-influenced South

Korea. Truman, under enormous pressure from conservatives to go with a more hard-line foreign policy, approved the development of the hydrogen bomb and, in a speech at the National Press Club, called for the vigorous defense of the Pacific perimeter—including Japan, the Philippines, and the Aleutian Islands—from potential Communist aggression. He would later approve measures beefing up the military budget to $50 billion, and putting American forces stationed overseas on constant high alert for an imminent conflict with the Soviet Union and its allies. Truman also established the Campaign for Truth, which would become a staple of American Cold War policy. The propaganda campaign included the creation of Voice of America and Radio Free Europe, the development of technology to make radio feeds into Russia (to counter Soviet state radio), and strengthening the communications structure of the armed forces to keep better track of Soviet and Chinese activities in Asia-Pacific. However, Truman's foreign policy initiatives were seen by many conservatives as not going far enough in stemming the spread of communism. Shortly after Alger Hiss's conviction on perjury, Joseph McCarthy made his infamous speech in Wheeling, West Virginia, asserting that there were no less than fifty-seven Communists in the State Department. His claim would effectively begin the era of McCarthyism, turning the government courts and law enforcement agencies into tools of an unofficial police state.

Though Paul's defense of the Soviet Union and the American Left was admirable, he clearly seemed out of touch with the pulse of the United States. He had even estranged liberals by browbeating them with his message. Robeson had tried to lump liberals and the Left together, the same flawed approach that doomed the Progressive Party from the very beginning. Liberals turned on Robeson for his insistence that the "true" progressives were the ones who endorsed the Soviet policy. A Unitarian pastor even made Robeson the topic of one of his sermons by pointing out that Paul and his "fellow leftists do cut a rather ridiculous figure in bellowing indignantly about the denial of your liberties when everybody who can read knows what would happen to liberties generally if your point of view came into power in America. So, in the name of honesty, let's ease up on this martyr pose. It's not fooling very many people." In perhaps one of the most even-handed critiques of Robeson's point of view, the pastor went on to note:

> Your remarkable loyalty to the Communist Party line in American public affairs, your zealous support of front organizations, and your uncritical and unquestioning attitude toward one particular nation not your own—all these suggest that your mind is made up on the point that a man has to be in or near the Communist camp to be a true liberal today. It is exactly here, Mr. Robeson, that you have completely lost touch with reality, I'm afraid. Not only do you make it especially difficult for liberals, whose name and language you still use but whose methods and philosophy you seriously twist; but you commit mayhem on the plain meaning of words.[20]

Despite the warnings, Robeson seemed oblivious to what the birth of McCarthyism would mean. In the last year, he had grown used to government attempts to censure and discredit him, but those efforts were to no avail. He was equally confident in this case, assuming that the rise of McCarthy would be followed almost immediately by the reactionary senator's fall. In June, Robeson was the keynote speaker for the National Labor Conference for Negro Rights, a coalition of black unionists that had remained militantly loyal to Paul in the wake of his recent controversies. Paul denounced Truman's Point Four Program as a tool of capitalists and fascists who "seek to restore power all over Europe and Asia."[21] He closed his diatribe against the administration and reactionaries by guaranteeing victory for progressive forces in the United States, saying that the organization of labor "sounds a warning to American bigotry and reaction. For if 15 million Negroes, led by their staunchest sons and daughters of labor, and joined by the white working class, say that there shall be no more Jim Crow in America, then there shall be no more Jim Crow!"[22] FBI agents—who were glued to Robeson's every move—took more detailed notes about Robeson's words.

The ramifications of Robeson's activism and his refusal to moderate his message would be felt in the coming weeks. In mid-June, the NAACP met in Boston and adopted a policy barring Communists. As Wilkins recalled, "the comrades were a problem that the NAACP had to face squarely."[23] The association's anti-Communist resolution reflected the growing edginess of American society about an imminent Communist takeover. Their fears seemingly were validated by the turbulence overseas. On June 25, North Korea crossed the 38th Parallel into the South, officially starting the Korean War. Anticommunists led the calls for the United States to intervene on South Korea's behalf, calling it a major test of the Truman

Doctrine. American troops confronted the North Koreans in Seoul on July 5; three days later, Truman named Douglas MacArthur head of the United Nations Allied Command. The United States had now juxtaposed itself into the lead of an international effort to defeat the North Koreans. Robeson upbraided the Truman administration for jumping into the war without using diplomacy first. "American intervention in Korea," he warned a Civil Rights Congress rally, "is the culmination of a wicked and shameful policy which our government has ruthlessly pursued with respect to the colonial peoples of the world." He repeated his claim that "the place for the Negro people to fight for their freedom is here at home—in Georgia, Mississippi, Alabama and Texas—in the Chicago ghetto, and right here in New York's Stuyvesant Town!" Robeson snickered at the possibility that "black Americans should one day be drafted to protect the British interest in Nigeria, whose proud people cannot be held in bondage for another ten years!"[24]

The CRC speech would be the breaking point for federal officials. Paul's suggestion that blacks wouldn't fight for a country that discriminated against them was poorly timed and smacked of treason. As the United States entered another conflict, his words were synonymous to enemy gunfire. In late July, the State Department issued an order demanding that Robeson, who was scheduled to leave for Europe, turn over his passport. The ruling placed FBI and customs agents on non-stop watch to make sure Paul did not leave the country. An August 23 meeting between Robeson, his attorneys, and the State Department did not change the government's position that Paul was a national security threat, and his international travel was "contrary to the best interests of the United States." What Robeson had privately feared—that the forces of fascism would try to silence him—became a reality. His lawyers prepped him on what they anticipated to be a lengthy legal struggle, given the political climate in the United States. With little hope of international travel, Robeson now had to fight for his citizenship.

As the age of Cold War paranoia got into full swing, Du Bois found himself in a similar position as Robeson. Having been rejuvenated by his interactions with young radicals following World War II, the Doctor had a sanguine outlook on the state of world affairs until the summer of 1949. Like Robeson, he was convinced that progressive forces would ultimately prevail in the war of philosophies and that colonial oppression would meet a quick and decisive end at the hands of Soviet-inspired intellectuals and activists. Encouraged by the development of a more militant intelligentsia in the United States, as well as the blossoming of Pan-Africanists overseas, Du Bois was confident he would live to see a new racial and socioeconomic reality for the world. It was this belief that inspired him to leave the confines of an office and take his message to the streets. The most influential man among three generations of Negroes had become black America's unofficial ambassador to the rest of the world, a role he enthusiastically shared with Robeson. The Doctor kept a grueling travel schedule, giving speeches on behalf of the numerous leftist causes he had become involved with following the war. In a 1948 speech at the Grand Boule of Sigma Pi Phi Fraternity, Du Bois offered a rebuttal to his Talented Tenth philosophy. "In the surroundings of my family in a little New England town," he told the gathering of young black men reared on his writings, "I felt myself always as a more or less isolated evangelist, who's going to teach the world what my people meant and what they could do." That philosophical arrogance, Du Bois admitted, led to the creation of the NAACP and Urban League, but failed to take into account "that the Negroes who were in school and getting an education were not by any means necessarily and inevitably the Negroes who ought to have had the chance. That large numbers of Negroes of great ability and talent never had the chance to learn, even to read and write. And that therefore the Talented Tenth had no right to preen itself upon the natural way in which it had risen to leadership; but rather should be extremely humble to think that by good fate they had the chance to be educated when others who deserved even more than they did, had no such opportunity."[25] The Du Boisian about-face on the concept to which his name has been most attached completed the transformation of the Doctor from a "bourgeois Democrat" into an uncompromising race and class radical. Whereas the Du Bois of twenty years earlier would have borrowed liberally from Fabian thought, his new incarnation was more in line with the economic teachings of Marx and the politics of Stalin.

The period of rejuvenation and idealism Du Bois enjoyed for the first time since the Harlem Renaissance abruptly ended with the downfall of the Progressive Party in the 1948 elections and his unceremonious dismissal from the NAACP. The Doctor began to share Robeson's belief that black leadership was useless in standing up for the gamut of issues facing the

Negro masses, a feeling that only grew with the chorus of denunciations from prominent blacks following the Robeson speech in Paris. The summer of 1949, marked by the advance of Mao's forces on Shanghai and Acheson's subsequent admission of futility on American backing of Chiang, turned Du Bois sour. He had become disillusioned by the HUAC hearings on Negro loyalty and the unchecked attacks on Robeson, fully aware that the witch hunt had only begun. Unlike Robeson, who clung to a tattered optimism, Du Bois was realistic in his assessment of what was happening in the Cold War era. Less than a month after Robinson's testimony criticizing the Robeson speech, Du Bois appeared before the House Committee on Foreign Relations in hopes of diffusing the anti-Soviet hysteria. "We are asked to believe that this country is in danger of attack from Russia or that Russia is ready to conquer the world," he told an unreceptive assembly of lawmakers. "We did not believe this when we asked ten million Russians to die in order to save the world from Hitler. We did not believe it when we begged Russian help to conquer Japan. We only began to believe it when we realized that the Russian concept of a state was not going to collapse but was spreading. . . . We want to rule Russia and we cannot rule Alabama."[26] His exasperation with American foreign policy driven by imperialists and capitalists drove him further into a Robesonesque justification of the Soviet imposition on Eastern Europe. "Russia has won the right to conduct her own economy as she wishes even if her plans no longer allow foreign capital to reap 50 percent profit on her serf labor," he noted. "Her main objectives have been advocated as strongly in the past in the West of Europe as in the East. . . . There is in them no threat to any kind of economic organization if that system can succeed poverty and bringing real democracy."[27]

The Sino-Soviet alliance was signed six days before Du Bois' eighty-second birthday. The Doctor saw the formation of the People's Republic of China as at least partial fulfillment of his prophecy of Asian supremacy. Like other leftists, he viewed the White Paper—and Truman's subsequent decision not to send American troops to defend Chiang in Formosa— as a blow against reactionaries in the U.S. government. However, his joy was short-lived. By the late spring, American policy hawks were preparing for what seemed like an inevitable entrance into the Korean conflict. Though he was privately resigned to war, Du Bois held out hope publicly for peace. That motivation led him to accept Progressive Party stalwart O. John Rogge's invitation for the Peace Information Center, an organization committed to encouraging the United States to disarm its nuclear arsenal. The Peace Information Center (PIC) was an avowed Leftist organization from the start, but what made it unique was that it had no official backing from the Communist Party. Rogge was a former Progressive Party attorney who had earned a strong reputation in activist circles and on Capitol Hill. Du Bois was comforted by the idea that he wasn't the only prominent name involved with the group. Robeson, Shirley Graham, John McManus, Albert Kahn, and Albert Einstein were among the impressive collection of activists who also joined. David Graham. Du Bois said the formation of the PIC was "thrilling" for his stepfather, who "really thought the organization would be an instrument of change."[28] The elder Du Bois had reason to be excited. Within its first three months of existence, the group had already done yeoman's work in promoting the Stockholm Peace Appeal. The PIC claimed 1.5 million people had signed the Stockholm Appeal by the second week of July. Abbott Simon, who served as the group's business manager, noted that the PIC appealed to a representative cross-section of the country "who didn't want another Holocaust."[29] The United States had gone beyond the point of return in its foray into Korea, but PIC members concentrated their efforts in ensuring that Truman would not resort to the nuclear bomb as he had in Hiroshima and Nagasaki five years earlier.

Du Bois's involvement with the Peace Information Center took his attention away, at least superficially, from the death of Nina. Du Bois's wife of more than fifty-five years passed away in a nursing home, ending what had been a life replete with maladies and unfulfilled promise. Her husband, as David Levering Lewis noted, had spent most of his life married to racial advocacy. Nina, as well as the other women in the Doctor's life, were mere mistresses.[30] Just weeks after Nina's passing, the Doctor mustered up the energy to challenge (in typical Du Boisian fashion) Acheson over the use of nuclear weapons by the United States. Disputing Acheson's assertion that the Stockholm Appeal was "a propaganda trick in the spurious `peace offensive' of the Soviet Union," the Doctor wrote[31]:

> The half billion persons who signed this Appeal and the billion who would have signed if given the chance, were moved not by the thought of defending the Soviet Union so much as by the desire to prevent modern culture from relapsing into primitive barbarism. The reputation of Dean Acheson, United

States Secretary of State, will never recover from his
deliberate attempt to misrepresent the origin, intent
and word of this great appeal.[32]

As Robeson had done with his speech on Korea less than a
month earlier, Du Bois infuriated government officials. His
antagonizing of Acheson and other members of the Truman
administration was no longer tolerable. Just days after the
State Department put its stop order on Robeson's passport, the
Justice Department issued a notice to Du Bois that the PIC
would have to register as a foreign agent. William E. Foley,
head of the Foreign Agents Registration division, explained in
his letter to Du Bois that the center was required to comply
under the foreign agents registrations act. During the Cold
War, the Justice Department used this tactic as a way of neu-
tralizing organizations it deemed as potentially seditious.
Though the PIC never openly attacked the U.S. government,
federal agents viewed most of the group's members (notably
Du Bois, Robeson, Graham, and Simon) as firebrands and
legitimate threats. In his response, Simon expressed incredu-
lousness at Foley's request.

I must admit I am at a loss to understand why you
consider that the Peace Information Center has an
obligation to register under the Act. The sole purpose of the Peace Information Center has been to
work with the American people for peace and the
avoidance of a Third World War and its terrible
consequences. . . . The Peace Information Center is
American in its conception and formation. Its

activities were intended to and do relate only to the people of the United States. It acts for and is responsible only to itself and to the people of this country. It has never agreed, either by contract or otherwise, to act as a "publicity agent" for a "foreign principal" as defined in the Act, nor does it purport or assume to act as one.[33]

Members of the group, sensing that the government was unlikely to withdraw its registration demand, retained the services of Gloria Agrin, a prominent liberal attorney whose clients included Julius and Ethel Rosenberg. Du Bois had concluded that the government was bent on making an example of the PIC in an effort to silence critics of its foreign policy. Seeing no recourse, the PIC membership voted to dissolve in October. Du Bois, smarting over Acheson's apparent vendetta, returned his attention to the leftist (and Communist-backed) groups he had already been a part of. His optimism about a peaceful solution in Korea died with the Peace Information Center.

CIVIL RIGHTS ACTIVISM in the early 1950s was dictated by the prevailing Cold War mentality: advocating black meant rejecting Red. The NAACP, which had shunned Du Bois and Robeson at the end of the previous decade, formalized its anti-Communist modus operandi with the formal exclusion and expulsion of Communists in 1950. Though Communist Party members represented only a fraction of the association's overall membership, Wilkins felt the NAACP was sending a message by adopting a zero-tolerance policy regarding Communists and other radicals. In February, Wilkins led a joint effort among various "friendly" civil rights groups in planning the National Civil Rights Mobilization in Washington, D.C. Patterson, on behalf of the Civil Rights Congress, entreated the leaders of the mobilization, particularly Wilkins, to allow the CRC to participate. Wilkins refused, claiming he did not want the "comrades" to "horn in on the mobilization."

> Part of my reasons were personal—I just didn't like the way Communists did business—but political considerations also dictated that they be shut out. We were having enough trouble getting Congress to consider even the most elementary civil rights legislation; the last thing we needed was to give ammunition to red-baiting Southern congressmen and senators, who would have loved nothing better than to paint us pink. If we had accepted help from the Communists, or had ducked the issue of keeping them out of the mobilization, Gabriel would have blown his horn for a long time before Congress did right by black Americans.[34]

Wilkins's personal animosity toward Communists and his desire for the NAACP to remain out of federal scrutiny led the association to adopt a formal statement barring the Left from participation in the mobilization. In doing so, the NAACP had reconstructed itself as a more moderate and digestible alternative to the militant civil rights platform advocated by the CRC. Again, the politics of the Cold War era put survival ahead of principles. As historian Wilson Record pointed out:

The NAACP leader was no doubt letting off a long-building head of steam. There was method in his public wrath, however, for the Association needed to forestall irresponsible charges that the Mobilization was Communist-inspired. Moreover, he was preventing in advance the almost certain split which would have come at the first session had the Communists been invited or admitted. (Wilkins) was determined that the Stalinists should not put the death sign on yet another coalition of liberal forces.[35]

In June, the NAACP wanted to send a resounding message to the Left *and* to anti-Communists. At the June convention, the association voted to expel Communists and revoke the charter of any NAACP branch suspected of harboring party members. The 6–1 vote essentially cemented the association's long-standing animus when it came to dealing with the Left. Wilkins later gloated, "I was happy to see them go. Ever since the twenties the Communists had been in a lather over ways to seduce Negroes. God knows it was hard enough being black; we certainly didn't need to be red, too."[36] But the NAACP's anticommunist stance went beyond simply shutting out Communists. As historian Manfred Berg later noted, the association struggled to fight claims that it had become the "left wing of McCarthyism."[37] The NAACP's refusal to condemn the witch hunts added to the prevailing notions among many non-leftist black leaders, including Frazier, Mary Church Terrell, and Rayford Logan, that it had gone soft in the civil rights struggle. The association had backed away from international suffrage issues, remaining silent on apartheid in South Africa and the

Korean War out of fears that conservatives might use such issues as measures to undercut its advocacy. Indeed, the "Red" label might have prevented the NAACP from launching its legal battles on behalf of school equality, which evolved into the desegregation.

While the association might have been justified in looking out for its best interests, it is harder to defend its rationale in collaborating with the government against the Left. As if Wilkins's moves against Robeson weren't enough, the NAACP leadership had kept the FBI regularly abreast of its efforts to shut out the Left. Wilkins, White, and Thurgood Marshall's correspondences with the FBI proved, in many scholars' eyes, that the association had broken ranks with its more radical counterparts and chose to "wrap itself in the flag."[38] The NAACP's decision to help the bureau identify and go after suspected Communist and leftist groups might have been a preemptive strike designed to eliminate potential competitors from the civil rights battlefield. As Horne noted, the CRC's high-profile legal defense of the Trenton Six, Martinsville Seven, and Willie McGee—however self-promoting it might have been—served as a wake-up call to the association that if it was not willing to go out on a limb for social justice, other groups were. White, who had returned to the position of executive secretary (though the title was nominal) in 1951, ascertained that leftist groups could hijack the NAACP's budding legal efforts against Jim Crow. Left-wing historians such as Horne have cited White's personal correspondences with FBI officials, including Hoover, as evidence of a cozy and mutually beneficial relationship between the association and the bureau.[39]

As it turned out, the FBI did not need the NAACP's assistance to help undermine the CRC. The bureau had already infiltrated many branches of the congress by the early 1950s, setting the stage for the IRS and the Subversive Activities Control Board (SACB) to take action against the CRC. The IRS levied a $75,000 tax claim against the congress, and the SACB charged the organization for failing to comply with the McCarran Act. The CRC's subsequent downfall paved the way for the NAACP to begin its legal assault on segregated schools and the concept of "separate but equal" unopposed. In later years, the association would find itself in territorial battles with King's Southern Christian Leadership Conference (SCLC) and Stokely Carmichael's Student Nonviolent Coordinating Committee (SNCC), leading to more clandestine relations with the FBI at the height of the civil rights struggle.

THE REVOCATION OF ROBESON'S PASSPORT and public response to his dilemma showed just how far he had fallen in the past year. No major mainstream black organization spoke out in his defense. In fact, most of the outcry came from overseas. Jawaharlal Nehru called upon the State Department to immediately return Robeson's passport and restore his right to travel. Only eight months earlier, Essie Robeson blasted Nehru for his alleged jailing of twenty thousand Indian radicals and his brutal repression of the Maoist rebellion in Andhra Pradesh. Claiming she was "embarrassed" about her previous support for India, Essie publicly disavowed her friendship with Nehru.[40] In spite of their public squabble, Nehru continued to hold Paul in very high regard. He would be one of the most prominent world leaders to vouch for Robeson during his passport battles. Though other notables, including Einstein, Terrell, Henry A. Wallace, and Frazier, would join in the passport fight, their support was exceptional at a time when Cold War politics dictated loyalties. McCarthy's crusade against Communists suffocated society while implicating almost everyone who espoused liberal tendencies. Robeson morbidly predicted that "the loyalty witch-hunts will soon catch up with Mr. Truman himself. Mr. McCarthy is gunning for him and all Rooseveltians and New Dealers. Even Mrs. Roosevelt may not escape."[41] Stifling political dissent through scare tactics only strengthened the conservative agenda. Secret police, night raids, and disappearances became commonplace as the McCarthy era fueled the wildest speculation that anyone's neighbor could be complicit in a conspiracy to overthrow the government. CRC leader George Marshall (imprisoned in 1950 for refusing to turn over the membership list of the congress) summed up the state of the times by declaring that "the House Un-American Committee will be free to demand membership lists and set up blacklists in an effort to destroy all other organizations which fight Jim Crow, Anti-Semitism and for the defense of the constitutional liberties of the American people. This would be a fundamental blow to basic American freedoms."[42]

As anti-Communist sentiment peaked, Paul's legal battle became almost impossible to wage. Newspaper articles about the State Department's decision to revoke his passport were published without any questions about *why* the government felt Robeson was a threat. In addition, very few news organizations publicized Robeson being awarded the International Peace Price from the World Peace Conference (an honor he shared with Pablo Picasso). At the same time, the press ran numerous stories about "patriotic" Negroes. Many of these stories were sourced from the NAACP offices. In their eagerness to discredit Robeson and distance themselves from the Left, White and Wilkins offered examples of blacks who gave lie to the notion that Paul's words and actions were reflective of his race. Conservative black publications followed suit, promoting black "patriots" and offering rebukes of Robeson. *Brown* and *Ebony* offered anecdotal accounts of the bravery of black soldiers in Korea (to go along with their pictorials of scantily clad women). Like the NAACP, many black organizations and publications lined up to pledge allegiance at a time when dissent was linked to Communism. Without any widespread support, Robeson and his lawyers filed a civil suit against the State Department in December 1950. In filing the suit, Robeson claimed that the State Department's revocation of his passport was meant to "divert discussion of the all-important explosive Negro and Colonial questions." The real enemy, he said, was the conservative oligarchy of American society who "have conspired with frightened elements of the Film, Theatre, Radio and Television industries to prevent me from earning my living by practicing my profession here in my own country" and overseas.[43] But Paul played into that enemy's hands with his unwavering support for China, claiming that he found it "ridiculous to even imagine [China and North Korea] embarking on a predatory war to conquer other peoples."[44]

As he grew more defiant, Paul's fight for his passport became less and less defensible. Patterson, who provided informal legal counsel to Robeson, hoped the court battle would cause such an international furor that the government

would be forced to concede defeat. But the State Department—
still reeling from McCarthy's charge that it harbored
Communists—had no such plans. To make matters worse for
Paul, other prominent blacks continued their campaign to
shame and ostracize him. Wilkins had been the most vocal of
the anti-Robeson effort, but up until 1950, White refrained
from attacking his estranged friend. That changed when
White, who returned to the NAACP after a one-year medical
leave of absence, wrote an article for *Ebony* claiming Paul had
become absorbed in his own idealistic fantasies about Russia.
White was disingenuous in his analysis of Robeson. He had
not known Paul intimately (as he had claimed to) in more
than twenty years, and his implication that Robeson was more
devoted to Russia than his own race seemed to be sour grapes.
Walter had always prided himself on developing the political
acumen of young talents; Paul was supposed to be *his* protégé.
But Robeson had gone astray from White after the Harlem
Renaissance, and without the help of the NAACP, had become
one of the most prominent political artists in the world.
White's *Ebony* piece was soaked in bitterness, but it was still
a powerful propaganda tool to taint Robeson.[45] Though it had
become fashionable for liberals to question Paul's political
convictions, the *Ebony* article had crossed the line for some.
Marie Seton upbraided White for twisting the facts and for
failing to note that Paul was "the one leading Negro of this
time to refuse, in the face of combined black and white attack,
to capitulate one iota from his convictions."

No one has the right to snipe with innuendo and
half-truths at Mr. Robeson in the way Mr. White

does when, right or wrong, Paul Robeson has show immense personal courage and been willing to say those very things which many people think but dare not say. Is there another living Negro celebrity who in our time forfeited his, or her, personal standing for conviction?[46]

Seton's defense did little to sway public opinion when it came to Robeson and his passport battles. Though some liberal anti-Communists worried that the persecution of leftists such as Robeson, Davis, and Patterson might make "heroes out of them," the political winds sustained in favor of reactionism.[47]

As Paul unsuccessfully fought for his passport and his reputation, the hammer dropped on Du Bois. In February, the Justice Department, not satisfied with the Peace Information Center's official dissolution, issued another order for the group to comply with the foreign agent registration act. When the PIC did not respond (ostensibly because it no longer was in existence), a federal grand jury indicted the group's officers, including Du Bois. In what was the most powerful example of how far Right the country had gone since the start of the Cold War, the U.S. government was now charging the elder statesman of the civil rights struggle with being a "subversive." Du Bois, Simon, Kyrle Elkin, Sylvia Soloff, and Elizabeth Moos were named as defendants in the *U.S. v. Peace Information Center* case. Many progressives quickly denounced the indictments, expressing shock that members of a defunct pro-peace organization (that had *no* connection to the CPUSA) could be held accountable for any crime against the government. Robeson and other prominent African Americans quickly mobilized in the Doctor's defense. Within two weeks of the indictment, more than seven hundred friends of Du Bois's crowded into Small's Paradise Restaurant in Harlem to celebrate the Doctor's eighty-third birthday and raise support for the embattled icon. Extolling the virtues of his fellow Cold War pariah, Robeson said, "Dr. Du Bois, by his full participation and dedication to the people's struggle, gives new meaning to the history of the Negro in his long and courageous fight for all liberation." He predicted that the indictment wouldn't stand because "the great masses will give their answer and set him free to labor on."[48]

As Robeson foresaw, the masses did respond. Prominent blacks flooded the Justice Department and the White House with letters and phone calls protesting the action against Du Bois and the other PIC officers. "They had acted against someone who was seen as untouchable," Simon recalled. "Dr. Du Bois *was* untouchable."[49] Unlike the Robeson case, the government found itself on the losing end of a public relations battle. Not even the staunchest anti-Communists could offer an eloquent defense of the Du Bois indictment. Though the Doctor was affiliated with Communists (and Simon was a member of the party), there was no evidence that the group had any ulterior motives behind its mission of peace. Even black moderates like former GOP Congressman Perry Howard spoke out against the prosecution of Du Bois. Bishop R. R. Wright Jr., head of the A.M.E. Church in Little Rock, Arkansas, implored Truman to intervene and stop the government's case. "Nothing," Wright wrote, "could happen to hurt and discourage the Negro people of America more than the conviction of Dr. Du Bois, whom no one of us could think of as disloyal to his country."⁵⁰ Wright seemed to capture the sentiment of black America, which was unwilling to see its most venerable leader be sacrificed in a Cold War witch hunt.

It is important to look at the response to the Robeson passport case and the Du Bois indictment under the Smith Act. The lack of outcry generated in the Robeson case stemmed from there being no formal charges against him; had Paul been arrested, it can be assumed that more blacks would have spoken out in his defense. In Du Bois's case, the charges were so incredible that even those who disagreed with his political views were inclined to support him. But on a deeper level, the reaction many African Americans had toward the Robeson case and the Du Bois trial reflected the "pay your dues to the race" mentality that has remained strong to this day. Robeson was an entertainer with a political view, a man whose radicalism was born well into his career as an artist. Many black leaders agreed with A. Philip Randolph's assessment that Robeson was a "Johnny-come-lately" to the civil rights struggle, despite the fact that Paul had been one of the most outspoken advocates of black suffrage and global emancipation for two decades. Though Robeson was a strong proponent of humanism and a dogged fighter for black empowerment, most of his reputation as an activist had been carved in Europe. His political outlook, shaped by an epiphany in a foreign land, was not grounded in the experience of black America. Robeson had traveled the world battling for racial and economic justice, but he had been unable to bring the idea of global struggle home to American Negroes. Rather than try to project black America's struggles outward, he tried to get blacks to embrace the struggles of others. But with Jim Crow an everyday reality, it was almost impossible for most African Americans to find any common ground with the Irish, the Czechs, Chinese, Panamanians, and other oppressed peoples Paul had fought for over the years. Robeson's message, twisted by Cold War politics, made him appear disconnected from the black experience in America. Du Bois, on the other hand, was an advocate for the Negro race from the start. His evolving theories on the advancement of blacks were applicable to every generation of African Americans born since the start of the twentieth century. He had fathered the Talented Tenth and, through his involvement with the Niagara Movement, laid the groundwork for two of the most prominent civil rights protest organizations in the country. Du Bois had earned, over nearly sixty years, an indubitable reputation as a champion of the Negro race in the United States and Africa. The Doctor's philosophies, ranging from those in *Souls of Black Folk* to the more militant ones in *Freedom* and the *Daily Worker*, reached almost every African American in some way. As the Peace Information Center trial began in November, he stood as an example of overzealous Cold War persecution.

"I have faced during my life many unpleasant experiences: the growl of a mob; the personal threat of murder; the scowling distaste of an audience. But nothing has so cowed me," Du Bois recalled, "as that day, Nov. 8, 1951, when I took my seat in a Washington courtroom as an indicted criminal. I was not a criminal. I had broken no law, consciously or unwittingly. Yet I sat with four other American citizens of unblemished character, never before accused even of misdemeanor, in the seats often occupied by murderers, forgers and thieves."[51] Though the Doctor had a groundswell of support and testimonials from prominent blacks calling for a dismissal of the indictment, as well as a skilled legal defense team, he remained skeptical about his chances for a fair trial.

> The jury system in the United States has fallen on evil days. The old English concept of a man's guilt being decided by presentation of the facts before twelve of his fellow citizens too often fails. Juries are selected in devious ways and by secret manipulation. Most Negroes are sent to jail by persons who hate or despise them. Many ordinary workers are found guilty by well-to-do "blue-ribbon" people who have no conception of the problems that face the poor. Juries are too often filled with professional jurors selected and chosen by the prosecution and expected to convict.[52]

Du Bois's supporters tried to enlist other high-profile lawyers to help in the case. Shirley Graham Du Bois thought of asking Thurgood Marshall to serve as cocounsel, but knew the NAACP officer would be unwilling to appear on her husband's behalf. Graham Du Bois instructed Agrin to tell potential defense witnesses "that their testimony would be, in essence, an attestation of Dr. Du Bois' reputation for veracity and patriotism. They should be asked to be available, on several days notice, to appear in Washington in early November, and informed that their expenses would be paid."[53]

Hoping to alleviate the burden for the beleaguered Agrin, Vito Marcantonio—who had lost his congressional seat a year earlier—offered to help in the defense. It would prove to be a decisive move. Marcantonio picked apart a weak prosecution case, asserting what many in the public had believed all along: There was nothing solid connecting Du Bois or the PIC to any foreign principal. Rogge took the stand against the PIC defendants, asserting that the PIC was connected to a foreign group called the Defenders of Peace. Du Bois later wrote how Marcantonio easily poked holes in the prosecution's theory of parallelism.

The prosecution then tried to say that the Defenders of Peace had said there was a terrible plot against humanity, and that the United States was the center of this plot, and for that reason the Defenders of Peace was attacking the United States. The defendants' lawyers objected to this. The judge reminded the prosecution that they had established the existence of a foreign group with headquarters in Paris. They should now indicate to the jury the evidence seeking to show the connection between that foreign group and the Peace Information Center.

This led to a long argument in which Marcantonio stressed the fact that it was absurd to argue that parallelism in thought or expression established the relationship of agency. Du Bois summed up Marcantonio's argument in *Battle for Peace*:

> Two people may have parallel views, one at the north pole and one at the south pole. That does not establish agency." The court agreed that two parallel lines never meet, but said that he assumed that the connection between the two lines of thought were going to be indicated. The court said that unless this nexus was shown, "I think that at the proper time you would be entitled to a directed verdict. This was the

first intimation that our case might never reach the jury; but this seemed at the time too good ever to become true.[54]

As Du Bois predicted, federal prosecutors could not overcome a lack of evidence and Marcantonio's brilliant courtroom performance. On November 13, Judge James McGuire dismissed the government's case against the defendants, scoring a rare legal victory for the Left during the Cold War. "I believe the happy end—if 15 million Negroes want it enough to stay right with it—will be freedom for all our militant Negro leaders who honestly and sincerely fight for Negro Rights," Essie Robeson wrote after the dismissal. "We Negro people slowly woke up, stood up, and angrily said NO! to the FBI and the Administration; No, you shall not lynch our Dr. DuBois, in or out of court."[55] Du Bois and his allies would have little time to savor the triumph, however. Within a year, he, like Robeson, would have his passport denied, setting off another round of legal skirmishes to win the right to travel.

Though Paul had battled vigorously for his freedom to leave the country, he found other ways to get his messages overseas. Accepting invitations from foreign groups, Robeson sent speeches and greetings exhorting the continued stand against "the most vicious and most powerful of the warmongers." During his domestic confinement, Paul sent greetings of support to the All-India Peace Council, the Natal Indian Congress, and the Congress of Soviet Writers. Boris Polevoy, who attended the Soviet Writers conference in Moscow in 1954, described to Robeson the audience's reaction when Paul delivered his speech via phone from the United States.

The ushers carried out a large speaker and put it on the rostrum, the chairman introduced you, a deathly quiet came over the hall, and once more we heard the hearty sound of your unique bass, enunciating the simple introduction of your words; a new wave of enthusiasm shook the hall, everyone jumped up and offered a longstanding ovation.[56]

The legal setbacks Paul suffered in getting his passport back only emboldened supporters to do more. A Left-wing Australian writers group wrote to President Dwight Eisenhower to immediately restore Robeson's traveling privileges. "Where is the America of democratic and liberal tradition?" the letter writer demanded to know. "You make a singer into a hero by robbing us of the right to listen to his songs." In 1954, a "Let Paul Robeson Sing" campaign was launched in London; Robeson allies, led by Left-wing writer Cedric Belfrage, tried to organize a mass petition to be delivered to the American Embassy to show that Robeson was still in great demand across the Atlantic. Einstein and Charlie Chaplin, along with the poet Pablo Neruda, also joined in the testimonials. Chaplin wrote that "to deny a great artist like Paul Robeson his right to give his art to the world is to destroy the very foundation upon which our culture and civilization is built. It negates every principle of democracy and freedom and follows a path of the worse type of tyranny."[57] Janet Jagan, the First Lady of Guyana, added, "In British Guiana, we can perhaps appreciate Mr. Robeson's plight more than others, for we too, are today encountering the terrible hysteria to act with such repression." An Israeli youth group sent a telegram urging Paul to "be strong. We are sure you will win if you stand in your opinion, Peace in the World!" But the testimonials did little to change the State Department's view on Robeson. In its denial of his application to attend the Congress of Soviet Writers, the passport division repeated the claim that "it was not in the national interest" to allow Robeson to leave the country.[58] The division would remain firm in its refusal for another four years, effectively clipping Paul's wings at the height of the Cold War.

LEGAL BATTLES WEREN'T DU BOIS and Robeson's only problems during the Cold War. The suffocating political atmosphere created by McCarthyism had robbed them of most of their political platform; both men found themselves censored in the mainstream. In October 1950, Du Bois took a crack at political office, accepting the American Labor Party (ALP) nomination for the U.S. Senate seat in New York. It was ironic timing, given that the Doctor was at the nadir of his popularity. His views no longer considered mainstream, Du Bois likely ran on principle and out of motivation to make a statement. His opponent, Democrat Herbert Lehman, was one of the few open liberals in Congress, and his civil rights record won him the endorsement of almost every prominent African American in the state. Lehman was likely as surprised as most when the ALP announced Du Bois, along with John T. McManus (governor), Clementina J. Paolone (lieutenant governor), Michael Jiminez (comptroller), and Paul L. Ross (mayor) as its political ticket. McManus, the radical former journalist, was closely associated with Du Bois and Robeson in the Council on African Affairs and the Peace Information Center. Ross, meanwhile, resigned from Mayor William O'Dwyer's administration to become a Left-wing activist. Du Bois's Senate bid was also a shot at Adam Clayton Powell Jr., who had publicly distanced himself from the Doctor and Paul after the 1948 elections. During his campaign, Du Bois and his supporters accused Powell of collaborating with "reactionaries" and going along with the Communist witch hunt. An ALP press statement read, "Despite the glamour surrounding him and his past activities, it is a fact that Congressman Powell has slipped tremendously in the past several months, especially since the Korean situation. . . . His former fight has left him." Robeson enthusiastically supported Du Bois's political bid, perhaps more optimistic (and idealistic) about the Doctor's chances of winning. At the party convention, Robeson revved up the delegates with a thunderous oratory praising Du Bois and promising "that our day of liberation is not far off."

> While Republicans and Democrats have nothing to offer but insults, abuse and excuses, the real party of labor in New York, the ALP . . . recognizes the full dignity of the Negro people and does honor to itself by placing at the head of its ticket one of the great Americans on our time. Should Dr. WEB Du Bois go to the United States Senate? One of the tragedies of American political life is that for so many years so many mediocrities, who do not deserve to sit in the same room with him, have gone to the head of the State Department, other places in

the cabinet and to the Presidency itself. Congratu-
lations to you. The Negro will not forget that the
ALP turns to a Du Bois for leadership, and not to
the sycophants and flunkies of monopoly wealth
and plantation power who clutter up the tickets of
the twin parties of reaction.[59]

As expected, Lehman easily won reelection; Du Bois captured
only 4 percent of the statewide vote, most of which came from
Harlem. But the Doctor's political bid had a greater significance
than what even he could see at the time: his completed transformation from militant academic to radical activist. Du Bois had
earned the stewardship of Black Thought with the pen,
expressing his brilliance from the confines of an office or a college campus. His larger-than-life status—a reward of a prolific
writing portfolio and an unmatched academic pedigree—had
afforded him the right to stay away from the public and expose
his vulnerability as a shy and aloof academic. But the professor
had left the safety of academia in 1944, hoping (in Gandhi's
words) to be the change he wished to make. Du Bois's activism
only grew as the Cold War heated up; he had no plans to abdicate
his throne as the "elder statesman" of the Negro race, even if the
current times had propelled him out of the mainstream. Like a
boxer on the ropes, Du Bois in his eighties would determinedly
fight back against his foes in the government and the upper echelon of black America. The conservatism of American society
only made Du Bois more dogmatic; he made up his mind to
spend his remaining days as an active combatant on the ideological battlefield, ultimately willing to be sacrificed in the name of
principle.

While his lawyers fought Dean Acheson in court, Robeson tried to find a forum to get his message out. By the end of 1950, most black publications expressed hesitance to publish his articles, fearful that they would become targets of anti-Left backlash. Paul took control of *Freedom*, a monthly black journal in Harlem geared toward a militant and leftist audience. Robeson expressed hope that the magazine would become "the real voice of the oppressed masses of the Negro people and a true weapon for all progressive Americans."[60] Du Bois joined him in the endeavor, publishing an article in the inaugural issue in November 1950. *Freedom* was more than a mouthpiece for Du Bois and Robeson, or, as some have suggested, an organ for the mortally wounded CPUSA; it provided an avenue for emerging black nationalist and left-wing writers to express their views without fear of censorship or modification. The journal's editors and contributors included Louis Burnham (who did most of the editing), Lloyd Brown, Alice Childress, Loraine Hansberry, Esther Jackson, Herbert Aptheker, Thelma Dale, Ossie Davis, and Ruby Dee. By assembling a youthful staff and soliciting young talent to contribute to the magazine, Robeson had allowed a new generation of black leftists to find their voice in his magazine. Though *Freedom*'s message was mostly heard in Harlem, its existence was a statement of defiance toward the "forces of reaction" Robeson had so openly despised. In its four-year existence, the magazine would launch writing careers, publish the works of leftists who had been blacklisted during the Cold War, and give a quality alternative to the conservative-leaning Negro publications (*Brown*, *Ebony*) that dominated the 1950s. However, like most of Harlem's black literary mediums, a small budget and an even smaller circulation precluded *Freedom*'s long-term success. Robeson managed to keep the publication running on pins and needles until it folded in 1955, collecting donations from sympathetic left-wingers around the country.

The *Freedom* experiment came at a crucial time in the repositioning of the Left. The old guard of Communists and black nationalists were disappearing, losing their freedom because of Cold War prosecution or their loyalty to the militant struggle Du Bois, Robeson and a few remaining leftists espoused. The McCarran Act took McCarthyism to another level. Now armed with federal prosecution powers against law-abiding citizens, government officials could demand left-wingers to sign oaths of loyalty. In 1951, federal prosecutors launched a second round of attacks against the CPUSA leadership, indicting the second echelon of party leadership under the Smith Act. James Jackson was among those charged. Rather than sign the loyalty oath or surrender to face prosecution, James took Esther and their two children "underground." The Jacksons would remain in hiding for more than five years, finally surrendering to federal authorities in 1956. Others weren't as bold or as lucky. Charismatic union organizer and Communist Party leader Elizabeth Gurley Flynn, who battled Hoover in the 1920s during the Palmer riots, was arrested and imprisoned in 1951 for violating the Smith Act. The conviction was the fulfillment of a vendetta Hoover had against Flynn for thirty years. Left-wing writer V. J. Jerome was also charged with "conspiring to teach and advocate the forcible overthrow of the government." He was convicted in 1954 and served three years in prison, joining Ben Davis Jr.,

Gus Hall, Eugene Dennis, Henry Winston, Dashiell Hammett, and other prominent radicals in the ranks of the incarcerated. Robeson, Du Bois, Howard Fast, John Howard Lawson, and Shirley Graham Du Bois were among the notable leftists who joined in the fight to free Jerome. "If Mr. Jerome can be indicted and sentenced for the publication of an article," Leftist Waldo Salt lamented, "there are few honest intellectuals in America who may not be subject to censorship for the expression, present or past, of non-conformist ideas."[61] Salt's assessment proved to be accurate. The threat of legal action by the government was enough to convince many prominent African Americans and progressive whites to leave the Left. By the end of 1951, former Communist Party members Joshua White, Canada Lee, and John Lautner had switched sides, testifying against the CPUSA and their old friends, including Robeson. Within five years, Fast and Doxey Wilkerson would also leave the Communist Party, though they opted not to turn against their comrades in the struggle.

The exodus in the wake of the Smith Act indictments and the vicelike grip of McCarthyism factored heavily in the collapse of the CPUSA and the Left in the early 1950s. The expulsion of Communists from the mainstream labor movement (engineered by anti-Communist union leader and civil rights activist Walter Reuther) forced leaders to reinvent the party yet again. By 1951, most Communist Party luminaries had realized that efforts to unite the white and black working classes had failed. Unions, though liberalized as a result of the advocacy of Reuther and George Meany, still refused to abandon the racial hierarchy system in their ranks. Blacks continued to be the "last hired and first fired" in union "shops." Communists focused their efforts on galvanizing the black working class, targeting rural sharecroppers and nonunionized tradespeople. But recruiting new members proved impracticable in the political climate; many of the party's recruits turned out to be FBI informants who would later testify about far-reaching schemes to overthrow the government. In the age of paranoia, joining the Communists was simply beyond reason. It did not help matters that the CPUSA was wrought with dissension during the Cold War. While Robeson remained loyal to old guard members such as Patterson, Foster, and Davis, Du Bois expressed a deep admiration for Henry Winston. Though Winston, Foster, and Davis were part of the infamous Communist twelve, there was an irreconcilable rift among them when it came to the direction of the party. Eugene Dennis, Gus Hall, and Winston still leaned toward a more practical approach for the party, given the dangerous political climate and their own legal troubles. But for Foster and Davis, a return to anything that resembled Browderism was out of the question. Foster tried to rally the party's remaining members against McCarthyism and in favor of Stalinism, which had already gone out of fashion for many Communist Party members. But the party's inefficacy in reaching blacks continued, and by the mid 1950s, many black Communists had either left or had been expelled. Claudia Jones, the Trinidadian Communist who reminded many in the Left of C. L. R. James and George Padmore, was deported to London in 1955 after being convicted under the Smith Act. At a rally shortly before Jones's banishment, Robeson declared, "Claudia belongs to us, belongs to America, and the reactionaries in power who have ordered her deportation have thereby delivered another grievous blow against the best interests of our country."[62]

Already teetering on collapse under the weight of McCarthyism, the Communist Party ultimately fell in 1956, when Nikita Khrushchev revealed the gory details of the Great Purge. Khrushchev had sought to de-Stalinize the Soviet Union, hoping to accomplish his goal by discrediting the architect of modern Russia. Though Khrushchev's revelation about the genocide furthered his own interests, the shock was too much for the CPUSA to bear. Most of the party's remaining members, as well as Soviet supporters, left soon after the full extent of the Great Purge came to light. Wilkerson, frustrated that he could not find a job because of his Communist ties, left the party in 1957, a decision that angered his close friends in the Left. Graham complained that "if Doxey Wilkerson is leaving the Communist Party because he thinks it will follow that he will thereby be able to get a better job under the repressive conditions now in force in our country, this is one thing. If, however, he is saying that the *goal* . . . of the Communist Party is *not* 'an America where men of all races and creeds can walk together in dignity and equality, where thought and speech are truly free, where political processes are genuinely democratic, and where the vast material resources of our nation are geared to the people's needs' this is quite something else."[63] Wilkerson's departure was especially shocking to Du Bois, who regarded Wilkerson and Robeson as two of the most profound influences in his conversion to the far Left. Fast simply left after realizing that the party's mission no longer fit his views. He and other white Communists, including lawyer Jessica Mitford, came to view the reshaped Communist Party as nothing more than a forum for black nationalists and unflinching Soviet loyalists. Following his departure from the party, Fast admitted to Gerald Horne that "the attitude toward the Communist Party on the part of Africans and even Black Americans, I would suspect, would be very different from what my attitude is."[64] Fast's admission articulated an unspoken truth about the CPUSA in the 1950s: Its most ardent supporters were gung-ho black radicals who came to see every other avenue of protest blocked off or tainted by white imperialism. The blacks who stayed with the party in its dying stages would later infuse the nationalist movement with a Marxist ethos.

The revelation of Stalin's purge traumatized Robeson more than Du Bois. Paul had spent more than twenty years defending the Soviet Union, only to find that the man he lionized as a defender of freedom was one of the most notorious mass murderers of the century. Robeson had blindly excused the repressive policies of Stalinism as a political necessity in times of global conflict. He never publicly questioned Stalin's actions, and even after Khrushchev's revelations, remained adherent to the bottom line: the USSR was anti-Fascist and anticolonial. "Through the years, we have watched the phenomenal development of this socialist society," he wrote in 1957. In his role as antiestablishment provocateur, Robeson glorified the Soviet Union as helping to bring about a "change in the balance of world power between the new defenders of the rights of peoples of all colors and the centuries-long imperialist oppressors of the West."[65] Paul's rationalization of Soviet genocide was likely the most sensible way to deal with the betrayal of his ideals. Though he would remain publicly supportive of the Soviet Union, his justification of Stalinism seemed hollow. Du Bois, on the other hand, was pragmatic. He defended the Great Purge and the consequences of Stalinism the same way he had contextualized the Japanese invasion of China. The Doctor was always willing to choose the lesser of evils; he had never wavered from the belief that Western imperialism and the exploitation of darker peoples by capitalism was the standard of atrociousness. In Du Boisian *realpolitik*, the executions of political dissidents and innocent civilians could be logically explained as a mere consequence of a continuing social and cultural experiment. He and Robeson ultimately concluded that a country that had been in existence for only forty years was inevitably dealing with growing pains. There was no excuse, however, for a country to continually oppress "a people who have suffered slavery for 300 years, who have been the primary source, in human bodies, in human toil, of much of the great wealth of this land—and who still live in poverty and in unspeakable ghettoes."[66]

As the Cold War losses mounted, both men found themselves making a last stand against anticommunist offensive. Though moderate blacks avoided scathing personal attacks on Du Bois (his age and his long-standing civil rights record made him somewhat of a symbolic sacred cow among Negroes), they did not show such refrain with Robeson. In November and December 1951, the *Crisis* published scalding assessments of Paul's political activism. The first, written under the pseudonym Robert Alan, said most Negroes "cannot recognize the Paul Robeson who today is so deep in the Communist morass that he even becomes involved in Communist internal fights, such as his rigid application of the Kremlin line to Yugoslav Communists—certainly not an issue for one to whom the Negro cause supposedly is paramount." The article, relying heavily on White and Yergan's commentary, asserted that Robeson had been led astray by the Communists and was now the party's goat. "How has Paul Robeson served the Communist cause in America? The evidence is that even his magnetic personality has failed the Communists."[67] The second, written with the Wilkins byline, claimed Robeson was part of the CPUSA's attempts to influence civil rights groups, and in doing so, undermine their reputations. In attacking communism among Negroes, Wilkins was as zealous as McCarthy and Hoover. Other publications followed the *Crisis* attack. In December 1954, *Brown* ran an anonymous piece (which might have been planted by the State Department) assailing Robeson as a hindrance to Negro advancement. "It's frustrating to any man, black or white, considered superior, to meet a world which offers him at best second rate employment, housing and equality because of his race. The fact remains that Robeson is but one of fifteen million Americans facing these same problems. Yet how many are 'performing services beneficial to the communists?'—Few if any." The author quoted Robeson allies-turned-adversaries Yergan and Randolph to underscore the point that Paul did not speak for the majority of Negroes. In fact, the author claimed, Robeson was no longer considered a national hero, but "a national casualty." The piece ended with a blunt estimate of Robeson's legacy as a civil rights fighter.

It's more than tragic to consider the good Robeson might have done had he chosen to fight his problem as thousands of others are doing. A few "overly aggressive" people may criticize the NAACP and the Urban League. But these "progressive' individuals don't realize how difficult it is for these groups to do their work. The fact remains that in the areas which count, housing and unemployment, the NAACP and the Urban League are first to do the most effective fighting. Robeson is indeed a tragedy. He is a disappointment to his race, his country and most of all to himself. Many of us at first felt sorry for Robeson. This sorrow in the face of our GIs combating an enemy supported by Robeson, is turning to general resentment.[68]

Robeson's public downfall sparked rumors that he would repudiate communism and return to the ranks of mainstream America. *Tempo* magazine reported in its May 1954 issue that "Paul (Ol' Man River) Robeson, the Red's showbusiness prize" would appear on Edward R. Murrow's *Person to Person* on CBS to "renounce communism, blast its doctrines." A CBS spokesman flatly denied the report, noting that "the singer has never been approached to appear on the show nor has Robeson ever asked us to be a guest."[69] Other media reports speculated the same outcome of Paul's long-standing affiliation with the Communist Party. Some black journalists openly questioned whether Robeson was staying with the party under his own free will (or, as some asserted, was being held captive by Essie and Paul Jr.).

The Doctor and Shirley Graham Du Bois offered a vigorous defense of Paul and a stern rebuttal to the claims of the anti-Communist press. "Communism was a friend of Negroes and not an enemy," Graham Du Bois opined. "The American Press under the monopoly of control which characterizes it today began a systematic attack on Robeson by misinterpretation, innuendo and significant omissions and silences. Robeson stood his ground and Negroes hesitated."[70] In a press statement presumably written by Essie, Paul finally spoke in his own defense. Chastising the media for engaging in "fantastic slander," Robeson said he remained "firmly and fully devoted to the struggle for peace and democracy throughout the world, for Negro liberation and colonial freedom, for friendship with the peoples of the Soviet Union, new China, and the people's democracies of Europe. The interests of the working people of every land are my guiding principle, and I know of no force that can make me change." Adding that "the doom of imperialism has been sounded in all of Asia" and Africa, Robeson (or in Essie's typical gusto) finished his statement with a stroke of defiance: "Change my mind? Gentlemen of the press, you'd better change yours, because what I believe in—is happening!"[71]

REALITY DID NOT SEEM to reflect Paul's optimism. In 1951, McCarthyism became the law of the land following the conviction and death sentences for Julius and Ethel Rosenberg on charges they were spies for the Soviet Union. Though the case against the Rosenbergs was shaky at best (prosecutor Roy Cohn relied primarily on the testimony of Ethel's brother David Greenglass), most Americans supported their prosecution. The Left rallied around the Rosenbergs. Led by Shirley Graham Du Bois, Abbott Simon, Theodora Peck, Robeson, and Du Bois, the remaining American radicals embarked on an international crusade to save the couple from execution. Armed with testimonials from Einstein and Pablo Picasso, Rosenberg advocates painted the case as textbook anticommunism and anti-Semitism. Robeson headlined several rallies for the Rosenberg defense fund, equating their case with the Scottsboro Boys and other blacks unjustly imprisoned or condemned. The same antiblack zeal that killed Willie McGee, Robeson argued, had "subjected Julius and Ethel Rosenberg to an unprecedented sentence for a crime no honest man believes they committed."[72] Robeson and Du Bois also made pitches to leading black churches to help in the defense of the death row political prisoners. Their efforts were to no avail, as on June 19, 1953, the Rosenbergs were executed, ending one of the most polarizing legal battles of the century.

McCarthyism also destroyed progressive politics during the 1950s. Wallace left the party soon after the North Korean invasion of South Korea, which he and other liberals blamed on Soviet support. Du Bois balked at the notion, ridiculing Wallace for falling into the trap of Cold Warriors.

> We were sure the Russians had started the Korean uprising, were furnishing arms and ready to march to war. Henry Wallace actually saw them and ran backward so fast that he tripped over his own resolutions, and stepped in the faces of his friends. Still the Soviets did not fight and began instead to call for world peace; for union against the atom bomb; for peace congresses. But the United States was not misled; not they. They stopped the peace

appeal. They picked up and jailed advocates of peace. They barred from our shores foreign advocates of peace, persons of the highest reputation.[73]

Du Bois's assessment of Soviet motives might have been oblivious to the facts, but he was right in questioning Wallace's retreat from progressivism. Had Wallace fallen victim to the oppressive conditions of McCarthyism? Arthur Schlesinger Jr. later noted that Wallace seemed happy to go back into private life, away from the political scene in which he had felt betrayed by so many people. Schlesinger hinted that Wallace might have felt used by the Communist Party and the Soviet Union to advance a clandestine agenda, embittering the "naïve" political idealist.[74]

Thus, the Progressive Party—minus a prominent leader who could draw liberal votes—chose to run Left-wing San Francisco lawyer Vincent Hallinan and Charlotta Bass for president and vice president, respectively. Hallinan made his name as an uncompromising leftist, angering authorities for defending union leader Harry Bridges on charges he was a Communist. He also sued the Catholic Church on the basis of whether there was a God. However, Hallinan and his wife Vivian were indicted in 1951 on charges of tax evasion; he served eighteen months in federal prison as a result. Though many of Hallinan's supporters believed his conviction was politically motivated, it was hard to muster support for a convicted criminal and an unabashed atheist at a time when Christian dogma was seen as the liberator against the "ungodly" ways of Soviet communism.[75] Bass became the first black woman to be nominated for vice president.

Robeson was not as fervent in supporting Hallinan and Bass as he had been with Wallace four years earlier; like many leftists, he felt the Wallace defection was a stunning blow to the Progressive Party. Paul seemed content to go through the motions, making not-so-emphatic endorsements such as: "You'll hear more about [Hallinan and Bass] and their platform before this is campaign, and I hope that you'll come to believe as I do that here is the only ticket for Negroes in November."[76] Instead of promoting Hallinan and Bass, Robeson focused on attacking the reactionary elements of the Democratic and Republican parties. He also joined in the Left's criticisms of Powell, who, like other black public figures, shifted to the center in order to survive politically. Powell, who had promised to fight tooth-and-nail for the FEPC and antilynching legislation in the 1940s, moderated his political stance and became known more for his bravado than his political action. In fact, by 1950, Powell had not only distanced himself from his mentor, Marcantonio, but had caused a rift with other progressive Democrats by not showing up for important congressional votes. What incensed Robeson even more was that Powell had endorsed Adlai Stevenson and his running mate, Alabama Dixiecrat John J. Sparkman.

> Not long ago Congressman Adam Powell threatened to call upon Negroes to boycott the presidential election unless real guarantees were forthcoming from his party, the Democrats. But it seems that Mr. Powell is built for speed but not endurance, for his hot words had hardly cooled off before he leaped publicly into the lap of Stevenson—*and Sparkman.*

Maybe Mr. Powell got some guarantees, but the
Negro people have received none whatsoever from
the two old parties.[77]

Du Bois was equally subdued in his support for the 1952
Progressive ticket, which ran on the motto: "Win or lose, we
win by raising the issues."[78] Perhaps out of loyalty to Robeson
and his friends on the Left, Du Bois endorsed Hallinan and
Bass, knowing that they had little chance to win. The Doctor
had already concluded that liberal dissent was intolerable to
reactionaries, and that no matter how hard the Left fought, its
struggles would be in vain against the juggernaut of
McCarthyism. The left of center political base had been all but
discredited by the fall. Du Bois blamed the NAACP and other
so-called liberal groups for trying to destroy the progressives
instead of working with them. He felt ashamed that blacks
would rather cow to the likes of McCarran, McCarthy, Gold-
water, and Cohn than use the repression of the Left as a galvanizing force. As he complained to Eurasian radical Cedric
Dover, "It is a great opportunity for a courageous stand
although few people seem it realize it."[79] Choosing principles
over political reality, Du Bois cast his ballot in November; it
would be the last time he would vote in a presidential election.

10

BONDING THROUGH DISGRACE

Paul Robeson how proudly your name flourishes on my
tongue even yet. Though there are those who ask: What
did you say? I always repeat, Paul Robeson speaks for me.
Even yet.

—Beulah Richardson, *Freedom*, June 1951

AT THE HEIGHT OF MCCARTHYISM, Du Bois and Robeson found themselves with few allies domestically and unable to reach out to their supporters abroad. Banished to the fringes by Cold War politics, they turned to the shadows to find solace and solidarity. Despite the near destruction of the Left during the 1950s, a galvanized cadre of radicals remained beneath the surface. The small pockets of left-wingers in New York, Chicago,

Philadelphia, and San Francisco provided a haven for the Doctor and Paul, allowing them to remain relevant to progressives. Young leftists looked to the men as inspiration for survival and adherence to principle in the face of enormous societal coercion to conform. The ruins of the Communist Party gave rise to a new generation of radicals whose perspectives had not been shaped by Moscow. Du Bois and Robeson embraced these new leaders of the Left, bridging the vestiges of Harlem Renaissance and Popular Front radicalism with Cold War–era progressive thought. This generational transition allowed both men to remain at the forefront of Cold War counterculture, as exemplified by the Doctor's whimsical Senate bid and Paul's defiant autobiography, *Here I Stand*.

Though McCarthyism fell because of overzealous prosecution and fabricated allegations of Communist plots, the legacy of anti-Communism would become ingrained in American society. McCarthy had fallen, but Hoover remained in power. Despite cooperating with various civil rights groups and prominent black leaders in an effort to discredit the Left, Hoover remained fundamentally opposed to any efforts at social equality and integration. As McCarthyism historiographer Ted Morgan later wrote, Hoover's initial misgivings about civil rights "mutated into irrational loathing" of black progress.[1] The transparency of the government's animosity toward black progress alienated many younger African Americans and shocked liberal whites, fostering an atmosphere of increasing discontent. By the mid-1950s, the start of a new grassroots struggle against Jim Crow was in full swing, spurred by those who had become frustrated with the constraints of pragmatic protest. That opened the door for a quiet resurgence of leftist thought and the partial rediscovery of Du Bois and Robeson as pioneers in progressivism. Despite being shunned by the mainstream, the Doctor and Paul reinvigorated left-wing activism among a younger generation, including those (Martin Luther King Jr., Malcolm X) who offered belated credit to their forerunners in the struggle.

DU BOIS AND ROBESON hit rock bottom in the early 1950s for a number of reasons: their political views had fallen out of step with acceptable civil rights dialogue; they advocated peace with the two biggest enemies of the United States—the Soviet Union and China; and their refusal to back down from their convictions alienated erstwhile allies who struggled for their own political survival. As P. L. Prattis lamented, "Bold defense of the Negro's rights is often a costly venture."[2] Anti-Communism became a convenient veil for racists and anti-Semites, as proven by the Rosenberg case. Du Bois and Robeson had already figured that the Republicans, led by McCarthy and Nixon, had mastered the politics of fear. Though the Venona encryptions would later validate some of the U.S. government's concerns about Soviet espionage, the overstatement of Communist influence in American society fostered malicious reactionism.[3] Du Bois believed the "witch hunt" that had marginalized the Left and prosecuted thousands of people on trumped-up charges was the creation of a nation insecure in its own democracy. In assessing the fate of the Rosenbergs, Du Bois was apoplectic:

The awful crime we threaten to commit in order to

protect a nation which thinks it needs this sacrifice of
blood to save its soul. Such a soul is not worth saving.
Such a sacrifice can be demanded of the chosen of
God only by the triumphant hosts of Hell.[4]

Robeson was equally distraught by the willingness of most
Americans to allow McCarthyism to reach unparalleled levels
of outrageousness. Following the election of Eisenhower, he
became even more convinced that the political storm would
hit minorities and the ranks of labor the hardest.
"McCarthyism is the American brand of fascism," Robeson
declared. "If this administration, which is a political vehicle
for the giant corporations and entrenched greed, embraces
fully as it seems prone to do, then the outlook for the Negro
people, labor, the foreign born and other minorities will be
gloomy indeed."[5] Paul realized that the anti-Communist stance
adopted by labor organizations and the NAACP would do
nothing to enhance their positions among conservatives.
Though McCarthy did not take swings at the NAACP, he tried
to implicate all black advocacy groups as part of a plot to
destroy America. In 1953, Joe subpoenaed prominent African
Americans, including Langston Hughes, Essie Robeson, and
Doxey Wilkerson, interrogating them on their intentions to
follow Communist Party philosophy in overthrowing the U.S.
government. Prosecutor Roy Cohn repeatedly questioned
Hughes about poems he had written in the 1930s, refusing to
accept Hughes's explanation that his musings about a "Soviet
America" were simply artistic interpretation. Essie Robeson
was not as accommodating to her questioners, going to toe-to-
toe with McCarthy. Essie, never one to back down, infuriated

senators with her coy answers and her insistence to invoke the Fifteenth Amendment.

> **McCarthy:** Negro or white, Protestant or Jews, we are all American citizens here and you will answer the question as such. The question is: Are you a Communist today? If you feel the answer will tend to incriminate you, you can refuse to answer. That is the only ground under which you can refuse to answer.
>
> **Mrs. Robeson:** What confuses me a little about what you said—you see I am a second-class citizen in this country and, therefore, feel the need of the Fifteenth. That is the reason I use it. I am not quite equal to the rest of the white people.[6]

While McCarthy and his companions might have knocked heads and gnashed their teeth over Essie's responses, they found more capable allies in former Communist Party members turned informants. At the apex of McCarthy's crusade, the government had enlisted professional witnesses in order to buttress its claim of a Communist conspiracy. Informants did the dirty work of their lawmaking bosses, often making fantastic allegations without fear of political retribution. Patriotic duty was hardly motivation for most government informants to willingly stake their (shoddy) reputations to destroy those of others. For instance, Ralph De Sola—a former Communist Party member of the New York Writers' Project—testified that Anna Rosenberg, a State Department nominee, was part of numerous Communist-front organizations. Rosenberg insisted she had never met De Sola, nor had she been part of any

Communist Party fronts. The facts backed her up, which cost De Sola his wings as the government's Abigail Williams.[7] But in a growing number of cases of Whittaker Chambers complex, other ex-Communists gladly filled De Sola's shoes as informants. Their stories gained them celebrity, and in a country that glorifies patriots, many viewed their roles as vehicles to stardom. Former Communists Louis Budenz and Harvey Matusow were among the most famous "star" witnesses for the government. They named hundreds of Communists, despite no facts to substantiate their claims. Budenz even named Shirley Graham Du Bois as a member of the Communist Party (which she was), though he admitted under cross-examination that he had never met her.[8] Despite inconsistencies in the informants' testimonies, their allegations fueled American paranoia that Communists were in every corner of the country, posing as good neighbors and civic leaders in order to gain a community's trust.

McCarthyites continued their attacks on suspected Communists, presumably to keep the GOP's influence on Capitol Hill. However, the castle built on a foundation of lies was doomed to crumble. McCarthy's witnesses became more careless in their allegations, more brazen in their attempts to destroy ordinary Americans and carry out personal vendettas, and more oblivious to the consequences. McCarthyism was an engine that was running off the rail, and Joe was the operator pressing the accelerator. By 1954, many of McCarthy's allies were turning against him. His star witnesses' testimony began to fall apart under closer scrutiny by government officials. Some would recant their testimony. As Joe began to unravel, his political opponents were emboldened to attack him.

Robeson, who had been one of the few to consistently speak out against McCarthyism (and defend the Communist Party), opined that "Americans are waking up to the fact that to be the victim of an attack by McCarthyites may not be fatal." Perhaps buying into his own perceived invincibility, McCarthy went after the U.S. Army, which in turn alleged improper conduct against McCarthy's staff. The nationally televised hearings would expose McCarthy as a self-serving political survivalist who had been held captive by his zealousness. Paul's public optimism that America would defeat McCarthyism was validated on December 2, 1954, when the Senate voted to censure McCarthy. A month later, Harvey Matusow—the former Communist Party member known for his self-promotion and concoction of far-reaching Communist plots—recanted his testimony in several Smith Act trials, admittedly perjuring himself. The McCarthy era had officially ended with Matusow's admission and Joe's subsequent implosion.[9] McCarthy died in 1957, a defeated man who had succumbed to depression and alcoholism. His destruction would not discourage the recklessness of his anticommunist comrades-in-arms. The FBI would continue to use informants to infiltrate the Communist Party and the civil rights movement, helping to destroy the former while creating rifts among the various groups involved in the latter. Hoover would impale himself by going after King, who had transcended reproach by the early 1960s.

Though Du Bois and Robeson had stood up to "American Fascism," they had become unwitting sacrifices for liberal America. Even after McCarthy's crusade was proven to be a "Big Lie," progressive forces were unwilling to help restore the

Doctor and Paul's reputations. The NAACP had bigger fish to fry, namely the fifty-eight-year-old doctrine of separation known as Jim Crow. The association filed suits in several states charging that black children were given inferior education to whites. Led by a legal team of Thurgood Marshall and Louis Redding, the NAACP and its allies launched an all-out legal attack on segregation. The case (*Brown v. Board of Education*) was argued in 1952, but a decision was not reached until May 17, 1954. In what would prove to be the landmark case in striking down segregation, the Supreme Court agreed with the plaintiffs. In his opinion, Chief Justice Earl Warren noted that to deal with the problem of separate and unequal, "we cannot turn the clock back . . . to 1896, when Plessy v. Ferguson was written. We must consider public education in the light of its full development and its present place in American life throughout the Nation. Only in this way can it be determined if segregation in public schools deprives these plaintiffs of the equal protection of the laws."[10]

The court's ruling signaled a turning point in the civil rights struggle. Even more significant was the timing of the ruling; Warren and his fellow justices did not bow to pressure from right-wingers who decried any attempts at civil rights as fodder for Communists. Though pointing out that "at best it will be a generation before the segregated Negro public school entirely disappears," Du Bois was thrilled with the legal victory. "It is going to be difficult," he predicted, "for the South and the Northern copperheads to treat the separate school decision as they have treated Negro disfranchisement since 1876."[11] Paul was convinced the legal victory would finally bring the Left its just due. "Far from being 'extremist,' [the demand for integration] had been voiced by Thurgood Marshall of the NAACP and . . . is backed by all sections of the Negro people. Yes, a ferment is growing among America's students, both Negro and white. Many are beginning to see that if a concern for future jobs has dictated conformity, a concern for their very lives requires that they think for themselves."[12]

Could the *Brown* decision have been possible without the help of the Communist-led Left? Walter White and Roy Wilkins thought so. White, who passed away a year after the *Brown* decision, opined that the NAACP's victory validated the notion that Negroes did not need communism and rejected the militant tactics of radicals. In crediting the Negro's "indestructible faith in democracy," White wrote, "Not even the very considerable aid given to the Communists by enforced segregation of Negroes, continuation of discrimination, filibusters against civil-rights legislation, and mob violence by American enemies of the Negro have been able to shake that faith."[13] His eulogy seemed fitting at the time, since the civil rights movement—minus the CPUSA—was picking up momentum following the *Brown* victory. The fact that only a few thousand party members remained in the wake of McCarthyism buttressed his claim. But what White failed to see was how the reverse psychology of anti-Communism factored into the civil rights struggle. Though Eisenhower, at Hoover's urging, refrained from enforcing *Brown*, his advisors soon convinced him that failure to enforce the Supreme Court's ruling would play into the hands of Communists. With their public praise of the Communist Party's militancy against Jim Crow, Du Bois and Robeson undoubtedly factored into the government's considerations. The last thing the Eisenhower administration wanted was to make martyrs out of Du Bois and Robeson *and* add fuel for Soviet rhetoric. Within a decade, American society would undergo its most radical change since the Civil War. The rise of the struggle for equality from the ashes of the old left would lay the foundation for Du Bois and Robeson's resurgence among a new generation of African Americans and progressive whites.

IF DU BOIS AND ROBESON represented the vanguard of the embattled Left during the Cold War, then Shirley Graham and Eslanda Robeson were the undisputed first ladies of the struggle. Shirley and Essie were more than just loyal life companions to their iconic husbands; they were prominent radicals in their own right, establishing themselves as prolific writers and complementary political voices to the Doctor and Paul. Though Shirley was Du Bois's second wife, her devotion to the Doctor stretched nearly forty years before their marriage.[14] Eslanda, meanwhile, had remained at Paul's side since 1921, bearing witness to and aiding his political transformation over the past three decades. For both women, taking care of their husbands went beyond spousal obligation; they both embraced that duty out of maternal instinct and a fervently held notion of territorialism.[15] The biggest challenge was dealing with husbands whose public stature belied their insecurity. "All that I can do is to surround him with every comfort and make him feel secure and loved," Shirley wrote Essie shortly before Du Bois's death. "You know something of that problem."[16] Buttressing their husbands' psyches and defending their political views became a trademark of Shirley and Essie's Cold War advocacy. Together, the Du Boises and Robesons stood unparalleled as the foremost couples of the Left during a decade of intense political repression.

Shirley Graham's rise from a young playwright and scholar to the inamorata of the most influential African American alive was unconventional, to say the least. Graham married her first husband, Shadrach McCants, the same year as Paul and Eslanda; unlike the latter, however, Shirley was doomed to a failed relationship. Six years and two sons later, she divorced McCants. As a young single mother, Shirley found it difficult to embark on her own career; she left her children, Robert and David, in the care of her parents and went to Paris, where she joined other African Americans whose romantic notions of the city made them oblivious to France's culpability in colonial oppression. Shirley returned several years later, embarking on an academic career that propelled her toward a life in academia. But another turn in the road led her into the heart of the black arts movement, and by 1932, Shirley was an accomplished playwright, having earned praise from Du Bois's *Crisis*.

By the mid-1930s, Shirley joined several other ambitious black women in pursuing Du Bois. Du Bois's larger-than-life status made him irresistible to those seeking even a small piece of his heart. To his numerous lovers, seducing the revered Doctor was tantamount to capturing the unattainable. Shirley was no different in her initial motivations, but her duty to Du Bois extended beyond worshiping his name and legacy. By the late 1930s, she would become an invaluable assistant in his research, "discovering" Africa and forming the roots of her own Afrocentric thought in the process. After a brief stint with the NAACP, which led to her own revelations about the association's commitment to grassroots uplift, Graham became nominally associated with left-wing groups in New York. Shortly after the death of her eldest son Robert in 1944, Shirley threw herself into radical political involvement, officially joining the Communist Party. One of her main goals in joining the party was attempting to provide "guidance" and "assurance" to her lover, the Doctor. Many historians later claimed that Graham was on a mission of conversion, but evidence indicates that Shirley's attempts to draw Du Bois to the Left were inspired by her own idealistic notions of Communism more than any Communist Party–sanctioned effort. Regardless of her motivations, Shirley's intensified affair with Du Bois corresponded with her political awakening. The two spent the latter part of the summer of 1944 in more frequent contact, including an escape to Lake Cobbosseecontee, an isolated retreat area in Litchfield, Massachusetts. "It is far enough from NY not be bumping into people," Graham wrote Du Bois.[17]

Graham's quest to draw Du Bois into the fold of the Left helped bring the Doctor and Paul closer together. Shirley, whose friendship with the Robesons stretched nearly twenty years, served as an intermediary between the two giants. Graham, who wrote Robeson's biography in 1946, lionized Paul as a champion of anticolonial thought. It was only fitting, she felt, that he would serve as the model for black progressivism—a paradigm she wanted Du Bois to follow. "When our world is crumbling to pieces,' she wrote Robeson, "you stand silhouetted upon the horizon—the perfect pattern for the coming 'world citizen.'"[18] Like other leftists, she hoped Robeson would act as a guide in political advocacy and catalyst to the radicalism that brewed within Du Bois. Graham also inserted herself into the social and political circle that was forming around the men as the political climate took a drastic turn to the Right. By the late 1940s, her efforts to bond Du Bois and Robeson would prove successful; within a few years, her attempts to become the woman in the Doctor's life yielded similar results.

The highlight of Shirley Graham's life came at the nadir of William's. One week after Du Bois was indicted for his involvement with the Peace Information Center, the couple wed. On February 16, 1951, Shirley became the second Mrs. Du Bois. In her new role as life partner to the father of black thought, Shirley Graham was the primary gatekeeper of her husband's social circle. Aware that government surveillance was a reality for her octogenarian husband, Shirley fiercely guarded the Doctor from anyone she did not know or trust. Shirley became Du Bois's secretary, political advisor, and most of all, the muse for his radical Cold War writings. As Gerald Horne noted in his biography of Graham Du Bois, Shirley embraced the role of caretaker for the aging civil rights icon. Putting her writing career on hold, Shirley was zealous in defending both her husband and Paul during the anti-Red crusade. She viewed the attacks on Du Bois and Robeson as the focus of conservatives' efforts to destroy the Left.

In her own political transformation from bourgeois liberal to staunch Communist (and later, a Maoist and black nationalist), Shirley Graham Du Bois found a kindred spirit in Eslanda Robeson. Like Shirley, Essie was weighted with the enormous role of being the other half of an internationally recognizable couple. Over the years, she was Paul's spokeswoman (though sometimes her attempts to speak for her husband only did more harm than good), ego masseuse, and often his ghostwriter. Essie, who felt she knew Paul well enough to espouse what she perceived to be his opinions, penned some of Robeson's most profound political observations during the Cold War. She was not one to take second place to Robeson. In fact, some biographers have written that Essie was driven by an intense competition with Paul, hoping to somehow carve her own legacy that paralleled his. She was fully aware that other prominent leftist women such as Graham and Louise Thompson were accomplished writers and activists long before they became Mrs. W. E. B. Du Bois and Mrs. William Patterson, respectively. Unfortunately, Eslanda's efforts in that regard fell short: despite an accomplished career as anthropologist, writer, activist, and linguist, she is still remembered mostly as Mrs. Robeson.

But Essie could claim success when it came to molding Paul philosophically. Unlike her husband, she did visit Africa, observing the firsthand conditions of disenfranchised blacks and Indians in South Africa. Though Essie shared most of Paul's observations on the Soviet Union, she was a more intense anticolonial than pro-Socialist in the 1930s. Most of the articles purportedly written by Paul in the 1930s were actually penned by Essie; her keen grasp of political dynamics, as well as her ability to use subtlety in some areas and emphasis in others, created some of Robeson's most intellectually provocative pieces. She tempered Paul's optimism with a strong dose of *realpolitik*, making—and keeping—alliances with people her husband might not have done on his own. It was Essie who kept in intermittent contact with Carl Van Vechten and Walter

White long after Paul's political transformation alienated him from both men. Essie "managed" her husband professionally and politically, but her style rubbed many of Paul's friends the wrong way. She came off as abusive and condescending toward Paul, and her constant desire to "butt in" on her husband's tête-à-têtes with political dignitaries only added to her reputation as a meddler.[19] But the image of Essie as a controlling figure who tried to monopolize Paul's name is not wholly accurate; beneath the standoffish demeanor was a woman who had a sincere passion for social justice.

Essie and Shirley had common characteristics that made for an "intense" friendship over many years. Both were resourceful, charismatic women who were determined to make the most of their opportunities in the limelight. They also had a flair for hyperbole when articulating their own political predicaments. Essie and Shirley painted themselves as victims in equal standing to their husbands, claiming that the persecution of Paul and William was an attempt to silence them as well. Essie embraced a bunker mentality in defending her political views. "Obviously, it would be impossible for anyone to be loyal to that part of any country which persecutes him, or to those people who do him harm and wish him evil," she wrote. "Such people are his enemies. Even animals recognize their enemies and make war on them or at least defend themselves."[20] Though Shirley was more charming than Essie, both women exuded savvy when it came to dealing with the public image of their husbands. Their alliance was only strengthened by the fact that both were members of Delta Sigma Theta Sorority, a black sorority known historically for cultivating women in leadership roles.

As it became more and more obvious that Shirley was priming to become Du Bois's next wife, Essie and Shirley grew even closer in their personal and political dealings. In 1950, Graham asked Essie—who had accumulated a lengthy FBI dossier of her own—to sponsor Du Bois's Senate bid. Mrs. Robeson, aware that her name would likely hinder the Doctor's candidacy, suggested Shirley "find a less controversial name than mine. People who would follow me would support Dr. DuBois anyway on their own. We want someone who would attract the more conservative non-political thousands. If this candidacy is properly sponsored, it would be very hard for any Negro not to vote for him, without being branded as anti-Negro." Essie was a key figure behind the scenes for Du Bois, actively supporting his candidacy and praising him as the antidote to the ignorance of Cold War hysteria. "I am willing to bet that Dr. Du Bois, with his long life of study and experience, has more theoretical and practical first-hand knowledge of the world problems now facing us, than all the members of the Senate and Security Council put together," she wrote.[21] During the PIC trial, Essie spearheaded guerrilla-style attacks on the media, the government, and so-called "Uncle Tom" Negroes, whom she blamed for not coming to Du Bois's defense. She did not refrain in using invectives against J. Edgar Hoover, Walter White, Roy Wilkins, and the entire Truman administration, lumping them together as coconspirators in a plot to discredit and humiliate Du Bois. But, as she would later gloat, "Dr. DuBois was the wrong Negro for the FBI to pick on."[22]

Shirley reciprocated the spousal advocacy by being one of Paul's chief advocates during his passport battles and HUAC hearings. She painted Robeson as a lone warrior whose only crime was speaking his mind. "The American Press . . . began a systematic attack on Robeson by misinterpretation, innuendo and significant omissions and silences. Robeson stood his ground and Negroes hesitated," she wrote in an epilogue to McCarthyism.[23] Graham Du Bois and Eslanda wore their husbands' martyrdom as badges of honor in the 1950s, using what happened to the Doctor and Paul as the embodiment of American oppression. Like their husbands, both women glorified the Soviet Union and the development of Marxist-inspired independence movements in Asia, Africa, and Latin America.

Essie's strong bond with Shirley was natural yet ironic. She had spent most of her married life looking over her shoulder, fretting about the possibility Paul would leave her for one of his many lovers. Though she would develop strong friendships with a few of her husband's paramours (Freda Diamond and Uta Hagen especially), Mrs. Robeson generally viewed the "other" women with disdain. After all, she viewed herself as the typical wife of a prominent black man, burdened with the role of providing emotional comfort and security while tolerating her husband's indiscretions. Shirley Graham was the "other" woman in the Doctor's life. She had beaten out the likes of Jesse Fauset, Georgia Douglas Johnson, and Virginia Alexander over the years to win the honor of becoming Du Bois's life companion. Essie could feel for Nina Du Bois, but her reverence toward the Doctor and her deeply professional and personal respect for Shirley likely mitigated any resentment she might have had over their affair.

Though Shirley and Essie were politically inseparable, their friendship was often volatile. David Graham Du Bois acknowledged that his mother and Essie did not always get along, a likely consequence of "first lady" complex. What had brought them together—being the lovers of two internationally recognized men whose careers had taken a dive—also caused friction. Shirley, like most of Paul's friends, felt that Essie had an overbearing and abusive style when dealing with Paul; in her opinion, Essie "didn't treat Paul right." Essie, meanwhile, might have harbored some bitterness over the fact that Shirley was an accomplished activist *before* her marriage to the Doctor.[24] Despite their differences, Shirley and Essie tirelessly worked together to defend their husbands' battered public reputations during the Cold War. Their efforts would ultimately implicate them, too, as evidenced by Eslanda Robeson's forced testimony before the McCarthy's bulldogs and the censorship of books written by Shirley Graham Du Bois. Still, their resilience and unwillingness to back down from controversial positions made them indispensible partners to the Doctor and Paul. Though both women would be recognized in later years as prolific radicals and feminist pioneers, their most important duty in the 1950s was to make sure their husbands did not face the witch hunt alone.

SHORTLY AFTER THEIR WEDDING, the Doctor and Shirley bought a town house in Brooklyn Heights from playwright Arthur Miller. Miller, who would write *The Crucible* in 1953 as an allegorical indictment of McCarthyism, became close to the Du Boises. He joined a New York social circle of leftists that would meet often at the Grace Court home throughout the decade; the impressive list of regular houseguests included the

Robesons, the Jacksons, Ossie Davis and Ruby Dee, Abbott and Priscilla Simon, Freda Diamond, Theodora Peck, Louis Burnham, Ed Strong, Howard Fast, Herbert Aptheker, and Alice Childress.[25] The Du Boises' new home would not only serve as their haven during the turbulence of the Cold War, but also as a base of operations for left-wing activists pushed underground by McCarthyism. Because of the Doctor and Paul's confinement, both men spent significant time together. Robeson would come over frequently to talk with Du Bois, where both men would "spend hours talking about the state of the world." David Graham Du Bois recalled a particular incident when Robeson, whose trips to the Grace Court home were not complete without a round of the grand piano, broke the piano bench. Unfazed by the awkwardness, Paul proceeded to sing in front of his shocked hosts and several guests. Such anecdotes were common, as Robeson made a third home out of the Du Bois residence (the second being the Manhattan apartment of Sam and Helen Rosen). The visits forged a stronger filial bond between the two men, who had long shared the same political vision and whose friendship was guaranteed by their similar circumstances. For Robeson, who was in his fifties, the notion of Du Bois being a father figure seemed only natural, given the Doctor's advanced age and wisdom. Du Bois appreciated and returned the regard, having "adopted" Paul as more than just a close comrade-in-arms. The Doctor's role as surrogate parent would extend beyond Robeson; by the end of the decade, he had similar relationships with David, Aptheker, James Jackson, and Simon.

Aptheker's relationship with Du Bois would grow beyond personal attachment; he would become one of the most noted preservationists of the Du Boisian legacy following the Doctor's death. Aptheker, a Communist Party member since 1939, remained loyal to the party despite growing reports of Soviet anti-Semitism following World War II. Having embraced the various incarnations of Du Boisian thought, Aptheker sought to publish the Doctor's correspondences, an endeavor William enthusiastically backed. However, few academic presses were willing to support Aptheker's efforts, owing to the hostile political climate and Du Bois's against-the-grain philosophies during the Cold War. Aptheker, however, loyally documented Du Bois's life and times, despite being blacklisted during McCarthyism. Du Bois appreciated Aptheker's steadfast commitment to the party, especially after Herbert had been shut out of teaching opportunities at most colleges and universities because of his political beliefs. In one instance, Aptheker had been banned from speaking at Ohio State University; he sat onstage as several students took turns reading his works. Aptheker, nearly fifty years Du Bois's junior, became one of the Doctor's closest confidants during the 1950s, and was one of the few the few whites who had not turned on Du Bois following the Doctor's final split from the NAACP and his assaults on white philanthropy. As editor of *Masses and Mainstream*, Aptheker frequently solicited Du Bois's editorials, allowing his mentor a forum for his increasingly marginalized opinions. Some have called Aptheker an "ideological sounding board" for Du Bois, since the pupil eventually guided his mentor into an official embrace of the Communist Party.[26] In later years, Aptheker would successfully publish the three-volume correspondences of Du Bois through the University of Massachusetts Press. He would also share biographical responsibilities with Shirley Graham Du Bois, who considered Aptheker the "only white American" she could fully trust.[27]

Aptheker wasn't the only acolyte committed to preserving his mentor's legacy; Lloyd Brown emerged as Aptheker's counterpart in documenting Robeson. Brown, a politically savvy wordsmith whose Marxist interpretations of history fueled a prolific writing career, became Paul's chosen scribe during the 1950s. Brown worked with *Masses and Mainstream*, and also became involved with Robeson's *Freedom*. Brown worshipped Robeson, viewing him as a self-effacing and self-sacrificing champion of oppressed peoples. Fiercely protective of Robeson's legacy, he routinely offered written rebuttals, replete with his uncanny wit, to any publication that dared to criticize Paul. Brown replaced Essie—who battled her own myriad health problems—as the chief caretaker of Paul's public philosophies, often helping Robeson write articles for various left-wing magazines at home and abroad. In doing so, he emerged as Paul's ad hoc spokesman.

> Robeson is the Douglass of today. He is a loyal American, the best kind of American, and only those who support the "100% Americanism" of the KKK lynchers can hold that his activities are not in the best interests of our country. . . . We— all of us, Negro and white, trade unionists, professionals, cultural workers, Jewish people and other minority groups—owe a large debt to Paul Robeson. His great art has inspired us; his strength and leadership have been given unstintingly over

the years; he has encouraged and helped every progressive cause of the people. He has given all, asking nothing.[28]

Brown's unswerving dedication to Robeson, along with his literary panache, made him the ideal choice to cowrite Paul's autobiography. With a willing and able ghostwriter in place, Robeson only needed to find a publisher—a nearly impossible task given the political atmosphere. Paul's reputation had been so tainted in the mainstream that publishing houses refused to even look at it, out of fear of government backlash. Finally, a small black publisher, Othello Associates, took on the manuscript. *Here I Stand* was released in March 1958, culminating a nearly decade-long effort to get Robeson's voice out in the open again. The book was more of a political manifesto than an autobiography; Robeson did not divulge much of his personal life, only referring to it when he connected to his philosophies. As he noted, the purpose of the book was to "present my ideas about a subject that is infinitely more important than any personal story—the struggle of my people."[29] He focused instead on the Negro's place in the changing world dynamics, referring to the spread of Socialism abroad and the budding civil rights struggle at home. Paul invoked the memories of freedom fighters such as Harriet Tubman and Frederick Douglass in hammering home his message of "decisive Negro action." Defiantly opening the book with the declaration: "I am a Negro," Robeson (and Brown) depicted his struggles through a macrocosmic lens. "When I, as a Negro American, can be restricted and charged with having acted against the 'best interests of the United States' by working in behalf of African liberation, some very important questions arise: What are the best interests of *Negro* Americans in this matter? Can we oppose White Supremacy in South Carolina and not oppose the same vicious system in South Africa?"[30] The tone of the autobiography was of reconciliation, militancy, and defiance. Brown claimed the book was "indispensable for an understanding of Paul Robeson's viewpoint."

In attempting to "set the record straight," Robeson also tried to rebuild the bridges he had burned with the more moderate elements of black America (even praising the NAACP for its inspiring heroism in the South). However, he stood by his claim that Negro action needed to be immediate. Rebuking "gradualism," Robeson attacked the "well-intentioned white liberals and various Negro spokesmen . . . who honestly believe that the advancement of colored people can be made only gradually, that progress cannot be forced, that the reactionaries should not be pushed too hard, that five years or ten years, or even generations must pass before our civil wrongs can become civil rights."[31] Throughout the book, Robeson was careful not to paint himself as a martyr (perhaps aware that the "woe is me" stance would engender more scorn), choosing instead to compare his struggles with other blacks, including Du Bois. "How monstrously evil it is," he wrote, "that the little men in high places have dared to say that such a man is not entitled to a passport, that he cannot travel abroad in a world which knows and honors him."[32] But Robeson also took some liberties to revise his own past, claiming that he had been race-conscious from a young age; a more accurate autobiographical assessment would have admitted that Paul did not get involved in race matters until his late twenties. Still, Robeson stated his case with eloquence, eagerly extending his hand to a civil rights struggle that might not have been possible without his outspokenness nearly a decade earlier.

Though McCarthy-era censorship of Robeson precluded reviews in white publications, many in the black press reviewed the book at home; overseas reviewers snatched it up following its release in Europe, Asia, and Latin America. Left-wing publications and writers concurred with the *New Times* assessment that *Here I Stand* was "a book wrought of the anguish, thoughts and hopes of America's 18 million Negroes. It is a book about their life, their interests, their struggle for freedom and civil rights."[33] Writer Dalton Trumbo declared that not reading the book would "miss a noble testimonial by one of the foremost Americans of our day."[34] Meanwhile, Louis Burnham wrote that the autobiographical manifesto epitomized "what Robeson stands and fights for. He believes in the worth of Africa's culture and fights for its liberation; he believes in the common humanity of all peoples and fights for world peace; he believes in Socialism and opposes its detractors; he believes in Negro freedom and is the scourge of its enemies."[35] Not surprisingly, the *Crisis* didn't share such a glowing appraisal of Robeson's book, despite his conciliatory remarks about the NAACP. A *Crisis* reviewer asserted that Robeson was "never regarded as a leader" by Negroes and that he imagined "his misfortunes to stem . . . from the persecution of the 'white folks on top.'" But the NAACP's reluctance to endorse the book did little to offset the surge of support for Robeson. As Brown later noted, "an important section of the Afro-American press moved with speed and energy to publicize and promote the sale of a book that expressed the ideas of a man considered by the dominant class to be Enemy Number One."[36] Two of Paul's biggest supporters in the black press, Carl Murphy of the Baltimore *Afro-American* and Prattis of the *Pittsburgh Courier*, also provided strong endorsements. *Here I Stand* soon became a staple of the literature of radical black protest; in later years, it would be interpreted as a guidebook for black nationalism.

When Grace Court wasn't available, the home of Abbott and Priscilla Simon became the alternate hub for the Left. Abbott Simon had been staunchly devoted to the Doctor since first meeting him in 1940; like the Jacksons, Ed Strong, and Louis Burnham, Simon was among the core of younger leftists who grew up idolizing Du Bois and inhaling his views on race, class, and world politics. He later boasted that he was given an uncanny insight into the Doctor's private disposition, which contrasted the trademark Du Boisian aloofness. "He was just a peach," Simon said. "He extended his heart out to me, because he knew I had lost my father at an early age."[37] The Du Boises frequently visited the Simons' home in Parkchester, an integrated neighborhood in the Bronx where left wingers and liberals were insulated from Cold War reality. Abbott's daughter Andrea recalled that as a young child, she would sit on the Doctor's lap and fall asleep listening to his renditions of German lullabies. "He would always sing German Leader to me because he knew I loved listening to it," Andrea Simon recalled fifty years later. Her father chimed in with a little-known observation about Du Bois: "He had a beautiful voice. Even at that age, he sang with such passion."[38] The Doctor and Shirley's arrival at the Simon home would undoubtedly prompt other visitors to drop by. Freda Diamond, Robeson's longtime confidant (and in her younger years, a lover), was a frequent houseguest. Like the Simons and the Rosens, Diamond continued adhering to leftist philosophies, staying not only because of idealism, but also because of the realization that the fervor of anti-Communism also bred anti-Semitism. Peekskill and the Rosenberg case was evidence to many Jewish left-wingers and some liberals that Cold War–era politics were as detrimental to them as they were to most blacks and Communist Party members. In fact, Du Bois and Robeson emphasized this point in their defense of the Rosenbergs and reprehension of McCarthyism. The Doctor preached that if Fascism were to rise in the United States, "it will be the Negro people first followed by the Jewish people who will feel the fury of barbaric sadism."[39]

Jewish antiracism advocacy was always ingrained in the civil rights struggle. Jews were among the cofounders of the NAACP and Urban League, working closely with Du Bois in the shaping of the Niagara Movement and the platform of integration and equality. During the Popular Front era, urban Jews became more radical in response to Hitler. Some, like Simon and Aptheker, joined the Communist Party out of the belief that its anti-Fascist stance was an effective weapon against anti-Semitism. Others, though not directly affiliated with the Communist Party, were not too far from the core of the Left. Du Bois believed the natural sympathies of Jews toward other oppressed groups made them the greatest domestic ally for the cause of Negro advancement, and vice versa. Fracturing such an alliance in the wake of Cold War politics would be folly, because "the only safeguard against the pernicious and pervasive virus of anti-Semitism among Negroes and anti-Negroism among Jews is for Negroes and Jews individually and in their organizations to act and work together on issues which either group or both groups face."[40] Robeson was even more emphatic, tying both groups' histories of oppression into their current struggle. He noted that in New York, "We saw progressive sections of the Jewish people united with the Negro people in a drive to make the racist walls come tumbling down."[41]

One prominent Jew who stayed in Du Bois and Robeson's corner until his death was Einstein. Despite his failing health, the physicist actively campaigned against McCarthyism and the HUAC, even urging witnesses not to testify at the hearings if called upon. Einstein's staunch support of the Left during the 1950s stemmed from his belief that the American government was suppressing civil liberties and quashing dissent in the name of ideological conformity—actions that eerily reminded him of Nazi Germany. Einstein had a profound admiration for Du Bois, sharing the Doctor's view that intellectualism was useless unless it was an instrument of social change. Einstein, already a target of FBI investigation by the late 1940s, refused to distance himself from Du Bois after the Peace Information Center indictments. He helped sponsor Du Bois' eighty-third birthday celebration, which former allies such as Arthur Spingarn, White, Wilkins, Bunche, and Tobias boycotted, and offered to testify at the Doctor's trial (though the case was dismissed before Einstein got the opportunity), something that most of the Talented Tenth refused to do. Einstein offered the same backing for Robeson after the latter's passport was revoked. In October 1952, Einstein asked Paul to visit him at his Princeton home. Robeson and Lloyd Brown met the ailing genius for lunch, which, according to Brown, "was a definite act of solidarity, especially after Peekskill."[42] The meeting touched Einstein and Robeson, who understood the gravity of maintaining their friendship at a time when their every action was scrutinized. Paul was especially appreciative of Einstein's gesture, recalling later that "it was good, once again, to clasp the hand of this gentle genius."

> We chatted about many things—about peace, for Dr. Einstein is truly a man of peace; about the freedom struggles in South Africa which interested him keenly; and about the growing shadows . . . being cast over freedom of thought and expression here at home. Though he is physically frail and not in good health, one can feel the strength of his spirit and the glowing warmth of his compassion for humanity. There was a note of deep sorrow and concern underlying his comments on what is happening in our land. As he spoke, one could sense something of what this must mean to Einstein, the giant of science and culture, who was driven from his homeland by the Nazi barbarians and who felt the immeasurable tragedy that his people suffered at their hands.[43]

The Doctor and Paul reciprocated the support they received from the Left, rushing to the defense of their embattled peers at a time when few would. Over the years, they would become spokesmen for the freedom of such noted Communist Party leaders as Ben Davis, Patterson, Winston, and Steve Nelson. Du Bois and Robeson would make the persecution of their fellow Leftists central to their argument that the notion of American democracy was a lie in the age of McCarthyism and Jim Crow. The imprisonment of Davis, who served five years in a federal prison in Terre Haute, Indiana, following his Smith Act Conviction, became a cause célèbre for the Left during the early 1950s. The Doctor's advocacy on behalf of Davis sprang from an intimate knowledge of the "bourgeois" Southerner turned New York proletarian. Du Bois knew Davis's father, Benjamin Sr., a Georgia journalist who went on to become a lawmaker. "He could have become," Du Bois noted of Davis Jr., "as so many young men who have his advantages do become, an easy-going man who did little work and had little serious thought; who lived his life largely upon what his father had accumulated."[44] In short, young Ben was destined for the typical Talented Tenth lifestyle, detached from the everyday hardships of Black America; but he had chosen a life of radicalism, becoming a longtime Communist Party loyalist and one of Robeson's principal advisors. The Doctor paralleled Davis's plight to that of his and Paul's, noting, "For a man in the prime of life and in the enthusiasm of deeply held beliefs, to be thus thrust into isolation and disgrace, is one of the most horrible of fates. It should never happen in a country which calls itself free and which tries to be great."[45]

Similarly, Robeson blamed McCarthy and his acolytes for trying to destroy Negro leadership, namely, the ones who were not afraid to challenge their country. As he complained to Soviet writer Boris Polevoy: "Militant leaders are persecuted, and some of the best and bravest of them are jailed. I think of a man dear to me as a brother—Ben Davis . . . whom the war-mongers imprisoned three years ago together with other leaders of the Communist Party."[46] Seeking to rectify the imprisonment and executions of thousands of black men based on Jim Crow prosecution, Du Bois and Robeson joined Patterson in petitioning the United Nations to take action against the U.S. government. In *We Charge Genocide*, the black Left scored one of its few public relations victories on the international stage during the Cold War. The Civil Rights Congress–endorsed statement was historic, as it was the first to charge the U.S. government with mass murder. The *Genocide* report read in part:

> There may debate as to the expediency of con-demning the Government of the United States for the genocide it practices and permits against 15,000,000 of its citizens who are Negroes. There can be none about the existence of the crime. It is an undeniable fact. . . . It is everywhere in American life. And yet words and statistics are but poor things to convey the long agony of the Negro people.

Patterson claimed the Left was "mounting an all-out ideo-logical attack."[47] Despite being shunned by mainstream groups such as the NAACP and Urban League, the CRC was able to collect a diverse collection of Leftists, representatives of church and fraternal organizations, and union leaders to back the petition. In addition to Patterson, Robeson, and Du Bois, the impressive list of signers included Bass, Davis, Alphaeus Hunton, Mary Church Terrell, Jessica Mitford,

Albert Kahn, Roscoe Dunjee, the Reverend Charles A. Hill ,and George Murphy Jr.[48] With widespread support among left-of-center activists, the petition was formally delivered by Robeson to the United Nations Secretariat on December 16, 1951. Patterson flew to Paris to lobby the UN General Assembly to hear the petition. The U.S. delegation, which included Channing Tobias, Eleanor Roosevelt, and Bunche, refused to accept the petition. Tobias accused Patterson of attacking the government and turned him away. Patterson subsequently tried in vain to lobby India and Egypt to support the petition, but both declined. Despite failing to secure an endorsement of *We Charge Genocide*, Patterson claimed an "ideological and moral victory" by exposing the "moral bank-ruptcy of the United States."[49] He would later lionize Du Bois and Robeson for their heroic efforts to defend the Left and the Negro race from persecution. Patterson hailed Robeson as a "great son of the American Negro people, renowned throughout the world as an artist and public figure . . . singled out for special persecution by the racists of the U.S.A. because of his passionate devotion to the cause of peace, freedom, equality and human dignity for the colored peoples of the world."[50] Du Bois and Robeson might have known that the *Genocide* petition would fail to be heard in the General Assembly, just as Du Bois's *Appeal to the World* had four years earlier; but in supporting the statement and lobbying for its consideration, both made it clear that Cold War persecution could not silence them.

Davis and Patterson weren't the only Communists whose struggles inspired Du Bois and Robeson. Jailed CPUSA leader Winston began to suffer violent headaches in prison. Federal prison officials ignored Winston's complaints, accusing him of being lazy and exaggerating his ailments. However, after months of petitioning the prison to allow him to see a doctor, Winston finally received medical attention—too little, too late. By that time, his optic nerves had been destroyed by a huge tumor, and he have to serve the rest of his prison term blinded in one eye. While he recovered from his tumor removal surgery in New York, Winston was able to enjoy temporary freedom. Esther Jackson recalled taking him to see Du Bois in 1960.

> We went over to Grace Court because Dr. Du Bois had wanted to meet Henry. We had breakfast, and Henry talked about his experience in prison. Henry had always worshipped Dr. Du Bois. Dr. Du Bois was in awe. He was amazed that Henry could stay firm in his convictions after all that he had been through. I think it really made him appreciate what was going on the time.[51]

Winston would later have his term commuted by President Kennedy, but his imprisonment—along with Davis's—proved to Du Bois that the jailed leftists were "suffering martyrdom for their opinions."[52] Winston would later be one of the principal revisionists of Du Boisian Pan-Africanism, inextricably linking with Communist ideology and attacking nationalist Pan-Africanists such as Padmore, James, Amiri Baraka, and Stokely Carmichael.[53] Though Robeson was not as close to Winston (owing to Communist Party factionalism prior to the Communist 12 convictions), he also came to regard him as one of the "brave working class leaders in the United

States."[54] Ditto for Steve Nelson, a former member of the Abraham Lincoln Brigade during the Spanish Civil War and a longtime Communist Party leader who had been charged with sedition in 1950. Nelson was convicted in 1952 and sentenced to twenty years in prison, but in 1956, the Supreme Court overturned the conviction. Many on the Left believed Nelson was another political victim of McCarthyism. Moe Fishman, executive secretary of the Lincoln Brigade, complained to Robeson that "anti-Francoism" had become "un-Americanism" in light of Franco's allegiance with the United States following World War II.[55]

Supporting Winston and Nelson—along with Claudia Jones, Elizabeth Gurley Flynn, Eugene Dennis, and other jailed or "underground" Communists—had become a central part of the Doctor and Paul's advocacy. Du Bois took on this role with special zeal, having come to accept that his political philosophies were more closely aligned with the Communist Party than any other group. The arrests of Communists based on wild allegations and false testimony only firmed his allegiance to the party's tenets. Like Robeson, Du Bois, who, only a decade earlier, viewed the Communist Party with suspicion, had unconditionally endorsed the efforts of Communists as the key to saving humanity from oppression. He believed the U.S. government, anti-Red zealots, and mainstream black organizations had slandered the name of the CPUSA and of the Soviet Union by insisting that the party was led by "conspirators who are enslaving peoples for selfish reasons. The attempts have failed yet the Soviet Union threatens to overthrow the world and the United States especially by force and violence." Such a malicious attempt to undercut another political ideology, Du

Bois declared, was part of American and European capitalists' goals in keeping oppressed people from realizing the dream of Socialism. Adopting Robeson's idealistic stance, the Doctor wrote that Communism "is an attempt to eliminate poverty, ignorance and disease among the majority of peoples, through efforts to achieve Socialism by Communist methods; that Socialism has long been regarded as the goal of modern civilization by great social philosophers; that the present Communist attempts to achieve Socialism are succeeding and spreading widely and are the hope of future civilizations."[56] Even after McCarthy's downfall, Du Bois held firm to his suspicions that the U.S. government would use anti-Communism to further its own capitalistic interests abroad. He soon became convinced that the United States was beyond reform and would be forever behind the revolution that was taking place abroad.

AMERICA'S WAR AGAINST THE LEFT continued after the fall of McCarthy and into the nascence of the civil rights movement. One by one, noted leftists fell, without so much as a mention of their legacy in the fight for equal rights. In August 1954, Vito Marcantonio—friend and close counsel to both Du Bois and Robeson—died of a heart attack. Marcantonio had been one of the most uncompromising radicals ever elected to Congress, giving the Left an unmuzzled voice on Capitol Hill for nearly two decades. But like many prominent leftists in the Cold War era, he became a victim of politics. The Democrats and Republicans colluded to run him out of office and successfully defeated him in 1950. Du Bois and Robeson reflected on the gravity of Marcantonio's loss. The Doctor praised him as "long the most intelligent and consistent of progressive congressmen," who happened to fall victim to "shameless gerrymander."[57] Robeson called Marcantonio "the people's tribune," lionizing his late friend as "the foremost spokesman for the rights of man the Congress of the United States has produced in the 20th century." Paul summed up his eulogy of Marcantonio with a call for the masses to remobilize in his name:

> He would expect us to fight on, to build ever stronger the people's unity; to rout the warmakers and exploiters; to send to Congress tens and scores of men and women who will serve the people in the style and spirit of Vito Marcantonio; to win the peace, happiness and equality for all the world's people to which he dedicated his life. As we do, we will be building a living monument to him who lived so well.[58]

But Robeson's call to arms fell on mostly deaf ears. Marcantonio's legacy might have been appreciated more than a decade earlier (or a decade after), but the Cold War had made pariahs out of even the most passionate social crusaders. His loss was compounded by the death of Einstein and the deportation of Claudia Jones and left-wing writer Cedric Belfrage (of the *National Guardian*) the following year. For Du Bois and Robeson, the censuring of McCarthy had done little to stem the venomous tide of Cold War conservatism.

But friends weren't the only ones to go. Walter White died in 1955, ending a tumultuous four-decade relationship he had with both men. White, one of the most relentless advocates of integration, left behind a mixed legacy. On one hand, he was among the few blacks who had managed to win consistent access to the White House and help influence government policies on civil rights. His charismatic leadership guided the association to the *Brown* victory; moreover, his philosophy of pragmatic protest would become the staple of NAACP practice for years to come. But the picture of Walter as a beneath-the-covers FBI collaborator is hard to shake, given his not-so-private disdain for the Left. His opposition to the Communists, black nationalists, and other left-of-center factions placed the NAACP's program of nonpartisanship at risk; by the early 1950s, the association had become a mouthpiece for the Democratic Party. In later years, the association's close ties with the Democrats and its anti-Republican rhetoric would lead to a federal investigation of its nonprofit status.[59] White had won the political battle, correctly sizing up the Communist sentiment among Negroes as nothing more than a mere fraction of black America. In a scathing rebuttal of the CPUSA's civil rights record (which conveniently ignored the work of the CRC and SNYC), White guessed the party's failure in winning over black America was because "the Negro's intense loyalty to democracy is a corollary of his dislike of over-rule.[60] But what White could not do was foster ill-will among the majority of African Americans toward Du Bois and Robeson. The prevailing notion among most blacks was that both men spoke for the common Negro, "saying the things which they would like to say." Du Bois and Robeson's appeal—in personality, not politics—among millions of African Americans precluded their exile from black consciousness.

IN HIS AUTOBIOGRAPHY, Robeson noted that "speaking the truth abroad has been of great value to the struggle for Negro rights in America."[61] But the truth, in this case, did not set him free. Instead, Paul was a threat because of his popularity abroad and his unwillingness to back down. Revoking Robeson's passport—and Du Bois's—seemed the best way to neutralize the threat. Though Paul and the Doctor refused to modify their positions, they were unable to continue their roles as ambassadors of black America. That role would go to Bunche, whose moderate views and prolific diplomatic portfolio made him the ideal candidate to represent the American Negro. Shut out from advocating international causes and alienated from the domestic struggles, Du Bois and Robeson concentrated on winning back their passports and their reputations.

But the psychological toll of confinement and scrutiny had a more negative impact on Robeson than Du Bois; unlike the Doctor, whose career in academia was defined by a proclivity toward solitude, Paul was unfamiliar with isolation. Traveling around the world had become second nature to him, and when that right was taken, Paul fought with bouts of depression and "island fever." By the mid-1950s, his income had dipped to about $6,000; by comparison, he earned $104,000 in 1944, at the height of his fame. Despite efforts by groups in Europe, Asia, Africa, and Latin America to persuade the State Department to return his passport, Robeson remained in confinement. But if the government's efforts were in part to muzzle Paul overseas, they backfired. Robeson remained popular overseas, owing partly to the continued influence of the Left outside of the United States, as well as Paul's reputation in Europe as a concert and theatrical performer which still outweighed his political beliefs. As Du Bois accurately wrote of Robeson's stature: "He is without doubt today, as a person, the best known American on earth, to the largest number of human beings. His voice is known in Europe, Asia and Africa, in the West Indies and South America and in the islands of the seas. Children on the streets of Peking and Moscow, Calcutta and Jakarta greet him and send him their love. Only in his native land is he without honor and rights."[62]

Robeson had a strong case that the government was deliberately and maliciously denying his right to earn a living, but his refusal to sign a waiver disavowing ties to the Communist Party made him an easy target for the State Department. The government's claims that granting Robeson his right to travel would go against the interests of the country were shaky at best. Without a legitimate reason for keeping Paul's passport, reactionary lawmakers tried to bury his already devastated reputation. In 1956, the HUAC, which continued its hearings even after McCarthy's downfall, summoned Robeson to testify. The hearings were to determine whether American passports were being used "in furtherance of the objectives of the Communist conspiracy." The committee's chair, Pennsylvania Representative Francis E. Walter—the cosponsor of the McCarran-Walter Act restricting immigration—was a rabid anti-Communist and noted racist; he served on the Pioneer Fund, a group promoting racial hierarchism and theoretical offshoots of eugenics. Robeson's appearance before the HUAC was testy from the start. When asked by HUAC staff member Richard Arens if he was a Communist, Robeson angrily replied, "Oh please, please, please." Pressed further about his involvement, Robeson lashed out at his interrogators.

Robeson: What do you mean by the Communist Party? As far as I know it is a legal party like the Republican Party and the Democratic Party. Do you mean—which, belonging to a party of Communists or belonging to a party of people who have sacrificed for my people and for all Americans and workers that they can live in dignity? Do you mean that party?

Arens: Are you a member of the Communist Party?

Robeson: Would you like to come to the ballot box when I vote and take out the ballot and see?[63]

Robeson then confronted Walter about his support for the McCarran Act. "You are the author of all of the bills that going to keep all kinds of decent people out of the country," he said. Walter smugly replied, "No, only your kind." Testy exchanges between Robeson and the committee members continued, especially when Arens introduced Manning Johnson and Max Yergan's testimony from several years earlier. Paul repeatedly invoked the Fifth Amendment, infuriating committee members. Robeson charged that the hearings were a cover-up to try him "for fighting for the rights of my people [who] are still second-class citizens in this United States of America. . . . You want to shut up every Negro who has the courage to stand up and fight for the rights of his people, for the rights of workers and I have been on many a picket line for the steelworkers, too. And that is why I am here today."[64] Robeson went on to defend his ill-fated Paris speech, which committee members insisted was part of his un-American sentiment. Paul, refusing to submit to the legislators' line of questioning, remained defiant, and dismissed the proceedings as "nonsense." When Representative Gordon Scherer of Ohio told Robeson that he was being questioned because of his involvement with a Communist conspiracy, Paul fired back: "I am here because I am opposing the neo-Fascist cause which I see arising in these committees." Unable to handle Robeson's barrage of accusations against them, including charges that they were fascists and warmongers, committee members adjourned. The committee subsequently began contempt proceedings against Robeson.[65]

The Communist conspiracy excuse barely held up under scrutiny. Paul had not been accused of any plots to overthrow the government, nor had he involved himself in any antiestablishment organizations. The State Department's rationale in withholding Du Bois and Robeson's passport seemed almost ridiculous, given the men's popularity (if they had been part of a shadowy Communist conspiracy, the FBI would have noticed) and their age: Du Bois was eighty-eight, and Robeson was fifty-eight. How could two men in the dusk of their lives be so much of a threat to the United States? And how could the U.S. government argue that it was fighting for democracy when it was denying it to two of its most prominent citizens, along with dozens of others? Legal experts began to poke holes in the government's justification, which had been built on a foundation of McCarthyite bluster and ideological xenophobia. As early as 1952, academics questioned the effectiveness of America's campaign against totalitarianism if it was employing the same tactics as totalitarian governments. Du Bois and Robeson's passport revocation became more than a political issue; it was now a constitutional one. In urging federal courts to reject the State Department's rationale, Warren H. Saltzman argued that "the days when the discretionary denial of passports had little effect on the right of exit are past."

> Even when it is no longer illegal for United States citizens to leave the country without a passport, there will be few places to which they can travel without one. The denial of passports to its citizens has long been one of the principal instruments of intimidation and of control used by totalitarian governments: of intimidation, since the individual is virtually imprisoned at home without a passport; of control, in that the government can thus determine what information and opinion about conditions abroad reach its people. The government of the United States has protested the refusal of totalitarian governments to allow their citizens freely to travel abroad as a denial of fundamental human rights, and has repeatedly urged a policy of enlarged human interchange as a step towards international understanding and the relief of international tension. It is the thesis of this Comment that under the circumstances of modern international life every American citizen has a constitutional right to a passport, and that the protection of that right has become an urgent matter of a national policy as well as of civil liberty. If our preaching is to accord with our practice, that right should be curtailed only for good cause and with that regard for fairness embodied in the phrase "due process."

Nothing less will achieve the objective envisioned in the Universal Declaration of Human Rights—free travel in a world society.[66]

International pressure helped Du Bois and Robeson's case as well. Du Bois had sought permission to go to Ghana, which gained its independence from Britain in 1956; his request was denied. Shirley Graham Du Bois complained to Padmore (who had moved to Ghana) that her husband, "in the evening of his life . . . has been cruelly deprived of the pleasures and free exchange of the world wide fellowship which has been a part of his entire life. This is the way it has been, but the past six months has given new force to the uniting voices of dark peoples."[67] Graham Du Bois was confident that an appeal from nonaligned African nations would play an important role in restoring her husband's passport. The pro-Robeson camp was based in England, making it extremely difficult for anticommunists to link him with any hostile governments. While Soviet and Chinese leaders offered support, neither country made a formal appeal for Paul's freedom. Instead, the Robeson "Right to Travel" movement came from diverse countries such as Ireland, India, Sweden, and the continent of Australia. The United States knew it had been put in an embarrassing public relations situation. However, the State Department refused to budge, and in repeatedly denying Du Bois and Robeson their passports, the answer remained the same: it was contrary to the best interests of the country.

The government's resistance could not overcome jurisprudence. Du Bois and Robeson's passport battles were ultimately resolved by two Supreme Court rulings in the spring of 1958.

In *Trop v. Dulles*, decided in March, Chief Justice Warren ruled that "citizenship is not subject to the general powers of the National Government and therefore cannot be divested in the exercise of those powers."[68] Simply put, the government had overstepped its bounds in revoking the passport rights of U.S. citizens. The court went on to note that citizenship could only be relinquished voluntarily; the ruling proved to be a major blow to anti-Communists, who had sought to deny "subversives" the same rights afforded to other American citizens. With the State Department's discretionary powers nullified, the Court's ruling in *Kent v. Dulles* was a landmark formality (though the 5–4 vote was a narrow victory). Justice William O. Douglas, on behalf of the majority, wrote, "The right to travel is a part of the 'liberty' of which the citizen cannot be deprived without due process of law under the Fifth Amendment."[69] Consequently, Du Bois and Robeson won their right to travel. The restoration of their passports proved to be a major victory for both men, who had exhausted legal and financial resources in a quest to regain their full citizenship. As Du Bois bitterly observed, the United States had simply resorted to pettiness in order to discredit two of its most vocal critics. "I had cooperated with millions of men who wanted war to cease. Even here my action had been simply to tell Americans what was being done by other countries to promote peace. For this I was accused of being the agent of foreign peacemakers and ordered to admit this or go to jail."[70] Almost immediately after getting his passport back, Robeson headed to England. A decade of imposed isolation had not tarnished his reputation in Europe, where he received a hero's welcome. With greetings from British parliamentarians and leaders of trade union movement, Robeson's warm reception proved even more embarrassing to the United States; after all, he was an American citizen who was being treated with more dignity overseas than he had been in his own country. Belfrage, Eurasian writer Cedric Dover, and Labour MP Tony Benn spearheaded the Robeson revitalization effort, helping to promote *Here I Stand* and enthusiastically rallying Paul's friends from the Old Left to support him in his return to the concert stage. After a short stay in England, Paul and Essie headed for the Soviet Union for rest and relaxation in Moscow and Yalta. Four months later, they returned to Moscow for a New Year's celebration at the Kremlin, where they were joined by the other honored guests of the state—William and Shirley Graham Du Bois.

The festivities focused on Du Bois and Robeson, who had returned to Moscow like prodigal sons. The two men, whose lives and reputations had suffered in America because of their Soviet idealism, had an emotional reunion in front of their applauding hosts. Shirley Graham Du Bois later wrote that "big Paul and small Du Bois threw their arms around each other in a bear hug and Mr. Khrushchev rose to his feet applauding. Then everybody in the hall was up, applauding and shouting their names."[71] Later that night, Khrushchev gave both men bear hugs, and Paul led the guests in singing "Fatherland." As the champagne of legal victory and a new year flowed, Du Bois and Robeson were seemingly oblivious to the precariousness of their situation: they were holdover Stalinists in a room full of Stalin's enemies. It apparently mattered little that Khrushchev was the man who had denounced Stalin only two years earlier. Though Khrushchev had labored to demonize his late comrade in front of the Communist world, neither the Doctor nor Paul offered any retrospective criticism of Father Joe. There was a sentimental value in hanging onto Stalinism; the "Red Czar" had created a utopia in Robeson's eyes while crafting the near-perfect state model for Du Bois's problem for the color and class line. Even if the Doctor and Paul knew that Stalin had encouraged anti-Semitism in his final years, they did not show it during their blissful Moscow stay. The splinter between Soviet-model Socialists and Maoists following Stalin's death didn't affect Du Bois and Robeson's political allegiances, either. The rise of Socialist governments in Asia, Latin America, Europe, and Africa was the only fitting response to imperialism, they reasoned; whether their guide was the Kremlin or Beijing was inconsequential in the Du Bois–Robeson world outlook. On cue with their visit to the USSR, the Cuban revolution culminated with the fall of Havana. Marxists Che Guevara and Fidel Castro commandeered a seemingly improbable bloody revolt against the American-backed dictatorship of Fulgencio Batista. The rise of a new Cuba, in the Doctor and Paul's opinion, only reinforced the rejection of imperialism and capitalism by darker nations. After their brief reunion with the Robesons, the Doctor and Shirley headed to China and became converts to Maoism. Upon his return to the United States later that year, Du Bois was a radically changed man. In his observations about the world he had seen for the first time in nearly a decade, the Doctor—in an assessment that eerily forecasted contemporary world opinions about America—reprehended the United States for its ideological arrogance.

I saw first that America and its actions since the first world war was thoroughly condemned by the civilized world; that no other country was so disliked and hated. The British and the Dutch while restraining their expression of dislike behind good manners and for fear of our wealth and power, nevertheless, did not like America or Americans. That the French could hardly mention America without calling them dirty; that the people of Czechoslovakia and Germany blamed America for the cruelities which they suffered and for the difficulties which they were facing. That the 200 million people in the Soviet Union regard Americans as their greatest threat and the 680 millions of China hate America with perfect hatred for treating them as sub-human.

Outside this matter of feeling was my discovery that the world was going socialist, that most of the people of the world, Europe, Asia and Africa were either socialists or communists. No matter what our attitude toward Socialism and communism may be, no matter how we judge the teachings of Karl Marx we must face the truth. Not only black but white Americans must know. We do not know.

The news gathering agencies and the periodicals of opinion in the United States are deliberately deceiving the people of the United States with regard to the rest of the world. For a long time they have spread the belief that communism is a crime or a conspiracy and that anyone either taking part

382

or even examining conditions in socialist lands is a
self-conscious criminal or a fool.[72]

Du Bois concluded that he could not live in a country where
"a group of military leaders backed by many who control our
organized industry and trade, determined to force us into a
war with the Soviet Union, to conquer China, and to control
Asia-Africa by invested capital."[73] Though the United States
had moved back to moderation (a rubber band effect following McCarthyism), the domestic currents were still far too
resistant to the fundamental change he and Robeson had
called for. Yes, integration was, for the most part, a good
thing. In an apparent about-face from "Segregation," Du Bois
agreed with the prevailing view among black leaders that
"separate schools are basically wrong."[74] But at what price?
Southern states still firmly resisted the Supreme Court's
Brown ruling, and without any teeth in existing civil rights
legislation, integrationists were still at the mercy of individual
states and school districts, whose discretion would determine
whether black students could get access to an equal education.
Exasperated, Du Bois realized he would never have the opportunity to see the full enfranchisement of black America.

ROBESON WOULD SPEND the next five years in Europe, working to
rebuild his finances by taking advantage of his undiminished
popularity abroad. Paul would quietly excuse the Soviet Union's
aggression in Eastern Europe while offering moral support for
the new Cuban government under Castro. He had little faith
that John F. Kennedy, a Catholic from Massachusetts whose

father had a chummy relationship with Joe McCarthy, would be much of an improvement over Ike. To Robeson, JFK was simply a younger and Northern version of Truman, advocating a civil rights platform that did enough to appease black leadership but not nearly enough to guarantee full enfranchisement. While enjoying his resurgence abroad, Paul would soon become an afterthought in the civil rights movement, which became a vehicle for a new generation of leaders such as King, John Lewis, Jesse Jackson, Stokely Carmichael, Julian Bond, C. Delores Tucker, and Maya Angelou. At the same time as the fight for black rights ascended to a new level of popularity, the anti–Vietnam War movement matured out of its infancy. Most peace activists disagreed with Robeson's veneration of Ho Chi Minh, but they were adamantly opposed to sending American soldiers to die in defense of abstract ideologies. King's antiwar stance was based on the needless deployment of black soldiers to die overseas when they could not live in full equality at home—the same idea Robeson had tried to articulate at the Paris Peace Conference. But King—despite his association with the likes of Jack O'Dell and Stanley Levison—opposed communism, making him the ideal protest leader during the Cold War. Wilkins would try to undo King as he had Robeson a decade earlier, but by the early 1960s, King was as revered as JFK in progressive white America.[75]

With the eye-opening visits to the Soviet Union, Eastern Europe, and China, Du Bois no longer needed shepherds such as Shirley Graham, James Jackson, and Herbert Aptheker to guide him to the Communist Party; he embraced communist ideology on his own. Whereas only fifteen years earlier, he had dismissed Communist attempts to unite the black and white working classes as misguided idealism, Du Bois now fully believed such solidarity was the only way to achieving humanity's salvation. "Consequently," he wrote, "the leadership of the Negro race will gradually pass from the educators to the businessmen and professional leaders and this industrial class will find alliance with white industry."[76] Du Bois had become as ardent a defender of party ideology as Robeson, perhaps even more so following his visit to China. While Robeson remained optimistic that progressives could once again retake American leadership and return to the liberalism of Roosevelt and the left-leaning open-mindedness of Wallace (before his burning bridges with the Left in 1950), the Doctor offered a more grim assessment: McCarthyism had not been a temporary malady in American politics, but rather the harbinger of terminal close-mindedness that would drag the country down. Du Bois knew King could become an instrument of change, but he also was aware that the "stooge" Wilkins would try to influence black thought away from the Left. The Doctor had become resigned to the idea that blacks wouldn't stray too far from the white masters who had created an illusory Talented Tenth—enough to trick Negroes into believing in the American Dream. This revelation he shared with an audience of Czechoslovakians in 1958: "By 1950, I saw clearly that the great machine of big business was sweeping not only the mass of white Americans into a mad race for individual wealth made through private profit in any kind of legal and often illegal enterprise; it had also and quite naturally swept Negroes into the same maelstrom."[77] Frustrated with America, Du Bois looked beyond its borders and took stock of the rapidly changing world, one that was being molded in accordance with neo–Du Boisian Socialism. "I know well that the triumph of communism will be a slow and difficult task, involving mistakes of every sort," he wrote. "It will call for progressive change in human nature and a better type of manhood than is common today. I believe this possible, or otherwise we will continue to lie, steal and kill as we are doing today."[78]

While the Doctor and Paul were overseas marveling the expansion of the Soviet Empire and communism, the CPUSA was experiencing a rebirth of sorts. In 1957, William Z. Foster stepped down as head of the party, making way for the younger and savvier Gus Hall. Longtime white members such as Fast, Steve Nelson, Jessica Mitford, and Albert Kahn were gone; Stanley Levison would join the new civil rights movement; and others, including brothers Jack and Morris Childs, would leave the party to become informants for the FBI.[79] With blacks now comprising much of the Communist Party membership, Hall and other leaders recognized that Communists needed to focus on recruiting young black radicals into their cause. To do this the Communist Party reincarnated the Black Belt thesis it had popularized during the 1920s and 1930s, hoping to entice young Negroes with nationalist tendencies. Hall also helped rebuild the party's finances, which were in shambles following its collapse, by raising money from Moscow. A $250,000 subsidy from the Kremlin helped get the party back on its feet, and subsequent funding would play an important role in reestablishing the Communists as small— but noticeable—contributors in the civil rights and black power movements.[80] A core of African American Communists, despite their philosophical disagreements over endorsing black nationalism or sticking with third-period dicta, spear-headed the task of remolding the party into a sounding board for pro-blackness. The Jacksons, the Pattersons, Davis, and John Pittman became the "new" faces of the party. For a short time, they would receive assistance from William and Shirley, both of who fully endorsed Hall's plan to bring back the Black Belt. By 1966, however, the Communists would find them-selves philosophically torn between promoting the interracial cooperation of King's movement and backing the calls of more radical blacks such as Carmichael, who would later become the head of the Black Panther Party.

Du Bois and Robeson took little comfort in the fact that the United States stood on the verge of revolution. Perhaps embit-tered by the decade-long effort by the U.S. government and moderate black leadership to destroy them, and traumatized by the decimation of the American Left, they remained distant from the new tide of protest. Du Bois would quit America in 1961, frustrated by the pace of progress in the United States and the stubbornness of Americans to accept global change. Robeson, already abroad, could offer little more than moral support for a movement that was passing him by. Indeed, both men would struggle for relevancy as the 1960s began. Their bond, welded by shared torment and a common vision for the world, had helped them survive hell. Unwillingly martyred in an age of hysteria, Du Bois and Robeson would now begin their quest for redemption.

11

THE LEGACY OF TWO FALLEN ICONS

Good name in man and woman, dear my lord,
Is the immediate jewel of their souls:
Who steals my purse steals trash; 'tis something,
nothing;
'Twas mine, 'tis his, and has been slave to thousands;
But he that filches from me my good name
Robs me of that which not enriches him
And makes me poor indeed.

—*Othello*, act 3, scene 3

"TIME! THE CORRECTOR WHEN OUR JUDGMENTS ERR," Lord Byron wrote, perhaps aware that only time could resurrect the damned. As the civil rights movement gained momentum at the start of the 1960s, two of its most vocal advocates were out of the country, living in self-imposed exile. Du Bois left for Ghana in 1961, having accepted Kwame Nkrumah's offer to undertake the extensive Encyclopedia Africana project. Robeson had moved to England three years earlier, continuing his stage career and political activism in a more friendly setting. While they were overseas, discontent bubbled over. Disquieting the American conscience were the images of white police officers attacking blacks with water hoses and dogs, of four black Alabama schoolgirls blown up in a terrorist attack on a black church, and National Guard members walking black students into white schools. Even Norman Rockwell, whose immortalization of everyday life popularized Americana, illustrated his dismay over the emergence of violent white resistance to black enfranchisement with "The Shame We All Live With." The *New York Times* predicted an imminent "social revolution" stoked by northern White America's increasing disdain for the Jim Crow South.

But the liberalization of the United States—emphasized by the election of Kennedy in 1960—came too little, too late for hundreds of prominent Left wingers scalded by the furnace of political persecution. Du Bois and Robeson were no different, but they benefited from international reputations that outlasted domestic confinement. Du Bois and Robeson's exodus from the United States during the rise of a new generation of mainstream black leaders was not entirely coincidental. The Doctor had become exasperated with the state of progress in the United States and the invitation to write the history of black Africa was too good to pass up. Paul, happy to be able to travel, was cognizant that his affiliation with Martin Luther King Jr. and other leaders of the SNCC might endanger black suffrage efforts in the South. By 1960, both the FBI and the Ku Klux Klan had King squarely in their crosshairs, making any formal connection with Robeson or Du Bois unwise and, more important, unsafe. Though King admired Du Bois and Robeson, his handlers steered him away from the black Left.

What the mainstream lost, the budding black power and black nationalism movements gained. Through a lens distorted by ambitious militants eager to offer a more radical alternative to the "within the system" struggle, Du Bois and Robeson became a paradigm of martyrdom: they were brothers who had made it, only to be cut down by the insidious forces of white racists and Uncle Toms. This image of both men as victims of a racist, capitalist system conformed to black nationalists, whose philosophy was an amalgamation of Garvey, Washington, and Du Bois with anticolonialism as a guiding principle. The re-creation of Du Bois and Robeson as the forerunners of black nationalism was the final evolution of their philosophies, although neither endorsed such a platform. But black militants weren't the only ones who revised the Doctor and Paul's political views. Du Bois's death in 1963 and Robeson's isolation following his return from Europe led to liberal co-option of their legacies into different political philosophies, creating incomplete—and often inaccurate— pictures of both men.

"GREETINGS FROM THE FIELD OF BATTLE, Comrades of the World!" Du Bois wrote from Ghana in 1962.[1] His arrival in Accra the year before fulfilled a lifelong destiny Du Bois had predicted in his writings for more than half a century: he was finally returning "home." Just as Harlem had become the spiritual home to the black intelligentsia, Africa—specifically the concept of independent Black Africa—as a destination was an integral notion to Pan-Africanists. For Du Bois, the move to Ghana represented a late-life realization that he would not die in the United States, *his* country for more than ninety years. "He wanted to be buried in Great Barrington," David Graham Du Bois said. "Going to Ghana was the most difficult decision of his life."[2] The Doctor had Shirley to thank for helping to make his decision. While Du Bois had reservations about leaving the country (knowing he wouldn't come back), Graham Du Bois—sold on Nkrumah's socialist government as a model for postcolonial Africa—enthusiastically pushed for Ghana. Shirley was convinced that "nothing would crown (Du Bois's) entire life work more fittingly and satisfactorily than a trip to the Gold Coast." Graham Du Bois was especially attuned to Du Bois's feelings for the young African leader, who seemingly built the newly independent nation from the Du Boisian Pan-African blueprint more than a decade earlier. "He has watched over Nkrumah's every step with such deep and warm concern," Graham Du Bois wrote of her husband.[3]

Du Bois's decision to join Shirley and leave for Africa was made in part by the U.S. government's unwillingness to ease its scrutiny of the remaining black Left. Though the end of McCarthyism had lessened the paranoia of Communism being seeped into every corner of society, the FBI and State Department's close observation of Du Bois and Robeson continued. FBI agents posted regular dispatches from abroad during

Robeson's five-year exile in Europe, signaling that the government was not ready to take him out of its sights. In addition to the government scrutiny, Du Bois was also exasperated with U.S. foreign policy, which had not softened after the Korean War. In fact, Cuban independence and China's growth into a military power in just one decade only underscored American national security concerns that communism needed to be stopped. Adding to this fear was the notion that African sovereignty movements were backed by Communists; Nkrumah himself was suspected of having Red ties, and the South African independence and antiapartheid struggle had an unabashed connection to the Communist Party. In Nkrumah's case, Washington let it be known that any official relationship with the Kremlin would meet with a response, an intimation that U.S. agents would help facilitate his overthrow or foment instability. Du Bois thought such efforts to contain communism were pathetic attempts to disguise American colonial interests. "America is impossible and I'm fed up," he wrote Robeson.[4] That view was shared by many African American and Afro-European expatriates who moved to Ghana as a token of support for the new republic. Until his death in 1959, Padmore served as a key advisor to Nkrumah. Padmore, as anti-Soviet as ever, likely kept Nkrumah from working too closely with Communists, for fear that their goals would favor Moscow's interests over Accra's. Other prominent blacks, including Richard Wright and Maya Angelou, also made the trip to Ghana, shrugging off U.S. government scrutiny to celebrate a liberated and emboldened African nation.

When William and Shirley arrived in 1961, Accra was a rapidly developing capital, reflecting the efficiency of Socialist economy and the dynamism of its ruler. The Du Boises were welcomed as special guests of the president and soon settled into their roles as VIPs in the Nkrumah government. While Du Bois embarked on the voluminous study of peoples of African descent, Shirley immediately took to the role of advising Nkrumah. Like Essie, Shirley's political savvy was invaluable to the men she guided and nurtured, including her husband, Nkrumah, and later, Malcolm X. Though the Doctor primarily labored on the Encyclopedia Africana, he didn't stray far from the activism that had made him a preeminent Leftist and pariah in the United States during the previous decade. Du Bois sensed a sweeping change in Africa was imminent, a feeling that grew more pronounced with the British government's decision to give Ghana full independence in 1961. "Revolution rides over all Africa," he wrote, perhaps cognizant that his Pan-Africanism was at the continent's fingertips as it wrested itself free from colonialism.[5] He had reason to be excited. The Mau Mau rebellion in Kenya was a protracted bloody struggle that the British were increasingly trying to wash their hands of; four months after Du Bois's death, Kenyans would gain independence, choosing Kenyatta as their first president. Congo, Malawi, Nigeria, and Uganda were also on the cusp of complete sovereignty. While Du Bois kept a close watch on the burgeoning African self-rule, Ghana remained *the* success story of Pan-Africanism.

With Roads, Schools, Industries, Contentment and their faces sternly toward Socialism. Capital they furnish themselves. Britain and the United States dare not deny them a hundred million dollars in

> loans at good interest because the USSR, China and
> East Europe gives three hundred million dollars at
> any interest they want to pay.[6]

Du Bois's overstated assessment of Ghana fell in line with his habit of aggrandizing countries that most closely matched his philosophical ideals of the time. As he had with Germany, Japan, Ethiopia, India, the Soviet Union, and later China, Du Bois viewed Ghanaian independence as a marvel in the development of the state. Ghana's faith in Nkrumah as the supreme leader defied the Doctor's traditional conceptions of how African countries dealt with the issue of power. Nkrumah was a president elected by the Parliament, which, in idealistic terms, was a reflection of the people. "No other modern country has dared to carry democracy so far as this, and this is a great advance," Du Bois gushed. "It faces frankly the danger that the people themselves will not always act wisely: but in the case of Ghana the ancient customs and history of the State have always been under the control of the chiefs and now, the chiefs, without political power, still hold the power of their knowledge and of the reverence which the people have for them." In the Doctor's worldview, the Pan-African Socialism that Nkrumah was putting into practice was the "weapon that Ghana is using" to overthrow "the Western Capitalists and investors in cheap labor and free land and materials in Asia and Africa."[7] Du Bois bought into the idea that Ghana was the model of Pan-Africanism and the founding state of a United States of Africa.

From now on it must be Pan-African nationalism,

and the ideology of African political consciousness and African political emancipation must spread throughout the whole continent, into every nook and corner of it. I have never regarded the struggle for the Independence of the Gold Coast as an isolated objective but always as a part of the general world historical pattern. The African in every territory of this vast continent has been awakened and the struggle for freedom will go on. It is our duty as the vanguard force to offer what assistance we can to those now engaged in the battle that we ourselves have fought and won. Our task is not done and our own safety is not assured until the last vestiges of colonialism have been swept from Africa.[8]

From a theoretical perspective, Ghana under Nkrumah was the prototype nation for Pan-Africanism. After all, the nation had won its independence from a colonizer and immediately established the kind of Socialism needed for guaranteeing postcolonial stability. Du Bois was especially impressed by Nkrumah's public unwillingness to cater to European and American industrial interests seeking to claim their stake in the Ghanaian economy. Nkrumah was bent on protecting the country's most desirable asset, cocoa, and build a Socialist economy around its export. The other half of the Socialist equation was the immediate uplift of Ghana's poor, which Du Bois saw as critical if the Pan-African Socialism model was to succeed. The Doctor seemed adamant that this form of Socialism, though inspired by the Soviets and Chinese, needed to be unique to the African experience.

Pan-African Socialism seeks the Welfare State in Africa. It will refuse to be exploited by people of other continents for their own benefit and not for the benefit of the peoples of Africa. It will no longer consent to permitting the African majority of any African country to be governed against its will by a minority of invaders who claim racial superiority or the right to get rich at African expense. It will seek not only to raise but to process the raw material and to trade it freely with all the world on just and equal terms and prices.[9]

Nkrumah seemed the perfect captain to execute such a plan. Du Bois held Nkrumah in filial regard, placing the utmost faith in the Western-educated Pan-Africanist who would lead his newly freed country to greatness. It was a feeling apparently shared by many young blacks in the United States, including Stokely Carmichael, who revered Nkrumah as an anti-imperialist folk hero in the same vein as Toussaint L'Overture. Du Bois and most African Americans who held Nkrumah in such high esteem were oblivious to his glaring weaknesses as a leader. Nkrumah was both quixotic and neurotic, two qualities that prevented him from ever putting his great ideas for Ghana and the rest of Africa into practice. Though considered a Communist by U.S. agents and even some African American expatriates in Ghana (including Richard Wright), Nkrumah feared Communists. In 1954, the Convention Peoples' Party banned Communists from taking leadership positions. After taking power, Nkrumah clamped down on trade unions, fearful that they would foment a revolt.

While W. E. B. and Shirley remained in sanguine ignorance, Nkrumah was making the necessary compromise to stay in power: balancing the ideals that brought him to leadership and the political reality of dealing with the West. Nkrumah symbolized Pan-Africanism's greatest success and its greatest failure. He was able to galvanize millions of common Ghanaians around the idea that they were the masters of their fate, but at the same time, he could not convince the political elites of the country that publicly reducing their influence would carry long-term benefits. Nkrumah was forced to fight off dissension in his ruling party while placating an army eager to flex its muscle. Scholars have assumed that much of the discord can be blamed on U.S.-backed anti-Nkrumah forces and Nkrumah's own bungling of diplomacy. By 1966, Nkrumah was overthrown by the military and forced into exile in Romania. He died in 1972 without having lived to see his vision for Ghana and United States of Africa fulfilled. Fortunately for Du Bois, he didn't live to see Nkrumah's downfall. The political realities in Accra apparently never affected the Doctor's sanguine outlook on the future of Ghana and the Dark Continent.

The Pan-Africanism adopted in 1945 and rubber-stamped thirteen years later in Accra never materialized. Though Ghana was close to practicing the form of Socialism both Du Bois and Robeson championed, Pan-Africanists who went on to lead their countries after independence found old habits hard to change. Nnamdi Azikiwie became the first president of independent Nigeria in 1963, only to be deposed in 1966 by military coup. Hastings Banda, whose Pan-African philosophies were molded by the likes of Du Bois and Padmore, took over as head of Malawi following its independence in 1964. But instead of adopting the Pan-African Socialism paradigm, Banda sought to unify the country by the sheer force of his political will. For the next thirty years, Banda ruled over the country as a dictator, suppressing political opposition while using Malawi's treasury as his own personal coffers. Jomo Kenyatta, another legendary figure in the Pan-African anti-colonial movement, developed into a similar leader in post-colonial Kenya. Kenyatta's security forces stifled dissent and created deep divisions among the nation's numerous tribes. Like Banda, Kenyatta went from Pan-African visionary to postcolonial despot, his legacy in Kenya mired by his own iron-hand rule for nearly two decades. The failures of Banda, Kenyatta, Azikiwie, and Nkrumah only underscored the fact that practicing Du Boisian Pan-Africanism was much more difficult than espousing it in theory. More than four decades after Du Bois's death, many Africans are still trying to re-create the Pan-African model, an effort complicated by civil wars, a clash between Christian evangelism and Islamism, and the West's reemergence as the caretaker of the continent in the wake of poverty, famine, and the AIDS epidemic.

Before leaving for Ghana, Du Bois symbolically signed his allegiance with the Communist Party of the United States. It was a token gesture, given that the CPUSA was in ruins and presented no political threat. However, Du Bois's "joining" of the party remains a controversial topic. Did Du Bois join because of his convictions about communism, or was it a final act of defiance by a man who had been a lifelong recusant of U.S. policy? Du Bois, like Robeson, was closely affiliated with Communists during the Cold War and expressed a strong admiration for Moscow until his death. But Du Bois was more of a pragmatic anticolonial than an idealistic, banging-the-party-drum Communist; he never fully aligned himself with any political cause because of his own tendencies to adjust his philosophies over time, although in his very last days (years) it became increasingly difficult to distinguish Du Bois's position on race, class and foreign policy from that of the official party line.[10] Yes, Du Bois was a Progressive Party supporter and a candidate for the Communist-backed American Labor Party. But he also backed Democratic candidates and had expressed some hope that John F. Kennedy would energize the country's liberal base. Though James Jackson and other Communist Party members had tried "converting" Du Bois, his registration with the party seemed more of a "sticking it" gesture to the U.S. government. Like Shirley, the Doctor adopted the Communist Party because it most reflected his radical philosophies on race, class, colonialism, and capitalism. But if cynics argue that the party used Du Bois's name to advance its cause among African Americans, an equal claim can be made that the Doctor used the party to formalize his philosophies into a political platform. The CPUSA after Du Bois would have a very Du Boisian outlook as it became involved in the cultural revolution of the 1960s. Party leaders, aware that most Communists were emerging from the ranks of young black radicals, tailored the late-life philosophies of Du Bois to their political message: the United States was a colonial power that continued to oppress minorities in its own land while opposing the suffrage of darker nations around the world. Though this was not significantly different from the party's tried-and-true path from previous years, there was a distinct flavor of black nationalism added into the Communist Party line. This only grew as the Communist Party became aligned with the Black Panther Party in the late 1960s and early 1970s, symbolically capped by William Patterson's defense of Angela Davis.[11]

Though his move to communism set off a firestorm in the United States, Du Bois didn't have to identify his political motives in Ghana. He was seemingly content with letting Shirley speak politically for the both of them, allowing him more time to focus on his research. However, the developments in the United States must have come as a blow to Du Bois as he approached the dusk of his life. A new generation of black leaders led by Martin Luther King Jr., seemingly untainted by the "Red" label, had drawn international attention to the conditions of the Negro in the South. Jim Crow, it seemed, was on its last leg. Du Bois was extremely optimistic about the future of postcolonial Africa, owing to his insulated placement in Nkrumah's Ghana; on the other hand, he became dispirited by not being able to witness the rapid changes taking place across the Atlantic, changes that he and Robeson had undoubtedly influenced. Du Bois's bouts of moroseness affected Shirley, who had hoped the progress in America would serve as validation for her husband. She wrote Essie that though Du Bois "and Nkrumah frequently get a real laugh together . . . he feels that his life is over and he is just waiting for the end. This is very distressing because he is not at all diseased. No doctor believes that he must go soon." But a broken heart over leaving America might have doomed Du Bois in the end. In his final days, Du Bois spent much time with Shirley and Nkrumah, sharing his hope that the vision

for Pan-Africa—born in 1919 and maturing over time—
would come true. As Malcolm X recalled in his autobiography,
"When Dr. Du Bois was failing fast, Dr. Nkrumah had visited,
and the two men had said goodbye, both knowing that one's
death was near—and Dr. Nkrumah had gone away in tears."[12]

Du Bois died on August 27, one day before the famous
march on Washington. Though he had lived nearly a century
and had outlasted almost all of philosophical rivals (except
Wilkins and Randolph), his passing was nonetheless shocking
to his closest friends on the Left. Shirley had expected the
move to Ghana to add years to the Doctor's life; like many
who knew him, she took for granted that Du Bois's keen
mental state would offset an aging body. Essie, in consoling
Mrs. Graham Du Bois, said most believed Du Bois to be indestructible. "Well, Doctor IS indestructible, and will stand as a
beacon, and be read for inspiration and reassurance by
Negroes and Africans for generations," Essie wrote. "I hope
you are not too worn out to be very proud of the very fine job
you did. Get some rest, and then get some more rest, and then
think about what you will do."[13] Though Du Bois had influenced generations of African Americans, his departure from
the United States had allowed his rivals to take his place at the
forefront of the civil rights movement. During the march on
Washington, organizers of the mass mobilization of blacks,
whites, and a mix of ages and incomes recognized A. Philip
Randolph for his contributions to the civil rights struggle. This
was the same Randolph who, for much of his life, had espoused
more radical views on race than Du Bois or Robeson. It was
Randolph who had frequently critiqued the NAACP for its
gradual approach to civil rights and whose black nationalist

perspective often clashed with those in the Left and in the mainstream. However, Randolph, whose own membership in the Socialist Party was cleverly obscured during the civil rights movement, wound up getting kudos as a pioneer in the struggle for black equality.

Du Bois's death would create a scramble to re-create his legacy by both black moderates and the Black Left. The architects of the civil rights movement portrayed Du Bois as the forebear of the modern struggle, although they were careful to avoid any of the Doctor's more radical disclosures on race and class. Wilkins, calling Du Bois "the voice of the militant heretics against the 'worthy serf' doctrine," claimed the NAACP and the voices of interracial progress would fulfill the Du Boisian prophecy of the color line. With chest-pounding bravado, Wilkins said the NAACP's actions, inspired by Du Bois and the Niagara Movement, would leave "the imprint of its declarations and its deeds . . . sharp and clear in the history of the United States in the twentieth century."[14] Though the long-term legacy of Du Bois as a liberal and "bourgeois democrat" would win out, his immediate remembrance was authored by the Left. Shirley Graham Du Bois, Herbert Aptheker, and others spearheaded an effort to depict Du Bois as a lifelong radical whose notions on race and class were far ahead of his time. The portrayal of Du Bois as a race visionary didn't conform to the more moderate tone of the civil rights movement, but it laid the groundwork for his resurrection as a Socialist-cum-nationalist during the height of black power. In the 1970s, Du Boisian thought would become a guiding force for black nationalism and, in some way, Afrocentric thought. In the meantime, scholars and activists would spend the decade after Du Bois's death deconstructing his philosophy and politics and revising them to fit their own notions about the undisputed Elder Statesman of Afro-America.

UNLIKE DU BOIS, Robeson saw his stay in Europe as a consequence of his ostracism in the United States. Despite being treated as a national hero and celebrity in Europe, Paul's realization that he could not receive the same treatment in his home country sent him into a tailspin from which never fully recovered. Though he kept himself busy with a flurry of speaking and singing engagements throughout Europe, Robeson viewed his stay there with ambivalence. In the United States, the forces of change that swept through the South beckoned someone of Robeson's stature to take part. But he was out of the loop, and by his absence, became a footnote in the civil rights movement. The mass mobilization by SCLC and SNCC was a dream of Paul's; he likely viewed the march on Washington with a mix of pride and sorrow, having failed to achieve similar success with the American Crusade to End Lynching years earlier. While it was true that Robeson's international fame had not diminished, the fact that he could never recapture his status as an American hero proved devastating to his psyche. Aware that CIA agents and other U.S. government informants were watching his every move, Paul began to wear down mentally and physically. Shortly after celebrating New Year's in Moscow with W. E. B. and Shirley, Paul was hospitalized with an unknown ailment. Though Doctors initially diagnosed Robeson's condition as exhaustion, it would later be revealed that he was suffering from a mental and physical breakdown resulting from "great strain."[15]

Paul's physical woes did not keep him from performing in his final rendition of *Othello* in 1959. At sixty-one, and a mere shadow of his former self, Robeson put on his gutsiest and most admirable performance as the lead role. With an all-star cast that included Sam Wanamaker, Mary Ure, and Albert Finney, *Othello* came off as a tribute to the old-school depiction of the Moor whose life had been destroyed by deceit and manipulation; there was no person better suited for that portrayal than Robeson. W. E. B. and Shirley managed to take in a show, to support their friend in the struggle. Many of Paul's friends in the United States visited the Robesons in London, if only to check up on how he was faring physically and emotionally. Bob and Clara Rockmore, Sam and Helen Rosen, Lloyd Brown, and Abbott Simon were among the houseguests who kept Paul and Essie company and up to speed on the social upheaval back home. While some friends left saddened, others were angered by what had happened to Paul. Physically, his body could not hide the fatigue that had caught up to him after years of fighting on the wrong side of political battles. Du Bois—nearing the end himself—was shocked by his friend's deterioration. In his autobiography, the Doctor would lay equal blame on a vindictive U.S. government and a disloyal black America, concluding that:

> The persecution of Paul Robeson by the government and people of the United States during the last nine years has been one of the most contemptible happenings in modern history. . . . And

above all his own people, American Negroes, joined in hounding one of their greatest artists—not all, but even men like Langston Hughes, who wrote of Negro musicians and deliberately omitted Robeson's name—Robeson who more than any living man has spread the pure Negro folk song over the civilized world. . . . Yet has Paul Robeson kept his soul and stood his ground. Still he loves and honors the Soviet Union. Still he has hope for America. Still he asserts his faith in God. But we— what can we say or do; nothing but hang our heads in endless shame.[16]

Paul's ailments didn't silence him in Europe. Politically, he was as outspoken as ever, espousing the ideals of scientific Socialism that had been a cornerstone of his philosophy for years. The USSR, Paul argued, was an incubator for postcolonial thought and a bulwark against capitalists. He pointed to the Soviet invasion of Hungary and the Kremlin's backing of the new Castro regime in Cuba as actions necessitated by the ever-constant threat of imperialism and Fascism. In Budapest, Robeson called China "the greatest country" that "has all along been standing on the side of our people." In his typical manner of shrugging off details or simply ignoring them, Paul's assessment of China failed to take into account Mao's Great Leap Forward, which would, by unofficial count, rival the Holocaust as the most extensive genocide of the twentieth century. Robeson was also conspicuously silent in 1962, when China ignited a border war with India, a conflict that would continue for the next three years and prove to be Nehru's greatest embarrassment as a leader. In the aftermath of the war, Nehru would sack Krishna Menon—Robeson's longtime friend and fellow scientific Socialist—as defense minister. China would seize Indian land in eastern Kashmir and take over Tibet, two occupation issues that have yet to be resolved. Following the outbreak of the Sino-Indian War, Robeson tempered his praise for China, careful to honor his loyalty to Nehru and Menon while avoiding taking sides in a conflict between two countries he held in high regard.

Equally murky in Paul's political philosophy is the extent to which he lost faith in the Soviet Union following the revelation about the Great Purge under Stalin. Though privately traumatized by Khrushchev's admission, Robeson put on a stoic face in defending the USSR. But by the early 1960s, rumors of Paul's disenchantment with Moscow and Soviet Socialism began to surface. In January 1963, the tabloid *The National Insider* ran an article purportedly written by Robeson in which he repudiated his belief in the Soviet model for society and admitted the error of blindly following the Kremlin line. The "confession" was picked by *Le Figaro* and printed without any verification. The U.S. media jumped at the chance to question Robeson about his supposed change of heart, but newspaper reporters found their access blocked by Essie. She publicly rebutted the *Le Figaro* article, calling the allegations of Paul's change of mind "pure fabrication." Still, American newspapers continued to speculate, and some of Robeson's peers proffered their views about his political flux. Actor Edric Connor claimed Khrushchev's revelation about destroyed Robeson. With Khrushchev's rise, Connor claimed, "Paul has never been the same man since." Journalists were

eager to write the story as an epilogue to a failed political idealist, claiming the tragic end to someone who "hitched his
wagon to a red star, moved his family to Moscow and began to
sing the praises of the Soviet Union."[17]

Though claims of Paul's jumping ship were greatly exaggerated (and *The National Insider* article obviously a fake), there
was some justification in questioning his allegiance to Moscow.
After all, Robeson had staked his entire reputation—and suffered for it—by asserting that the Soviet Union was a society
without race and class, where the serfs had risen to equal status
of their former masters. The highly integrated, intellectually
advanced utopia that Robeson had seen in his initial visits to
the USSR was proving to be an elaborate mirage constructed
by the Politburo to keep international visitors such as Paul and
Du Bois in its corner. By the 1950s, Soviet anti-Semitism was
beginning to leak out of its borders with the Russian Jews who
fled to Israel and the United States. Stalin, who had been
depicted as an anticolonial hero sympathetic to the Jewish
struggle, led the effort to oppress Jews in the USSR. In fact,
Father Joe had readied concentration camps in Siberia to relo-
cate Jews; only his death would save thousands from a fate similar to that of the victims of Auschwitz. Soviet anti-Semitism
continued to drive Jews from the USSR to Israel, Western
Europe, and the United States. Many of them would become
powerful anticommunist voices during the Cold War. Even
racism, which Robeson publicly denied existed in the Soviet
Union, began to rear its ugly head in Moscow. African students,
who received stipends to study, reported getting attacked by
Russians. The idea of the black boogeyman, which was the justification for Southern lynch mobs, had become an excuse for

Russians to lash out against visiting Africans and other non-whites. In fact, the Youth Communist League, through *Komosomolskaia Pravda*, in Russia issued "official warnings to Russian girls against dating Africans."[18] Though Robeson never made mention of these kinds of prejudice in the Soviet Union, his son later claimed that Paul had been aware that they existed. Paul Jr. alleged that Soviet leaders even encouraged anti-Semitism. Those claims set off a public battle between Paul Jr. and Lloyd Brown, who had labored to keep alive the image of Paul Sr. as a political romantic who had never been exposed to the ugly realities of Soviet society. Despite Brown's best efforts to downplay his friend's astuteness, Robeson had clearly seen facets of the USSR that upset him. Though some biographers have claimed that the shock of what he saw in later years led to his mental collapse, it was likely the combined weight of government persecution and the pressures of living up to the international status that ultimately aided in Robeson's breakdown.

On December 22, 1963, ten days after the independence of Kenya, Robeson returned to the United States. Since his departure, American society had changed dramatically, nearing the inevitable goal of substantive civil rights legislation and an official end to Jim Crow. John F. Kennedy had been assassinated a month earlier, replaced by the unlikeliest of civil rights champions, Lyndon B. Johnson, a former Texas Dixiecrat. Others had fallen, too. Louis Burnham died in 1960, cutting short a life that had been committed to the Left. Paul's brother Ben, who had been one of his most steadfast supporters, died a few months before his return. Within a year, Ben Davis would die. Their deaths would weigh heavily on

Paul's conscience, adding to his feeling that all of his loved ones were leaving him. Robeson, in one of his last public speaking appearances, delivered a eulogy for Davis, expressing "deep grief at the loss of a precious friend, whose courage and dedication to the fight for freedom has always been a glowing inspiration." He summed up his brief oratory with a poem dedicated to Davis, as well as to Du Bois and Ben Robeson. "Farewell Beloved Comrade / We make this solemn vow / The fight will go on / The fight must still go on Until we win / until we, the people, win."[19]

The poem captured Robeson's desire to fight. Though weary, he pressed on with his commitment to the civil rights struggle, a movement that had gained most of its momentum while he was away from the country. Paul tried to interject himself into the fray almost immediately upon his return from Europe. "A reporter . . . said very nastily, I think, that I have arrived home belatedly to join the fight for Civil Rights. I have been fighting for Civil Rights all my life." The disconnection between Robeson and the cadre of leaders from the SCLC and SNCC did not lessen his affinity for them and support for their cause. Paul was determined to help the movement in whatever way he could, although he realized his worsening health precluded him from active participation. In what would be a fitting epilogue to his life as a political artist, Robeson painted himself as a man who overcame odds, only to find more challenges awaiting him.

> I was a sort of illustration of the mythical American
> Boy who made good. Only I was a black American
> Boy, and mythical, typical American Boys, are, of

course, white. I would have been acceptable if I was the "Yes, Sir, No, Sir" type Negro who would not have disturbed the wishful picture of Americans. My success as an artist in my country has always seemed a contradiction to me. I could, as a singer and actor, receive acclaim and awards and full recognition, but as a man, a Negro, a human being, I and my people could be denied any or all our constitutional rights, and even could be denied life itself, because of the color of our skin.[20]

Robeson also softened his defiance, fine-tuning his radicalism into conciliation with the elements of liberal white America and moderate black America that abandoned him during the McCarthy era. "I do not believe the Negro is essentially different from the white man, that the European, the Asian, the African is a different species of humanity," he said, sounding more like vintage 1930s Robeson than Cold War Robeson. "I believe we are all members of one wonderful Human family, with a common origin, a common culture with a wealth of art and music, a common purpose, a common destiny."[21] But though his words were in line with the sentiment of the civil rights movement, Robeson himself was still out of step with the pace of the struggle. Most of the SCLC and SNCC leaders did not even know who Robeson was, and by careful design, Wilkins tried to keep them in ignorance. In the NAACP's dogged anti-Communism, not even the sentimental value of having Robeson's name in the effort was worth the risk of undermining the civil rights movement. The SNCC was already battling allegations that it had been infiltrated by

Communists, a fact that John Lewis pointed out in a 1965 tribute to Robeson. The sentiments of Lewis and others, including Bob Moses, didn't go beyond sympathy. It appeared Robeson's desire to reach out to the new generation of civil rights leaders wouldn't be reciprocated.

Robeson's final year of active life was also his most tragic. In January 1965, Claudia Jones died in London, spending her final years as a deportee from the United States under the Smith Act. Jones was one of the highest-ranking CPUSA functionaries, and in retrospect, pioneered the role of black women in political organizations. As Mary Helen Washington noted years later, Jones was also a vocal critic of the subordination of black women in the Left, championing the black working-class woman as the focal point of radical thought.[22] Within days of her death, another Robeson protégé, Lorraine Hansberry, succumbed to cancer at age thirty-four. Hansberry, who worked with Robeson on *Freedom*, was one of the young inspirational forces in the Left. Though best known for *Raisin in the Sun*, Hansberry had been a tireless writer and activist, openly affiliating with marginalized Communist Left. Robeson attended Hansberry's funeral in New York, somberly reflecting on the life of a young playwright who had committed her life to political artistry. The next month, Robeson and many others in black America would become distraught over the death of a popular and controversial black leader.

According to Duberman's biography, Malcolm X had wanted to meet Robeson for several years. Even during his days with the Nation of Islam, Malcolm expressed an almost reverent devotion to Robeson, casting him as a victim of malicious white persecution and conspiracy. In the racialized world of Malcolm, Robeson exemplified martyrdom. Paul, on the other hand, despised the politics of the Nation of Islam and its racially chauvinistic leader, Elijah Muhammad, choosing to distance himself from the Nation's unwanted admiration. However, Malcolm X's defection from the Nation and his newfound internationalism paved the way for the two, through intermediaries, to meet. That encounter would never take place; Malcolm X was assassinated in Harlem on February 21, 1965, ending the life of someone who could have bridged the gap between Robeson and many young blacks. Though Robeson did not attend the crowded funeral for Malcolm, the fact that Robeson's close friend and follower, Ossie Davis, delivered the eulogy signified how close both men could have become had they gotten to know one another. Malcolm's death had a profound private impact on Paul, as it hammered home his long-felt belief that blacks could be their own worst enemy. Though the FBI and white racists might have wanted to kill Malcolm, those who actually pulled the trigger were members of the Nation.

Hoping to keep Robeson's name relevant to the 1960s civil rights struggle, *Freedomways* organized a tribute for him in April. The *Freedomways* event brought together some of Paul's friends from the Left, as well as the younger generation of activists. Some SCLC members were on hand; however, John Lewis, one of those charged with honoring Robeson, embarrassed event organizers by reading from scribbled notes. Still, as the magazine noted, "Many from the Harlem and Bedford-Stuyvesant communities of New York came out . . . because they felt 'our freedom movement has now caught up with many of the things Paul Robeson fought for all these years; it's time we openly acknowledge his contribution.'"[23] Robeson, noticeably older and weaker, still captivated the crowd with his keynote speech. Paul spoke of the progress the American Negro had made over the past forty years, but he also made a plug for Socialism. He echoed Du Bois's sentiments that the world was moving toward Socialism, but refrained from attacking U.S. capitalism. Instead, Paul diplomatically mused, "The large question as to which society is better for humanity is never settled by argument. The proof of the pudding is in the eating." He went on to add that Americans were taking a path that might reopen the doors of Socialist thought and bring back true democracy.

It is clear that large sections of the American people are feeling and accepting their responsibility for freedom and peace. It also is clear that from the Negro people has come a tremendous initiative and dynamic power in the forward thrust of our march toward freedom. It is clear that the Negro people are claiming their rights and they are in every way determined to have those rights and nothing can turn us back!

Most important is the recognition that achieving these demands in no way lessens the democratic rights of white American citizens. On the contrary, it will enormously strengthen the base of democracy for all Americans. So, the initiative, the power and independence of the Negro Movement are all factors which strengthen the alliance between the Negro people and the white citizens of our country at every level in our society. Now we must find and build a living connection, deeper and stronger, between the Negro people and the great mass of white Americans who are indeed our natural allies in the struggle for democracy. In fact, the interests of the overwhelming majority of the American people as a whole demand that this connection be built and that the "Negro question" be solved. It is not simply a matter of justice for a minority.[24]

The *Freedomways* event marked Paul's last major public appearance. He was hospitalized two months later in New York and spent the rest of the year under constant supervision as doctors, family, and friends tended to his depression and mental fatigue. In December, Paul lost the one woman who had remained at his side. Eslanda Goode Robeson—Paul's manager, ad hoc political advisor and the unswerving loyal wife in public—died on the two-year anniversary of Kenya's independence, a fitting date given her commitment to Africa. Essie's death might have been the final straw for Paul. Essie had long ignored her own health problems for the sake of her husband's rise to fame, standing firmly beside him at the apex and nadir of his career. Without anyone to appropriately "manage" him the way Essie had so successfully done, Paul would turn to seclusion as the only solution. His family and friends moved him to West Philadelphia to live with his sister Marian, where he spent the last ten years of his life away from attention. Historian Charles L. Blockson, who was among the few people to have personal interaction with Robeson in his final years, recalled that even in the 1970s, "You couldn't even whisper Paul Robeson's name in Philadelphia."[25]

For a man who had made headlines since his teens, Robeson's disappearance from public life essentially ended his; even before his death in 1976, contemporaries would refer to the Robeson legacy and Paul in the past tense. In what sounded like a preemptive obituary, one Philadelphia writer wrote:

> Perhaps Paul Robeson was born 30 years too soon. His protest that scandalized Americans in the 1930s and 1940s would hardly cause a ripple today. The same Robeson who in the 1950s was deprived of his passport, blackballed by a frightened artistic establishment and shunned as a Redlining pariah, would be the toast of the talk-shows, the ambassador of goodwill, the people's champion today. Thus have times change, and not least because of the courage of Paul Robeson, singer, actor, activist.[26]

As the country underwent radical social and political changes during the late 1960s and 1970s, Paul Leroy Robeson watched his life fade away from Marian's home at 4951 Walnut Street. Loften Mitchell bemoaned the fact that Paul's ostracism had been so complete that youngsters had never been able to see a man whose face was once a fixture on the front pages of newspapers and magazines during the 1930s and 1940s. "It is interesting to note that Mr. Robeson was effectively kept off TV in this country and this explains in large part why the present generation, a TV generation, may have members who ask: 'Who was Paul Robeson?'"[27] It would be another decade before his resurrection in the American conscience.

IN THE YEARS AFTER DU BOIS'S DEATH and Robeson's disappearance from public life, their contemporaries fought to control and reinvent their political legacies. Leading the charge in molding the Du Bois name were Shirley Graham Du Bois and her son, David. After Du Bois's death, Shirley began to affiliate more with the black nationalist movement; consequently, her interpretation of her late husband's life began to center around his nationalist philosophies, which had evolved significantly over the course of the century. Graham Du Bois feuded with Esther Jackson—who was now editing *Freedomways*—over the Jackson's decision to allow some of the Doctor's political enemies, including Roy Wilkins and Rufus Clement, to write articles paying tribute to Du Bois. Graham Du Bois and other nationalist-leaning black Leftists would begin a tug-of-war with the Communists over the right to author the appropriate tribute to Du Bois's life. The Communists had an initial edge; Du Bois identified closely with party members such as James and Esther Jackson, Louis Burnham, and Alphaeus Hunton in his later years, not to mention Graham Du Bois herself was a registered Communist. Presenting Du Bois as an Afrocentric Communist also posed problems for his white followers, namely, Herbert Aptheker. Aptheker and Jackson had a falling out over Jackson's apparent refusal to allow Aptheker to contribute to *Freedomways*; her justification was that the magazine was to be a forum for black writers. Undeterred by the black Left's memorializing of Du Bois, Aptheker offered his own analysis of the Doctor in writings throughout the 1960s. In 1971, Aptheker wrote the foreword for the rerelease of *Dark Princess*, explaining the novel as Du Bois's foray into Marxism and its role in the anticolonial struggle. He also wrote *The Literary Legacy of W. E. B. Du Bois* and edited the Doctor's correspondences, making him one of the most visible Du Boisian disciples until his death in 2003.

Du Bois would also have a place in the nationalist ideology championed by the likes of John Henrik Clarke and Harold Cruse and put into practice by the Black Panthers and the black arts movement of the late 1960s and 1970s. As Jim Smethurst noted, many young black nationalists were "drawn to the figure of the uncompromising anti-imperialist believer in national self-determination."[28] The reconstruction of Du Bois in the black nationalist paradigm was apt for the times. Frustrated by the apparent lack of immediacy in the civil rights movement, many urban blacks gravitated toward a more militant view of social progress, summed by Malcolm X's proclamation: "By any means necessary." Du Bois—like Robeson—fit the image of a martyr, a leading black icon dragged down by an oppressive government and the treachery of milquetoast moderates. It was hardly the image of Du Bois as a champion of interracial cooperation that both the Communists (and Communist-aligned Left) and the mainstream elements of black leadership advocated. But the turbulence of the 1960s prevented any sort of common ground among the diverse forces seeking to re-create Du Bois in their own light. For Shirley Graham Du Bois, the nationalistic and anticolonial ruminations of the Doctor needed to be the foundation of his memory. For the Communists who had not aligned themselves with black nationalism, Du Bois was a preeminent internationalist and a man persecuted for his political leanings. Even the moderates who had nearly disowned Du Bois a decade earlier came back to him, taking some of his earlier philosophies— considered radical at the time he espoused them—and incorporating them into the calls for desegregation and just application of civil rights laws. Indeed, the beauty of Du Bois's political transformation was in the flexibility of his philosophy over time; there was something for everyone. Perhaps King put it best when, two months before his assassination, he called Du Bois "a tireless explorer and a gifted discoverer of social truths." The Doctor's politics were irrelevant, King argued, when putting the life of a civil rights pioneer into context. "It is time to cease muting the fact that Dr. Du Bois was a genius and chose to be a Communist. Our irrational obsessive anti-Communism has led us into too many quagmires to be retained as if it were a mode of scientific thinking."[29]

Du Bois's scholarly contributions, particularly in Pan-Africanism, took center stage in the early 1970s in Africa. While living in Cairo, David Graham Du Bois spearheaded an effort to make Du Boisian Pan-African thought a permanent part of African education. In Ghana, Du Bois and other staunch Pan-Africanists founded the W. E. B. Du Bois Centre for Pan-African Culture in Accra, hoping to spread the political philosophy fathered by Du Bois and practiced by Nkrumah (and to a lesser extent, Kenyatta and Azikiwie). David Graham Du Bois, however, interpreted his stepfather's political evolution through the eyes of a black nationalist, lessening the Pan-Africanist appeal to those who read Du Bois from a Socialist perspective. Graham Du Bois acknowledged his stepfather's "conversion" to the Communist Left, but maintained that Du Boisian philosophy was predicated on the notion of racial identity—and African Americans' grasping of it—as the key to black advancement. Graham Du Bois maintained that stance until his death in January 2005. However, Pan-Africanism—both as a philosophy beyond the borders of the Dark Continent and as political practice within—never caught on with most African Americans, or for that matter, Africans. Though Nkrumah became a folk hero for his anticolonial leadership, his failure as a ruler was a cautionary tale about the limitations of visionary politics. During the 1970s, much of sub-Saharan Africa reattached itself to European and American patronization, reverting to the colonial-era dependency the Doctor had railed against for most of his life.

Though Du Boisian Pan-Africanism was a precursor to Afrocentricity in the United States, not all Afrocentrists embraced Du Bois. Molefi K. Asante, one of the leading Afrocentrists and a proponent of African political solidarity, claims Du Bois was a "European man" in his views on Africa. According to Asante's definition of Afrocentricty, "All human cultures must be centered, in fact, subject or their own realities." Asante argues that Du Bois consistently viewed Africa—even in his desire for Pan-African Socialism—through a Eurocentric construct shaped by his education and upbringing in the United States. Though not denying Du Bois's passion for social justice, Asante essentially labeled Du Bois an outsider in the world of true Afrocentrism.[30] Asante even criticized his role model, Harold Cruse, for deifying Du Bois as a trailblazer in Afro-cultural thought. "Cruse had deliberately separated Africa from African Americans and in so doing believed that he was following Du Bois' notion that the African American was truly an American product. But Du

420

Bois was wrong and Cruse's support of him was to compound the problem of culture and further conceal the source of the lack of cultural will."[31] Afrocentrists, as it turned out, were the most moderate of Du Bois's critics. Ultimately, it was the Doctor's politics that made him an enemy to social conservatives long after his death. In 1978, Georgia Representative Larry McDonald blasted the United Nations for celebrating Du Bois's 110th birthday. McDonald (who attacked efforts to honor Robeson two years earlier) claimed Du Bois was "essentially a black racist who worked with the Communists, but understood what they really were."[32] The stigma of Du Bois's affiliation with the Communist Party and the Soviet Union remained fresh in the minds of many conservatives; in fact, it would become the primary reason for opposition to naming a school in Great Barrington after him.[33]

As Du Bois's contemporaries and revisionists battled for ownership of his legacy, his image split into two. For the consumption of laymen and the compatibility of American history books, Du Bois the scholar became narrowly defined as the founder of the NAACP, the originator of the Talented Tenth, and one of the most prolific writers on race in the twentieth century. In the academic world, battles raged over what contributions the Doctor should be most remembered for: his philosophies or his politics. Some academics would argue that in assessing Du Bois's politics, his age (and questions of his lucidity after eighty) should be taken into consideration. However, given the intense political activity during his last fifteen years, there was little doubt that Du Bois had his full mental faculties until his death. David Levering Lewis would write the definitive two-volume biography on Du Bois in 1994 and 2000, respectively, painting the picture of a man whose political restlessness over time reflected the rapidly changing world around him. Lewis depicted Du Bois as an against-the-grain political firebrand whose meditations on race and society often bordered on iconoclastic; he also noted the Doctor's fallibility in espousing philosophies that he would later disavow. Though Lewis blended Du Bois's philosophical transformation with his evolving politics, the biography could not counter the prevailing image of Du Bois as a philosopher and academic whose greatest contribution to civil rights was cofounding the NAACP. The modern image of Du Bois, linked forever with the Talented Tenth and the Niagara Movement, is a testament to moderate black America's victory over its more radical counterparts. Du Bois the Communist and Du Bois the quasi-nationalist have been all but erased from the mainstream contemporary interpretation of his life, though, as a testament to his prolific activism, he continues to be remembered as a race radical for the ages.

Capturing Robeson's legacy proved more difficult and controversial. While Du Bois wore many hats and evolved both philosophically and politically over a seventy-year span, Robeson's philosophical awakening and political activism—though intense—lasted only thirty years. His core views were also in stasis, making it harder for a flexible interpretation of his views. Still, Robeson was an icon of the Communist Left *and* black nationalists, two seemingly incompatible groups that would find more common ground during the rise of the black power movement. Ironically the debate over Paul's political legacy raged while he was living in solitude in Philadelphia. His contemporaries began speaking of him in the past tense, perhaps aware that Robeson was too far gone mentally to make any sort of comeback to public life. His friends in the Communist-affiliated Left took great pains to preserve his legacy as an intrepid internationalist and anti-colonial, a black man whose only crime was to profess love for the Soviet Union and the United States. As Lloyd Brown wrote, "Any honest appraisal would show that Robeson's internationalism, his all-embracing humanism, was developed *through* his deep communion with the Afro-American heritage. . . . The record also shows that not only as an artist but an activist Robeson firmly based himself on Afro-American tradition."[34] Brown fervently promoted and protected the prevailing notion among leftists that Paul was an international renaissance man felled by "a boycott . . . that was meant both to silence him and to deny him any opportunity of making a living." Communists and other left-wing intellectuals stuck to this notion of Robeson, glorifying his global citizenship and noting that his acceptance in other countries was a sign of American intolerance. William Patterson called Robeson a "statesman . . . of art and culture" and "an artist of the revolution."[35] This notion of Robeson as a political artist with deeply rooted loyalties to labor and suffrage of oppressed peoples was also advocated by Ossie Davis, Ruby Dee, Sidney Poitier, and Harry Belafonte, who followed in the tradition of merging art and activism.

Though Brown and Patterson led the effort to promote Robeson's internationalism and activism for the common man, nationalist scholars began to view Robeson as a racial self-determinist. Brown was livid when Sterling Stuckey (who would later write a new introduction to *Here I Stand*) asserted that Robeson was a "lifelong black nationalist." Stuckey claimed Robeson supported nationalism since his days at Rutgers, only becoming more nationalistic through the influence of Garveyites upon moving to Harlem. Brown complained to Patterson that he had "accumulated . . . mass material that refutes that statement, not to mention my own first-hand knowledge." Patterson, who expressed more nationalistic sympathies by the end of the 1960s, concurred, saying that he never recalled "Paul . . . taking a narrow nationalist position" or "speak in favor of any position espoused by Garvey."[36] But the black nationalist label—trendy because of the black power movement among urban blacks following the 1968 riots—stuck, and many young intellectuals swarmed to a revised image of Robeson as a race man destroyed by racism. Black nationalists played up the idea that "Uncle Tom" Negroes were complicit in Robeson's destruction, taking special aim at Jackie Robinson and Roy Wilkins for their roles. Malcolm X attacked Robinson for allowing himself to "be used by the whites . . . against your own kind. You let them sic you on Paul Robeson. You let them use you to destroy Paul Robeson . . . to dispute and condemn Paul Robeson, because he had these guilty American whites frightened silly."[37] Malcolm would use Robeson's downfall—and his betrayal by Robinson and the NAACP—as fodder for his own militant activism. The black power movement, a mix of Marxism, Garveyism, and urban black angst, also lionized Robeson—not as a champion of oppressed peoples, but as a victim of "white America." Other nationalist interpretations of Robeson emerged in the 1970s, with prominent black intellectuals such as Amiri Baraka likening him to Sisyphus.

Cruse, however, was among a core of Negro writers who did not agree with the idea of making Robeson into an archetype for black nationalism. In *The Crisis of the Negro Intellectual,* Cruse painted Paul as a tool of "Communist Left political propaganda." He even questioned whether Robeson's loyalty to his friends in the Communist Party had cost him his legacy as a Negro cultural advocate. To Cruse, Robeson was a "broken symbol." Such an assessment undercut the martyr image advanced by the Left and many anti-Communist black nationalists. Cruse went so far as to disparage Robeson for his "innocent idealism." *Here I Stand,* in Cruse's opinion, did not merit serious analysis by Negro intellectuals because it was "weak, sentimental" and "lacking a single paragraph on Negro problems."[38] But his opinion of Robeson seemed to be the juice of sour grapes rather than a convictive appraisal. Cruse had been loosely involved with the Communist Party in the 1950s, including a short stint with the *Daily Worker.* The fact that he had not been able to distinguish himself as a Leftist writer in the vein of Hansberry or Brown probably inspired *Crisis* more than a genuine epiphany on the state of black intellectualism. As Esther Jackson noted, "He was a very bitter man."[39] Cruse's book provided for "shock and awe" reading at the height of the 1960s revolution, propelling him from an unknown into a leading voice in black nationalism. His views also influenced Afrocentric thought, though Cruse became known more as an "African Americanist" for his emphasis on the uniqueness of the African American struggle compared with the rest of the black world. Though some black nationalists took their cue from Garvey, Cruse was as opposed to Garveyism as he was communism; both, Cruse argued, were concepts not native to black America. After Cruse's death, some black scholars tried to point out that Cruse was simply misguided in his analysis. Asante, for instance, asserted that Cruse—in seeking the prototypical Negro intellectual—weighed too heavily on Robeson's political ties and not enough on his personal philosophies. If he had, Asante noted, Cruse might have realized that Robeson was a "true race man."[40]

Evidence of Asante's claim came from C. L. R. James, who had dreamed of Robeson becoming the voice of Black Zion. If only Paul had taken his cues from Garvey instead of the Kremlin, James wrote, the Black World would have had a new Moses. Like Cruse, James concluded that Robeson was a victim of Communist manipulation, unable to express his true Blackness in a way that would have galvanized millions.

> I was in the United States busily noting all that was going on in politics concerning Black people, and I became certain, and all the people whom I talked to were absolutely certain, that if Paul had wanted to he would have built a movement in the United States that would have been the natural successor to the Garvey Movement. Further, Paul, being what he was and his ideas being what they were, the movement would have been of a far higher intellectual quality than was the Garvey Movement, which had laid a foundation for future movements. I can say, and it will be easy to prove, that people were looking to Paul to start such a movement. There were numbers of people, dozens

and scores of people, who would have been ready to work with him if he had begun, and the mass of the Black population would have followed him as they were ready to follow him everywhere he went. But the plain fact is that Paul felt himself committed to the doctrines and the policies of the Communist Party. The Black movement which could have burst and swept the United States around Paul Robeson did not come because Paul did not see it that way. That is a part of the history of the United States, which everybody in the United States should know. What was there, what was possible, what was missed, and why.[41]

One important aspect in viewing the divide between the Communist Left and the nationalists on Robeson (and Du Bois) was the era in which the battles were fought. In the 1960s, black power became more appealing to some prominent black Communists, who viewed the struggle of militant black nationalists as a natural offshoot of Communist philosophy. In defending the Black Panther Party, many Communist leaders rationalized the Panthers' militant tactics as a "response . . . to the racist crimes of police power."[42] In fact, black Communists began to shift their sympathies to the black power movement. John Pittman, former editor of the *Daily World*, recalled that "the party . . . supported the cause of the Panthers. We see the Panthers as an expression of militant black youth who refuse . . . to be pushed around, accept racist practices and so forth."[43] This justification of black power as a sister struggle with communism appealed to many, including Patterson, who urged the party to back the Black Panther legal defense. However, some Communists remained at odds with the notion of nationalism and communism going hand-in-hand. James Jackson called the ideas of black self-determinism championed by the Black Panther Party and the Nation of Islam "Marcus Garvey nationalist fantasy." He added:

> It makes no difference that the separatist outlook is presented in terms of the Black Panther Party's demand for a plebiscite; it is still a boost for a separatist way out. Such a thrust in emphasis is disorienting to the Black freedom movement and is confusing to the anti-monopoly allies in the struggle. When the progressive movement is confused, only the reactionary ruling circles benefit.[44]

Jackson's assessment showed that for at least some of Du Bois and Robeson's contemporaries, attempts to bridge two schools of thought into harmonious compromise were impractical. It also proved that despite some alchemic revisions of both men's lives, the pure Communist and pure nationalist interpretations of Du Bois and Robeson were irreconcilable.

Though the Communist Left and the nationalists were at odds over the most accurate depiction of Robeson, each side had a legitimate case in interpreting his life. Robeson espoused themes that were nationalist *and* Marxist. His brand of scientific Socialism, based on the notion of the Negro and other groups as the oppressed class in capitalism, resounded on both a racial and class-oriented level. As Baraka accurately concluded, Robeson "understood that the only way to measure

428

the 'racial oppression' was in terms of its class nature. . . .
That one people is forced to live a *lower*, more depressed and
uncertain marginal existence, that other people 'live better'
than they—this is the ultimate disposition of class."[45]
Robeson's declaration in his autobiography that firstly, "I am
a Negro" added fuel to nationalists' claims that he was a black
man whose identity came before any of his global politics. But
to his Communist friends, that statement underscored the
reason why Paul chose to align himself with the Soviet Union
and leftist politics: he was an oppressed black man who could
never find full freedom under the clamps of imperialistic capitalism. The shoe fit for both camps. Communists in the
United States and leftist anticolonial writers abroad would
immortalize Robeson as the consummate political artist,
whose core political philosophy was built around an opposition to oppression, fascism, and injustice. Black nationalists
brought Robeson "home" to a new generation of African
Americans as they had done with Du Bois, making him a
paragon of the antiestablishment in the vein of Malcolm X,
Muhammad Ali, and Marcus Garvey. This partial compromise
led to Robeson's resurgence among black activists following
his death in 1976; he would be "reintroduced" to mainstream
America in 1998, during the extensive celebration of his cen-
tennial anniversary.

But beneath the revisionist rhetoric, a strong argument
exists for making Robeson the precursor to modern Afrocentrism. Though Du Bois might have introduced the notion,
Asante asserts that it was Robeson who put Afrocentric
thought into practice. Robeson might have distanced himself
from the nationalists, but he never shied away from espousing

a state of black consciousness. For Paul, the expression of his blackness did not need to be politicized; rather, he emphasized black as a state of mind. Robeson might have considered himself an Afrocentric Socialist who emphasized Afro humanity and promoted class solidarity.

Robeson's critique of capitalism and its exploitative nature might have also made him the first contemporary political economist. The late radical writer and media analyst Herbert Schiller, who is generally regarded as one of the most prolific political economists and an influence to modern media critics like Robert McChesney and Ben Bagdikian, was profoundly influenced by Robeson's activism. Schiller biographer Robert Maxwell wrote that Schiller once spoke at an Australian dock where "Robeson . . . stood . . . years earlier, inspiring the 'wharfies' with speech, song and protest. The memory always seemed to fill him with that special delight of living in the big picture of historical processes and the world struggle for progressive change."[46]

Historians have been frustrated by their efforts to label Robeson because he simply does not fit into any classification. Paul transcended categorization and moved in diverse and often conflicting circles. In addition to being Du Bois's pupil-turned-political compass, he was a philosophical disciple of Douglass, Marx, Nathaniel Turner, Harold Laski, and Henry David Thoreau. He had been able to promote labor, champion integration, and espouse black pride. Duberman's attempt to portray Robeson as a "tragic hero" missed the mark because it failed to weigh Paul's significant impact on the Left. Lloyd Brown's writings on Robeson might have leaned too heavily to the Communist Left, but his eloquence and exclusive access to

Paul provided rare insight into the life of one of the most complex men in modern history. While numerous historians have had their opportunity to present Robeson, Paul Jr. has devoted the last thirty years trying to reconstruct his father's legacy; however, in the process, he has distanced and alienated himself from many in the Left. In the years after Robeson's death, Paul Jr. openly attacked some in the Communist Left, accusing them of using his father for their own gain. In his revelation about Soviet anti-Semitism, Paul Jr. made public his feud with Lloyd Brown, who claimed to be Robeson's designated biographer. Brown attacked Paul Jr. for his "incredible slander of his father" and "grotesque falsehood directed against the integrity of a great and good man whose stand against fascism made him the No. 1 target of America's white supremacists and anti-Semites."[47] Paul Jr. angrily called Brown's allegation "absurd," countering that Brown was likely spilling sour grapes over being terminated as the designated biographer of Paul Sr.

After ending his relationship with Brown, Paul Jr. sought out Duberman, whose excellence as a writer (he had previously won the Bancroft Prize and was a finalist for the National Book Award) and attention to detail seemingly made him the perfect choice to chronicle the complex life of Paul Sr. But there were immediate roadblocks. As Esther Jackson noted, many of Paul's friends on the Left refused to cooperate with Duberman. "We knew what he was trying to do," Jackson said. As it turned out, the Duberman biography of Robeson came across as a portrait of a tragic hero, and in many ways, paralleled Paul's life with Othello's. Sculptor Antonio Salemme, a close friend of Paul during the 1920s, called Duberman "a son of a bitch" for intimating that Robeson had an affair with his first wife Betty.[48] Brown had other choice words to describe Duberman, taking special notice of Martin's decision to dedicate the book to his "friends in the rooms," a veiled homosexual reference. Paul Jr. took strong exception to the book, especially in its psychosexual analysis of Robeson and not-so-veiled references to his private life. He also upbraided Duberman for his intimations that Essie was often more detrimental to Robeson than she was helpful; there were also several references to Essie's apparent infidelity, including speculation that she might have carried on an affair with Nehru (an allegation Paul Jr. fervently denied).[49] Frustrated by the Duberman book, which he called a "prurient exploration of Robeson's life," Paul Jr. set to write his own biography of his father. Robeson released *The Undiscovered Paul Robeson* in 2001, with the intent of "clearing up" past interpretations of his father. Academics generally viewed the book as an effort by Paul Jr. to erase his father's faults, or at least contextualize them in a way that made Paul Sr. appear less culpable for his mistakes. Paul Jr., however, has soldiered on in trying to represent his father's views and re-create his image.

REWRITING DU BOIS AND ROBESON has undoubtedly eroded their legacies. Many revisionists have sought to "tame" both men for mainstream consumption, to the point of Du Bois's radicalism (and disavowal of the NAACP) being ignored and Robeson's political involvement glossed over. The tendency of history to be viewed through the eyes of the "winners" reflects the modern interpretations of Du Bois and Robeson. The defeat of the Left during the Cold War—and the fall of the Soviet Union in 1991—eliminated the need for including Du Bois and Robeson's leftist ties in their biographies. In fact, most of Du Bois's political involvement has been omitted from modern studies of his life. While *Souls of Black Folk* is a rite of passage reading for most college students, the Doctor's more militant musings on race, class, and politics—eloquently and emphatically expressed in *Darkwater*, *Black Reconstruction*, and *Autobiography*—are mere footnotes when examining his impact. Revisionist history has been harsher on Robeson. Baraka concluded that "Robeson's pitiless harassment, character assassination, career destruction, and ultimate physical sickness and death, are another legacy of American slavery and the continuing rule of money."[50] While such an assessment may seem extreme, its validity is demonstrated by the fact that Robeson—once the most lionized black man in the world—is now irrelevant to the American mainstream and mostly forgotten in global dialogue. A generation of young Americans—with the exception of those who have graduated from Rutgers or Penn State University—is oblivious to one of the great political figures of the twentieth century. At Penn State, most students refer to the student center named after him as "The Robe," unaware of the insult to Robeson's legacy.[51] In laymen's understanding, Robeson was an accomplished singer and actor, known primarily for "Ol' Man River" and *Othello*, respectively. When rapper Kanye West—a product of black middle-class angst—proclaimed, "George Bush doesn't care about black people!" his career did not suffer; in fact, many Americans might have secretly agreed with such a harsh assessment.[52] But West (and the Dixie Chicks) at least had an opportunity to criticize the government and the commander in chief without significant backlash; on the other hand, Robeson was excoriated for speaking his mind and standing firm on his political convictions. As a result of Cold War–inspired revisionism, Paul's politics have been conveniently left out in many of the contemporary readings of his life. Though Robeson made invaluable contributions to arts and culture, especially as a breakthrough black male lead actor, the downplaying of his political involvement seemingly misses the main point of Robeson's life—combining the notions of artistic achievement with political activism. As Robeson himself noted, "the Negro artist . . . had a responsibility to his people who rightfully resented the traditional stereotyped portrayals of Negroes on stage and screen."[53] By not capturing the beauty of Robeson's political artistry, revisionists have done a disservice to the first African American entertainer to combine those notions on such a prominent scale.

Revisionism has also made it nearly impossible to resurrect warriors of the Left like Du Bois and Robeson, especially after the spread of far Right-wing ideology in American society over the last decade. In fact, reactionary talk radio hosts have justified McCarthy-era tactics, and many conservatives have even used the same public fear-mongering in the so-called War on Terror. Critics of conservative ideology have been publicly lambasted as threats to national security, and almost everything pushed forward by the Bush administration—tax cuts for the wealthy and for oil companies, cuts in social programs, racial profiling, torture and illegal wiretaps—has been justified as part of a strategy to "fight our enemies." Civil liberties have become a mere inconvenience for Right wingers, who have opposed illegal immigration, abortion, gay marriage, and affirmative action on the same shaky grounds as McCarthyites had for opposing civil rights more than fifty years ago. The conservative revisionists who played a significant part in obscuring Du Bois and Robeson have attempted to paint America's most despicable acts and most heinous individuals in a more sympathetic light. For instance, conservative blogger and commentator Michelle Malkin, the daughter of Filipino immigrants, wrote a 2004 book arguing that the internment of Arab Americans should be a viable option in the war on terror, despite the American government's own admission that such a policy was an embarrassment to democracy when used against Japanese Americans more than sixty years ago. Similarly, right-wing ideologue Ann Coulter has attempted to recast Joseph McCarthy as an American patriot felled by the treachery of American liberalism. In essence, conservative demagoguery has made it nearly impossible to give the Left its proper due in helping to shape twentieth-century America, and its heroes—many of who have not been mentioned in this book—continue to linger in the shadows.

Today's interpretations of Du Bois and Robeson are, as historian Alfred Moss puts it, "the inevitable result of how history affects what people see in and value about a great person."[54] But attempts to separate the men from their politics—as mainstream organizations like the NAACP have done—are the utmost dishonor to Du Bois and Robeson. Politics made both men, and ultimately destroyed them; denying their political affiliation would be tantamount to censorship. Du Bois and

Robeson chose political paths that diverged from the American mainstream and paid for it with their reputations, making attempts to erase their leftism only seem like added punishment to their legacies. Both men took their political ties and their global outlook to their graves, defying calls by their contemporaries to moderate their positions. Whether viewed through the lefist or nationalist lens, their impact on anticolonial and radical thought is undeniable. They forged a path for black nationalists, Pan-Africanists, and other leftists to find their own voice. In the end, W. E. B. Du Bois and Paul Robeson's contributions to culture, politics, and philosophy are immeasurable. That is why appreciating *every* aspect of their lives is the most fitting tribute to the Professor and the Pupil.

NOTES

INTRODUCTION
1. David Graham Du Bois interview with author in Amherst, MA, July 11, 2004.
2. Dick Russell, "All the World's Their Stage," in *Black Genius* (New York: Carroll & Graf, 1998), 123.
3. W. E. B. Du Bois, "The Negro and Communism," *Crisis* (September 1931).
4. W. E. B. Du Bois, *An Appeal to the World: A Statement on the Denial of Human Rights to Minorities in the Case of Citizens of Negro Descent in the United States of America and an Appeal to the United Nations for Redress* (New York: NAACP, 1947).
5. Paul Robeson, unpublished notes, 1940, Paul Robeson Archives, Howard University.
6. Speech by W. E. B. Du Bois, "The Talented Tenth, the Re-Examination of a Concept," August 12, 1948, Sigma Pi Phi Grand Boule, Wilberforce, Ohio. Used with permission of the David Graham Du Bois Trust.
7. W. E. B. Du Bois, *The Autobiography of W. E .B. DuBois: A Soliloquy on Viewing My Life from the Last Decade of Its First Century* (New York: International Publishers, 1968), 397–8.
8. Speech by Du Bois, "The Talented Tenth."
9. Ernest Allen, "DuBoisian Double Consciousness: The Unsustainable Argument," *Massachusetts Review* (Summer 2002), 217–53.
10. Du Bois, *An Appeal to the World*.
11. W. E. B. Du Bois letter to Vito Marcantonio, December 6, 1951, W. E. B. Du Bois Archives.
12. Du Bois, "The Talented Tenth."
13. Paul Robeson, *Here I Stand* (Boston: Beacon Press, 1988), 20.
14. Elizabeth Shepley Sergeant, "A Portrait of Paul Robeson," *New Republic*, March 3, 1926.
15. Robeson, *Here I Stand*.
16. Speech by Paul Robeson, (Untitled), April 20, 1949, Paris Peace Conference, France. Historians have had trouble verifying the full text of Robeson's speech, but have generally agreed that an Associated Press dispatch from the event was inaccurate.

17. Speech by Robeson, "Nehru." Welcome Home Rally for Jawalarhal Nehru, London, June 1938.
18. Amiri Baraka, "Paul Robeson and the Theater. *Black Renaissance/Renaissance Noire* (Fall–Winter 1998), 13.
19. P. L. Prattis, "Why Has Robeson Been Called One of the World's Great Intellects?" *Horizon*, November 18, 1944.
20. Several publications, including *Collier's* magazine, gave Robeson that title during the 1940s.
21. Speech by Paul Robeson, "Anti-Imperialists Must Defend Africa." Council on African Affairs Rally, June 6, 1946, New York.
22. Ossie Davis, excerpts of interview with *NewsHour with Jim Lehrer*, April 9, 1998. Courtesy of PBS.
23. W. E. B. Du Bois, "The Souls of White Folk," in *Darkwater: Voices from Within the Veil* (New York: Harcourt Brace, 1920).

1. THE HARLEM RENAISSANCE AND THE BIRTH OF A FRIENDSHIP

1. A. Philip Randolph, "Truth about Lynching," in *Truth about Lynching: Its Causes and Effects* (New York: Cosmo-Advocate, 1917), 8.
2. Ibid., p. 297.
3. Introduced by Congressman Leonidas Dyer of Missouri, the Dyer Anti-Lynching Bill was championed as both legal and moral legislation against lynching. However, the bill was filibustered several times before ultimately dying in the House of Representatives. On June 13, 2005, Congress formally apologized for failing to enact antilynching legislation.
4. W. E. B. Du Bois, "Returning Soldiers," *Crisis* (May 1919), 13.
5. W. E. B. Du Bois, "Strivings of the Negro People," *Atlantic Monthly* (August 1897), 197
6. Du Bois, *The Souls of Black Folk* (Chicago: A. J. McClurg, 1903). Reprinted by Dover Publications, 1994. Du Bois made numerous references to the new black intelligentsia as the ambassadors of the race, which is probably why so many contemporary interpretations of Du Bois's legacy continue to dwell on the Talented Tenth.
7. Du Bois, "The Possibility of Democracy in America," *Crisis* (October 1928).
8. *Rutgers Daily Targum* (June 1919), 563.
9. Bud Schultz and Ruth Schultz. "Paul Robeson Jr.," in *The Price of Dissent: Testimonies to Political Repression in America* (Berkeley: University of California Press),133.
10. Speech by Paul Robeson, "The New Idealism," at Rutgers University, June 10, 1919. Reprinted in *Paul Robeson Speaks: Writings, Speeches, Interviews, 1918–1974,* edited by Philip S. Foner (Secaucus, NJ: Citadel, 1978), 62–5.
11. Numerous scholars of the Harlem renaissance have written extensively about Carl Van Vechten's patronization of Harlem artists and intellectuals. In his biography of Robeson, Martin Duberman implies that Van Vechten was as sexually drawn to the new Negro as he was intellectually (*Paul Robeson*, 78). One could easily compare Van Vechten's regard for black culture in the 1920s to current infatuation with hip-hop culture by suburban

whites. See Duberman, *Paul Robeson: A Biography* (New York: Alfred A. Knopf, 1988; The New Press, 2005).

12. David Levering Lewis, *When Harlem Was in Vogue* (New York: Penguin, 1997).

13. Elizabeth Shepley Sergeant, "A Portrait of Paul Robeson," *New Republic*, March 3, 1926.

14. Jeffrey C. Stewart, "The Black Body: Robeson as a Work of Art and Politics," in *Paul Robeson: Artist and Citizen*, edited by Jeffrey C. Stewart (New Brunswick, NJ: Rutgers University Press, 1998), 156.

15. Robeson made numerous references to the fact that whites were using colored peoples purely for physical labor. He came to realize, as Stewart noted in *Paul Robeson: Artist and Citizen*, that the glorification of the physical aspects of the Negro took away from his intellect.

16. W. E. B. Du Bois, "The Souls of White Folk," in *Darkwater* (New York: Harcourt, Brace and Howe, 1920), 50.

17. Ibid.

18. W. E. B. Du Bois, "The Social Equality of Whites and Blacks," *Crisis* (November 1920), 16, 18.

19. A. Philip Randolph, "Truth about Lynching."

20. A. Philip Randolph, "The New Negro—What Is He?" *Messenger* (August 1920), 7–9.

21. William Patterson letter to Lloyd Brown, May 31, 1973, William L. Patterson Papers, Howard University.

22. Robert C. Smith, *Racism in the Post-Civil Rights Era: Now You See It, Now You Don't* (New York: SUNY Press, 1995).

23. W. E. B. Du Bois, "Marcus Garvey," *Crisis* (December 1920), 58.

24. Ibid., p. 60.

25. W. E. B. Du Bois, "Back to Africa," *Century Magazine* (February 1923), 548.

26. Ibid., p. 539.

27. Ibid., p. 547.

28. W. E. B. Du Bois, "The Pan African Congress," *Crisis* (April 1919), 273–4.

29. Du Bois, "Back to Africa," 539–48.

30. Paul Robeson, *Here I Stand* (Boston: Beacon Press, 1988), 103.

31. "'The Emperor Jones' by a Giant Negro Actor." *The Sphere* (London), September 19, 1925.

32. Sergeant, "A Portrait of Paul Robeson," 40–4.

33. Paul Robeson, "Tribute to W. E. B. Du Bois," *Freedomways* (December 1964).

34. W. E. B. Du Bois, "American Negro Art," *Modern Quarterly: A Journal of Radical Opinion* (October–December 1925), 53–6.

35. W. E. B. Du Bois letter to Paul Robeson, April 17, 1927, W. E. B. Du Bois Papers, reel 22, frame 1302.

2. Dual Epiphanies

1. W. E. B. Du Bois, *Dusk of Dawn: An Essay toward the Autobiography of a Race Concept* (New York: Harcourt Brace, 1940), 286.

2. The Fabian Society, formed in 1884, is a leftist think tank in England. Its early members included H. G. Wells, George Bernard Shaw, and Harold Laski.
3. W. E. B. Du Bois, "Judging Russia," *Crisis* (February 1927), 189–90.
4. Ibid.
5. Ibid.
6. Robert C. Tucker, *Stalin in Power: The Revolution from Above, 1928–1941* (New York: W. W. Norton, 1990).
7. Du Bois, "Judging Russia," 190.
8. W. E. B. Du Bois, "Russia, 1926," *Crisis* (November 1926).
9. Robeson, *Here I Stand*, 33.
10. John Maynard Keynes, "Liberalism and Labor in England," *New Republic*, March 3, 1926, 39.
11. Claude McKay, "Soviet Russia and the Negro," *Crisis* (December 1923), 61–5.
12. Doris Evans McGinty and Wayne Shirley, "Paul Robeson: Musician," in *Paul Robeson: Artist and Citizen*. Edited by Jeffrey C. Stewart (New Brunswick, NJ: Rutgers University Press, 1998), 119.
13. Robeson, *Here I Stand*, 32.
14. Sheila Tully Boyle and Andrew Bunie, *Paul Robeson: The Years of Promise and Achievement* (Amherst, MA, 2001), 203.
15. Kenneth Little, *Negroes in Britain*. (London: Routledge and Kegan Paul, 1972).
16. Matthew Fort, "The Savoy Grill," *Guardian*, August 2, 2003.
17. Robeson's letter to the press and was reprinted in dozens of newspapers, including the Manchester *Guardian*, October 23, 1929, and the *New York Times*, November 17, 1929.
18. Numerous Robeson biographies, including Duberman's and Boyle and Bunie's, make reference to this revelation in his life.
19. Robeson, *Here I Stand*, 31.
20. Rose Henderson, "Paul Robeson, Negro Singer," *Southern Workman*, ca. 1933, 166–72.
21. W. E. B. Du Bois, "Gandhi and India," *Crisis* (March 1922).
22. Shyam Dua, *The Luminous Life of Lala Lajpat Rai* (New Delhi: Printline Books, 2004).
23. Lala Lajpat Rai letter to W. E. B. Du Bois. October 6, 1927, Du Bois Papers, R-22, F-1261.
24. W. E. B. Du Bois, "Indians and American Negroes," published as "The Clash of Colour," *Aryan Path*, March 1936 Du Bois Papers, R-82, F-464.
25. Herbert Aptheker, Foreword to W.E.B. Du Bois, *Dark Princess* (Millwood, N.Y.: Kraus, Thomson, Ltd., 1974).
26. Dua, *Lala Lajpat Rai*, 116.
27. Du Bois, "Souls of White Folk," 49.
28. Du Bois, *Dark Princess*, 235.
29. Ibid., p. 233
30. W. E. B. Du Bois, "Strivings of the Negro People," *Atlantic Monthly* (August 1897), 195.
31. Ibid., p. 243

32. Karl Marx, manuscript of *Critique of Hegel's Philosophy in General*, 1844.
33. Du Bois, *Dark Princess*, 247.
34. Ibid., p. 262.
35. Dorothea Mann's review was reprinted in the forward to *Dark Princess* (Millwood, NY: Kraus, Thomson, Ltd., 1974).
36. W. E. B. Du Bois, "The Negro and Communism," *Crisis* (August 1931).
37. George Schuyler letter to W. E. B. Du Bois, August 19, 1931, Du Bois Papers, R-36, F-530.
38. James Smethurst interview with author in Amherst, MA, September 28, 2004.
39. Ibid.
40. Paul Robeson, "The Culture of the Negro," *Spectator*, June 15, 1934, 916.
41. Speech by Paul Robeson, Foyle's Twenty-Ninth Literary Luncheon, Grosvenor House, London, March 1, 1933.
42. Paul Robeson,"What I Want from Life," *Royal Pictorial Screen* (April 1935), 28–29, 48.
43. Robeson, *Here I Stand*, 33.
44. Ibid., p. 31. Several of Robeson's friends, as well as contemporary biographies of Robeson, have also confirmed this.
45. William Patterson, *The Man Who Cried Genocide* (New York: International Publishers, 1971).
46. Paul Robeson, unpublished notes. Courtesy of Paul Robeson Papers, Howard University.
47. Boyle and Bunie, *Paul Robeson*, 309
48. Paul Robeson, "Robeson Weighs Equal Rights Practices of US and the Soviet Union," *Soviet Russia*, (August 1949), 425.
49. Paul Robeson, "Why I Left My Son in Moscow," *Russia Today* (February 1938), 7, 14.
50. Paul Robeson, personal notes. Courtesy of the Paul Robeson Papers, Howard University.
51. Robeson, "When I Sing." *Sunday Worker*, February 7, 1937.

3. Du Bois, Robeson, and the Popular Front

1. Paul Robeson, unpublished notes, 1940s, Robeson Papers, Howard University.
2. W. E. B. Du Bois, "Inter-Racial Implications of the Ethiopian Crisis," *Foreign Affairs* (October 1935): 87–8.
3. W.E.B. Du Bois, "Dr. Du Bois Resigns," *Crisis* (August 1934), 245–46.
4. Patterson, *The Man Who Cried Genocide*.
5. Ibid.
6. Ibid.
7. W. E. B. Du Bois, "Marxism and the Negro Problem," *Crisis* (May 1933), 104.
8. W. E. B. Du Bois, "The Negro and Communism," *Crisis* (October 1931).
9. James Jackson interview with author in Brooklyn, NY, October 28, 2004.
10. Mark Naison, *Communists in Harlem during the Depression* (Urbana: University of Illinois Press, 1984), 57–89.
11. Du Bois, "The Negro and Communism."

12. "Dr. Du Bois Resigns," 245.
13. W. E. B. Du Bois letter to committee of Spingarn, Harry E. Davis, George W. Crawford, Lillian A. Alexander, and Louis T. Wright, April 21, 1933, Du Bois Papers, R-40, F-556.
14. Spingarn letter to Du Bois, April 26, 1933, Du Bois Papers, R-40, F-1037.
15. Marcus Garvey, "An Expose of the Caste System among Negroes," *Philosophy and Opinions of Marcus Garvey* (Dover, MA: The Majority Press, 1986), 61.
16. W. E. B. Du Bois, "The NAACP and Race Segregation," *Crisis* (February 1934).
17. Robert Bagnall letter to Walter White, March 23, 1934, NAACP Archives, Library of Congress, Washington, D.C.
18. Abram Harris letter to Walter White, May 22, 1934, NAACP Archives, Library of Congress, Washington, D.C.
19. W. E. B. Du Bois, "Segregation in the North," *Crisis* (April 1934).
20. Ibid.
21. W. E. B. Du Bois, "William Monroe Trotter," *Crisis* (May 1934), 134.
22. Dr. Du Bois Resigns," 246.
23. Du Bois, "The Negro and Communism."
24. W. E. B. Du Bois, *Black Reconstruction: An Essay toward a History of the Part Which Black Folk Played in the Attempt to Reconstruct Democracy in America, 1860–1880* (New York: Russell & Russell, 1935), 728.
25. Roi Ottley, *No Green Pastures* (New York: Charles Scribner's Sons, 1952).
26. C. L. R. James interview with Andrew Bunie, *Paul Robeson*, 365.
27. Anonymous, "Paul Robeson Speaks for His People and All Humanity," *Sunday Worker*, November 14, 1937.
28. E. A. Baughan review of "Toussaint L'Overture." *News Chronicle*, March 17, 1936.
29. Sheila Tully Boyle and Andrew Bunie, *Paul Robeson*. 343.
30. C. L. R. James letter to Bunie, *Paul Robeson*, 366.
31. American League against War and Fascism letter to NAACP, March 26, 1934, NAACP Archives.
32. Naison, *Communists in Harlem*, 170–87.
33. William Pickens letter to American League against War and Fascism, March 27, 1934, NAACP Archives, Library of Congress, Washington, D.C.
34. Abbott Simon interview with author in Brooklyn, NY, October 28, 2004.
35. Canute Frankson letter to wife, July 6, 1937. Reprinted in Cary Nelson's "Legacy of American Volunteers in Spain." *Left of the Color Line: Race, Radicalism and Twentieth-Century Literature of the United States*, edited by Bill V. Mullen and James Smethurst (Chapel Hill, NC: University of North Carolina Press, 2003), 302.
36. Robeson, "When I Sing."
37. Duberman, *Paul Robeson*, 218.
38. Speech by Paul Robeson, "Nehru." Welcome Rally for Nehru, June 1938, London, Robeson Papers.
39. The Japanese invasion and the subsequent rape and massacre of Chinese were both called "The Rape of Nanking." Iris Chang, *The Rape of Nanking: The Forgotten Holocaust of World War II* (New York: Basic Books, 1997).

40. Ibid.
41. In 1937, the Germans—who had sided with Franco—bombed the seaside city of Guernica.
42. W. E. B. Du Bois, "Neuropa: Hitler's New World Order," *Journal of Negro Education* (July 1941), 380–6.
43. W. E. B. Du Bois, "Inter-Racial Implications of the Ethiopian Crisis," *Foreign Affairs* (October 1935), 88.
44. Ibid, 92.
45. Waldo McNutt letter to W. E. B. Du Bois (re: Japanese propaganda), February 13, 1939; Du Bois's response, February 25, 1939, Du Bois Papers, reel 50, frame 494-5. Used with permission of the David Graham Du Bois Trust.
46. Paul Robeson. Unpublished notes, undated, Robeson Papers, Howard University.
47. "Paul Robeson's Message. Great Negro's View of the War," May 12, 1944, Robeson Papers, Howard University.
48. Abram Harris letter to Walter White, May 22, 1934, NAACP Archives.
49. Du Bois, "Inter-Racial Implications of the Ethiopian Crisis," 88–9.
50. Speech by W. E. B. Du Bois, "The Meaning of Japan," Morehouse College, March 12, 1937, Du Bois Papers, R-80, F-654. Used with permission of the David Graham Du Bois Trust.
51. Du Bois, "Inter-Racial Implications of the Ethiopian Crisis," 85.
52. Du Bois, "Meaning of Japan."

4. STALIN'S PURGE, THE PACT, AND FALSE JUSTIFICATION

1. Robeson, "Why I Left My Son in Moscow," 7, 14.
2. W. E. B. Du Bois, "The Soviets and the Negro," unpublished, 1933, Du Bois Papers, R-82, F-112. Used with permission of the David Graham Du Bois Trust.
3. Speech by Paul Robeson, National Maritime Union Convention, July 8, 1941. Reprinted in *Paul Robeson Speaks: Writings, Speeches, Interviews, 1918–1974*, edited by Philip S. Foner (Secaucus, NJ: Citadel, 1978), 137–8.
4. Speech by Paul Robeson on Soviet foreign policy, 1940, (Date and location not provided) Robeson Papers, Howard University.
5. Paul Robeson, "On Stalin," unpublished notes, 1953, Robeson Papers, Howard University.
6. Robert Tucker, *Stalin in Power: The Revolution from Above, 1928–1941*. (New York: W. W. Norton, 1990), 26.
7. Edward Radzinsky, *Stalin* (New York: Anchor Books, 1996), 335.
8. Report of Court Proceedings, "Trotskyite-Zinovievite Terrorist Centre," August 19–24, 1936. Published by the People's Commissariat of Justice of the USSR, Moscow, 1936.
9. Radzinsky, *Stalin*, 339.
10. Nikhil Pal Singh, "Retracing the Black-Red Thread," *American Literary History* (Winter 2003), 830–40.
11. Radzinsky, *Stalin*, 405.
12. Robeson, *Soviet Worker*, 1937.

13. Naison, *Communists in Harlem*, 176–7.
14. Adam Clayton Powell Jr., "The Soapbox." *New York Amsterdam News*, September 18, 1937.
15. Paul Robeson Jr. *The Undiscovered Paul Robeson* (New York: John Wiley, 2001), 289.
16. Ibid., p. 294.
17. Benjamin Davis Jr. "U.S.S.R.—The Land for Me," May 10, 1936. Reprinted in *Paul Robeson Speaks: Writings, Speeches, Interviews, 1918–1974*, edited by Philip S. Foner (Secaucus, NJ: Citadel, 1978), 109.
18. Robeson, "On Stalin."
19. The Dewey Commission, headed by American philosopher John Dewey, was established by supporters of Trotsky to clear his name. The commission accused Stalin of creating an anti-Trotsky movement to eliminate a political nemesis.
20. Du Bois, "The Soviets and the Negro."
21. Du Bois, The Meaning of Japan.
22. David Levering Lewis, *W. E. B. Du Bois: The Fight for Equality and the American Century, 1919–1963* (New York: Henry Holt, 2000), 463.
23. *"Birth of a Nation* Will Have Sequel," Raleigh *News and Observer*, October 22, 1937.
24. W. E. B. Du Bois, "As the Crow Flies," *New York Amsterdam News*, March 23, 1940.
25. Paul Robeson speech on Soviet foreign policy, 1940, Robeson Papers.

5. WORLD WAR II AND THE DOMESTIC BATTLEFRONT

1. W. E. B. Du Bois, "As the Crow Flies," *New York Amsterdam News*, January 27, 1940. Coulborn's speech was reprinted in Du Bois's column. Du Bois Papers, R-84, F-274.
2. W. E. B. Du Bois, *Dusk of Dawn: An Essay toward an Autobiography of a Race Concept* (New York: Harcourt Brace, 1940), 306.
3. Ralph J. Bunche, "The Negro in the Political Life of the U.S." *Journal of Negro Education*. Reprinted in *Ralph J. Bunche: Selected Speeches & Writings*, edited by Charles Henry (Ann Arbor: University of Michigan, 1995), 111.
4. W. E. B. Du Bois letter to George Padmore, July 9, 1945, Du Bois Papers, R-57, F-1028.
5. Jerome Beatty, "America's No. 1 Negro," *American* (May 1944), 28–9, 142–44. Other publications also referred to Robeson by this title.
6. "CIO Builds Unity," *News of Connecticut*, August 1, 1941m 1, 4.
7. Speech by Paul Robeson, Win the Peace Conference, 1940, Robeson Papers.
8. Paul Robeson, "In What Direction Are We Going?" *Friday* vol. 1 no. 25 (August 30, 1940).
9. Though the Soviet Union had conquered Finland, Finnish military leaders allowed Germany secret penetration into the country, setting up a Nazi invasion of the Soviet Union on June 22, 1941. The breaking of the pact allowed Paul to espouse full support for American intervention.
10. James W. Ford, *The War and the Negro People*. (New York: Workers Library, 1942).

11. Du Bois, *Dusk of Dawn*, 289.
12. George Schuyler, "The Double-V," *Pittsburgh Courier*, January 10, 1942.
13. Du Bois, "As the Crow Flies," January 6, 1940.
14. David Levering Lewis. *W.E.B Du Bois: The Fight for Equality and the American Century, 1919–1963* (New York: Henry Holt, 2000), 463.
15. W. E. B. Du Bois, "As the Crow Flies," *New York Amsterdam News*, March 14, 1942.
16. W. E. B. Du Bois, "Communism and the Negro," *New York Amsterdam News*, March 23, 1940.
17. Bunche biographer Charles Henry makes note of this in his book, *Ralph Bunche: Model Negro or American Other?* (New York: New York University Press, 1999). Bunche's research would later be used as part of Myrdal's groundbreaking *An American Dilemma: The Negro Problem and Modern Democracy* (c. 1944; reprint Piscataway, NJ: Transaction Publishers, 1995), which many blacks hailed as a comprehensive look at race relations. However, Marxist scholars offered a stinging critique of the book, noting how Myrdal had completely ignored economics as a factor in creating "caste."
18. Thelma Dale Perkins phone interview with author, May 19, 2005.
19. MacArthur letter to Houston, August 20, 1934, NAACP Archives.
20. Littleton Mitchell interview with author in Delaware City, DE, July 19, 2005.
21. Paul Robeson, "American Negroes in the War," November 16, 1943, *New York Herald Tribune* Forum on Current Problems.
22. Camp Wo-Chi-Ca has been hailed by many left-wing thinkers as a model of interracial cooperation among children. June Levine and Eugene Gordon detail the experiences of camp participants, and Robeson's impact on them, in their book, *Tales of Wo-Chi-Ca: Blacks, Whites and Reds at Camp* (Walnut Creek, CA: Avon Springs Press, 2002).
23. Many biographies of Robeson have included mentions of Communist influence on his development as a labor supporter. However, Mark Naison noted in a 1998 essay, "Paul Robeson and the American Labor Movement," that Paul's prolabor convictions stemmed from his long-held connection to working-class people.
24. Paul Robeson, "Negroes Should Join the CIO," *CIO News*, December 23, 1940. Reprinted in *Paul Robeson Speaks: Writings, Speeches, Interviews, 1918–1974*, edited by Philip S. Foner (Secaucus, NJ: Citadel, 1978).
25. Sidney B. Whipple, "Paul Robeson Brilliant in Bradford's John Henry," *New York World-Telegram*, January 11, 1940.
26. Remarks by Paul Robeson, "A Plea for Earl Browder," Madison Square Garden Rally for Browder, September 29, 1941. Reprinted in *Paul Robeson Speaks: Writings, Speeches, Interviews, 1918–1974*, edited by Philip S. Foner (Secaucus, NJ: Citadel, 1978).
27. Bunche's biographer, Henry, makes note of Bunche's 1942 interview with the FBI regarding his supposed ties to the Communist Party. Bunche was cleared and went on to join the State Department.
28. Esther Jackson interview with author in Brooklyn, NY, April 8, 2005.

29. Paul Robeson, "We Must Come South," October 29, 1942. New Orleans. Robeson Papers.

30. *Othello* had a run of 296 performances, more than any Shakespeare play on Broadway at that time.

31. Langston Hughes, "Black Eye for D.C.," *Chicago Defender*, July 22, 1944.

32. Paul Robeson, "Labor and the Minorities Must Save Democracy Here," Conference on Racial and National Minorities, August 8, 1943, San Francisco. Reprinted in *People's Voice*, August 19, 1943.

33. Robeson, "American Negroes in the War."

34. Ibid.

35. Du Bois, "Communism and the Negro."

36. Ford. *The War and the Negro People.*

37. Du Bois, *Dusk of Dawn*, 305.

38. Ibid. p. 304–5.

39. W. E. B. Du Bois, "If I Were Young Again." Published as "Reading, Writing, and Real Estate," *Negro Digest* (October 1943).

40. W. E. B. Du Bois, "What He Meant to the Negro," *New Masses*. April 24, 1945.

41. Ibid.

42. W. E. B. Du Bois, *The Color of Democracy: Colonies and Peace* (New York: Harcourt Brace, 1945), 114.

43. "Colonial Questions Ignored at Dumbarton Oaks Peace Session," *Pittsburgh Courier*, October 28, 1944. It is ironic that Du Bois made this assessment in 1944, at the height of U.S.-Soviet relations. Perhaps he knew Churchill would never accept the alliance as anything more than a temporary arrangement.

44. In February 1942, President Franklin D. Roosevelt issued Executive Order 9066, which authorized military commanders to designate military areas from which "any or all persons may be excluded." The military chose to establish curfews for Japanese Americans, to remove all people of Japanese ancestry from the West Coast and southern Arizona, and to confine them in detention camps until their loyalty could be determined. About 110,000 Japanese were confined in ten detention camps scattered over seven states: Arizona, Arkansas, California, Colorado, Idaho, Utah, and Wyoming. They lost their homes and their jobs as a result.

45. Greg Robinson, "Internationalism and Justice: Paul Robeson, Asia and Asian Americans," in *AfroAsian Encounters: Culture, History, Politics*. Edited by Heike Raphael-Hernandez and Shannon Steen. (New York: New York University Press, 2006), 260–75.

6. AFRICA, ASIA, AND THE GLOBAL VISION

1. W. E. B. Du Bois letter to Manmohan Gandhi, August 19, 1931. Gandhi's response was written in September 1931. Du Bois Papers, R-36, F-49, 52.

2. Ibid.

3. Speech by E. Franklin Frazier prior to Robeson concert in Washington, D.C., October 13, 1949, Robeson Archives.

4. In his biography of Du Bois *(W. E. B. Du Bois: The Fight for Equality and the*

American Century, 1919–1963), Lewis goes into detail about Hikida's influence on Du Bois and his connection to the Japanese government.

5. W. E. B. Du Bois, "Listen, Japan and China," *Crisis* (January 1933).

6. Du Bois, "The Meaning of Japan."

7. Du Bois, "Indians and American Negroes."

8. Ibid.

9. W. E. B. Du Bois, *Color and Democracy: Colonies and Peace* (New York: Harcourt Brace, 1945), 17.

10. W. E. B. Du Bois, *Black Folk: Then and Now* (New York: Henry Holt, 1939), 345.

11. W. E. B. Du Bois, "Black Africa Tomorrow," *Foreign Affairs* (1938), 109.

12. Paul Robeson, Meeting for Jamaica, Canning Town Hall, London, July 17, 1938.

13. J. C. O'Flaherty, "An Exclusive Interview with Paul Robeson," *West African Review* (August 1936): 12–3. Reprinted in *Paul Robeson Speaks: Writings, Speeches, Interviews, 1918–1974,* edited by Philip S. Foner (Secaucus, NJ: Citadel, 1978), 113.

14. Paul Robeson. "What I Want from Life," *Daily World,* January 5, 1935.

15. Jawaharlal Nehru, *The Discovery of India* (Calcutta: Signet Press, 1946), 420.

16. Speech by Paul Robeson, "On Nehru," June 1938, London.

17. Mohandas K. Gandhi, *Gandhi's Autobiography* (Washington, D.C.: Public Affairs Press, 1948), 141–2.

18. Speech by Paul Robeson, rally for India hosted by Council on African Affairs, September 8, 1942.

19. Daniel W. Aldridge III, "Opportunity Lost: African American Public Intellectuals, the Roosevelt Administration, and the Creation of the UN Trusteeship Council, 1941–1945." *Perspectives on International and Multicultural Affairs,* vol. 1, no. 1 (2003).

20. Henry A. Wallace, diary entry, May 22, 1943, Henry A. Wallace Papers. University of Iowa.

21. Walter White letter to W. E. B. Du Bois, June 5, 1942, Du Bois Papers, R-54, F-1.

22. Gerald Horne, *Race Woman: The Lives of Shirley Graham Du Bois* (New York: New York University Press, 2000), 6.

23. Not much is known about Kumar Goshal, who made a living in the United States as an actor, writer, and activist. However, E. S. Reddy noted Goshal's influence in the Council on African Affairs and his role as a liaison to the Indian freedom struggle. Goshal would later emerge as one of the few Leftists who publicly backed Du Bois and Robeson during the Cold War.

24. Ralph Bunche, "Africa and the Current World Conflict," *Negro History Bulletin* (October 1940), 14. Reprinted in *Ralph J. Bunche: Selected Speeches & Writings,* edited by Charles Henry (Ann Arbor: University of Michigan, 1995).

25. Speech by Paul Robeson, "China: Promise of a New World," Sun Yat-sen Day rally in New York, March 12, 1944.

26. Speech by Paul Robeson, conference on Africa at the Institute for International Democracy in New York, April 14, 1944.

27. Ibid.
28. Du Bois, *Color and Democracy*, 57.
29. Max Yergan letter to W. E. B. Du Bois, November 18, 1939, Du Bois Papers, R-50, F-343.
30. Charles Henry makes note of this in his biography of Bunche.
31. W. E. B. Du Bois, "Colonial Questions Ignored at Dumbarton Oaks Peace Session," *Pittsburgh Courier*, October 28, 1944.
32. W. E. B. Du Bois, "India." Published as "Du Bois, White Run from Photo with White Stooges,"*Chicago Defender*, May 12, 1945.
33. W. E. B. Du Bois, "Lauds Molotov's Frankness in 'World Equality' Speech." *Chicago Defender*, May 26, 1945.
34. Edward R. Stettinius letter to Paul Robeson, June 6, 1945, Robeson Papers.
35. W. E. B. Du Bois letter to George Padmore, July 9, 1945, Du Bois Papers, R-57, F-1028. Used with permission of the David Graham Du Bois trust.
36. Statement by David Sibeko, representative of Pan Africanist Congress of Azania, at an international tribute to Du Bois sponsored by the United Nations Special Committee against Apartheid, February 23, 1978.
37. Esther Jackson interview with author in Brooklyn, NY, April 10, 2005.
38. W. E. B. Du Bois, *An Appeal to the World*, Du Bois Papers, R-60, F-945.
39. W. E. B. Du Bois, "Gandhi," *Unity* (May–June 1948).
40. According to Charles Henry's biography, Bunche distanced himself from groups that advocated more radical platforms than diplomacy. Bunche might have sensed early on that the CAA was too aligned with Soviet interests to be viewed as a legitimate instrument of change.
41. Enuga S. Reddy interview with author in Manhattan, September 1, 2005.
42. Paul Robeson, "Never Again Can Colonialism Be What It Was," *New Africa* (March 1945). Reprinted in *Paul Robeson Speaks: Writings, Speeches, Interviews, 1918–1974*, edited by Philip S. Foner (Secaucus, NJ: Citadel, 1978).
43. Paul Robeson, "Africa: Continent in Bondage," *New York Herald Tribune*. June 5, 1946.
44. Lewis, *W. E. B. Du Bois*, 539.
45. E. S. Reddy confirms this point. He said Yergan fired Hunton for questioning his financial management of the organization. Hunton's firing spurred a revolt in the council.
46. W. E. B. Du Bois letter to Alphaeus Hunton, March 26, 1948, Du Bois Papers, R-62, F-80.
47. Max Yergan letter to Council on African Affairs, March 12, 1948, Du Bois Papers, R-61, F-770.
48. *New York Herald Tribune*, April 6, 1948.
49. Eslanda Robeson letter to Council on African Affairs, April 17, 1948. Paul Robeson Papers at the Schomburg Center for Research in Black Culture, Harlem.
50. Statement by Council on African Affairs, April 25, 1948. Documents obtained in the W. Alphaeus Hunton and Paul Robeson Papers, both at the Schomburg Center for Research in Black Culture, Harlem.

51. Du Bois, "A Review of African Movements for Freedom," *Africana* (December 1948).
52. Speech by Paul Robeson, "Racialism in South Africa," Friends' House, London, March 25, 1949. Reprinted in *Paul Robeson Speaks: Writings, Speeches, Interviews, 1918–1974*, edited by Philip S. Foner (Secaucus, NJ: Citadel, 1978), 195.
53. Council on African Affairs news release, May 11, 1949.
54. E. S. Reddy interview with author in Manhattan, August 5, 2005.
55. The Monroe Doctrine, enacted in 1823, gave the United States the ability to intervene in Latin American affairs. Truman invoked the doctrine to help stop the spread of leftist and Communist influence in South America. The Truman Doctrine was designed to stop communism in Greece and Turkey.
56. Notes by Eslanda Robeson, "Labor Conditions in Asia," Paul Robeson papers at the Schomburg Center.
57. W. E. B. Du Bois, "As the Crow Flies," *Chicago Globe*, August 4, 1950.
58. This seems very ironic, given Du Bois's justification for Japanese aggression against China only a decade earlier. He likely had not given up completely on this notion of racialist internationalism when excusing Communist aggression in Tibet and Korea.
59. Du Bois, *The Autobiography of W. E. B. DuBois*.
60. Paul Robeson, "Happy Birthday, New China!" *Freedom* (October 1952). Reprinted in *Paul Robeson Speaks: Writings, Speeches, Interviews, 1918–1974*, edited by Philip S. Foner (Secaucus, NJ: Citadel, 1978).
61. Paul Robeson, "Ho Chi Minh Is the Toussaint L'Ouverture of Indo-China," *Freedom* (March 1954). Reprinted in *Paul Robeson Speaks: Writings, Speeches, Interviews, 1918–1974*, edited by Philip S. Foner (Secaucus, NJ: Citadel, 1978).
62. Speech by W. E. B. Du Bois, "The American Negro and the Darker World," April 30, 1957. Reprinted in *Freedomways*, 1968.
63. Esther Jackson interview with author in Brooklyn, NY, October 28, 2004.

7. CONVERGENCE AND DIVERGENCE

1. NAACP press release. Reprinted in the *Pittsburgh Courier*, October 17, 1945.
2. Esther Jackson interview with author in Brooklyn, NY, May 9, 2005.
3. "Robeson Lauds Russia at Spingarn Medal Banquet," *Pittsburgh Courier*, October 17, 1945. Reprinted in *Paul Robeson Speaks: Writings, Speeches, Interviews, 1918–1974*, edited by Philip S. Foner (Secaucus, NJ: Citadel, 1978), 162–3.
4. Esther Jackson phone interview with author, May 15, 2005.
5. Roy Wilkins with Tom Matthews, *Standing Fast: The Autobiography of Roy Wilkins* (New York: Viking, 1982), 193.
6. Ibid.
7. W. E. B. Du Bois, "Bound by the Color Line," *New Masses*, February 12, 1946, 8.
8. W. E. B. Du Bois, "Colonies and Moral Responsibility," *Journal of Negro Education*, (Summer 1946), Du Bois Papers, R-80, F-535. Used with permission of the David Graham Du Bois Trust.

9. An outstanding book on the murders of Roger and Dorothy Malcolm and George and Mae Dorsey is *Fire in a Canebrake: The Last Mass Lynching in America* by Laura Wexler (New York: Scribner, 2003).

10. "Robeson Asks Truman Action on Lynching," *Daily Worker*, July 29, 1946. Reprinted in *Paul Robeson Speaks: Writings, Speeches, Interviews, 1918–1974*, edited by Philip S. Foner (Secaucus, NJ: Citadel, 1978), 171.

11. Paul Robeson letter to W. E. B. Du Bois, August 30, 1946, Du Bois Papers, R-59, F-463.

12. Fred Jerome, "The Hidden Half-Life of Albert Einstein: Anti-Racism." *Socialism and Democracy*, vol. 17, no. 1 (Winter-Spring 2003): 227–44.

13. "Robeson Tells Truman: Do Something about Lynchings or Negroes Will," *Philadelphia Tribune*, September 24, 1946; "Truman Balks at Lynch Action," *Chicago Defender*, September 28, 1946; "Robeson to President Truman—'Government Must Act against Lynching or the Negroes Will,'" *New York Times*, September 24, 1946.

14. Excerpts from testimony before the Tenney Committee, October 7, 1946.

15. Wilkins with Matthews, *Standing Fast*, 193.

16. The letters are correspondence between Du Bois and White, September 19–October 2, 1946, Du Bois Papers, R-59, F-709-13. Used with permission of the David Graham Du Bois Trust.

17. W. E. B. Du Bois letter to Arthur Spingarn, April 2, 1948, Du Bois Papers, R-63, F-179.

18. Speech by Paul Robeson, ICC-National PAC Meeting, Madison Square Garden, September 12, 1946.

19. Notes by Paul Robeson for meeting of Civil Rights Congress in New York, October 17, 1946.

20. Gerald Horne, *Communist Fronts? The Civil Rights Congress, 1946–1956*. Cranbury, NJ: Farleigh Dickinson Press, 1988.

21. *Time*, May 14, 1951.

22. Patterson, *The Man Who Cried Genocide*, 165.

23. Horne, *Communist Fronts?*

24. Speech by Paul Robeson at the Longshore, Shipclerks, Walking Bosses & Gatemen and Watchmen's Caucus, August 21, 1948. Reprinted in *Paul Robeson Speaks: Writings, Speeches, Interviews, 1918–1974*, edited by Philip S. Foner (Secaucus, NJ: Citadel, 1978).

25. W. E. B. Du Bois, "The Sane Liberal," *Soviet Russia Today* (September 1949).

26. Henry Luce, "The American Century." *Life*, February 7, 1941.

27. Speech by Paul Robeson, Council on African Affairs Rally, New York, April 25, 1947. Paul Robeson Papers, Howard University.

28. Du Bois, "Gandhi."

29. Du Bois, responding to a letter from Cuban missionary E. Pina Moreno, said that he could "see no proof to sustain belief, neither in history nor in my personal experience." But, as Du Bois went to on add, if God was "vague force which in some incomprehensible way dominates all life and change, then I . . . recognize such force, and if you wish to call it God, I do not object." November 15, 1948, Du Bois Papers, R-63, F-381.

30. Ford, *The War and the Negro People*, 9.
31. David Levering Lewis interview with author in Manhattan, October 27, 2004. I had the pleasure of knowing Abbott Simon in the later part of his life. He was extremely passionate about social justice and was among the many people who fought hard to preserve Du Bois and Robeson's legacies.
32. James and Esther Jackson interviews with author in Brooklyn, NY, October 28, 2004. Also noted in Lewis's *W.E.B. Du Bois* (2000).
33. Shirley Graham letter to Earl Browder, April 27, 1945. Shirley Graham Du Bois papers, Schlesinger Library, Radcliffe Institute, Harvard University.
34. Esther Jackson interview with author, February 19, 2005.
35. From Robeson's FBI files, 1946–1949.
36. Speech by Paul Robeson, Council on African Affairs Rally, New York, April 25, 1947.
37. Speech by Henry Wallace, "The Way to Peace," ICC-National PAC Meeting, Madison Square Garden, September 12, 1946.
38. Ibid.
39. Reference to *Mr. Smith Goes to Washington* (1939), a movie, starring James Stewart, about an idealistic man who tries to reform the U.S. Senate, but finds his job complicated by machine politics.
40. Wallace, "The Way to Peace."
41. Speech by Paul Robeson at the Longshore, Shipclerks, Walking Bosses & Gatemen and Watchmen's Caucus, August 21, 1948. Reprinted in *Paul Robeson Speaks: Writings, Speeches, Interviews, 1918–1974*, edited by Philip S. Foner (Secaucus, NJ: Citadel, 1978).
42. Wilkins with Matthews, *Standing Fast*, 199.
43. Harry Truman, "Presidential Civil Rights Message" February 2, 1948. Civil rights rally in Washington, D.C.
44. Walter White, *How Far the Promised Land* (New York: Viking Press, 1955), 223.
45. According to Powell biographer Charles Hamilton, Truman and Powell had great animus toward each other. But Powell—ever the political pragmatist—knew that Truman was a more legitimate option in the White House than Wallace. This mirrors the sentiments of many African American leaders in recent years who have backed moderates such as John Kerry and Al Gore over social progressives such as Dennis Kucinich and Ralph Nader.
46. Interview with Paul Robeson in Copenhagen (Telepress), March 5, 1949.
47. Du Bois, "The Sane Liberal."
48. Interview with Paul Robeson interview in Copenhagen (Telepress), March 5, 1949.

8. THE "WITCH HUNT" AND THE NAACP'S BETRAYAL

1. Shirley Graham letter to W. E. B. Du Bois, July 24, 1944, Du Bois Papers, R-56, F-128.
2. White, *How Far the Promised Land*, 224.
3. An excellent book on this topic is Manfred Berg's *"The Ticket to Freedom": The NAACP and the Struggle for Black Political Integration* (Gainesville,

FL: University Press of Florida, 2005). Berg notes that the NAACP's determination for civil rights was often motivated by its vanity as the sole owner of black progress. As a result, the NAACP leadership often moved against more the radical elements of black America, including Martin Luther King Jr., whom Wilkins called a "sexual degenerate" to FBI officials.

4. During the 1950 NAACP Convention, Wilkins pushed forward a resolution to investigate Communist influence of association branches. The resolution passed with an overwhelming majority.

5. Both David Levering Lewis and Raymond Wolters make note of the Doctor's political restlessness in their biographies of Du Bois.

6. Walter White letter to W. E. B. Du Bois, May 17, 1944, Du Bois Papers, R-56, F-422. Used with permission of the David Graham Du Bois Trust.

7. Arthur Spingarn letter to W.E.B. Du Bois. May 23, 1944. Du Bois Papers. Used with permission of the David Graham Du Bois Trust.

8. NAACP figures put their wartime membership as high as 600,000, but contemporary historiographies place the number at closer to 400,000.

9. In September 1944, White admonished Du Bois for the Doctor's trip to Haiti on association time. Du Bois Papers, R-56, F-436-8.

10. W. E. B. Du Bois memorandum to NAACP Board, October 10, 1946, Du Bois Papers, R-59, F-160-9.

11. Ibid.

12. Walter White letter to W. E. B. Du Bois, October 23, 1946, Du Bois Papers, R-59, F-173-4.

13. W. E. B. Du Bois letter to White, November 14, 1946, Du Bois Papers, R-59, F-177.

14. William Howard Melish, chairman of National Council of American Soviet Friendship, letter to W. E. B. Du Bois, November 14, 1946, Du Bois Papers, R-59, F-22.

15. Summary of *Appeal to the World*, NAACP Papers II, A637.

16. In *Ticket to Freedom*, Berg noted that the association used *Appeal* as more of a propaganda tool. White was undoubtedly aware that pushing for the document to be delivered to the UN would have an adverse impact on the association's relationship with Truman and Mrs. Roosevelt.

17. W. E. B. Du Bois letter to Marcelle Bruyn, May 24,1948, Du Bois Papers, R-61, F-514.

18. Roy Wilkins, "Voluntary Segregation—A Disaster," *Daytona Journal Herald*. March 29, 1969. Reprinted in *In Search of Democracy: The NAACP Writings of James Weldon Johnson, Walter White and Roy Wilkins (1920–1977)*, edited by Sonra K. Wilson (New York: Oxford University Press, 1999), 429–30.

19. W. E. B. Du letter Bois to NAACP Board (Spingarn, Wright), Du Bois Papers, R-62, F-727-8.

20. NAACP memorandum to Branch Officers, September 15, 1948, Du Bois Papers, R-62, F-742.

21. James Malley letter to Louis T. Wright, October 6, 1948, Du Bois Papers, R-62, F-756.

22. Alphaeus Hunton letter to Arthur Spingarn, September 20, 1948, Du Bois Papers, R-62, F-751.

23. John Hudson Jones, "Walter White Ducks Query on Sellout," *Daily Worker.* September 14, 1948.

24. W. E. B. Du Bois to George Padmore, April 7, 1949, Du Bois Papers, R-62, F-1013.

25. W. E. B. Du Bois, "The Negro and Communism," *Crisis* (September 1931).

26. W. E. B. Du Bois, "To the American Negro," August 1954, unpublished, Du Bois Papers, R-83, F-606.

27. Berg notes that McCarthy's lack of direct attack on the NAACP was one of the reasons why the association did not condemn McCarthyism until 1952.

28. Arthur M. Schlesinger, "The U.S. Communist Party." *Life*, July 29, 1946, 84–96. White's subsequent letter to the editor caused Schlesinger to clarify his position.

29. Horne, *Communist Front?*

30. White, *How Far the Promised Land*, 218.

31. Wilkins, *Standing Fast*, 211.

32. In *Invisible Man*, Ellison paints an allegorical picture of the black man's myriad flirtations with political ideologies; however, in each of them, the protagonist is ultimately conned by other interests.

33. White, *How Far the Promised Land*, 218.

34. In numerous writings in the late 1940s, White and Wilkins referred to the Communists as Kremlin-influenced agitators. Wilkins smugly called them "comrades."

35. P. L. Prattis, "Why Has Robeson Been Called One of the World's Great Intellects?" *Horizon*, November 18, 1944.

36. Eleanor Roosevelt letter to Harry S. Truman, April 17, 1947. Courtesy of the Harry S. Truman Library.

37. Harry S. Truman to Eleanor Roosevelt, May 7, 1947. Courtesy of the Harry S. Truman Library.

38. Speech by Paul Robeson, Council on African Affairs, June 6, 1946, Madison Square Garden rally, New York City.

39. Hazel Rowley, *Richard Wright: The Life and Times* (New York: Henry Holt, 2001), 511.

40. Vito Marcantonio letter to W. E. B. Du Bois. January 29, 1949, Du Bois Papers, R-63, F-1246.

41. It should be noted that in 1947, Walter White implored J. Parnell Thomas, chairman of the House Committee on Un-American Activities, not to "fall into the dangerous error of labeling 'subversive' honest American doctrine of freedom, justice and equality." Report of the secretary for the board meeting of November 1947. Reprinted in *In Search of Democracy: The NAACP Writings of James Weldon Johnson, Walter White and Roy Wilkins (1920–1977),* edited by Sonra K. Wilson (New York: Oxford University Press, 1999).

42. Speech by Paul Robeson, "Racialism in South Africa," Friends' House, London. March 25, 1949. Reprinted in *Paul Robeson Speaks: Writings,*

Speeches, Interviews, 1918–1974, edited by Philip S. Foner (Secaucus, NJ: Citadel, 1978), 194–7.

43. Speech by Paul Robeson. Congress of the World Partisans of Peace, April 20, 1949.
44. *Associated Press* dispatch, April 20, 1949. Robeson papers, Howard University.
45. Max Yergan, "The American Negro and Mr. Robeson," *New York Herald Tribune*, April 23, 1949.
46. Walter White, "Paul Robeson: Right or Wrong. Wrong: Says Walter White," *Negro Digest* (March 1950), 9, 14–8.
47. Television transcript from "Paul Robeson: Here I Stand." Produced by WNET, New York, in *American Masters*. First aired February 24, 1999.
48. J. A. Rogers, "Paul Robeson May Be Wrong but His Speech Was Food for Thought," *Pittsburgh Courier*, May 7, 1949.
49. W. E. B. Du Bois. "Paul Robeson: Right or Wrong. Right: Says W.E.B. Du Bois," *Negro Digest* (March 1950), 8, 10–4.
50. Charles DeBiew, "Thanks to God We Now Have Robeson," *Afro-American*, August 12, 1949.
51. Anonymous, "Robeson Speaks for Robeson," *Crisis* (May 1949), 137.
52. Charles P. Howard letter to Roy Wilkins, May 26, 1949. NAACP Papers.
53. Wilkins, *Standing Fast*, 206.
54. Ibid.
55. Editorial, "Paul Robeson Doesn't Speak for the American Negro," *Columbia* (SC) *Record*, April 26, 1949.
56. Du Bois. "Paul Robeson: Right or Wrong."
57. "Two Million People Can't Be So Wrong." The date and name of this newspaper clip, found in the Robeson Papers at Howard University, could not be verified. However, the tone of the story suggests it is a Southern newspaper.
58. This is supposition, but the link here is Thurgood Marshall. Marshall defended Bellanfant, and by the late 1940s, was already working with anti-communists to discredit the Left.
59. Dan Burley, "On Black Suddenly Turned Red," *New York Age*. July 23, 1949.
60. A great inside story of the Rickey influence on Robinson's decision to testify can be found in Roger Kahn's *The Era* (New York: Ticknor & Fields, 1993), 198–207.
61. Jackie Robinson, *I Never Had It Made* (New York: Putnam, 1972), 82.
62. Testimony of Manning Johnson, transcript of "Hearings Regarding Communist Infiltration of Minority Groups," July 14, 1949.
63. Testimony of Lester Granger, "Hearings Regarding Communist Infiltration," July 14, 1949.
64. See Kahn, *The Era*. 200.
65. Robinson, *I Never Had It Made*, 83.
66. Testimony of Jackie Robinson. "Hearings Regarding Communist Infiltration." July 18, 1949. Reprinted in Robinson, *I Never Had It Made*.
67. Charley Cherokee, "Your Lips Tell Me No, No," *Baltimore Afro-American*, July 18, 1949.
68. Paul Robeson interview with the *Daily Worker*, July 21, 1949.

69. Robinson, *I Never Had It Made*, 85.
70. "Robeson Weighs Equal Rights Practices of U.S. and the Soviet Union," *Soviet Russia* (August 1949): 425
71. Excerpts from "Eyewitness: Peekskill, USA," a September 1949 report published by the Westchester Committee for a Fair Inquiry into the Peekskill Violence. Courtesy of the Robeson Collection at the Schomburg.
72. Ibid.
73. Paul Robeson interview with Dan Burley. Published as "My Answer," *New York Age*, September 17, 1949.
74. Excerpts from "Eyewitness: Peekskill, USA."
75. David Graham Du Bois phone interview with author, July 14, 2004.
76. Excerpts from "Eyewitness: Peekskill, USA."
77. Robeson interview with Dan Burley, *New York Age*, September 17, 1949.
78. Speech by Paul Robeson to the open-air rally of the International Fur and Leather Workers Union, September 12, 1949.
79. David Levering Lewis letter to author. June 23, 2004.

9. CRASH

1. James H. Gilliam Sr interview with author in Wilmington, DE, July 21, 2005. Gilliam, a World War II veteran, became acquainted with Robeson in the late 1930s while living Baltimore. Gilliam later founded the Metropolitan Wilmington Urban League.
2. "Halls in 2 Ohio Cities Closed to Paul Robeson," *Afro-American*, September 24, 1949.
3. Statement in support of Ben Davis for New York City Council, September 11, 1949.
4. Anonymous letter to J. Edgar Hoover, June 20, 1949. FBI files of Paul Robeson.
5. Letter to J. Edgar Hoover, July 6, 1949. (Writer's name was blacked out.) FBI files of Paul Robeson.
6. Paul Robeson FBI fact sheet, June 9, 1949, FBI files of Paul Robeson, file #100-25857.
7. The McCarran Act, named after Nevada Senator Patrick McCarran, was also known as the Internal Security Act.
8. Speech by Paul Robeson, "The Negro People and the Soviet Union," address at banquet sponsored by the National Council of American-Soviet Friendship. November 10, 1949, New York City. Reprinted as a pamphlet in January 1950.
9. "Robeson Weighs Equal Rights Practices of U.S. and the Soviet Union" *Soviet Russia* (August 1949), 425.
10. Robeson, "The Negro People and the Soviet Union."
11. "Robeson Sees Soviet A-bomb as Peace Force," *Daily People's World*, October 3, 1949.
12. *Congressional Record*, September 21, 1949, 13375
13. Robeson statement in support of Ben Davis for New York City Council, September 11, 1949.

14. Cedric Belfrage, *American Inquisition, 1945–1960: A Profile of the "McCarthy Era"* (London: Bobbs Merrill, 1973).
15. "Robeson Sees Soviet A-bomb as Peace Force," *Daily People's World*, October 3, 1949.
16. Statement by prominent African Americans in Washington, D.C., regarding Robeson's October 13, 1949 concert.
17. Speech by E. Franklin Frazier in Washington, D.C., October 13, 1949.
18. Carl Murphy, "Paul Robeson, The Man," *Afro-American*, March 11, 1950.
19. Speech by Paul Robeson at Progressive Party Convention, February 25, 1950, New York.
20. Peter Samsom, "A Letter to Paul Robeson." Speech delivered in the First Unitarian Church of San Diego, California, November 27, 1949. This speech is one of the most accurate assessments of Paul's position during the height of McCarthyism. Rather than condemning him, Samson points out that Robeson has alienated many of his liberal friends by insisting that only one path is correct. Samsom argues that this mentality goes against the principles of liberalism.
21. Speech by Paul Robeson at National Labor Conference for Negro Rights, June 12, 1950, New York.
22. Ibid.
23. Wilkins, *Standing Fast*, 219.
24. Speech by Paul Robeson at Civil Rights Congress rally, June 28, 1950, New York.
25. Speech by W. E. B. Du Bois, "The Talented Tenth, The Re-Examination of a Concept," August 12, 1948, Sigma Pi Phi Grand Boule, Wilberforce, Ohio, Du Bois Papers, R-80, F-1090-2.
26. W. E. B. Du Bois testimony, U.S. House Committee on Foreign Relations, August 8, 1949.
27. W. E. B. Du Bois statement to National Council of American-Soviet Friendship. c.1949. Du Bois Papers. Used with permission of the David Graham Du Bois Trust.
28. David Graham Du Bois interview with author, September 7, 2004.
29. Abbott Simon interview with author, August 12, 2004.
30. Lewis makes note of this in his biography of Du Bois (*Du Bois: The Fight for Equality and the American Century, 1919–1963*, 545–6). Du Bois himself admits this in "I Bury My Wife," *Chicago Globe*, July 15, 1950.
31. *New York Times*, July 13, 1950.
32. First written as a response to Acheson, Du Bois rewrote this in his recounting of the Peace Information Center Trial. *Battle for Peace: The Story of My 83rd Birthday* (New York: Masses and Mainstream, 1955).
33. Abbott Simon letter to William E. Foley, August 23, 1950, Du Bois Papers, R-65, F-440-2.
34. Wilkins, *Standing Fast*, 210.
35. Wilson Record, *Race and Radicalism: The NAACP and the Communist Party in Conflict* (New York: Cornell University Press, 1966), 155.
36. Wilkins, *Standing Fast*, 211.

37. Berg, *Ticket to Freedom*, 118.
38. See Carol Anderson, *Eyes off the Prize: The United Nations and the African American Struggle for Human Rights, 1944–1955* (New York: Cambridge, 2003).
39. In *Communist Fronts*, Gerald Horne cites a correspondence between Walter White and an FBI special agent in which White urged the feds to move against the Civil Rights Congress.
40. Jimmy Hicks, "Mrs. Robeson Regrets Having Defended Nehru," *Afro-American*, January 28, 1950, 1, 2.
41. Paul Robeson letter to Carl Murphy, August 9, 1951. Robeson Papers, Schomburg Center.
42. George Marshall press release, April 10, 1950.
43. Passport statement by Paul Robeson, undated, 1950s. Paul Robeson Papers.
44. Paul Robeson, "Conversation about the New China," *Freedom* (May 1951).
45. Walter White, "The Strange Case of Paul Robeson," *Ebony* (February 1951).
46. Marie Seton, "Letter to the Editor," *Ebony* (March 1951).
47. Editorial, "The Reactionaries Making Heroes out of Paul Robeson, Ben Davis and Patterson," *National Baptist Voice*, July 15, 1950.
48. Paul Robeson, "Set Him Free to Labor On—A Tribute to W. E. B. Du Bois," *Freedom* (March 1951).
49. Abbott Simon interview with author in Brooklyn, NY, October 28, 2004.
50. Bishop R.R. Wright Jr. letter to Harry S. Truman, April 27, 1951. Shirley Graham Du Bois Papers, Schlesinger Library, Radcliffe Institute at Harvard University.
51. Du Bois, 119.
52. Ibid., pp. 120–1
53. Gloria Agrin letter to Shirley Graham Du Bois, October 18, 1951. Shirley Graham Du Bois Papers, Schlesinger Library, Radcliffe Institute at Harvard University.
54. Du Bois, *Battle for Peace*, 127–9.
55. Eslanda Robeson, "Let's Go!" Baltimore *Afro-American*. November 27, 1951.
56. Boris Polevoy letter to Paul Robeson, December 21, 1954.
57. Unsourced press release, "Chaplin Urges Passport for Robeson," May 24, 1954.
58. "Paul Robeson Again Denied Passport," *Los Angeles Herald Dispatch*, December 2, 1954.
59. Speech by Paul Robeson at American Labor Party rally, Madison Square Garden, New York, October 24, 1950.
60. Paul Robeson, "Here's My Story," *Freedom* (November 1950).
61. Waldo Salt letter to Paul Robeson, et al., September 25, 1951.
62. Farewell speech by Paul Robeson to Claudia Jones, December 7, 1955, Hotel Theresa, New York.
63. Shirley Graham Du Bois letter to Ben Davis, December 15, 1957. Shirley Graham Du Bois Papers, Schlesinger Library, Radcliffe Institute at Harvard University.
64. Gerald Horne, *Race Woman: The Lives of Shirley Graham Du Bois* (New York: New York University Press, 2000), 142.

65. Paul Robeson, "Greetings on the Anniversary of the Great October Revolution," *New World Review* (November 1957).
66. Paul Robeson response to rumors he was breaking with the Communist Party, January 28, 1954.
67. Robert Alan, "Paul Robeson—The Lost Shepherd," *Crisis* (November 1951), vol. 1, 569–73.
68. "Is Paul Robeson Hurting the Negro?" *Brown*, vol. 1, no. 2 (March 1954), 44–50.
69. *Tempo Magazine*, May 3, 1954. CBS's response was printed in several magazines, including *Jet*, May 13, 1954. Robeson also fired off a testy response to the rumors he had renounced support for the Soviet Union. See note 75.
70. Shirley Graham on Paul Robeson, unpublished manuscript, 1957. Shirley Graham Du Bois Papers, Schlesinger Library, Radcliffe Institute at Harvard University.
71. Press statement by Paul Robeson, May 3, 1954.
72. Speech by Robeson, Rally for the Rosenbergs. January 8, 1953. New York.
73. W. E. B. Du Bois, "I Take My Stand," *Masses and Mainstream* (April 1951), 10–6.
74. Arthur Schlesinger Jr., "Who Was Henry A. Wallace?" *Los Angeles Times*, March 12, 2000.
75. In *Reds: McCarthyism in Twentieth-Century America* (New York: Random House, 2003). Ted Morgan notes that McCarthy and his supporters created the witch hunt based on the theory that Communists threatened to destroy Christian civilization. Many of McCarthy's zealous followers were Christian conservatives.
76. Paul Robeson, "We Can't Sit Out This Election," *Freedom* (August 1952).
77. Remarks by Paul Robeson during Vincent Hallinan/Charlotta Bass campaign, Progressive Party, New York, September 26, 1952.
78. Some historians have asserted that the Progressive Party of 1952 essentially ran as an informative campaign. It is unlikely that even the staunchest progressives believed the Hallinan-Bass ticket had a realistic chance of winning.
79. W. E. B. Du Bois to Cedric Dover, March 30, 1951, Du Bois Papers, R-66, F-500.

10. BONDING THROUGH DISGRACE

1. Morgan, *Reds*, (New York: Random House, 2003), 549.
2. P. L. Prattis, "Paul Robeson," *Pittsburgh Courier*, March 9, 1957.
3. The Venona program was established in 1943 by the U.S. government to translate encrypted Soviet communications. The program later involved surveillance of reported Soviet spies and included the cooperation of British intelligence. The program was discontinued in 1980.
4. Rosenberg Rally, January 8, 1953, New York City Committee for Clemency for the Rosenbergs, Du Bois Papers, R-81, F-536.
5. Paul Robeson, "Civil Rights in '54 Depends on the Fight against McCarthyism," *Freedom* (November 1952).
6. Testimony of Eslanda Robeson before the Senate Permanent Subcommittee

on Investigations of the Committee on Government Operations, Washington, D.C., July 7, 1953.

7. In Arthur Miller's *The Crucible*, Abigail Williams accuses Goody Proctor of witchcraft, sparking a series of accusations against other women.

8. Richard Morford, executive director of National Council of American-Soviet Friendship, to Graham Du Bois, June 29, 1954. Shirley Graham Du Bois Papers.

9. Robert M. Lichtman and Ronald D. Cohen, *Deadly Farce: Harvey Matusow and the Informer System in the McCarthy Era* (Urbana: University of Illinois, 2004).

10. From *Brown v. Board of Education*, 347 U.S. 483 (1954) (USSC+).

11. W. E. B. Du Bois, "200 Years of Segregated Schools." *Jewish Life* (February 1955). 7–9

12. Paul Robeson, unpublished notes, 1950s, Robeson Papers, Howard University.

13. White, *How Far the Promised Land*, 224.

14. Horne, *Race Woman*, 123. David Levering Lewis also makes substantial mention of Graham's devotion to Du Bois in the second volume of his biography of the Doctor.

15. Horne and Duberman make these references about Shirley and Essie in their respective biographies of Shirley Graham Du Bois and Paul Robeson. This notion was backed by several people who knew both women.

16. Shirley Graham Du Bois letter to Eslanda Robeson, June 7, 1963, Robeson Papers.

17. Shirley Graham letter to W.E.B. Du Bois, August 10, 1944, Du Bois Papers.

18. Shirley Graham letter to Paul Robeson, March 9, 1944, Robeson Papers.

19. Several biographers have noted Essie's controlling tendencies. Esther Jackson and David Graham Du Bois confirmed this in later interviews.

20. Eslanda Robeson, "Loyalty—Lost and Found," unpublished, Paul Robeson Collection at the Schomburg, box 2, folder 9, reel 2.

21. Eslanda Robeson letter to Shirley Graham, September 23, 1950. Enclosed letter was an endorsement of Du Bois's Senate bid. Shirley Graham Du Bois Papers, Schlesinger Library, Radcliffe Institute, Harvard University.

22. Eslanda Robeson, "Let's Go!" *Afro-American*, November 27, 1951, Robeson Papers.

23. Unpublished writing by Shirley Graham Du Bois, 1956, Shirley Graham Du Bois Papers, Harvard University.

24. Interview with David Graham Du Bois, July 7, 2004; Gerald Horne interview with David Graham Du Bois, May 16, 1996 (published in Horne's biography of Shirley).

25. Author interviews with David Graham Du Bois, July 7, 2004; and Esther Jackson, October 28, 2004.

26. Smethurst noted the importance of Aptheker as an ideological counselor to Du Bois. Aptheker remained loyal to the party even after its collapse in 1956.

27. Horne interpreted a 1950 correspondence between Shirley Graham Du Bois and Herbert Aptheker as evidence of Graham Du Bois's growing frustration with white America.

28. Lloyd L. Brown, "Lift Every Voice for Paul Robeson," *Freedom* (November 1951).
29. Paul Robeson, *Here I Stand* (Boston: Beacon Press, 1971), 27.
30. Ibid., p. 64
31. Ibid., p. 75
32. Ibid,, p. 72
33. A. Ulyanov, "Paul Robeson Speaks for the American Negro." *New Times.* (April 1958): 31–2
34. It's unclear whether Trumbo's review of *Here I Stand* was actually published. The manuscript can be found in the Robeson Papers, Howard University.
35. Louis Burnham, "Paul Robeson—Where He Stands." *New World Review* (May 1958), 22–4.
36. Lloyd L. Brown, Preface to *Here I Stand*, xii.
37. Abbott Simon interview with author in Brooklyn, NY, October 28, 2004.
38. Abbott Simon and Andrea Simon interviews with author in Brooklyn, NY, October 28, 2004.
39. Speech by W. E. B. Du Bois, "Negro-Jewish Unity," ca. 1950, Du Bois Papers, R-81, F-60
40. Ibid.
41. Paul Robeson, "Bonds of Brotherhood," *Jewish Life* (November 1954).
42. Jerome, "The Hidden Half-Life of Albert Einstein: Anti-Racism."
43. Paul Robeson, "The Brave Trumpets of Albert Einstein and His Fellow Scientists," *Freedom* (November 1952).
44. W. E. B. Du Bois, "This Man I Know," *Masses and Mainstream* (February 1954).
45. Ibid.
46. Paul Robeson letter to Boris Polevoy, October 1954, Robeson Collection at the Schomburg, box 1, folder 6, reel 1.
47. Patterson, *The Man Who Cried Genocide*, 177.
48. Roscoe Dunjee was the editor of the Oklahoma City *Black Dispatch*; Murphy was the editor of the Baltimore *Afro-American*. The Reverend Charles A. Hill was a noted Detroit clergy leader.
49. Patterson, *The Man Who Cried Genocide*. 197.
50. William Patterson to Robeson supporters. 1955. Robeson Papers, Schomburg Center.
51. Esther Jackson interview with author in Brooklyn, NY, April 9, 2005.
52. Du Bois, "This Man I Know."
53. Winston wrote *Strategy for a Black Agenda* (New York: International Publishers, 1973) as a Communist response to the black power movement. Deeply critical of black nationalism, Winston dissected notions of black empowerment and dismissed neo-Marxist interpretations by Baraka, Eldridge Cleaver, and other black intellectuals as diluted reincarnations of Trotskyism.
54. Paul Robeson, Foreword to *Born of the People*, Robeson Papers.
55. Moe Fishman letter to Paul Robeson, March 14, 1951, Robeson Collection at the Schomburg, box 1, folder 4, reel 1.

56. W. E. B. Du Bois, "To the American Negro," Du Bois Papers, R-82, F-606.
57. Shirley Graham Du Bois, *His Day Is Marching On: A Memoir of W.E.B. Du Bois* (New York: J. P. Lippincott, 1971).
58. Paul Robeson, "Negro Americans Have Lost a Tried and True Friend," *Freedom* (August 1954). Robeson Papers, Howard University.
59. In June 2004, NAACP Chairman Julian Bond's statements admonishing the Bush administration were scrutinized because of the association's status as a nonpartisan, nonprofit organization.
60. White, *How Far the Promised Land*, 225.
61. Robeson, *Here I Stand*, 66.
62. Speech by W. E. B. Du Bois, "Paul Robeson." Dinner for Robeson sponsored by *New World Review*, October 14, 1954, Du Bois Papers, R-81, F-925.
63. Transcripts from House Un-American Activities Committee Hearings, "Investigation of the Unauthorized Use of United States Passports—Part 3. June 12, 1956.
64. Ibid.
65. "House Group Favors Citing Paul Robeson," *New York Times*, June 13, 1956.
66. Warren Hall Saltzman, "Passport Refusals for Political Reasons: Constitutional Issues and Judicial Review," *Yale Law Journal* (February 1952), 171–203.
67. Shirley Graham letter to George Padmore, September 30, 1956, Shirley Graham Du Bois Papers.
68. *Trop v. Dulles*. 356 U.S. 86 (1958).
69. *Kent v. Dulles*. 357 U.S. 116. (1958).
70. W. E. B. Du Bois, "Whither Now and Why," *Quarterly Review of Higher Education among Negroes* (July 1960), 139–40.
71. Shirley Graham Du Bois, *His Day Is Marching On*.
72. Ibid., 140–1.
73. Speech by W. E. B. Du Bois, "The Wrongs Which Suppress Our Rights," June 3, 1960, Emergency Civil Liberties Committee, New York, Du Bois Papers, R-81, F-1349.
74. Speech by W. E. B. Du Bois, "Integration," August 18, 1956, New York, Du Bois Papers, R-81, F-1022.
75. As previously noted, Wilkins tried to undercut King without hurting the civil rights struggle. He knew King was invaluable as a frontman for the movement, but continued to provide information to the FBI about King's private life.
76. Du Bois, "Integration."
77. Speech by W. E. B. Du Bois, "The American Negro and Communism," October 23, 1958, Charles University, Prague, Czechoslovakia, Du Bois Papers, R-81, F-1203.
78. Du Bois, *The Autobiography of W. E. B. DuBois*, 57.
79. Jack and Morris Childs became informants for Hoover in the 1950s and 1960s in an attempt to discredit King. However, they were unable to find a "smoking gun."
80. Morgan, *Reds*, 567.

11. THE LEGACY OF TWO FALLEN ICONS

1. W. E. B. Du Bois, "Greetings to the World from Africa!" (January 1962), Du Bois Papers, R-81, F-1423.
2. David Graham Du Bois e-mail to author, November 9, 2004.
3. Shirley Graham letter to George Padmore, September 30, 1956, Shirley Graham Du Bois Papers.
4. W. E. B. Du Bois letter to Paul Robeson, July 25, 1961, Robeson Papers.
5. Du Bois, "Greetings to the World from Africa!"
6. Ibid.
7. W. E. B. Du Bois, "Pan-Africanism," *Voice of Africa* (June 1961), 15–6.
8. W. E. B. Du Bois, "The Prime Minister of Ghana," *Masses and Mainstream* (May 1957), 11–6.
9. Du Bois, *The Autobiography of W. E. B. DuBois*, 448.
10. David Levering Lewis interview with author in Manhattan, August 25, 2005.
11. In 1970, Davis—a Black Panther Party and CPUSA member—was charged with murder, kidnapping, and conspiracy. Her arrest led to an international "Free Angela Davis" campaign, ultimately leading to her acquittal in 1972. Patterson was the lead lawyer in the case.
12. Malcolm X, *The Autobiography of Malcolm X* (New York: Ballantine Books, 1992), 393.
13. Eslanda Robeson letter to Shirley Graham Du Bois, October 5, 1963. Robeson Papers.
14. Roy Wilkins, "Emancipation and Militant Leadership," excerpted from *100 Years of Emancipation* (Chicago: Rand McNally, 1963), 22.
15. Duberman, *Paul Robeson*.
16. Du Bois, *The Autobiography of W. E. B. DuBois*, 397–8.
17. Robert G. Spivack, "A Voice Is Silenced," *New York Herald Tribune*, September 17, 1963.
18. Henry W. Morton, "Moscow Conversations," *Columbia University Forum* (Fall 1964).
19. Eulogy for Ben Davis, August 26, 1964. Robeson Papers, Howard University.
20. Unpublished notes (December 1963), Robeson Papers, Howard University.
21. Ibid.
22. Mary Helen Washington, "Alice Childress, Lorraine Hansberry and Claudia Jones: Black Women Write the Popular Front," in *Left of the Color Line: Race, Radicalism and Twentieth-Century Literature in the United States* (Chapel Hill, NC: University of North Carolina Press, 2003), 183–204.
23. *Freedomways* (Summer 1965).
24. Speech by Paul Robeson, "It's Good to Be Back," Tribute to Paul Robeson, April 23, 1965. Reprinted in *Freedomways* (Summer 1965).
25. Charles L. Blockson interview with author in Philadelphia, October 21, 2005.
26. Hans Knight, "Born 30 Years Too Soon," *Philadelphia Evening Bulletin*, May 15, 1975.
27. Loften Mitchell, "Who Is Paul Robeson?" *Equity*, vol. LVII, no. 5 (May 1972), 16.
28. Interview with James Smethurst, May 21, 2005.

29. Speech by Martin Luther King, February 23, 1968. Reprinted in *Freedomways Reader: Prophets in Their Own Country*, edited by Esther C. Jackson (Boulder, CO: Westview Press, 2000), 31–9.
30. Molefi K. Asante interview with author in Philadelphia, October 21, 2004.
31. Molefi K. Asante, "Harold Cruse and Afrocentric Theory." Online journal article (www.asante.net). Courtesy of Molefi K. Asante.
32. *Congressional Record*, March 8, 1978, E1133.
33. Controversy continues to rage in Du Bois's hometown over naming a school after him. According to the *Berkshire Eagle*, much of the anti–Du Bois sentiment stems from FBI "planted" articles in the now-defunct *Berkshire Courier* during the 1970s.
34. Lloyd Brown, preface to *Here I Stand*.
35. William Patterson speech on Robeson, April 8, 1969, New York, Robeson papers, Howard University.
36. William Patterson to Lloyd Brown, May 31, 1973, Robeson Papers, Howard University.
37. Excerpt from Malcolm X letter to Jackie Robinson. Published in *I Never Had It Made*, 85.
38. Harold Cruse, *The Crisis of the Negro Intellectual* (New York: William Morrow, 1967).
39. Esther Jackson interview with author in Brooklyn, NY, October 16, 2005.
40. Molefi K. Asante interview with author in Philadelphia, October 10, 2005.
41. C. L. R. James, "Paul Robeson: Black Star," *Black World*, (November 1970), 107.
42. Charlotte Mitchell, foreword to William Patterson, *The Man Who Cried Genocide*.
43. Transcripts of recordings by John Pittman. Courtesy of Howard University archives.
44. James E. Jackson, *Revolutionary Tracings in World Politics and Black Liberation* (New York: International Publishers, 1974), 221.
45. Amiri Baraka, "Paul Robeson and the Theater," *Black Renaissance* (Fall/Winter 1998), 13–34.
46. Robert Maxwell, *Herbert Schiller* (Lanham, MD: Rowman & Littlefield, 2003), 25.
47. Morris U. Schappes, "The Record—Paul Robeson Jr. Refutes Lloyd Brown," *Jewish Currents* (February 1982), 13, 25–30.
48. Charles L. Blockson interview with author in Philadelphia, PA, October 21, 2005.
49. Ella Dutt, "Robeson's Son Recalls Nehru Link," *India Abroad*, April 28, 1989.
50. Baraka, "Paul Robeson and the Theater,"
51. "Da Robe" is a common expression used to describe the Paul Robeson Student Center at Penn State University's main campus in University Park, PA.
52. On September 2, 2005, rapper Kanye West spoke at a nationally televised fund-raiser for victims of Hurricane Katrina. In words that sounded inspired by *We Charge Genocide*, West said that the United States was "set up to help the poor, the black people, the less well-off as slow as possible. . . . We

already realize a lot of people that could help are at war right now, fighting another way—and they've given them permission to go down and shoot us!"

53. Robeson, *Here I Stand*, 31.
54. Alfred A. Moss interview with author in College Park, MD, September 9, 2005.

INDEX